THE KURDISH NOBILITY
IN THE OTTOMAN EMPIRE

Edinburgh Studies on the Ottoman Empire
Series Editor: Kent F. Schull

Published and forthcoming titles

Migrating Texts: Circulating Translations around the Ottoman Mediterranean
Edited by Marilyn Booth

Ottoman Translations: Circulating Texts from Bombay to Paris
Edited by Marilyn Booth and Claire Savina

Death and Life in the Ottoman Palace: Revelations of the Sultan Abdülhamid I Tomb
Douglas Scott Brookes

Ottoman Sunnism: New Perspectives
Edited by Vefa Erginbaş

Jews and Palestinians in the Late Ottoman Era, 1908–1914: Claiming the Homeland
Louis A. Fishman

Spiritual Vernacular of the Early Ottoman Frontier: The Yazıcıoğlu Family
Carlos Grenier

Armenians in the Late Ottoman Empire: Migration, Mobility Control and Sovereignty, 1885–1915
David Gutman

The Kizilbash-Alevis in Ottoman Anatolia: Sufism, Politics and Community
Ayfer Karakaya-Stump

Çemberlitaş Hamami in Istanbul: The Biographical Memoir of a Turkish Bath
Nina Macaraig

The Kurdish Nobility in the Ottoman Empire: Loyalty, Autonomy and Privilege
Nilay Özok-Gündoğan

Nineteenth-Century Local Governance in Ottoman Bulgaria: Politics in Provincial Councils
Safa Saraçoğlu

Prisons in the Late Ottoman Empire: Microcosms of Modernity
Kent F. Schull

Ruler Visibility and Popular Belonging in the Ottoman Empire
Darin Stephanov

The North Caucasus Borderland: Between Muscovy and the Ottoman Empire, 1555–1605
Murat Yasar

Children and Childhood in the Ottoman Empire: From the 15th to the 20th Century
Edited by Gülay Yılmaz and Fruma Zachs

euppublishing.com/series/esoe

THE KURDISH NOBILITY
IN THE OTTOMAN EMPIRE

LOYALTY, AUTONOMY AND PRIVILEGE

Nilay Özok-Gündoğan

EDINBURGH
University Press

To Roza Perî and Azat Zana

Edinburgh University Press is one of the leading university presses in the UK. We publish academic books and journals in our selected subject areas across the humanities and social sciences, combining cutting-edge scholarship with high editorial and production values to produce academic works of lasting importance. For more information visit our website: edinburghuniversitypress.com

© Nilay Özok-Gündoğan, 2022, 2024

Edinburgh University Press Ltd
The Tun – Holyrood Road
12 (2f) Jackson's Entry
Edinburgh EH8 8PJ

First published in hardback by Edinburgh University Press 2022

Typeset in Jaghbuni by
Cheshire Typesetting Ltd, Cuddington, Cheshire

A CIP record for this book is available from the British Library

ISBN 978 1 3995 0861 2 (hardback)
ISBN 978 1 3995 0862 9 (paperback)
ISBN 978 1 3995 0863 6 (webready PDF)
ISBN 978 1 3995 0864 3 (epub)

The right of Nilay Özok-Gündoğan to be identified as author of this work has been asserted in accordance with the Copyright, Designs and Patents Act 1988 and the Copyright and Related Rights Regulations 2003 (SI No. 2498).

Contents

List of Figures, Maps and Tables   vii
Acknowledgements   viii

Introduction: Rethinking Kurdish Nobility in the Ottoman Empire   1

PART I   A TENUOUS ACCORD

1. At the Beginning: The Formation of the Kurdish-Ottoman Nobility of Palu in the Sixteenth Century   43
2. Noble Privilege on the Ground, from the 1720s to the 1830s   62

PART II   A QUASI-RIFT

3. The Kurdish Nobility and the Making of Modern State Power in Kurdistan   107
4. A System in Transition: Negotiating Nobility in the Locality   132
5. The Weşin Incident: the Spark that Burnt a Village … and the Arsonist   157

PART III   RESTRUCTURING AND VIOLENCE

6. After Abdullah Beg: The Politics of Dividing the Kurdish Nobles' Lands   177
7. Provincial Administration after the Palu Nobility   219

8. The Beginning of the Endgame? The Road to the 1895
   Massacres in Palu   242

Conclusion: The End of the Nobility in Kurdistan   280
Postscript   286

Glossary   288
Select Bibliography   291
Index   330

Figures, Maps and Tables

Figures

I.1	The ruins of the old city of Palu	21
5.1	A contemporary view from Weşin – now called Erimli	158
8.1	The Palu Memorial	261

Maps

I.1	Palu in the Ottoman Empire	23
1.1	Emirates that were granted *hükümet* status (c. 1520)	49

Tables

I.1	Total male population of Palu in 1841	24
6.1	Latif Efendi's account of the lands sold by the Treasury in Abrank village (c. 1860)	196
6.2	Muhtar Efendi's account of land sales	200
6.3	Amount of money collected from all the non-Muslim villages of the Palu district	205
6.4	Amount of money collected from all the Muslim villages of the Palu district	206

Acknowledgements

Writing this book was a long and arduous journey across institutions, libraries and countries. I am grateful that many people supported me during this time. My late adviser Donald Quataert had an unconditional belief in the significance of a project on the socio-economic history of Kurdistan. He was a great mentor who encouraged and supported his students with endless patience, and I feel deep regret that he did not live to read the final product of this project. The late Rifa'at Ali Abou-El-Haj was a source of scholarly inspiration. His unrelenting critical approach to conventional histories of the Ottoman Empire, his insistence on bringing the society back into historical analysis and his call for comparative approaches enormously enriched my historical thinking. I owe gratitude to Nancy Appelbaum, who opened the door to the exciting world of Latin American history. She kindly stepped in to chair my dissertation committee after we lost Donald. Her support and mentorship over the years have been invaluable. Fa-ti Fan guided me through the rich historical scholarship on rural societies in Qing China. I have also had the privilege of working with Raymond Craib from Cornell University. I thank him for reading and sharing his helpful insights with me on this project.

This project would not have been possible without Kent Schull's support. I have been fortunate to have had him as a mentor, colleague and friend. Our afternoon coffee hours brightened the gloomy Binghamton winters and gave me much-needed hope and strength. Janet Klein has left an indelible mark on this project. It was her work that triggered my interest in the history of Ottoman Kurdistan. She is an inspiring scholar and also a generous mentor whose example I can only hope to follow.

At Cornell College, where I spent a year as an ACM-Mellon Postdoctoral Fellow, I had the pleasure of working with Phil Lucas, Catherine Stewart and Michelle Herder. I also had supportive colleagues

Acknowledgements

at Denison University. I owe an enormous debt to Trey Proctor and Megan Threlkeld for their friendship, care and support. I also thank Adam Davis, Karen Spierling, Barry Keenan and Mitchell Snay. I am grateful to have wonderful friends in Granville: Rebecca Futo Kennedy, Jo Tague, Kyle Bartholomew, Hannah Weiss Muller, Hanada al-Masri, Rana Odeh, Michele Stephens, Olivia Aguilar, Yadi Collins and Nida Bikmen. I also thank Nurten Kilic-Schubel and Vernon Schubel for their friendship. Sohrab Behdad, a caring colleague and friend, and I have had inspiring exchanges about life with all of its colours and shades.

The writing process of this book witnessed many important life events. I had a child, and my family moved back to Turkey from the United States. Shortly after this, Turkey witnessed one of the biggest political crackdowns of its history, and unexpected circumstances forced us to leave the country again, facing an unknown future. Many people and institutions made it possible for me to have a safe place to continue my academic work back in the United States. I am grateful to the Institute of International Education Scholar Rescue Fund (IIE-SRF) for providing me with a grant that allowed me to continue working on this project. Danielle Alperin, Emily Borzcik, James King and Sarah Willcox are more professional, caring and supportive than I can express in words. Kent Schull and Mostafa Minawi generously helped during my search for a host institution. My alma mater, Binghamton University, welcomed me back into a vibrant and collegial academic milieu where I worked on this book. I thank Nathanael Andrade, Dina Danon, Heather D. DeHaan, Sean Dunwoody and Ekrem Karakoç for their collegiality. The late Jean Quataert supported me in numerous ways during this time in Binghamton. I would also like to thank the president of Denison University, Adam Weinberg, and the Provost Kim Coplin for their generous offer to provide me with an academic home after I left Turkey. I owe a special debt of gratitude to four formidable women – Aslı Iğsız, Aslı Bâli, Beth Baron and Gaye Özpınar – who supported me enormously during this process. My valiant lawyer Helîn Beştaş also deserves heartfelt thanks.

I have been fortunate to be a part of the History Department at Florida State University and work with wonderful colleagues. I am grateful to Will Hanley for his mentorship and friendship, and for his unrelenting efforts to make justice, equality and solidarity an integral part of human relations in and outside of academia. I would also like to thank Rafe Blaufarb for providing me with invaluable insights which helped me to think about Ottoman history from a comparative historical perspective. Special thanks to Edward Gray for the support and encouragement he provided as the department chair. Thanks are also due to Cathy McClive,

Jennifer Koslow, Claudia Liebeskind, Suzanne Sinke, Annika Culver, Laurie Wood, Charles Upchurch, Maximillian Scholz, Jonathan Grant, Kurt Piehler, George Williamson, Ben Dodds, Nathan Stoltzfus, James Palmer, Sam Holley-Kline, Hadi Hoseiny, Adam Gaiser, Aline Kalbian and Peter Garretson for their collegiality.

Numerous other people and institutions assisted me during the research and writing processes of this book. Derya Satır, Elif Feyyat, Nışan Güreh, Abdusselam Ertekin and Ben Goff provided research assistance. My friend and colleague Jelle Verheij generously shared documents and always made himself available to answer my questions about place names. I am indebted to him for his help. I also thank the staff of the Başbakanlık Osmanlı Arşivi in Istanbul, Glenn Bartle Library in Binghamton, Denison University Library, and Florida State University Libraries. A summer research grant from Denison University Research Foundation (DURF) allowed me to conduct research in Palu. The First-Year Assistant Professor (FYAP) award from Florida State University granted me funds to conduct further research. Also, I would like to extend a big thank you to my brilliant editors, Martha Schulman and Allison Bramblett.

My undergraduate and graduate students have been a constant source of inspiration, especially Dena Sutphin, Chelsi Arellano, Jill Hopkins, Adam Hunt, Daniel Zylberkan, Sibel Algı, Ömer, Topal, Ahmet Yusuf Yüksek, Bahadin Kerborani and Timur Saitov.

Writing is a solitary experience, but friendship is one of the best things to enjoy in life. Can Nacar has supported me in many different ways during this long journey. I am grateful to have him as my *ahretlik*. Mostafa Minawi has been someone I would describe as a *can yoldaşı*, a friend with whom I can walk down any path no matter what. Our writing sessions, to which we have been religiously committed every day, produced two books (as I write this acknowledgement, my writing companion is crafting the acknowledgement to his book). David Gutman has been a great friend and an inspiring scholar. Yiğit Akın has always been a supportive and caring friend. I have been blessed to have had wonderful women as friends/sisters: Hillary Gleason, Zülâl Fazlıoğlu-Akın, Canan Tanır, Sezen Bayhan, Suzan Bayhan and Sandrine Bertaux. Thanks are also due to Ege Özen, Sinem Silay Özen, James Parisot, Alper Ecevit, Ümit Kurt, Murat Akan, Ebru Öztürk, Emma Buckthal, Laura Warren Hill, Heather Laube, Jennifer Alvey, Rushika Patell Lipp, Hişyar Özsoy, and the late Ananth Aiyer. Josie Fliger, Jeremy Deese and Morgyn Elizabeth Fliger Deese made my life in Tallahassee more colourful and joyful. I would also like to thank Teagan Dunn for her support and for the cups of tea she offered while I was writing this book.

Acknowledgements

I have been fortunate to work with an outstanding team at Edinburgh University Press. Kent Schull and Rachel Bridgewater have generously given their support and invaluable advice. I also thank the two readers for the helpful comments they provided on the manuscript. I have no words to express my gratefulness to Nurettin Erkan for the gorgeous cover image he made. The beauty of his painting of Palu that he generously shared with me is beyond my imagination. I also owe gratitude to the descendants of the Palu begs, especially Mehmet Karacimşit, for their hospitality and for sharing their family archive with me.

My family has always been a source of unconditional support. My late father, Süleyman İrfan Özok, instilled in me the love of books and left his legacy as a person committed to equality and justice. My mother, Nadide Özok, taught me the significance of education for a woman's self-realisation and continually supported my efforts to this end. My brother, Özyay Özok, supported and encouraged me with his love. The moments that I spent with İrfan Rüzgâr Özok reminded me of the beauty of life. I would also like to thank the members of my now-expanded family, Meral Gündoğan, Yaşar Gündoğan and Ceren Cevahir Gündoğan, for their warmth, care and encouragement. I am grateful to Yaşar Gündoğan for the stunning pictures that he took of Palu and its vicinity.

Last but not least, my deepest thanks go to my team at home. Seeing me lost in documents written in different scripts or sitting at a desk for hours at a time, my daughter Roza found creative ways to get into my world. In a confident voice, she would say, 'Mom, in the late Ottoman Empire, people liked pizza.' She wrote 'Play with Roza' in my calendar with her glitter markers. 'When your book is finished …' became the standard opening for any sentence about the future. My only consolation is that maybe this book dedicated to her name will inspire her one day to feel the extraordinary pleasure of writing as a woman in a room of her own. Azat – my husband, colleague and comrade – and I started the academic journey together. He read every page of this book, guided me with his *good sense*, and reminded me of what I was trying to achieve when I felt lost in the complexity of the historical material that I was working with. Without his love and compassion, this venture would have not been possible.

Introduction: Rethinking Kurdish Nobility in the Ottoman Empire

In the last days of August 1848, the inhabitants of Weşin,[1] a village nestled in a secluded valley on the banks of the eastern Euphrates, woke early. The men met at the village mosque to perform the pre-sunrise prayer marking the beginning of a three-day Muslim holiday celebrating the end of Ramadan. Just before the prayer began, they heard the sound of distant gunfire. As the noise approached, the prayer-goers saw that it was being made by Abdullah Beg, the *hâkim* (ruler) of the Palu emirate and at least six hundred armed men. They were coming to collect 1.5 tons of clarified butter from the villagers in payment for four years of back taxes owed to Abdullah Beg. The villagers responded by opening fire. *Eid* turned bloody, with three villagers dead and four wounded. The despairing villagers then fled to the surrounding hills. The next day Abdullah Beg came back with his men and set the village on fire, burning sixty-five houses and buildings to the ground, along with stored grain, animals and their fodder, poplar trees and vineyards.[2]

On the surface, this event seems like just one among many conflicts about agrarian surplus extraction the world over. What neither Abdullah Beg nor the villagers knew was that the incident would trigger a series of events that would break up the Kurdish begs' hereditary rule.[3] Abdullah Beg was a descendant of the Palu *ûmera* (pl. of *emîr* – alternatively *begs*/*bey*s or *mîr*s)[4] that had ruled the emirate for more than three centuries. Successive Ottoman sultans recognised the Palu begs' hereditary rulership over the emirate from the 1500s – the time when it came under Ottoman suzerainty – onward. Within a year, this violent encounter would cost Abdullah Beg his position as *hâkim*, his landholdings and, when the Ottoman state exiled him to Tekfurdağı in Rumelia, 900 miles away from the lands that his ancestors had ruled for centuries, his bond with his homeland. And with the end of Abdullah Beg's career came the end of the begs' hereditary rule in Palu.

Kurdish emirates and the elite families have been the cornerstones of both popular and academic historical renditions of the Kurds and Kurdistan. From the late medieval era through the modern age, the rise and fall of the Kurdish emirates has constituted a key aspect of Kurdish history. But, although the emirates feature in popular notions of Kurdish history, they are barely addressed in actual historical research. The scant existing scholarship has focused on the most powerful Kurdish ruling houses, namely the Baban (based in Sulaimania), Bohtan (based in Cîzre/ Cızîr) and Soran (based in Rawanduz).[5] All three disappeared from the political arena in the second half of the nineteenth century as a result of Ottoman military campaigns. Bedirkhan Beg of the Botan emirate has attracted the most attention from historians, not least because his descendants constituted the leading cadres of the budding Kurdish nationalist movement at the turn of the twentieth century.

Abdullah Beg, who wreaked havoc on Weşin village on that hot August day, was also a member of an elite Kurdish family, the leaders of the Palu (Palo in Kurdish; Balu in Armenian) emirate. This emirate was geographically smaller and politically less significant in the nineteenth century than the previously-mentioned emirates. The Palu begs did not respond to the Ottoman state's mid-nineteenth-century centralisation policies with large-scale uprisings. It is true that Abdullah Beg, like the emîrs of the three formidable emirates, was exiled by the Ottoman imperial state at around the same time period. The rest of the family, however, stayed in their historic homeland and continued to claim rulership of the emirate for several decades after Abdullah Beg's exile. Thus, the Palu begs' modern history does not fit with the nationalist interpretations of the Kurdish past in which the Kurdish ruling families represent heroic resistance to the Ottoman state's military and political encroachments during the long nineteenth century.[6] Additionally, unlike Bedirkhan Beg's sons and the Babans, who became the flag-bearers of Kurdish national identity, the majority of the Palu begs' descendants were integrated into the mainstream Muslim-Turkish identity.[7] In the nineteenth century the family's relationship with Kurdish identity was debatable. In their dealings with the Ottoman state, the begs hardly ever mentioned being Kurdish, and when they talked about tribes or other groups they perceived as recalcitrant or unlawful, the begs referred to them as '*ekrad* and *aşair*' (Kurds and tribes). This derogatory tone echoed the Ottoman state's dominant usage towards these groups. While distinguishing themselves from Kurdishness as such, the Palu begs embraced and emphasised the claim that they were a family of begs descended from Cemşîd Beg, who was granted this position by Sultan Suleyman the Magnificent.

Introduction

This book is the first comprehensive account of the transformation and eventual disappearance of a Kurdish elite family's hereditary privileges in the Ottoman Empire. It focuses on the Palu begs and examines their changing position in the locality and vis-à-vis the Ottoman imperial state from the eighteenth through the end of the nineteenth century. What attracted my interest in this family were the events of Weşin in 1848. As I read the archival documents, I was puzzled by the drastic consequences of this seemingly ordinary happening. Because the event resulted in the deaths of villagers and the destruction of the village, the villagers' insistent appeals eventually brought about a criminal investigation that led to a court case and Abdullah Beg's eventual exile. But how and why did this incident culminate in the abolishing of the Palu begs' hereditary privileges, privileges that had existed in the Ottoman politico-economic system for over three centuries? The documents about the incident revealed a fierce underlying negotiation between local and imperial actors about the economic, political and military privileges of the Palu elites. For the begs, these privileges were legitimate hereditary rights bestowed upon them because of their noble position. From the Ottoman state's perspective, however, these old claims were invalid, a remnant of the past. One thing was clear: the Palu begs saw themselves as a noble family, and while that nobility preceded the Ottoman entry into Kurdistan, it was bolstered by the family's acceptance of Ottoman suzerainty in the sixteenth century. Their identity was not based on a negation of or antagonism towards the Ottoman imperial state. It was the Ottoman sultans who recognised the family's entitlement to their privileges, who reinforced and legitimated their noble claims. Notwithstanding ups and downs in their relationship, their noble identity connected the Palu begs to the Ottoman imperial centre from the mid-sixteenth century through the empire's end.

This book tells three intertwined stories about the Palu begs. First, it describes the transformation of the relations between the Ottoman imperial state and the begs from the time they came under Ottoman rule through the late nineteenth century. Second, it considers the Palu begs as an elite group whose wealth derived primarily from land. The book examines the transformation of land tenure in the Palu countryside in relation to the Palu begs' changing fortunes. Third, it uses this backdrop of the Palu begs' changing economic and administrative power to consider the ways in which their relations with the local population changed. The book offers a granular account of the Palu begs' changing position in the locality and their relations with local actors including provincial Ottoman administrators, cultivators, Armenian creditors (*sarraf*s) and Kurdish tribes. In doing so, the book demonstrates how local socio-economic structures and relations changed in relation to the changing position of the Kurdish nobility vis-à-vis the Ottoman state while highlighting the role played by local actors. These locals were not passive observers; they were actively involved in the negotiations over the Palu begs' hereditary privileges, using the newly-established *Tanzimat* (Re-organisation) institutions, especially the provincial councils, to challenge the Palu begs.[8] We will see how the transformation of land ownership and local power configurations set the ground for the ethno-religious clashes between the Armenians and Muslims that plagued Palu in the last decade of the nineteenth century.

The Question of the Autonomy of Kurdish Emirates in the Ottoman Empire

Questions about the autonomy of the emirates ruled by the Kurdish begs have constituted a common underlying theme in studies on Kurds and Kurdistan – historical or otherwise.[9] This interest stems from a presentist agenda related to the Kurdish population's current statelessness. In their search for the origins of the Kurdish plight, nation-state-centred renditions of Kurdish history rely on an oft-cited schema of the degree of autonomy the Ottoman Kurdish emirates held. According to the standard narrative, Kurdish emirates came under Ottoman rule in the sixteenth century when they received privileges that accorded them autonomy vis-à-vis the Ottoman central state. The narrative then shifts to the mid-nineteenth-century Tanzimat era, when the Ottoman state destroyed their autonomy via large-scale military operations and centralisation policies. The period between is described as a static time during which the political system of Kurdistan remained unchanged.[10] This picture has come to constitute the standard 'historical background' or 'Ottoman background' part of almost every book written on Kurdish history and politics in the past century.[11]

At the centre of this schematic portrayal of the Kurdish emirates' autonomy is the hegemony of the nation-state paradigm in the historical accounts of an imperial setting. This portrayal sees the emirates' history during the Ottoman era either in terms of their autonomy from and resistance to the Ottoman state or as a precursor of the twentieth-century nationalist movements. Either way, the relationship between the Kurdish elites and the Ottoman state is described primarily as a zero-sum game. I am not the first to take issue with the nation-state fallacy in the analysis of the provincial elites. Albert Hourani's conceptualisation of politics of notables opened up a significant strain in the historiography of the Arab provinces by situating provincial elites of the Arab provinces within the Ottoman imperial context.[12] Deploying the Weberian notion of the patriciate, Hourani argued that what he described as the 'politics of notables' was key for understanding the urban politics of Ottoman (specifically the Muslim) provinces.[13] The urban notability's political influence rested on their intermediary position between the imperial state and the local population. They had access to authority and held social power of their own that was not dependent on the ruler. In Hourani's account, the concept of 'notable' was a political, not a sociological one: different groups with varying forms of social power could play this intermediary role between the state and the provincial society.[14] In this sense, the framework Hourani presented was prescriptive than descriptive. Nevertheless, he also provided a description of the groups which he thought constituted the notability in the Arab provinces (i.e. the 'ulama, the leaders of the local garrisons, and the secular notables – a'yan, aghas and amirs).[15] Regardless of which group ended up seizing the leadership position, and notwithstanding the varying socio-economic bases of their power, they played this role as intermediaries between government and people. Hourani's notability paradigm found great resonance among the historians of the Arab provinces in different time periods from the medieval era to the twentieth century.[16]

More recently, historians working on different parts of the empire sought a comprehensive analytical framework to examine the provincial elites in Ottoman imperial formation. The distinction between elite formation and elite incorporation was replaced by a more relational perspective that emphasised 'the interactive process of *localization* and *Ottomanization*'. This relational process of elite formation produced what Toledano describes as '*Ottoman-Local elites*'[17] who benefited from the Ottoman presence in the locality by seizing administrative and military posts and fiscal opportunities. In this way, 'provincial elites "localised" the hegemony of the state'.[18] More recent studies questioned historians' overemphasis on Arab provincial elites and brought a more comprehensive and comparative approach to the study of Ottoman provincial elites.[19] Examining local power-holding families in the Balkans and Anatolia, Ali Yaycıoğlu described their relationship with the Ottoman state as 'partnership'.[20]

These epistemological interventions in the study of the provincial elites in the Ottoman Empire were echoed in scholarly work on the Kurds and Kurdistan later and to a lesser extent. New generations of Kurdish historians complicated the ethno-national and teleological accounts of Kurdish history by considering it within an imperial context.[21] Janet

Klein's work is one of the earliest attempts to debunk the nationalist and ethnic-conflict-centred accounts of Kurdish history. In her study of the Hamidiye Light Cavalry, Klein examined the emergence of this armed militia group from the Kurdish tribes within the conceptual framework of Ottoman colonialism in Kurdistan.[22] Similarly, Sabri Ateş's study of the making of the Ottoman–Iranian borderlands considered the changing relations between the Kurdish local elites and the Ottoman state within the context of the tension between the territorialisation of the state-space and local desires for autonomy.[23]

This book contributes to this line of thinking by situating the question of the Kurdish emirates' autonomy within the Ottoman imperial framework. It contends that the relationship between the Ottoman state and the Kurdish elites was shaped within the context of the political, economic and military exigencies of the imperial setting rather than by a preconceived antagonism between the two. In this light, there was nothing unusual about the Palu begs or the Kurdish elites more generally. Just like other ethnically, religiously and linguistically different local notables, Palu begs were a provincial elite group operating in an imperial context. Nevertheless, we must avoid any temptation to disregard the specificity of each region or group in terms of their position within the Ottoman political system and the privileges, prerogatives and obligations this position accorded them. As Dina Khoury states, it is 'impossible to make blanket generalizations about political power-holders applicable to the whole of the Ottoman Empire'.[24]

One key characteristic of the Kurdish begs that distinguished them from the majority of the elite groups that became the subject of these revisionist historiographies following Hourani's conceptualisation of the politics of notables: their de jure hereditary control over their land, and the security of property it gave them despite constant threats of state confiscation.[25] This de jure recognition was based on the Ottoman state's acceptance that the Kurdish begs' rights over the land preceded the Ottoman arrival in the area and its recognition of their hereditary privileges within a specific type of politico-administrative organisation – one that granted autonomy to the Kurdish elites in various fiscal, military and administrative realms. This book situates the Kurdish elite formation within the context of this specific administrative model.

Ottoman political formation is characterised by the diversity of the administrative arrangements through which different elite groups were incorporated into the Ottoman system. Geo-strategic location, local socio-economic characteristics and the existing power configuration in a newly-conquered area determined its administrative position in the

Introduction

Ottoman realm.[26] In the areas where the classical Ottoman military and fiscal regimes were not implemented, local elites were incorporated into the Ottoman imperial realm through administrative arrangements that accorded them varying degrees of autonomous rule. However, the major discussions of the Ottoman provincial elites have centred on areas where the classical Ottoman military and fiscal regime was implemented. But as Adanir states, 'the complex issue of provincial elites in the Ottoman Empire cannot be studied adequately without due attention to pre-Ottoman leadership groups'.[27]

When Kurdistan came under Ottoman rule in the sixteenth century, the Kurdish elites of the existing principalities in the area were incorporated into the Ottoman realm mainly through a system that recognised their hereditary rulership. Palu was one of five emirates that were granted a special position as *hükümet* (lit. government).[28] *Hükümet* was how the Ottoman state recognised the hereditary rights of the Kurdish begs over their dominions. What separated the *hükümet*s from the more typical Ottoman sanjaks and other hereditary Kurdish estates (*yurtluk-ocaklıks*)[29] was that they were designated as *mefrûzü'l-kalem* and *maktû'ü'l-kadem* in the administrative system. *Mefrûzü'l-kalem* refers to the *hükümet*s' protection from *timar*s – fiefs granted to cavalrymen by the state in return for military service. With this immunity came another: Palu and the other Kurdish *hükümet*s were free of *tahrir*s. Literally meaning 'enregisterment', *tahrir* was the 'Ottoman system of periodical surveying of populations, land and other sources of revenue'.[30] Once a new region was annexed, detailed surveys were conducted and the data was recorded in detailed registers.[31] *Maktû'ü'l-kadem* meant that both military and civilian Ottoman administrators were barred from having any authority in the emirate; this meant both tax collectors and the Janissary troops.[32] This left the begs free to maintain private forces and to seize the agrarian surplus from the areas under their dominions. Together these designations meant that *hükümet*s had extensive administrative and fiscal autonomy within the Ottoman system.

To varying degrees, precedents for the Ottoman state's recognition of local dynasties' rule existed outside Kurdistan. Early Ottoman sultans had granted lands to the frontier lords from the newly-conquered lands in Rumelia with *mefrûzü'l-kalem* and *maktû'ü'l-kadem* status that gave them fiscal and administrative rule over these lands. After the conquest of Trabzon, Christian elites there were granted hereditary landownership – continuing an established practice from the pre-Ottoman Byzantine era.[33] Similarly, members of the prominent Mihaloğulları family were granted lands in Pleven (modern Bulgaria) by Sultan Bayezid I (r. 1389–1402).[34]

There were cases of entire regions being granted along with similar immunities and privileges to ruling families present in the area before the Ottoman conquest. By the end of the sixteenth century, Transylvania, Wallachia, Moldavia and the Crimean Khanate were ruled by native dynasties.[35] These areas, previously described as 'vassal states', have recently been renamed in Ottoman historiography as 'tributary states', evoking the Ottoman concept of *haraçgüzâr* (tributary) – even though some of them, like Crimea, did not actually pay tribute.[36] We can also add other configurations of autonomous rule, including Hejaz, Tunis, Algeria, Tripolitania, Yemen and Egypt – to name just a few. Ottoman historians have examined the extent and nature of the autonomy these ruling families had vis-à-vis the Ottoman state.[37] In a recent volume on the European tributary states of the Ottoman Empire, scholars scrutinised the historicist, nation-state-centred assumptions of autonomy in these areas. For instance, Viorel Panaite warns about the ahistorical usages of 'autonomy' in an imperial context since 'autonomy could exist only within another state – in this case, the Ottoman Empire – and not outside of it'.[38] The *mefrûzü'l-kalem ve maktû'ü'l-kadem* formulation attests to the de jure position of Wallachia and Moldovia *within* the system of what Panaite describes as *pax ottomanica*, not outside of it.[39]

This approach is useful in understanding the nature of the Kurdish begs' autonomy in the Ottoman imperial context. Broad surveys of Ottoman provincial organisation always treat the Kurdish *hükümet*s as sui generis, exceptions to be mentioned in parentheses. The lack of comprehensive monographic studies of the *hükümet*s in the Ottoman realm, coupled with the prevalent historicist notions of the Kurdish past, has pushed the question of Kurdish emirates' autonomy to the margins of Ottoman historical writing. Historians mention the specific position the Kurdish emirates had within the Ottoman administrative system without actually investigating that position. The Kurdish *hükümet*s' position was different from that of the classical Ottoman sanjaks, but it was by no means unique. This book considers the Palu emirate's autonomy as one example of the manifold modalities of the organisation of autonomy within the Ottoman imperial system.

The book pushes the examination of the Kurdish *hükümet*s' autonomy beyond the usual focus on their administrative position, considering them in relation to the hereditary position of the ruling family and the actual fiscal, military and administrative prerogatives and exemptions this position gave them. The *hükümet* status tied the rulership of the emirate to a family in a hereditary fashion. From the sixteenth until the eighteenth century, the Ottoman state recognised the Kurdish begs as a corporate body that

Introduction

collectively made decisions about the administration of the region. The imperial decrees mentioned them as *Kurdistan begleri* (or alternatively as *ûmera-ı Kurdistan*). According to the Ottoman documents defining the hereditary rights of the begs (*temessükname*), when a beg died without an heir (since succession was based on primogeniture), the Kurdistan begs could choose someone from among themselves to rule the emirate. This changed in the late seventeenth century, when the Ottoman provincial administrators increased their efforts to intervene in the appointment processes of the Palu begs, despite the begs being technically immune to such interventions. The Kurdish emirs' horizontal relations in the early centuries of Ottoman rule, the mechanisms they deployed to collectively rule the region, and the way in which their sense of being a part of a larger unit (e.g. *ûmera-ı Kurdistan*) shaped their relations with the Ottoman administration are questions for Ottoman historians. For the purposes of this book, the point is that the Palu begs entered the Ottoman realm as a noble family whose de jure hereditary rights and privileges manifested in the degree to which they were exempt from Ottoman oversight.

Nobility as a Historical Category of Analysis

On a hot summer day in 2013, I visited Palu in search of descendants of the Palu begs. My initial inquiry led me to a young man. Dressed in a suit, he pointed out of the window and said that he owned the quarry by the hill – his voice could not hide his pride. This was one of several references to his wealth. He was proud of his connection to the *begs*, but they were totally fabricated. The actual descendant of the *begs*, a retired teacher in his mid-fifties, came to meet me in a decrepit Renault 12, probably from the early 1990s. He seemed happy to have the attention of a historian interested in his ancestors, and mentioned that the quarry owner was a *nouveau riche* whose desire for a noble past had led him to the Palu begs. In Palu, a small district that is now an impoverished backwater, the title of *beg* had survived into the twenty-first century; the begs' wealth, however, had not. I found it puzzling that the title persisted when its bearers had long since fallen from grace, that it was potent enough that a well-to-do person would claim it. The begs' real descendants could prove their noble identity via a *temlîkname*[40] (alternatively *temlîk* or *mülkname*) – a title deed from the Ottoman sultans that recognised their hereditary rulership over the Palu emirate – that they kept in a chest in their attic.

The absence of hereditary nobility in the Ottoman Empire is a foundational assumption in Ottoman historical writing. Generations of historians have based their theories, conceptualisations and narratives of the Ottoman administrative system on the idea that hereditary nobility had no legal place in the Ottoman politico-administrative order. According to this widely accepted view, the Ottoman state diverged from its European counterparts in terms of its persistent opposition to hereditary rights and privileges. This theory is based on references to three institutions seen as the building blocks of the classical Ottoman regime: gradual Ottomanisation of ruling aristocracies in the newly-conquered areas, the *devşirme* (child-levy) system and *müsadere* (confiscation of wealth).

Let us look at these one by one, beginning with the idea that early Ottoman methods of conquest worked by gradually incorporating local aristocracies.[41] According to this claim, the Ottoman state followed a two-stage policy towards incorporating the newly-conquered territories. First, it established a form of suzerainty, and then it tried to eliminate the local dynasties by establishing direct control through instituting the *timar*.[42] Starting from Bayezid I (r. 1389–1402), the policy of using vassals to administer newly-conquered places was replaced by the appointment of Ottoman governors.[43] One important way the Ottoman state approached the question of the indigenous noble families was to appoint them to important positions within the administrative machinery. With Mehmed II's reign (r. 1444–1446; 1451–1481), the doors of the highest offices in the central administration, including the Grand Vizierate, were opened to Balkan aristocrats – Greek, Bulgarian, Serbian and Albanian elites. Even the fallen Byzantine ruling dynasty was subsumed into the Ottoman ruling elite.[44] The logic for incorporating the former Balkan and Byzantine aristocracies into the Ottoman administration was that it prevented them from becoming rival nodes of power.

The second pillar that supports the claim of the lack of a hereditary nobility in the Ottoman Empire is the system of meritocracy that served as a primary instrument of elite formation in Ottoman statecraft through the *devshirme* (child-levy) system. That system, which forcibly recruited young Christian boys from across the Ottoman territories, created a slave (*kul*) army and court bureaucracy of Ottoman civilian and military officials whose sole loyalty lay with the Sultan.[45] The purpose of the system was to counteract the emergence of hereditary nobility by creating a select group of military and civilian officials loyal to the ruler. Starting from the mid-fifteenth century, these formerly Christian, peasant-origin children filled the ranks of the highest positions in the Ottoman system, including the Grand Vezir's office, gradually replacing the former Balkan and Byzantine aristocracies who had filled this position up until this period.[46]

Last, Ottoman historians have seen *müsadere*, the state's confiscation of the wealth and property of deposed elites (*ehl-i örf*), as another indication of the empire's intolerance towards elite groups accumulating inheritable wealth and power. From the rule of Mehmed II (r. 1444–6, 1451–81), Ottoman sultans institutionalised *müsadere* to prevent the formation of hereditary nobility.[47] The practice of *müsadere* was closely related to political execution (*siyaseten katl*), since oftentimes the confiscation of wealth and property followed this.[48]

This belief that the Ottoman state was different from its European counterparts in terms of being fundamentally inimical to hereditary offices and privileges also found an echo in the writings of the European political philosophers. The Renaissance political theorist Machiavelli described the Ottoman state as ruled by 'a prince with a body of servants', different from the French state, which was ruled by 'a prince and barons' who 'hold that dignity by antiquity of blood and not by the grace of the prince'.[49] Ottoman observers of the later centuries also emphasised what they considered the unique method of elite formation by the Ottoman state. For instance, in his political treatise, İbrahim Müteferrika stated that the Ottoman state was not comparable to other states because 'in the latter, posts belong to the nobility and are hereditary, while the sultan grants offices to whoever is worthy'.[50] Originating from the writings of the Ottoman and European observers alike, the idea that de jure hereditary nobility was non-existent in the Ottoman politico-administrative system trickled into Ottoman historical writings as one of the most widely accepted and rarely questioned doctrines of the field.

These assumptions about the absence of hereditary nobility in the Ottoman Empire are reminiscent of similar arguments surrounding the non-feudal nature of the Ottoman state. From the 1930s through the 1980s, the question of an Ottoman feudalism caused the most heated debates within Ottoman historiography. Generations of historians argued that the Ottoman state was not feudal, that its fiefdoms (*timar*) were different from those in Europe. First, they were handed out by the Sultan and were non-hereditary. Second, compulsory labour was not prevalent in the agrarian sectors since the system was based on in-kind tax and rent collection. Finally, the *timar*-holders did not have juridical authority over the *reaya*.[51] Halil Berktay criticises this approach because of its rigid legalism, arguing that this understanding of feudalism comes from Ottoman historians' tendency to take state legal and political discourse at face value. Given the state's vested interest in presenting itself as an autonomous monolithic entity, Berktay suggests going beyond a legal and juridical definition of feudalism and considering it within the larger socio-economic context of pre-capitalist societies:

the fundamental social classes that could be found in virtually any pre-capitalist peasant society were here recast by the state as legally differentiated estates or orders, bolstering the illusion that classes were 'made' by the state instead of state being derived from a certain class structure, whilst also making it more difficult to detect the universal behind the specific, the suppressed sociological spontaneity underneath the legal garb.[52]

In the past few decades, paradigmatic shifts in Ottoman historiography have added nuance to previously dominant idealist portrayals of the Ottoman political system. The depiction of the classical Ottoman state as centralised and absolute has been reassessed. Historians of the Ottoman provinces have established that the Ottoman state deployed a variety of administrative models and flexible ruling techniques in its provincial periphery, even during periods when it was supposedly most centralised. More recent scholarship has shown that it was not centralism but adaptability, flexibility and accommodation that gave the Ottoman administration its longevity.[53] Meanwhile, the meta-narrative of decline that had long been the major analytical framework for understanding the Ottoman seventeenth and eighteenth centuries came under serious criticism.[54] At the same time, critiques of modernisation theory and orientalist perspectives rendered dominant assumptions about the Ottoman Empire's uniqueness highly problematic.[55] Comparisons of the Ottoman politico-administrative system with its European and Eurasian contemporaries gained currency. These changing paradigms are echoed in approaches to Ottoman modernity. Critiques of Europe-centred modernisation narratives in light of an emphasis on the interconnectedness of the world and multiple routes to modernity have revealed the indigenous roots of transformation of Ottoman society in the long nineteenth century.[56]

Despite this sea change regarding Ottoman state power and the question of elite formation, the assumption that hereditary nobilities were non-existent in the Ottoman realm remains unquestioned. This thesis is based on the persistence of the assumption that the state meant the central administration at the capital, that it successfully abolished any rival dynastic claims with the policies mentioned above, and that it had absolute control over other elite groups at the centre and in the provinces. In a way, despite the revisionist accounts that have complicated the notion of the state, the idea of the all-powerful Ottoman state has remained intact in Ottoman historians' unquestioned acceptance of the lack of a de jure nobility. Additionally, the field's foundational works about the nature of the early Ottoman state and its approach to hereditary nobility were based on the early Ottoman conquests, mostly in the Balkans and Anatolia. As such, in Ottoman historiography, the pre-Ottoman nobility in

Introduction

the newly-conquered territories refers primarily to Byzantine, Balkan and Turcoman aristocracies. These regions' experience of Ottoman conquest did not necessarily reflect the experiences of other areas that came under the Ottoman rule much later. That is, as the empire expanded with more conquests, the reality of elite formation became more complex, but the meta-narrative of the lack of hereditary nobilities based on these early centuries' experiences remained intact.

In his survey of eighteenth-century provincial magnates, Ali Yaycıoğlu argues that '[t]hese new provincial elites also differed from the nobilities we know in Europe and elsewhere, which were clustered as corporate bodies with hereditary rights and privileges'.[57] Ottoman magnates did not have hereditary rights over their offices and contracts, and the 'Ottoman sultan reserved the right to dismiss officeholders, revoke contracts, and even confiscate property and order executions without judicial process'.[58] Although Yaycıoğlu draws a clear line between European nobilities and Ottoman provincial elites, he is careful to mention exceptions, referring to 'the dynasties in distant provinces that were integrated in the empire with special vassalage arrangements, such as Crimea (until 1774), Bosnia, Kurdistan, the Caucasus, and the Hejaz'.[59] While this recognition is worth noting, it remains a rarity as the consensus is that there was no hereditary nobility in the Ottoman Empire.[60] But if there are so many 'exceptions' in so many different parts of the empire, on what conceptual and historical assumptions is the consensus about the Ottoman state's attitude towards hereditary nobility built?

In its essence, this argument is based on the belief that there was one type of nobility in Europe, uniform across time and space with no historical variations. For Ottoman historians, the French nobility is usually *the* prototype of European nobility. More broadly, most comparative studies of nobility are defined by a research agenda 'derived from French history'.[61] Based on an entrenched estate system, constituting a corporate body, and with hereditary rights that the monarch could not seize, the French model was considered the ideal and, thus, the basis for comparisons and conclusions about the Ottoman case. What if the mirror image of Ottoman nobility discussions, that is the European nobility, was instead a kaleidoscopic reality?

In fact, however, European nobility was more heterogeneous than this.[62] Revisionist approaches within various strands of European historiography have presented a more nuanced and historicised portrait instead of the long-prevalent ideal-type definition of nobility.[63] The single term 'nobility', Paul Fouracre states, 'should comprehend a spectrum of people which stretched from the leaders of small communities of several hundred people, through to an élite group of families which dominated a single county, to that supra-regional élite which would later make up the *Reichsaristokratie*'.[64]

Unlike the French model, not all noble groups were legally defined as an estate by the monarch.[65] Nobility not only had regional variations; it was a group in which 'complex gradations, forming bewildering sub-hierarchies existed everywhere'.[66] Urban–rural divisions, power and wealth differentials, variations in manners and etiquette make it impossible to discuss nobility as a uniform category. And the nobility's political power varied across place and time. Not all nobles in or out of Europe were represented in a representative body.[67] In his comparative analysis of the European nobilities, Asch states that 'England was one of the few European countries in which nobility with the exception of its highest ranks, the peerage, never became a legal estate. The gentry was always a much more informal social status group.'[68] Along similar lines, in his survey of the British nobility, John Cannon points out methodological problems in the definition of the titled nobility and its various constituents. Compared to continental nobilities, the British nobility was distinguished by its small size. This was the result of nobility being bestowed by the monarch – as opposed to being attached to office or service. In addition, the practice of primogeniture resulted in the ongoing shrinking of both the size and wealth of the nobility.[69] All of this made it imperative for historians to 'include the gentry as "a lesser nobility" in their definition of the English aristocracy'.[70]

Seeing nobility as an ideal type rather than a variable historical phenomenon, and guided by the absence of an estate system in the Ottoman Empire, Ottoman historiography categorically rejected the usefulness of the concept for understanding elite formation in the imperial domains. And as far as European historiography is concerned, notwithstanding the revisionist approaches that have complicated the concept of nobility and showed its protean character, historiography on European nobles rarely ventured east of Hungary.[71] This regional bias was a corollary of a long-standing orientalism that drew a thick line between the Ottoman (read Islamic) political formation and Europe and emphasised the former's difference and peculiarities. In rare instances when Ottoman imperial formation was considered as part of Europe, it was still treated as an exception in terms of having 'notables' but not 'nobilities'.[72] As Peter Haldén states, '[a] long tradition in Western political and social thought argues that the Ottoman Empire terminated hereditary elite groups and established an impersonal despotic state in which all subjects, from the most exulted vizir to the most humble Anatolian peasant, were slaves of the sultan'.[73]

Introduction

This view is also buttressed by the writings of Ottoman historians which until quite recently were based on the notion of the absolute power of the Ottoman state. This Eurocentric political thought, as Haldén rightly argues, 'cast the Ottoman Empire as the radical "other" of European realms'.[74] The result is an Ottoman history without nobility, and a history of European nobility without Ottoman representation.

But if nobility is an 'an elite which was open, imperfectly defined, and subject to regional variation',[75] one may legitimately ask what nobility actually entails. Despite the variations, there are patterns that allow us to deploy the concept to understand certain elite groups. Originating in a pre-capitalist socio-economic milieu, nobility at its most basic entails 'entitlement or pre-emptive claims on resources by virtue of one's own distinguished position'.[76] The historians Leonhard and Wieland state that the notion of 'distinctiveness' that nobility entails goes beyond 'mere inequality with its dominantly legal and socioeconomic connotations'.[77] Furthermore, nobility must be acknowledged by both external and internal groups.[78]

Nobilities are formed as a result of the coalescence of service with privilege. In return for performing services and fulfilling duties, nobilities are assigned hereditary rights, privileges and prerogatives. The form and the degree of the noble privileges were not static, but historical and contextual. But as this book demonstrates, military roles and responsibilities were critical in the initial formation of nobility as a privileged group. In addition to honour and lineage, 'military valor' constituted one foundation of noble identity.[79] Above and beyond their military functions and entitlement to landed wealth, the making of the nobility also involved a process of ideological construction that allowed them to justify their status and wealth by virtue of descent from noble ancestors.[80] This construction was fortified through a special code of conduct used only with other nobility and the ruler; by the concept of honour; and by the use of honorific titles that differentiated them from others.

In light of the comparative revisionist perspectives, this book approaches the notion of nobility as a historical phenomenon – a type of elite formation found in the pre-capitalist imperial context and the flexible ruling strategies of early modern empire – as opposed to an ideal type defined solely by shared legal and technical characteristics. The differences between the Ottoman political system and the European cases do not mean the Ottoman Empire had no nobles. While lacking a European-style estate system that gave nobility political representation, the Ottoman politico-administrative system included provincial elites who had been granted hereditary economic and political privileges. By focusing on the Palu begs, this book provides the first systematic study of nobility and the hereditary privileges that came with it within the Ottoman imperial domains. From the sixteenth until the mid-nineteenth century, the rulership of the Palu emirate (*hâkim*) came from the descendants of the Palu begs by virtue of the *temlîknâme* granted to them in the sixteenth century and renewed by successive Ottoman sultans. With this *temlîknâme*, the position of the *hâkim* was attached to a family name for three centuries. The *temlîknâme* was renewed for the last time in 1841 by Sultan Abdülmecid I (r. 1839–61),[81] and the census registers of 1841 specifically noted that the lands of Palu were under the hereditary ownership of the Palu begs. In addition to the imperial state's recognition of the family's rulership, the begs who ruled the Palu emirate in a hereditary fashion had all the characteristics of an elite group defined as hereditary nobility in an imperial setting: a sense of entitlement referring to noble pedigree; titles (*beg/mîr/emîr*) that distinguished them not only from commoners, but from other elite groups with no similar claims to noble ancestry; and a privileged position that accorded them inalienable authority over land, both as an economic resource (i.e. control over agrarian surplus) and a territorial entity (i.e. administrative authority), as well as tax exemptions – and all of this was hereditary. This sense of having a privileged position was further galvanised by the fact that their status had a de jure character granted by the imperial decrees of successive Ottoman sultans over three centuries, decrees that linked them to the Ottoman imperial state that recognised and legitimised their entitlement. For the Palu begs, this noble consciousness and its accompanying sense of entitlement showed a striking continuity from the time they came under Ottoman suzerainty to the end of the empire. What changed was the nature and extent of the privileges that came with their noble position. This means that the degree of *autonomy* they held vis-à-vis the Ottoman state and the latter's authority in the begs' jurisdiction changed over time according to politico-economic and military circumstances.

Beyond the notions of privilege that concern the nobility's relationship with the imperial state, a key aspect of hereditary nobility is control over land and the nobles' position vis-à-vis the agrarian producers. Land stands at the centre of the book's analysis of the Palu begs' privileges. The begs of the Kurdish *hükümet*s held inalienable control over land and labour, and until the mid-eighteenth century issues related to agrarian relations of production in the areas under the begs' ownership remained largely outside the Ottoman imperial state's reach. This, of course, means that the idea that the Ottoman state's control over land was absolute and uniform throughout the empire, and that it protected a presumably independent peasanty, does not hold up when it comes to the Kurdish emirates.

A related aspect of the Kurdish begs' privileged position concerns the administration of justice in the *hükümet*s. In Palu, there was a judge (*qadi*) of the local Islamic court appointed and paid by the imperial centre.[82] The records of the Islamic court constitute vital sources for Ottoman historians, both for legal history and because they are rich in information about socio-economic hierarchies and disputes.[83] But there are no records of Palu's Islamic court. And this does not apply just to Palu; no records of any of the other Kurdish emirates' (e.g. Cîzre, Eğil or Hazzo) courts are available.[84] Ottoman official correspondence shows that the imperial state rarely sent decrees to the *qadi* of Palu, and when it did, it almost always involved the state asking the *qadi* to go after the *hâkim* to make him pay his annual tribute to the central treasury, which was almost always in arrears. Occasionally, the state asked the *qadi* to monitor the repair of churches. Outside these issues, Ottoman archival records show no signs that the local Islamic courts functioned as a major legal mechanism to resolve disputes in the locality. Nearby Harput, which was an ordinary Ottoman sanjak, had a functioning court and its records from 1630 through 1830s are available.[85] They indicate that cases concerning Palu inhabitants were handled by the *qadi* of Harput, especially from the eighteenth century on. But these cases were mostly related to day-to-day economic and administrative issues that required the *qadi*'s supervision, particularly his notary services, not actual dispute resolution. The court records of Amid – the provincial centre of Diyarbekir – also handled cases related to Palu. These suggest that Palu inhabitants used justice mechanisms outside Palu's local Islamic court. In the countryside, this would have been tribal justice.[86] The role of *hâkim* in the administration of justice in that realm – an area outside the imperial state's reach – must have been more pertinent. This is the context in which we must consider the begs' legal autonomy.

Hereditary Privilege and Modernity: The Question of the Nobility's Decline

Nobility's fate in modernity has been widely discussed in comparative studies of nobility. Before the 1970s, historical approaches to nobility often portrayed it as a relic of the traditional order, opposed to the values and ideas represented by the bourgeoisie: a social group doomed to vanish in the dustbin of history.[87] For some scholars, there was a seventeenth-century crisis of the elites, while others saw a long-term decline of the nobility 'in face of the twin threats of Leviathan state and the rising middle class'.[88] More recently, however, this narrative of crisis and decline has been replaced by one of adaptation, accommodation and survival.[89]

In the mid-nineteenth century, the Ottoman state set out to abolish the Kurdish begs' hereditary privileges *in toto*. The historical processes that resulted in the abolition of the Kurdish begs' autonomous rule were no less complex than the concept of nobility. Histories of Kurdistan rightfully see the abolition of the Kurdish emirates as a significant turning point in the region's history – but they do so mostly from a presentist point of view. The disappearance of the Kurdish noble families is understood as the termination of 'potential nuclei' of a forceful group with a modern, nationalist agenda.[90] And discussions of the disappearance of the Kurdish elites' autonomy do not examine how modernisation transformed the previously privileged elite status of the Kurdish begs within the Ottoman system. Existing historical narratives of the Kurdish emirates have emphasised the Ottoman state's military campaigns against the powerful emirates. According to this oft-told tale, these military campaigns resulted in the uprooting of the Kurdish begs from their homelands and the confiscation of their property. It is true that the Ottoman state deployed force to undermine the Kurdish *emîrs* in the mid-nineteenth century. But at the core of this process – both before and after the military operations – was a negotiation about what to do with the hereditary fiscal, military and administrative privilege of the Kurdish emirs. The standard account, already limited, also focuses only on the experiences of the most powerful emirates, those known for their fierce resistance to Ottoman state-making, at least initially. What happened in greater Kurdistan with the lesser elites whose wealth and authority did not match these big ones requires a more nuanced historical perspective.[91] The history of the Palu begs is not one of heroic resistance but of a noble family who justified their fiscal, military and administrative privileges by referring to the imperial state's recognition. By examining the Palu begs' modern history, this book makes four important interventions in the historiography of the Kurdish emirates' disappearance.

First, contrary to the dominant narrative that starts the emirates' transformation with the intervention of the Tanzimat state, this book pushes the periodisation back to the eighteenth century. From the 1720s on, well before the Ottoman state abolished their hereditary privileges, the Palu begs' control over their land had already undergone significant transformations. Palu was near two important mining areas: Keban and Ergani in the Euphrates basin. This proximity gave the Palu nobility the significant role of providing for these mines' logistical needs. Above and beyond the economic burden that the mines put on the local population,

Introduction

the establishment of the Ma'âdin-i Hümâyun Emâneti – a special mine, fiscal and administrative body established to oversee the administration of the Keban and Ergani mines – meant the begs had to contend with mine administrators who significantly challenged their political and fiscal authority. As the mine superintendents' interventions increased, the begs started to lose their control over the appointment processes to the rulership (*hâkim*) of the emirate. The established practice of primogeniture vanished, and the *hâkim* position became monetised, as the superintendents imposed exorbitant fees on candidates for the position. It was within this context that the Palu begs increasingly leased out or sold their hereditary lands. The commodification of land resulted in the fragmentation of the Palu begs' control over land from the 1730s on.

Second, the Palu begs let us analyse the Ottoman state's approach to the hereditary privileges of the landed elites in the context of modern state-making during the Tanzimat era. For the Ottoman state, Palu was important mainly for its fertile agricultural land. But seizing the agrarian surplus in the form of tithe required the abolition of the begs' hereditary rights. Oddly, while the Ottoman administrators were leading a series of large-scale military operations against the powerful Kurdish emirates (e.g. Baban and Bohtan), they were not reckless or heavy-handed towards the Palu begs. In the mid-nineteenth century, the Palu begs could not have resisted a military assault from the Ottoman state. Nevertheless, there were serious discussions at the *Meclis-i Vâlâ-i Ahkâm-i Adliyye* (The Supreme Council of Judicial Ordinances) aimed at justifying the abolition of the begs' hereditary privileges.[92] Why? The discussions among the various echelons of the imperial and provincial bureaucracy demonstrate that the existence of the imperial decrees which granted the begs these hereditary privileges was not a light issue for the Ottoman administrators. There was an effort to justify the annulling of the imperial decrees by referring to how much had changed since the Kurdish begs were first granted these privileges. The idea was that since the Ottoman state now had a regular army, the begs' military service was redundant, and thus they no longer merited hereditary privileges. But even after the state confiscated the Palu begs' lands, the begs' reference to the imperial decrees to justify their hereditary rights did not always fall on deaf ears. As far as the Palu begs are concerned, the Ottoman state was neither categorically inimical nor oblivious to the notion of hereditary rights.

Third, the processes leading to the transformation and eventual dissolution of the Kurdish begs' noble privileges were shaped within the context of their relations with *local actors*. When the state confiscated the begs' lands in the 1840s and opened them up for sale, landownership and local power structures changed drastically. At the core of these changes was the emergence of local Armenians as major purchasers of Palu begs' confiscated land. This brought about a fierce, protracted conflict between the two groups, with the Armenians working to undermine the begs' hereditary claims by insisting on their legal rights as the land's new owners. The Palu begs' status was challenged not just at the imperial level, but within the locality by local actors, mainly wealthy Armenians who became the primary voice of modern property rights based on individual land ownership with title deeds – all anathema to the noble privilege ardently defended by the begs.

Fourth, conventional historical accounts of the Kurdish emirates indicate that a political vacuum emerged in Kurdistan that would be filled by newly-powerful religious leaders (sheiks) who went on to lead the nationalist revolts at the end of the century. While the rise of religious leadership in Kurdistan is important for understanding the region's modern history, this narrative obscures the multifaceted nature of the political scene that emerged in the aftermath of the emirates' abolishment. Modern state-making entailed creating new posts in the provincial bureaucracy and co-opting the begs into this system by granting them positions. It is true that the Tanzimat was a huge blow to the begs' leadership position, but they did not disappear overnight. Instead, they used their contacts with various echelons of the central and provincial Ottoman administration to vie for administrative positions, even when the system wanted to eject them.

Historical Geography of Palu

The Palu begs' identity as a noble family was tied to their control over the fortressed town of Palu and its fertile land. Thus, to understand the career of this family, we must understand the land over which they claimed hereditary ownership. From Istanbul, one could reach Palu via three different routes. Someone coming from the south would arrive at the port city of Mersin, then take a caravan to the east and arrive at Palu after a ten-day journey. From the north, one would arrive at Samsun – a port city on the Black Sea – and take a caravan to the south to Palu. This route took longer, about sixteen days. The last route went north-east to south, from Trabzon through Gümüşhâne, Erzincan and Kiğı to Palu. This route took about ten days.[93]

Palu's old town was built on the west and east sides of a steep hill on the banks of the fertile areas of the Aradzani/Murad River, which flowed round it on three sides. The summit of this cone-shaped hill was 3,292 feet and was crowned by an Urartu-era castle.[94] The famous seventeenth-century traveller Evliya Çelebi poetically likened the castle to the head of

Introduction

Figure I.1 The ruins of the old city of Palu. Photo by Yaşar Gündoğan, 2019

a snake reaching up to the sky – Murad River surrounding the hill being the snake's curled-up body.[95] It was so unreachable, he noted, that even Tamerlane bypassed it. When Evliya Çelebi visited the castle, İbrahim Beg, the then *hâkim*, was there with his armed forces. In addition to a mosque, the castle featured an arsenal, cellars and cisterns.[96]

Palu's ancient history as an Urartu provincial centre made it a point of interest for European Orientalists from the late nineteenth century on. A natural stronghold of the town housed a ninth-century rock inscription engraved in cuneiform by the king of Urartu Menua (or Menuas) (810–785 BCE).[97] It recorded Menuas' military marches and conquests through the country of the Hittites.[98] Below the tablet are said to be 'three sets of rock-hewn chambers, apparently the burial places of the princes of Palu'.[99] One observer in the 1850s noted that 'a Syriac MS. of the New Testament exists, ascribed to the third century', in Palu.[100] As a fortressed city, Palu also featured in medieval accounts and crusade history. It was the scene of the battles between Emir Balak of the Artuqid dynasty based in Harput and Jocelyn of Courtenay, count of Edessa (Urfa) in the twelfth century.[101]

Palu also has a unique place in Armenian ethno-national imagination as an ancient Armenian city. Ancient accounts describe it as part of the 'Fourth Armenia' of Armenia Major (or the Kingdom of Armenia).[102] In a map showing ancient Armenia on the eve of the Arab invasions, Palunik is indicated as a region that roughly corresponds to the modern town of Palu with an area of 475 square kilometres.[103] Palu is also significant in Armenian historical memory because it was the homeland of

Mesrob Mashtots (or St Mesrob) – the saint who invented the Armenian alphabet and translated the Bible from Syriac and Greek into Armenian (c. AD 431).[104] In the words of Armenian ecclesiast Karekin Sırvantsdyants, who toured the region in 1878, the Palu castle was the 'womb of Armenian enlightenment'.[105] In the twentieth century, Palu's place as a key site of historic Armenia was tarnished by grim memories of the pogroms of 1895 and the Armenian Genocide of 1915. Armenian villages had been reduced to ruined churches, cemeteries and houses.

In Kurdish historical memory, Palu's significance stems mainly from its being the home town of Sheikh Said (Şêx Seîd in Kurdish) – the famous leader of the Nakşibendî- Hâlidiyye order.[106] Born in 1865, the sheikh was one of the leaders of the 1925 Kurdish nationalist revolt against the Turkish government. The state's response to the revolt was brutal – it even used its meagre air force against the rebels.[107] Despite its significance during the rebellion, contemporary Palu has lost its 'Kurdish' character and is now a centre of Turkish-Islamic conservatism. As mentioned, the descendants of the Palu begs are distant from, if not inimical to, Kurdishness and identify with the mainstream Turkish ethnic identity.

Palu's current location is not the same as during the Ottoman period. The old town, called Zeve, moved to its current position on the west side of the castle after fires destroyed the city centre completely in 1928 and 1941. From the sixteenth century through the eighteenth, Palu was attached for administrative purposes to the Diyarbekir province. In the eighteenth century, when the Ma'âdin-i Hümâyun Emâneti was established, it came under the roof of this special mine administration because of its role in providing charcoal for the mines. In the mid-nineteenth century, it became a district of the newly-established Harput province. From the late nineteenth century onward, Palu was again a district of the Diyarbekir province. Throughout this process, Palu kept getting smaller, especially after the Ottoman state began centralising in the mid-nineteenth century. The emirate of Palu under the hereditary rule of the Palu begs covered a much larger area than its twentieth-century namesake does. Until the Tanzimat era, all of Palu was under the Palu *hâkim*'s jurisdiction as an emirate. As the Ottoman state made more inroads into Palu's politico-administrative scene, it began rearranging the emirate's administrative divisions in accordance with its fiscal, military and bureaucratic priorities. It removed villages from Palu and attached them to the nearby districts, a policy continued during the twentieth century by the republican regime. The fertile villages on the northern bank of the Murad River were under Palu's administrative scope until 1934, when they were attached to Kovancılar, a newly-established district intended for the settlement

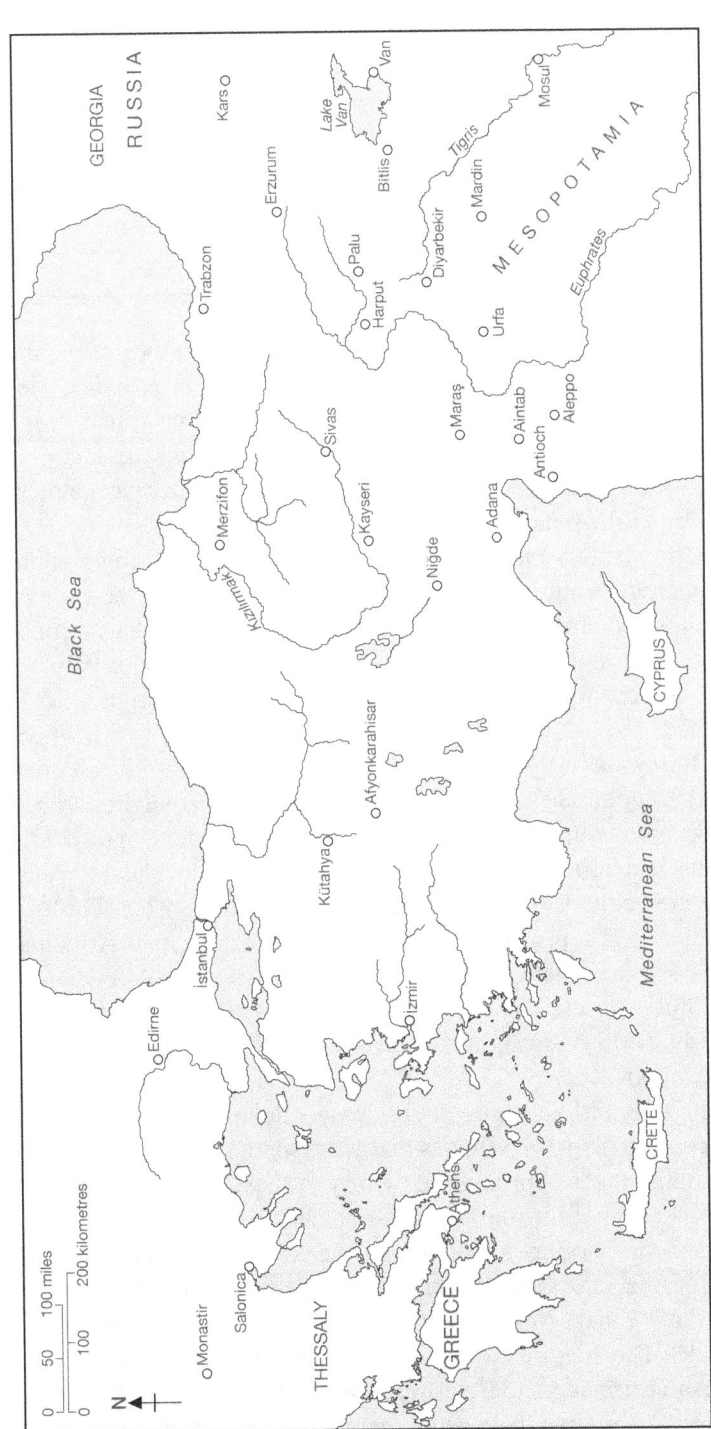

Map I.1 Palu in the Ottoman Empire[108]

Table I.1 Total male population of Palu in 1841

Palu's Male Population in Various Areas	
Palu's Muslim male population (city centre)[109]	2,397
Muslim male population in the countryside (Palu, Hun, Weşin, Sivan, Gökdere, Bulanık, Ohi, Karaçor *nahiye*s [sub-districts])[110]	13,718
Palu's non-Muslim population (city centre)[111]	1,687
Non-Muslim population in 51 villages[112]	4,282
Total male population	22,065

of Romanian refuges.[113] Over time, more villages, sub-districts and districts were extracted and attached to the neighbouring provinces, leaving the once-sizeable Palu emirate only a fraction of what it had been. And when the government focused on Turkification during the late Ottoman and republican periods, Kurdish, Zazakî and Armenian place names were replaced by Turkish names.[114]

Palu stood largely outside of the Ottoman record-keeping system until the nineteenth century because of its previously mentioned *mefrûzü'l-kalem* status. The first modern Ottoman census of 1830–1 was conducted in Palu in 1841 and provided the first systematic data about Palu's population.[115] According to this census, Palu's total population was around 45,000. The 1881–2 census data shows its population as 50,496.[116] The overwhelming majority of Palu's Christian population were Armenians. They had four churches in the city centre, each with a neighbourhood that had grown around it.[117] Mostly traders and manufacturers, in the 1870s, the Armenians had 200 looms (a dying establishment) and a tannery, and they manufactured cloth using native cotton.[118] Almost every household had its own vineyards. There were forty households of Protestant Armenians.[119] In the city centre, there was also a small community of Jews – around eleven families in the 1840s.[120] The Muslim population of the city centre was mostly Turkish-speaking and Sunni, and they lived in three separate neighbourhoods.

The majority of Palu's population was made up of the agrarian inhabitants of its more than 300 villages that were spread over the plain between the mountain ranges. Approximately fifty of these villages, located on the north and south-west of the Murad/Aradzani River, contained Armenian populations of varying sizes, as well as Kurdish settlements. Habab (Havav), Kapıaçmaz (Tset), Sakrat, Uzunoba, Hoşmat (Khoşmat), Bağın, Srin, Abrank, Çınaz, Nacaran and Nerkhi had the largest Armenian communities.[121] The majority of Palu's Muslim rural population consisted of Kurdish (Kurmanc and Zaza) groups. Some lived as settled agrarian-pastoral groups in the villages, but there were other groups of nomadic or

Introduction

semi-nomadic Kurds in the greater Palu area – Karaçor in the north-west, Karabegan and Weşin in the south, and Sivan, Gökdere and Karabegan in the south-east. Semi-nomadic Kurds inhabiting these areas moved to mountain pastures with their herds of sheep, horses and cattle in the summer.[122] They produced significant amounts of dairy, which they traded with the settled villagers around the Murad/Aradzani River.

Three interconnected elements defined Palu's socio-economic-geographical scene: river, forest and mines. The emirate was based on the fertile alluvial lands of the Murad/Aradzani River – one of the two main tributaries of the Euphrates River. The Murad originates at Mount Ararat at the north of Lake Van and flows approximately 450 miles before merging with the Karasu to form the Euphrates. The river stood at the centre of the district's socio-economic life. Inhabitants enjoyed a variety of fish; its water was a gathering place for women; and it provided transportation for people and goods in *kelek*s. A *kelek* consists of 'goatskins inflated with air, tied beneath a framework of light poles. Often as many as eight hundred such skins are used to give the boat the desired buoyancy … When [the cargo] reaches its journey's end it is broken up and sold as skins and timber.'[123] The timber needed for the rafts came from the forests in the mountains surrounding the district, while the skins were provided by livestock raised mainly by the Kurdish population in the district's east and south-east. In the eighteenth century, with the revitalisation of the mining industry in Keban and Ergani, *kelek*s now carried charcoal to these mine areas, further increasing the interdependency between animal husbandry (because more livestock skin was needed for *kelek*s), forestry (because of the charcoal needed for the smelters and the timber needed for the *kelek*s) and the mining industry. Operations at the Keban mines ceased in the late 1870s because of lack of wood.[124] Along with providing charcoal for the nearby mines, Palu itself housed important mine resources that remained largely unexploited before the twentieth century.[125]

Throughout the period examined in this book, agriculture was at the centre of Palu's economy. Grains, specifically wheat, cotton and rice, were cultivated on the fertile alluvial lands on the northern bank of the Murad River. During the long wars of the eighteenth century, the grains sold in Palu fed the Ottoman troops in their military campaigns against Iran. Cotton primarily went to local markets, where it was used by families and small workshops in spinning and weaving.[126] The majority of the agrarian population worked as sharecroppers (*maraba*) who paid half of the harvest, on top of the tithe, to the landowning begs. More than anything else, it was Palu's agrarian potential that brought it to the Ottoman administrators' attention in the mid-nineteenth century, as the central government emerged as a new party claiming shares in agrarian surplus. This process accelerated the commodification of land and the privatisation of land ownership in Palu and posed an important challenge to the Palu begs' control over land ownership. Nevertheless, from the time they came under the Ottoman realm until the end of the empire, the Palu begs continued to be a landed elite. Their major wealth and authority derived from the agrarian surplus they seized from Palu's fertile lands. And it was what brought them under the Ottoman imperial state's radar in the mid-nineteenth century.

Organisation of the Book

The book consists of three parts. The first focuses on the period prior to the Tanzimat era. Chapter 1 examines the first encounter between the Ottoman state and the Palu begs in the sixteenth century within the context of the Ottoman imperial rivalry with the Safavids – the Iranian ruling dynasty in the sixteenth century (r. 1501–1736). Through an analysis of the earliest imperial decrees granted to the Palu begs and of the notion of privilege, the chapter shows the Palu begs' transformation into a noble group in the Ottoman realm. The second chapter puts flesh on the begs' hereditary privileges by focusing on interplay between the different realms in which the Palu begs engaged with the Ottoman state. Throughout the eighteenth century, the Palu begs interacted with the Ottoman state through three interconnected sectors: economic (the mines); fiscal (taxation); and military (providing soldiers in times of military campaigns). Each realm granted prerogatives and entailed responsibilities. The chapter demonstrates that the level of autonomy of the Palu begs was constantly being negotiated between the begs and the state. Prerogatives and responsibilities were defined by the permutations of mining, taxation and the military, and the leverage each party held in each realm. This period also was a time of unprecedented land commodification; needing cash in an increasingly monetised economy, the Palu begs leased out their lands to non-nobles. The last part of the chapter examines the begs' changing control over land in this context.

Part two consists of three chapters focusing on the early Tanzimat era from the 1820s through the 1840s. This is a key period to understand the transformation of the Ottoman state's policy towards the Kurdish elites. Chapter 3 analyses the logic underlying the Ottoman state's goal of abolishing the Kurdish emirates' hereditary privileges, focusing on this transformative moment in the Ottoman state's approach to the begs. Starting in the 1820s, the Ottoman state began trying to undercut the economic and political power of the long-established Kurdish nobility.

Introduction

This was a clear deviation from the previous centuries during which the Ottoman state's approach to Kurdish nobility was based on how much specific Kurdish begs co-operated with the imperial Ottoman state. This moment represents a rupture, as the Ottoman state began to consider the complete annulment of the three-century-old contract made with the begs' ancestors. This analysis compares the Palu case with other emirates. Chapter 4 turns to the local context and examines how the begs' hereditary privileges were negotiated by and among local actors. At the centre of these discussions was the Palu begs' right to the agrarian surplus. The chapter illuminates the ways local power dynamics and events influenced governmental decision-making processes about hereditary land ownership in Palu. Chapter 5 focuses on the Weşin incident, providing a micro history of this pivotal event. It first considers the career of the *hâkim* Abdullah Beg, giving an account of the exploitative labour system he imposed, then turns its attention to Weşin and its aftermath. The incident and its investigation activated different levels of the central and local bureaucracies, with the governor and the local councils created by the Tanzimat programme serving as platforms for parties to voice their versions of the event. The chapter shows that the fate of the Palu nobility was not just determined by the powerbrokers in the meeting rooms of the imperial bureaucracy, but by local actors, their power conflicts and the way those were reflected in the capital.

Part three highlights the developments after the de jure abolishment of the Palu begs' hereditary privileges. Chapter 6 focuses on land ownership, examining the government order confiscating the begs' lands and the ensuing conflict-ridden process of land sales from the 1850s through the 1870s. It offers a granular account of land sales and the resulting alterations in land ownership and relations of agricultural production. Chapter 7 focuses on the bureaucratic realm to demonstrate the making of a new administrative order in the district as the authority of the *hâkim* became contested. It examines the central state's efforts to deepen its control in Palu by establishing modern administrative machinery. What position would the begs hold in this changing administrative scheme with its expanded provincial bureaucracy? Chapter 8, the last chapter, focuses on the 1895 Massacres in Palu. Analysis of Palu's socio-economic and political scene on the eve of the massacres shows that the internationalisation of the Armenian Question, the politicisation of the Palu Armenians, and the ongoing socio-economic tensions set the ground for violent attacks on the Armenians in the fall of 1895. This analysis shows that this violence occurred in a context defined by the deterioration of the military and symbolic authority of the begs and increasing tensions in the rural setting over land. After maintaining de jure hereditary rights for over three centuries, the Palu begs were now a group that lost its identity as a collective body, the majority of their landholdings, and positions in provincial bureaucracy. What remained of a glorious past was a tarnished prestige because of their ill-reputed acts during the Armenian massacres and faded imperial decrees which they still kept as the only proof of a noble pedigree.

Notes

1. In Ottoman archival sources, the village's name is transliterated as 'Veşin'. I heard villagers pronounce this with a 'W' sound at the beginning. The village is a Zaza-speaking one. In Zazakî, the language spoken by the Zaza people, 'W' sounds exist. Therefore, I transliterate the name of the village as Weşin.
2. Başkanlık Osmanlı Arşivi (henceforth BOA) İ.MVL 139/3859, 15 Rebîülâhir 1265 [10 March 1849].
3. Palu is one of the areas where the Zazas constituted a significant portion of the population. There is an ongoing scholarly and political debate over whether the Zazas are a branch of the Kurds or a separate ethnic group, along with the related question of whether Zazakî is a dialect of Kurdish. This question is important both for Zazakî-speaking and Kurmancî-speaking groups and scholars of ethnicity, linguistics and nationalism. In Ottoman archival documents of the period discussed in this book, the two groups are not distinguished, and are invariably described as Kurds (*ekrad*). The difference between the two groups in scholarly and political discourse became pertinent only in the twentieth century. Not differentiating between them here should not be read as a denial of the Zazas' claim for difference, nor as ignoring the question, but rather as a corollary of the historical context and the Ottoman archival documentation on the region. For a study that describes Zazas as Kurds, see Mehmed S. Kaya, *The Zaza Kurds of Turkey: A Middle Eastern Minority in a Globalised Society* (London; New York: I. B. Tauris, 2011). For works that emphasise the separateness of the Zaza identity, see Serdar Karabulut, *Zazalar* (İzmit: Altın Kalem Yayınları, 2013). Recently, an emphasis on the Zaza identity of the Palu begs – as opposed to them being Kurdish – has emerged. See Murat Alanoğlu, 'Zaza Beylikleri, Şeyhler ve İslam', *Tarih ve Gelecek Dergisi* 5, no. 3 (27 December 2019): 792–804.
4. Ottoman archival sources addressed the members of the Kurdish ruling households as '... Beg of the Palu ûmera'. The members of the family also described their position as 'from the begs' [lineage]'. The 'beg' title referred to their distinguished position in the society. Hence, I refer to them as 'the Palu begs' in this book.
5. In his study on the Baban Emirate, Metin Atmaca points out the tendency in the literature on the Kurdish emirates to focus on the Bedirkhans.

Introduction

His scholarship brings to light the significance of the Baban emirate in Kurdish political history as well as literary tradition. Metin Atmaca, 'Politics of Alliance and Rivalry on the Ottoman–Iranian Frontier: The Babans (1500–1851)' (Ph.D. dissertation, Albert Ludwigs University of Freiburg, 2013). For Bedirkhan Beg's emirate of Botan, see Malmîsanij, *Cızira Botanlı Bedirhaniler ve Bedirhani Ailesi Derneği'nin Tutanakları*, 1. baskı (Istanbul: Avesta, 2009); Mehmet Alagöz, 'Old Habits Die Hard: A Reaction to the Application of Tanzimat and Bedirhan Bey's Revolt' (MA thesis, Boğaziçi Üniversitesi, Istanbul, 2003). For an approach to the Bedirkhan family that is more focused on dynastic and family history, see Barbara Henning, *Narratives of the History of the Ottoman-Kurdish Bedirhani Family in Imperial and Post-Imperial Contexts: Continuities and Changes* (Bamberg: University of Bamberg Press, 2018), https://fis.uni-bamberg.de/handle/uniba/43114 (last accessed 15 March 2020).
6. In the Ottoman state's view, they were a part of the Kurdistan emîrs (*Kürdistan ûmerası*), which the former perceived as a collective entity.
7. One descendant is an exception. Feyzullah Demirtaş openly expressed his Kurdish identity and was persecuted for it. He was one of the 52 Kurds who were arrested in 1959 and imprisoned for 195 days. Their number decreased to 49 during their trials, leading to them being called '49s' (49'lar). Azat Zana Gündoğan, 'The Kurdish Political Mobilization in the 1960s: The Case of "the Eastern Meetings"' (MA thesis, Middle East Technical University, 2005), 186–8.
8. The *Tanzimat* period refers to a period of intense fiscal, military and administrative reforms in the Ottoman Empire that began in 1839 with the issuing of the Gülhane Imperial Rescript (Gülhane Hattı Hümayunu).
9. In 1846, the Ottoman state designated a sizeable province of Kurdistan and defined it for the first time as an official Ottoman administrative unit. It covered the areas of Diyarbekir Province, Van, Muş and Hakkari districts and Cîzre, Botan and Mardin sub-districts. However, both before the establishment and after the liquidation of the Kurdistan *Eyaleti*, Ottoman authorities used the term 'Kurdistan' to refer to the eastern provinces that were predominantly populated by Kurds and Armenians and that had historically been under the command of the Kurdish emirates. They referred to the rulers of these emirates as 'Kurdistan Begleri or ûmera-ı Kurdistan'.
10. Metin Atmaca, 'Three Stages of Political Transformation in the 19th Century Ottoman Kurdistan', *Anatoli. De l'Adriatique à La Caspienne. Territoires, Politique, Sociétés*, no. 8 (1 October 2017): 44.
11. From a Kurdish ethno-national point of view, the era of the Kurdish emirates' rule is important because it represents or proves the existence of a Kurdish self-rule that was lost with the centralisation of the Ottoman Empire and the establishment of a modern nation-state system in the Middle East. Turkish historians of a nationalist-conservative bent discuss the Kurdish emirates with a completely opposite agenda, seeking to minimise

the degree of autonomy held by the Kurdish begs in order to delegitimise present-day Kurdish political claims. For this position, see Mehmet Ali Ünal, 'XVI. Yüzyılda Palu Hükümeti', *Ondokuz Mayıs Üniversitesi Eğitim Fakültesi Dergisi* 7, no. 1 (1992); Orhan Kılıç, 'Yurtluk-Ocaklık Sancaklar Üzerine Bazı Tespitler', *Ankara Üniversitesi Osmanlı Tarihi Araştırma ve Uygulama Merkezi Dergisi*, no. 10 (1999): 119–37. For a critique of these positions, see Christopher Houston, '"Set Aside from the Pen and Cut off from the Foot": Imagining the Ottoman Empire and Kurdistan', *Comparative Studies of South Asia, Africa and the Middle East* 27, no. 2 (1 January 2007): 411. Houston concludes that 'the current perceptions of the Ottoman history of the Kurdish provinces are refracted through a nationalist prism'. See also Murat Alanoğlu, 'Osmanlı İdâri Sistemi İçerisinde Palu Hükûmeti' (Ph.D. dissertation, Istanbul, Istanbul University, 2017), 19–21.

12. James L. Gelvin, 'The "Politics of Notables" Forty Years After', *Middle East Studies Association Bulletin* 40, no. 1 (2006): 25.
13. Albert Hourani, 'Ottoman Reform and the Politics of Notables', in *The Modern Middle East*, eds Albert Hourani, Philip Shukry Khoury and Mary Christina Wilson (Berkeley: University of California Press, 1993), 83–110.
14. Hourani, 89–90.
15. Hourani, 89–91.
16. For a useful overview, see Philip S. Khoury, 'The Urban Notables Paradigm Revisited', *Revue Des Mondes Musulmans et de La Méditerranée* 55, no. 1 (1990): 215–30. Scholars working on other parts of the empire, mainly the Balkans and Anatolia, also used the concept but focused mostly on the a'yan dynasties of the eighteenth century. For a bibliography of this expansive literature on the a'yan, see Hamit Karasu, 'Osmanlı Ayanları Üzerine Yapılan Çalışmalar (Tanzimata Kadar)', *Journal of Turkish Studies* 13 (1 January 2018): 127–50. For two most recent works on the a'yan dynasties, see Ali Yaycioglu, *Partners of the Empire: The Crisis of the Ottoman Order in the Age of Revolutions* (Stanford, CA: Stanford University Press, 2016); Yonca Köksal, *The Ottoman Empire in the Tanzimat Era: Provincial Perspectives from Ankara to Edirne* (London; New York: Routledge, 2019).
17. Ehud R. Toledano, 'The Emergence of Ottoman-Local Elites (1700–1900): A Framework for Research', in *Middle Eastern Politics and Ideas: A History from Within* (London: I. B. Tauris, 1997), 148–9.
18. Dina Rizk Khoury, 'The Ottoman Centre versus Provincial Power-Holders: An Analysis of the Historiography', in *The Cambridge History of Turkey: The Later Ottoman Empire*, ed. Suraiya Faroqhi (Cambridge: Cambridge University Press, 2006), 136.
19. A recent edited volume showcases studies on the Ottoman provincial elites in diverse areas of the empire, primarily the Balkans and Anatolia. ed. Antonis Anastasopoulos, *Provincial Elites in the Ottoman Empire: Halcyon*

Days in Crete V: A Symposium Held in Rethymnon 10–12 January 2003 (Rethymon: Crete University Press, 2005).
20. Yaycioglu, *Partners of the Empire*.
21. For a critique of the nationalist historical rendition of the Ottoman Balkans, see Isa Blumi, *Reinstating the Ottomans: Alternative Balkan Modernities, 1800–1912* (New York Palgrave Macmillan, 2011), 5–9.
22. Janet Klein, *The Margins of Empire: Kurdish Militias in the Ottoman Tribal Zone* (Stanford, CA: Stanford University Press, 2011), 15. Since the 2000s, scholars have increasingly used post-colonial perspectives to approach the nineteenth-century Ottoman state's modernisation policies for its provincial periphery, describing them within the frameworks of Ottoman Orientalism, colonialism or imperialism. For discussions of these frameworks, see, among others, Ussama Makdisi, 'Ottoman Orientalism', *The American Historical Review* 107, no. 3 (2002): 768–96; Selim Deringil, '"They Live in a State of Nomadism and Savagery": The Late Ottoman Empire and the Post-Colonial Debate', *Comparative Studies in Society and History* 45, no. 02 (April 2003): 311–42; Thomas Kühn, 'Shaping and Reshaping Colonial Ottomanism: Contesting Boundaries of Difference and Integration in Ottoman Yemen, 1872–1919', *Comparative Studies of South Asia, Africa and the Middle East* 27, no. 2 (18 September 2007): 315–31; Edip Gölbaşı, '19. Yüzyıl Osmanlı Emperyal Siyaseti ve Osmanlı Tarih Yazımında Kolonyal Perspektifler', *Tarih ve Toplum Yeni Yaklaşımlar* 13, no. Güz (2011): 199–222; Özgür Türesay, 'The Ottoman Empire Seen through the Lens of Postcolonial Studies', *Revue d'histoire Moderne et Contemporaine* 60, no. 2 (February 2013): 127–45. For a study of Ottoman colonial approach to Sub-Saharan Africa, see Mostafa Minawi, *The Ottoman Scramble for Africa: Empire and Diplomacy in the Sahara and the Hijaz* (Stanford, CA: Stanford University Press), 2016. For a critique of Ottoman colonial historiography's inordinate focus on the Arab provinces, see Vangelis Kechriotis, 'Postcolonial Criticism Encounters Late Ottoman Studies', *Historein* 13 (2013): 39–46. Recent studies have also examined new forms of autonomous or semi-autonomous regions that emerged in the nineteenth century within the context of a Eurocentric international legal order. See Aimee M. Genell, 'Autonomous Provinces and the Problem of "Semi-Sovereignty" in European International Law', *Journal of Balkan and Near Eastern Studies* 18, no. 6 (1 November 2016): 533–49; Elektra Kostopoulou, 'Autonomy and Federation within the Ottoman Empire: Introduction to the Special Issue', *Journal of Balkan and Near Eastern Studies* 18, no. 6 (1 November 2016): 525–32.
23. Sabri Ateş, *Ottoman–Iranian Borderlands: Making a Boundary, 1843–1914*, reprint edn (Cambridge: Cambridge University Press, 2015), 38–9.
24. Khoury, 'The Ottoman Centre versus Provincial Power-Holders: An Analysis of the Historiography', 138.

25. In his 2001 study, Hakan Özoğlu examined the Kurdish elites through the prism of Hourani's concept of notables. He argued that in the Kurdish provinces notables came from 'the Sufis, especially the Naqshbandis, the Kurdish tribal nobility, and also from families whose leaders managed to secure local administrative positions'. Hakan Özoğlu, *Kurdish Notables and the Ottoman State: Evolving Identities, Competing Loyalties, and Shifting Boundaries*, revised edn (Albany, NY: State University of New York Press, 2004), 12–13. For two other studies which overemphasise the similarities between the *ayan* in Hourani's conceptualisation and the Kurdish begs/mîrs, see Uğur Bahadır Bayraktar, 'Erken 19. Yüzyılda Kürt-Osmanlı İlişkileri: Zirki Begleri ve Hazro'da Yerel Siyaset', in *Osmanlı Devleti ve Kürtler*, eds İbrahim Özcoşar and Shahab Vali (Istanbul: Kitap Yayınevi, 2017), 137; Atmaca, 'Politics of Alliance and Rivalry on the Ottoman–Iranian Frontier: The Babans (1500–1851)', 10.
26. Gabor Agoston, 'A Flexible Empire: Authority and Its Limits on the Ottoman Frontiers', *International Journal of Turkish Studies* 9, nos 1–2 (2003): 15–32.
27. Fikret Adanır, 'Semi-Autonomous Provincial Forces in the Balkans and Anatolia', in *The Cambridge History of Turkey: The Later Ottoman Empire*, ed. Suraiya Faroqhi (Cambridge: Cambridge University Press, 2006), 158.
28. The others were Cîzre, Eğil, Genç and Hazzo. For a general overview of the Kurdish emirates, see Michael Eppel, 'The Kurdish Emirates', in *Routledge Handbook on the Kurds*, ed. Michael M. Gunter (Boca Raton, FL: Taylor & Francis, 2018), 37–47.
29. Both *hükümet* and *yurtluk-ocaklık* sanjaks consisted of lands belonging to the Kurdish chiefs who ruled the area and declared their allegiance to the Ottoman state. Both were based on principles of hereditary ownership that left the rule of the emirate in the hands of the same ruling family and promised that the Ottoman state would not intervene in succession except in situations in which the chiefs were found guilty of treason, disobedience or oppressive behaviours. The difference between them was that *yurtluk-ocaklık*s were not exempt from *tahrir*s and *timar*. Outside Kurdistan, there were *yurtluk-ocaklık* sanjaks in Bosnia, Anatolia, Damascus, Rakka and Baghdad.
30. Halil İnalcık and Donald Quataert, eds, *An Economic and Social History of the Ottoman Empire: 1300–1914* (Cambridge: Cambridge University Press), 1001. On occasion, the Ottoman state violated this principle by trying to conduct *tahrir* in *hükümet*s. Tom Sinclair, 'The Ottoman Arrangements for the Tribal Principalities of the Lake Van Region in the Sixteenth Century', in *Ottoman Borderlands: Issues, Personalities, and Political Changes*, eds Kemal H. Karpat and Robert W. Zens (Madison, WI: University of Wisconsin Press, 2003), 119–44.
31. İnalcık and Quataert, 133.

Introduction

32. According to the seventeenth-century traveller Evliyâ Çelebî, there was a market inspector (*muhtesib*) and a voivoda in Palu. Yücel Dağlı, Seyit Ali Kahraman and İbrahim Sezgin eds, *Evliya Çelebi Seyahatnâmesi*, vol. III (Yapı Kredi Yayınları, 2001), 134.
33. Heath Lowry examines the geneology of *zemin/baştina* – privately held plots of land – that he observed in the *tahrir* surveys of Maçuka. He traces the concept to Bosnia and Herzegovina, where it referred to 'freeholds the inhabitants of these areas had possessed under their former rulers'. This, Lowry argues, attests to 'the Ottoman recognition of pre-existing *status quo*'. Heath W. Lowry, 'Privilege and Property in Ottoman Maçuka in the Opening Decades of the Tourkokratia: 1461–1553', in *Continuity and Change in Late Byzantine and Early Ottoman Society*, eds Anthony Bryer and Heath W. Lowry (Birmingham: University of Birmingham, Centre for Byzantine Studies, 1986), 113.
34. Ömer Lütfi Barkan, 'Timar', in *Türkiye'de Toprak Meselesi: Toplu Eserler* (Istanbul: Gözlem Yayınları, 1980), 819.
35. Colin Imber, *The Ottoman Empire, 1300–1650: The Structure of Power*, 2nd edn (Basingstoke: Palgrave Macmillan, 2009), 181. Joseph von Hammer-Purgstall, the Austrian orientalist who wrote the monumental, multi-volume history of the Ottoman Empire in the nineteenth century, made an analogy between the Muslim Bosnian aristocrats of Bosnia and Herzegovina and the Kurdish Begs. Nedim Filipović, 'Ocaklık Timars in Bosnia and Herzegovina', *Prilozi Za Orijentalnu Filologiju*, no. 36 (1986): 153.
36. Sándor Papp, 'The System of Autonomous Muslim and Christian Communities, Churches, and States in the Ottoman Empire', in *The European Tributary States of the Ottoman Empire in the Sixteenth and Seventeenth Centuries*, eds Gábor Kármán and Lovro Kunčević (Leiden: Brill, 2013), 375.
37. Bruce Masters examines the Arab provincial elites' autonomy vis-à-vis the Ottoman state in relation to their proximity from Istanbul. Bruce Masters, 'Semi-Autonomous Forces in the Arab Provinces', in *The Cambridge History of Turkey: The Later Ottoman Empire*, ed. Suraiya Faroqhi (Cambridge: Cambridge University Press, 2006), 186–206.
38. Viorel Panaite, 'The Legal and Political Status of Wallachia and Moldavia in Relation to the Ottoman Porte', in *The European Tributary States of the Ottoman Empire in the Sixteenth and Seventeenth Centuries*, 20.
39. Panaite, 17.
40. *Temlîk* literally means to give something to someone as their property. *Temlîknâme* refers to a title deed given by the ruler that grants someone specific lands in return for a service. Another term used for this is *mülknâme*. Both are used to refer to the document granted to the Kurdish begs by Ottoman sultans. Mehmet İpşirli, 'Temlîknâme', in *TDV İslâm Ansiklopedisi* (İstanbul: Türkiye Diyanet Vakfı, 2011), https://islamansiklopedisi.org.tr/temlikname (last accessed 15 September 2020).

41. Halil İnalcik, 'Ottoman Methods of Conquest', *Studia Islamica*, no. 2 (1954): 103–29.
42. İnalcik, 103–4.
43. Imber, *The Ottoman Empire, 1300–1650*, 180.
44. Heath W. Lowry, *The Nature of the Early Ottoman State*, 1st edn (Albany, NY: State University of New York Press, 2003), 118. Lowry demonstrated that between 1453 and 1516, of the fifteen individuals who held the position of Grand Vezir, six, and possibly seven, of them were members of the 'Byzantine and Balkan aristocrats turned Vezirs'. Lowry, 128. In this work, Lowry also discusses the descendants of the co-founders who joined forces with Ottoman rulers as *akıncı* in early raids of the Balkans as a group of hereditary nobility in the Ottoman realm. He notes that 'even two-hundred-fifty years after the founding of the Ottoman polity, the importance of the descendants of Mihal, Evrenos, Turahan and Malkoç, was still recognised. They were as close to a hereditary nobility as the Ottomans produced.' Lowry, 142.
45. For a classical account of *devşirme*, see V. L. Ménage, 'Some Notes on the "Devshirme"', *Bulletin of the School of Oriental and African Studies, University of London* 29, no. 1 (1966): 64–78.
46. Lowry, *The Nature of the Early Ottoman State*, 129.
47. Mehmet Ali Ünal, 'Osmanlı İmparatorluğu'nda Müsâdere', *Türk Dünyası Araştırmaları Dergisi* 49 (1987): 95–111.
48. Yasin Arslantaş, 'Confiscation by the Ruler: A Study of the Ottoman Practice of Müsadere, 1700s–1839' (Ph.D., London School of Economics and Political Science, 2017), 24, http://etheses.lse.ac.uk/3729/ (last accessed 1 March 2021).
49. Niccolò Machiavelli, *The Prince*, trans. W. K. Marriott, eBook #1232 (Project Gutenberg Ebook, 1998), https://www.gutenberg.org/files/1232/1232-h/1232-h.htm#chap04 (last accessed 15 April 2021). Metin Kunt elaborates on this point. İ. Metin Kunt, *The Sultan's Servants: The Transformation of Ottoman Provincial Government, 1550–1650* (New York: Columbia University Press, 1983), 31–5.
50. Marinos Sariyannis, *A History of Ottoman Political Thought up to the Early Nineteenth Century* (Leiden; Boston: Brill, 2018), 393.
51. Halil Berktay, 'The Feudalism Debate: The Turkish End – Is "Tax-vs.-Rent" Necessarily the Product and Sign of a Modal Difference?', *The Journal of Peasant Studies* 14, no. 3 (1 April 1987): 293.
52. Halil Berktay, 'The Search for the Peasant in Western and Turkish History/Historiography', *The Journal of Peasant Studies* 18, nos 3–4 (1 April 1991): 135.
53. Agoston, 'A Flexible Empire'; Karen Barkey, *Empire of Difference: The Ottomans in Comparative Perspective* (Cambridge: Cambridge University Press, 2008).
54. Cemal Kafadar, 'The Question of Ottoman Decline', *Harvard Middle East and Islamic Review* 4 (1998): 30–75; Donald Quataert, 'Ottoman History

Writing and Changing Attitudes towards the Notion of "Decline"', *History Compass* 1, no. 1 (2003): 1–9.

55. Rifa'at Abou-El-Haj, *Formation of the Modern State: The Ottoman Empire Sixteenth to Eighteenth Centuries*, 2nd edn (Syracuse, NY: Syracuse University Press, 2005); Ariel Salzmann, 'An Ancien Régime Revisited: "Privatization" and Political Economy in the Eighteenth-Century Ottoman Empire', *Politics & Society* 21, no. 4 (1 December 1993): 393–423.
56. Huri Islamoglu and Peter C. Perdue, 'Introduction', *Journal of Early Modern History* 5, no. 4 (1 January 2001): 271–81.
57. Yaycioglu, *Partners of the Empire*, 67.
58. Yaycioglu, 67–8.
59. Yaycioglu, 67. Another study refuted the idea of the non-existence of hereditary nobility in the Ottoman political system by demonstrating the Ottoman state's protectionist policies towards the Crimean Khans and the descendants of the Ramazanoğulları family in the nineteenth century. Mehmet Yavuz Erler, 'Osmanlı'da "Asil Kan" Aristokrasisinin XIX. Yüzyıldaki Yansımalarına Dair Birkaç Örnek: Cengiz Han ve Ramazanoğlu Soyu', *Journal of International Social Research* 1, no. 2 (2008). In Bosnian historiography, hereditary landownership of the Bosnian Muslim elites was debated in relation to the question of continuity between the pre-Ottoman Bogomil nobility and the Muslim elites in the Ottoman period. For more on this, see Michael Hickok, *Ottoman Administration of 18th Century Bosnia* (Leiden ; New York: Brill, 1997), 42–53.
60. For a recent work reproducing this notion of the absence of formal provincial aristocracy in the Ottoman Empire, see Antonis Anastasopoulos, 'Introduction', in *Halcyon Days in Crete V: A Symposium Held in Rethymno: Provincial Elites in the Ottoman Empire*, xi–xxviii.
61. Ronald G. Asch, *Nobilities in Transition 1550–1700: Courtiers and Rebels in Britain and Europe* (London: New York: Bloomsbury USA, 2003), 5.
62. Historical scholarship on the European nobilities is extensive. For a wonderful bibliography, see H. M. Scott ed., *The European Nobilities in the Seventeenth and Eighteenth Centuries*, 2nd edn (New York: Palgrave Macmillan, 2007), 322–35.
63. Paul Fouracre, 'The Origins of the Nobility in Francia', in *Nobles and Nobility in Medieval Europe: Concepts, Origins, Transformations*, ed. Anne Duggan (King's College London: Boydell & Brewer, 1998), 20.
64. Fouracre, 20. According to Scott and Storrs, '[t]he nobility throughout Europe resembled a pyramid, though the steepness or otherwise of the sides varied according to the characteristics and the composition of the individual élite'. In this pyramid, the apex consisted of 'a small number of wealthy and powerful families who together composed an aristocracy'. The original meaning of aristocracy as 'rule by the best' was later inceasingly used to describe 'a group of leading nobles who enjoyed immense social and political authority'. In this sense, 'aristocracy' is a much more specific term

than 'nobility' and it implies a sense of economic and political superiority over other noble groups. *The European Nobilities in the Seventeenth and Eighteenth Centuries*, 21.

65. Asch, *Nobilities in Transition 1550–1700*, 29. Scott, *The European Nobilities in the Seventeenth and Eighteenth Centuries*, 21.
66. Jerzy Lukowski, *The European Nobility in the Eighteenth Century*, 2003 edn (Houndsmills, Basingstoke, Hampshire; New York: Palgrave Macmillan, 2003), 3.
67. Lukowski, 3.
68. Asch, *Nobilities in Transition 1550–1700*, 25.
69. John Cannon, 'The British Nobility, 1660–1800', in *The European Nobilities in the Seventeenth and Eighteenth Centuries: Western Europe*, vol. 1 ed. H. M. Scott (London; New York: Longman, 1995), 62–3.
70. Cannon, 63.
71. See for instance, Scott, *The European Nobilities in the Seventeenth and Eighteenth Centuries*.
72. M. Safa Saraçoğlu, 'Resilient Notables: Looking at the Transformation of the Ottoman Empire from the Local Level', in *Contested Spaces of Nobility in Early Modern Europe*, eds Matthew P. Romaniello and Charles Lipp (Routledge, 2016), 257–77.
73. Peter Haldén (ed.), 'The Ubiquitous and Opaque Elites of the Ottoman Empire c.1300–c.1830', in *Family Power: Kinship, War and Political Orders in Eurasia*, ed. Peter Haldén, *500–2018* (Cambridge: Cambridge University Press, 2020), 252.
74. Haldén, 252.
75. Fouracre, 'The Origins of the Nobility in Francia', 17.
76. Gail Bossenga, 'A Divided Nobility: Status, Markets, and the Patrimonial State in the Old Regime', in *The French Nobility in the Eighteenth Century: Reassessments and New Approaches*, ed. Jay Smith, 1st edn (University Park, PA: Penn State University Press, 2012), 48.
77. Jörn Leonhard and Christian Wieland, 'Noble Identities from the Sixteenth to the Twentieth Century: European Aristocratic Cultures in Law, Politics, and Aesthetics', in *What Makes the Nobility Noble?: Comparative Perspectives from the Sixteenth to the Twentieth Century*, eds Jörn Leonhard and Christian Wieland (Vandenhoeck & Ruprecht, 2011), 9.
78. Leonhard and Wieland, 7.
79. Asch, *Nobilities in Transition 1550–1700*, 9.
80. Anne Duggan, 'Introduction: Concepts, Origins, Transformations', in *Nobles and Nobility in Medieval Europe: Concepts, Origins, Transformations*, ed. Anne Duggan (King's College London: Boydell & Brewer, 1998), 1.
81. İ.MVL 237/8388 1 Şevvâl 1257 (14 November 1841).
82. Martin van Bruinessen and Hendrik Boeschoten eds, *Evliya Çelebi's Book of Travels: Evliya Çelebi in Diyarbekir* (Leiden; New York: Brill Archive, 1988), 26.

Introduction

83. For a recent examination of court records as sources for Ottoman historiography, see Yavuz Aykan and Boğaç Ergene, 'Shari'a Courts in the Ottoman Empire before the Tanzimat', *The Medieval History Journal* 22, no. 2 (1 November 2019): 203–28.
84. Alanoğlu, 'Osmanli İdâri Sistemi İçerisinde Palu Hükûmeti', 44.
85. Mehmet Beşirli, '385 Numaralı Harput Şer'iye Sicili'nin Tanıtımı ve Osmanlı Şehir Tarihi Açısından Önemi', *OTAM* 10 (1999): 9.
86. Tribal justice and *qadi* courts were not entirely separate. In the seventeenth century, customs and practices emanating from tribal justice found their way to the *qadi* court. Ercan Gümüş, '17. Yüzyılda Aşiret Geleneklerinin Şer'i Hukuktaki Yerine Dair Diyarbekir Mahkemesi'den Bir Örnek: Kan Davalarında Sulh Amacıyla Kız Verme Âdeti ve Aşiretli Toplumlar Hakkında Bazı Değerlendirmeler', *Journal of Turkish Studies* 13, vol. 13, issue 1 (1 January 2018): 29–50. Plaintiffs preferred *qadi* court resolution over tribal justice if they thought it would be to their benefit. Yavuz Aykan, *Rendre la justice à Amid: Procédures, acteurs et doctrines dans le contexte ottoman du XVIIIème siècle* (Leiden: Brill, 2016), 141.
87. Jay M. Smith, 'Introduction: Nobility after Revisionism', in *The French Nobility in the Eighteenth Century: Reassessments and New Approaches* (University Park, PA: Penn State University Press, 2006), 1–18.
88. Scott, *The European Nobilities in the Seventeenth and Eighteenth Centuries*, 6.
89. For an overview of approaches to the question of the 'decline of the nobility', see Seymour Becker, *Nobility and Privilege in Late Imperial Russia*, 1st edn (DeKalb, IL: Northern Illinois University Press, 1988), 1–27.
90. Michael Eppel, 'The Demise of the Kurdish Emirates: The Impact of Ottoman Reforms and International Relations on Kurdistan during the First Half of the Nineteenth Century', *Middle Eastern Studies* 44, no. 2 (1 March 2008): 240.
91. For a study focusing on the Zirki Begs, see Uğur Bayraktar, 'Reconsidering Local versus Central: Empire, Notables, and Employment in Ottoman Albania and Kurdistan, 1835–1878', *International Journal of Middle East Studies* 52, no. 4 (November 2020): 685–701.
92. *Meclis-i Vâlâ-i Ahkâm-i Adliyye* was established in 1838 within the context of the re-organisation of the Ottoman bureaucratic structure in the Tanzimat era. It would act as an advisory body for the Tanzimat reforms. After 1839, the authority of the council was broadened and it functioned as a legislative organ in the Ottoman bureaucratic organisation. The members of the council were selected from the viziers, the military, *ulama* (clergy) and upper-level bureaucrats. Initially, the Council consisted of the chair and five members, but the number of members gradually increased and by the 1850s it had twenty-five members. Mehmet Seyitdanlıoğlu, *Tanzimat devrinde Meclis-i Vâlâ, 1838–1868* (Ankara: Türk Tarih Kurumu Basımevi, 1994), 37–41.

93. Arsen Yarman, *Palu-Harput, 1878: Raporlar*, vol. 2 (Derlem, 2010), 83.
94. C. H. Wheeler, *Letters from Eden; or, Reminiscences of Missionary Life in the East*. (Boston, 1868), 169.
95. Dağlı, Kahraman, and Sezgin, *Evliya Çelebi Seyahatnâmesi*, III: 134. *Murâd nehri kenarında hakkâ ki mânend-i kahkahâ eflâke ser çekmiş bir seng-binâ bir küçük kal'adır ...'*
96. Dağlı, Kahraman and Sezgin, III: 134.
97. Altan Çilingiroğlu, *The History of the Kingdom of Van, Urartu* (Ofis Ticaret Matbaacilik Limited, 1988), 19.
98. A. H. Sayce, 'The Kingdom of Urartu (Van)', in *The Cambridge Ancient History: The Assyrian Empire, 1925*, vol. 3 eds John Bagnell Bury, Stanley Arthur Cook, Frank E. Adcock, Martin Percival Charlesworth and Norman Hepburn Baynes. (Cambridge: Cambridge University Press, 1925), 174.
99. John Murray (Firm), *Handbook for Travellers in Asia Minor, Transcaucasia, Persia, Etc.* (J. Murray, 1895), 243.
100. George Percy Badger, *The Nestorians and Their Rituals with the Narrative of a Mission to Mesopotamia and Coordistan in 1842–1844, and of a Late Visit to Those Countries in 1850: Also, Researches into the Present Condition of the Syrian Jacobites, Papal Syrians, and Chaldeans, and an Inquiry into the Religious Tenets of the Yezeedees* (London, 1852), 319.
101. Charles Henry Wheeler, *Odds and Ends; or, Gleanings from Missionary Life*. (Boston, [c. 1888]), 3.
102. Fourth Armenia refers to the two banks of the Euphrates River. The other three were Armenia Major (Greater Armenia), Armenia Minor (Lesser Armenia) and Syria. Boğos Natanyan, 'Ermenistan'ın Gözyaşı veya Palu, Harput, Çarsancak, Çapakçur ve Erzincan Hakkında Rapor, in Arsen Yarman, *Palu-Harput, 1878: Raporlar*, vol. 2 (Derlem, 2010), 93.
103. Hewsen, R. H., 'Armenia According Asxar hac'oy', Macler, F., Association de la revue des études arméniennes, Fundação Calouste Gulbenkian, Société des études arméniennes. *Revue des études arméniennes*. Paris: Association de la revue des études arméniennes, [etc.], 328.
104. S[usan] A[nna] (Brookings) Wheeler, *Daughters of Armenia* (New York, [c. 1877]), 16–17.
105. Yarman, *Palu-Harput, 1878*, 2: 487.
106. The Nakşibendî is one of the most popular Sufi orders in the Muslim world. The Hâlidiyye branch is attributed to Mevlânâ Hâlid-i Bağdâdî and has been the most popular religious order in Kurdistan. For the spread of the Nakşibendî order in nineteenth-century Kurdistan, see Martin van Bruinessen, 'The Naqshbandi Order in Seventeenth-Century Kurdistan', in *Naqshbandis: Cheminements et Situation Actuelle d'un Ordre Mystique Musulman* ed., Marc Gaborieau (Istanbul–Paris: Éditions Isis, 1990), 337–60.
107. Robert Olson, *The Emergence of Kurdish Nationalism and the Sheikh Said Rebellion, 1880–1925* (Austin, TX: University of Texas Press, 2013), 120.

Introduction

108. Elnathan Ellsworth Strong, *Mission Stories of Many Lands: A Book for Young People. With Three Hundred and Forty Illustrations* (American Board of Commissioners for Foreign Missions, 1885), 76.
109. BOA.NFS.d 2687 c.29 Zilhicce 1256 [21 February 1841]. The census register showing the Muslim population of Palu's city centre.
110. BOA.NFS.d 2688 c.29 Zilhicce 1256 [21 February 1841]. The census register showing the population of Palu's seven sub-districts (*nahiye*s).
111. BOA.NFS.d 2689 c. 29 Zilhicce 1256 [21 February 1841]. The census register showing the non-Muslim population [*reaya*] of Palu.
112. BOA.NFS.d 2689 c. 29 Zilhicce 1256 [21 February 1841]. The census register showing the non-Muslim population [*reaya*] of Palu.
113. T. C. Elazığ Valiliği (Elazığ Governorate of Turkey) http://www.elazig.gov.tr/kovancilar (last accessed 13 March 2021).
114. According to the 1841 census, in the seven sub-districts of Palu there were 323 villages. Süleyman Yapıcı, '1841 Nüfus Defterlerinde Palu', in *Fırat Üniversitesi Harput Uygulama ve Araştırma Merkezi Uluslararası Palu Sempozyumu Bildiriler Kitabı*, vol. 1 (Elazığ: Fırat Üniversitesi Matbaası, 2018), 231–56.
115. The implementation of the first Ottoman census was an uneven process throughout the empire. For more on the Ottoman censuses in Kurdistan, see Nilay Özok-Gündoğan, 'Counting the Population and the Wealth in an "Unruly" Land: Census Making as a Social Process in Ottoman Kurdistan, 1830–50', *Journal of Social History* 53, no. 3 (28 March 2020): 763–91.
116. Kemal H. Karpat, 'Ottoman Population Records and the Census of 1881/82–1893', *International Journal of Middle East Studies* 9, no. 02 (May 1978): 134.
117. Yarman, *Palu-Harput, 1878*, 2: 101.
118. *Cyprus and Asiatic Turkey: A Handy General Description of Our New Eastern Protectorate. From 'The English Cyclopaedia'* (London : 1878), 83–4.
119. BOA.NFS.d 2689 c. 29 Zilhicce 1256 [21 February 1841]. The census register showing the non-Muslim population [*reaya*] of Palu.
120. BOA.NFS.d 2689 c. 29 Zilhicce 1256 [21 February 1841]. The census register showing the non-Muslim population [*reaya*] of Palu.
121. BOA.NFS.d 2689 c. 29 Zilhicce 1256 [21 February 1841]. The census register showing the non-Muslim population [*reaya*] of Palu. The largest Armenian presence was in Havav, with 478 males, followed by Hoşmat (174).
122. Helmuth Moltke, *Essays, Speeches, and Memoirs of Field-Marshal Count Helmuth von Moltke* (New York: 1893), 280–1.
123. Mariposa Gazette, Vol. LXII, No. 2, 17 June 1916.
124. G. Bie Ravndal, *Turkey: A Commercial and Industrial Handbook* (Washington: G.P.O., 1926). 150.

125. For instance, the Sivan sub-district of Palu contained iron reserves. *Cyprus and Asiatic Turkey*, 83. In 1884, a coal mine was discovered in Palu but at the time it was considered unsuitable for smelting. 'Reports from Her Majesty's Consuls on the Manufactures, Commerce, &c. of Their Consular Districts' (London: Harrison & Sons, 1884), 1,423; 'Reports from Her Majesty's Consuls on the Manufactures, Commerce, &c. of Their Consular Districts' (London: Harrison & Sons, 1885), 1,927. In the early twentieth century, the presence of coal in this area would trigger British and German commercial interest, but no actual investments resulted. 'Reports from Her Majesty's Consuls on the Manufactures, Commerce, &c. of Their Consular Districts' (London: Harrison & Sons, 1884), 1,423; 'Reports from Her Majesty's Consuls on the Manufactures, Commerce, &c. of Their Consular Districts. 1884', 1885, 1,927. Frech, *Die Grundlagen Türkischer Wirtschaftsverjüngung* (Berlin: 1916), 70, http://hdl.handle.net/2027/njp.32101073305946 (last accessed 15 January 2020).
126. Donald Quataert, *Ottoman Manufacturing in the Age of the Industrial Revolution* (Cambridge: Cambridge University Press, 2002), 82.

PART I
A TENUOUS ACCORD

Chapter 1

At the Beginning: The Formation of the Kurdish-Ottoman Nobility of Palu in the Sixteenth Century

Soon after, Kethüdabey appeared at the door: 'It is the hâkim of Palu, Cemşit Bey,' he called out. [Cemşit Bey] looked to be in his fifties. He was very tall and had a dark complexion. He was wearing an *abani* turban and an embroidered cardigan. There was an empty scabbard for a dagger on his belt wrapped around his waist. His dagger was taken before he entered; it was forbidden to appear before the sultan with a weapon. Cemşit Bey was one of the Kurdish beys who declared their loyalty to the Sultan during the Çaldıran Battle where he distinguished himself and he showed significant achievements. He put in effort and had a share in victory. [Bey] stopped three feet from the throne, put his hand on his chest and greeted the Sultan. The Sultan responded, 'Aleykümüsselâm, Cemşit Bey; it makes us pleased to see you among us. How are our brethren along the borderlines?'[1]

[…]

'I represent the Sunni Kurdish Beys in your presence. They chose me from among themselves. They asked me to convey their loyalty.' He took out a *kozak*[2] from his belt and passed it to Sultan: 'Here is the deed of alliance. It is sealed by twenty-five Kurdish beys.' Sultan Selim opened the *kozak*, took the paper out and read it carefully. Kurdish beys were proclaiming their unconditional acceptance of the sublime and just rule of the Ottomans. There were twenty-five seals on the bottom of the page. The hâkim of Bitlis Emir Şerefüddin, the melik of Hizan Emir Davud, the emir of Hisnakeyfa from the Ayyubid [descent] Melik II. Halil, the hâkim of Imadiye Sultan Hüseyin and others. The Sultan's face lightened up. He said 'thanks.' 'God bless you all. Now we will get a *menşur* written and give it to you. We are appointing these beys whose names appear here as the emirs of the places where they are [situated]. Praise be.' Cemşit Bey reached out to Sultan to kiss his hand. Yavuz stood up hastily, grabbed Cemşit Bey from his shoulders and pulled him towards himself: 'We like hugging our brethren, brother Cemşit.'[3]

Cemşîd Beg was to the Palu nobility what Osman Gazi was to Ottomans.[4] A ruler of the Palu emirate within the Ottoman realm, Cemşîd Beg's ancestors, the Mîrdasi begs, pre-dated Ottoman rule in the area. According to Şeref Han's *Şerefnâme* (1596–7), arguably the most comprehensive historical account of the Kurdish noble families, Mîrdasi begs led an emirate centred on neighbouring Eğil around the eleventh century.[5] The Palu emirate was established by one branch of this family based in the Bağın castle near Palu. When his uncle died without an heir, Cemşîd Beg became the leader of the emirate and brought it under Ottoman suzerainty in the early sixteenth century.

The scene in the epigraph is from *Mısır'a Doğru: Sefer-i Hümayûn*, a novel that came out in 2010 by Yavuz Bahadıroğlu, a novelist and columnist known for his Islamist-conservative bent. The last volume of a trilogy narrating Sultan Selim I's reign, the book covers his eastern campaigns. Bahadıroğlu's dramatic description of Cemşîd Beg's encounter with the Sultan obviously employs several leaps of imagination – it would be an Ottoman historian's dream to know what Cemşîd Beg actually wore, how he comported himself, or the Sultan's exact words.

Two things in this scene are true, however. Cemşîd Beg did have an audience with Sultan Selim I in Karaman, when the latter was on his way to Tabriz.[6] And, as this scene implies, Cemşîd Beg's military achievements during the Ottoman-Safavid wars of the 1510s made him stand out among the Kurdish begs. He defended the Palu fortress from Safavid forces and was one of the Kurdish begs who accepted Ottoman suzerainty as a result of the ardent diplomacy of the Ottoman envoy, İdris-i Bidlîsî. This made Cemşîd Beg the architect of the Palu begs' incorporation into the Ottoman-Kurdish nobility in the sixteenth century. His descendants maintained their hereditary rule over Palu until the mid-nineteenth century.

Şerefnâme, includes a story about Cemşîd Beg from before he ruled the Palu emirate, when he served Halid Beg of the Pazuki emirate. As the story goes, Cemşîd Beg, who was known as Kara Cemşîd at the time,[7] was hunting with his master, and Halid Beg's bird soared high, staying in the sky longer than usual. When it finally came back, it landed on Cemşîd Beg's head, which witnesses understood to mean that he would someday have a magnificent state. A few days later, Cemşîd Beg's uncle, the emirate's ruler, died without an heir, and Cemşîd Beg succeeded him.[8] This is the foundation myth of the Palu emirate under the charismatic leadership of Cemşîd Beg – reminiscent of the Ottoman Empire's foundation myth under Osman Gazi.[9] Cemşîd Beg did not lead a world empire that lasted six centuries, but he proved his leadership, valour and diplomatic skills in the context of the Ottoman–Safavid Wars, and he solidified the rule of his noble family, who maintained their hereditary rights for the next three centuries.

We begin our exploration of the origins of the Ottoman realm's Kurdish nobility in the sixteenth century in the context of the Ottoman–Safavid Wars. The rivalry between the Ottomans and the Safavids, the ruling dynasty of Iran (1501–1736), was critical for the formation of Kurdish noble families as a privileged group within the Ottoman administration. A fundamental assumption of Ottoman historiography is that hereditary privilege was anathema in the Ottoman Empire. Yet the Kurdish begs maintained de jure hereditary rights over their land for three hundred years. How did this peripheral group gain an elite status in the Ottoman political system?

First Encounter: War, Diplomacy and the Ottoman Entry into Kurdistan

'In the sixteenth century of our era', writes Marshall Hodgson, the pioneering historian of the Islamic world, 'a visitor from Mars might well suppose that the human world was on the verge of becoming Muslim.'[10] In this period, the Islamicate empires of the east – the Ottomans, Safavids and Mughals – had the political, economic and strategic upper hand. If our Martian were to travel to the lands where these empires ruled around the 1510s, she would see that the Ottomans and Safavids were on the verge of war over this frontier zone where tribes, tribal confederations and emirates ruled in a decentralised fashion. Kurdistan became the major battle zone between these two formidable empires in their competition for riches, authority and legitimacy in the Islamic world. If the Martian were near the zone where the ruling Kurdish begs held court, she would witness them enacting a delicate political dance between the two powers, alternating between negotiation and accommodation. This first encounter between the local Kurdish rulers and the Ottoman imperial state took place in crisis, with actors of varying degrees and types of leverage seeking alliances in hopes of emerging from a political collision with their power either intact or enhanced. This first encounter shaped the Kurdish begs' military, fiscal and administrative prerogatives in the Ottoman politico-administrative system. It defined who the Kurdish-Ottoman nobles were and how they saw their role in the broader Ottoman Empire.

In the summer of 1514, Ottoman and Safavid armies met at Çaldıran, and the Ottomans emerged victorious thanks in part to their cannons, which the Safavids lacked.[11] However, the Ottoman strategy of territorial expansion had never been based solely on force and military tools. Instead, a key element was negotiation with local power holders, to whom the Ottomans offered concessions and administrative flexibility in exchange for loyalty.[12] During his eastern campaign, Sultan Selim I pursued this strategy with the Kurdish ruling elites of the area. After Çaldıran, İdris-i Bidlîsî, a seasoned scribe in the Ottoman court, was tasked with persuading the Kurdish emirs to side with the Ottomans against the Safavids.[13] He was provided with blank imperial orders (*temessüknâmes*) with the sultan's seal on them. The content of these *temessüknâmes* would be defined as a result of İdris-i Bidlîsî's diplomacy and it would shape the terms of the Kurdish rulers' incorporation into the Ottoman realm and define their prerogatives.[14] But İdris-i Bidlîsî's role was more than just an intermediary. In a letter to the Sultan, İdris-i Bidlîsî enthusiastically highlighted the significance of bringing the Kurdish lands under Ottoman control, saying it would open the way to the Ottoman conquest of Baghdad, Basra, Azerbaijan, Aleppo and Damascus – which it did.[15] Bidlîsî also exaggerated the loyalty of the Kurdish begs to convince the Ottoman sultan of the success of his venture, even though at that point they were still negotiating with the Safavids.[16] At one point, twelve Kurdish begs pledged loyalty to Safavid leader Shah Ismail, but İdris-i Bidlîsî concealed this and other such acts from the Sultan, emphasising instead that the Kurds, who, like the Ottomans, were Sunni Muslims, would have a religious motivation to ally with the Sultan.[17]

Meanwhile, the Kurdish begs were by no means passive: they wanted to use İdris-i Bidlîsî. His Kurdish origins and his familiarity with the socio-political realities of Kurdistan likely afforded him a degree of prestige and authority from the Kurdish point of view, as well as giving him legitimacy when he represented them to the Ottoman sultan.[18] According to the seventeenth-century chronicler Hüseyin Efendi, the ûmera [the begs] of Kurdistan sought to reach out to the Sultan through a letter they sent with İdris-i Bidlîsî.[19] In this letter, which Hüseyin Efendi quotes at length, the begs declared their allegiance to the Ottoman sultan, whom they describe as the 'Sultan of Islam', strategically gesturing to the religious aspect of the imperial rivalry. Pointing out the proximity of their lands to the Safavids, they emphasised the damage the Safavids had caused and demanded help from the Ottoman sultan to defeat the Kızılbaş menace (referring to the Shi'ite population of Anatolia supporting Shah Ismail). The letter indicates the proactive strategies Kurdish begs employed to gain the best possible alliance once it was clear that the lands over which they ruled were desired by two of the most powerful political entities of the time. The question was what they could gain through their incorporation into the Ottoman system.

İdris-i Bidlîsî's ambassadorial skills proved critical in this regard. Not only was he familiar with the region but he also most likely witnessed the Kurdish leaders' negotiation tactics with the Akkoyunlu and Karakoyunlu rulers during his tenure at the Akkoyunlu court.[20] He also understood the socio-political organisation of Kurdish leadership and the way their noble lineage allowed them to claim the right to rule over these territories. In his negotiations, İdris-i Bidlîsî highlighted the Kurdish leaders' hereditary claims to rule and addressed them with the titles that indicated their noble pedigree, such as *beg/bey* or *emîr/mîr*.[21] His deep familiarity with Kurdistan and its noble families convinced him that recognising the Kurdish begs' hereditary claims to leadership was essential to securing their loyalty. Besides, the Sultan himself specifically asked İdris-i Bidlîsî to pay the utmost attention to the hierarchies between the Kurdish begs while designing the administrative structure of Ottoman Kurdistan and granting titles to the begs.[22] In the administrative model that emerged after the Kurdish begs accepted Ottoman suzerainty, the recognition of the hereditary character of the begs' rule was an essential parameter.

Kurdish Nobility in the Ottoman Politico-administrative System

In his formative work 'The Ottoman Methods of Conquest', Halil İnalcık lays out an oft-cited framework for understanding Ottoman policies and strategies of conquest. He describes Ottoman conquest as a two-stage process. In the first, the Ottoman administration followed a flexible policy of suzerainty that did not aim for the total obliteration or alienation of indigenous elites.[23] In the second, the Ottomans tried to gain direct control by recording the population and revenue-bringing resources of the area (*tahrir*) and establishing the *timar* system, the main fiscal-military institution of the Ottoman imperial state. İnalcık's model is useful as it demonstrates that the Ottoman policy of conquest was less rigid and more pragmatic than it was hitherto assumed. Recent works add further depth by highlighting the different ways the Ottoman state implemented its instruments, policies and strategies in different provinces. As Agoston argues, '[f]ormer historical reconstructions of Ottoman administrative practices and capabilities are based on random evidence, often from the core provinces of the Balkans and Asia Minor, that have very little to say about regional variations outside the core zones'.[24] Fiscal and administrative models that emerged through the conquest of different regions varied across the empire, and the process of negotiation between the Ottomans and indigenous elites was one factor that led to varied administrative models with varying degrees of autonomy.

In Kurdistan, the fiscal and administrative model reflected a compromise between Kurdish leaders and the Ottoman state, and it is possible to see traces of İdris-i Bidlîsî's approach to Kurdish begs as autonomous entities and noble households in that model. After the Çaldıran battle, Diyarbekir was under siege by the Safavids for about a year. In mid-September of 1515, Ottoman forces entered the city and, according to the famous chronicler Hoca Sadeddin, they 'raised the standard of victory' on the city's towers.[25] Over the next few years, other cities, towns and fortresses in Kurdistan were brought under Ottoman administration. Afterward, two sizeable administrative units, *Diyarbekir Beylerbeyliği* (1515) and *Van Beylerbeyliği* (1548), were created. This model reflected a 'compromise' between imperial control and local autonomy and was based on a 'coexistence' of administrative units with different degrees of autonomy.[26] The imperial state was able to institute classical Ottoman military-fiscal administration in some parts of the region, such as the sanjak (sub-province) of Amid where it conducted a *tahrir* – the land, population and income surveys characteristic of the Ottoman imperial state's control over a newly-conquered area – and assigned *timars*.[27] But for much of the rest of the territory, the Ottoman state developed new administrative structures, reflecting its inability to establish unmediated control over Kurdistan's economy and administration.

As a result, there were two types of administrative organisation in Kurdistan, namely, *yurtluk-ocaklıks* and *hükümets*. *Hükümet* and *yurtluk-ocaklık* were both used to describe sanjaks granted to local begs with administrative and fiscal privileges that classical Ottoman sanjaks did not enjoy. Both designations indicated the Ottoman state's acknowledgement that 'succession to the office would remain within the family and the ruler would not be deposed by the sultan or any other Ottoman authorities'.[28] Thus, this codified the imperial state's acceptance of local Kurdish leaders' hereditary rule. The difference between the two was that *hükümets* held *mefrûzü'l-kalem* and *maktû'ü'l-kadem* designations. Literally, these terms meant that *hükümets* were 'set aside from the pen and cut off from the foot', with *mefrûzü'l-kalem*, indicating that the Ottoman imperial state could not conduct *tahrir* surveys, while *maktû'ü'l-kadem* meant that the state would not send tax collectors or any other Ottoman officials to these lands.[29] In other words, neither the pen of the state nor the feet of its tax collectors were allowed to do their usual jobs: *hükümets* were essentially exempt from the *timar* system and many other state taxes and extractions such as *avarız, sürsat, nüzul*.

At the Beginning

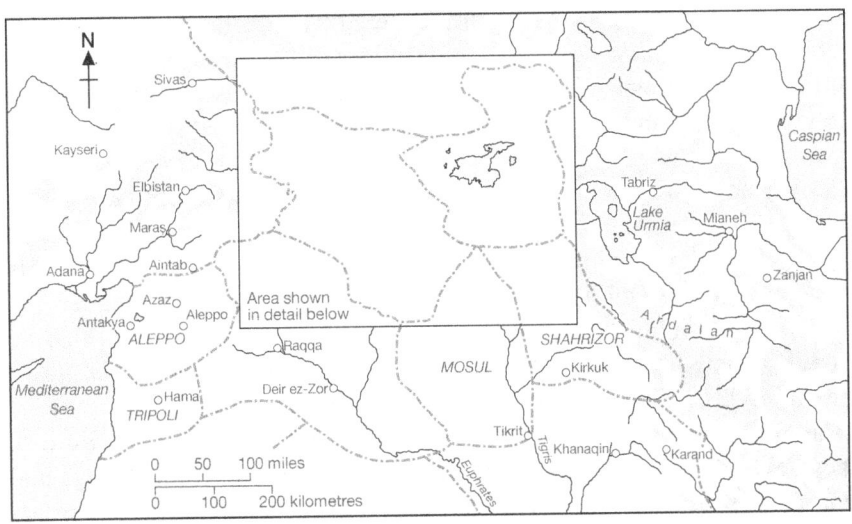

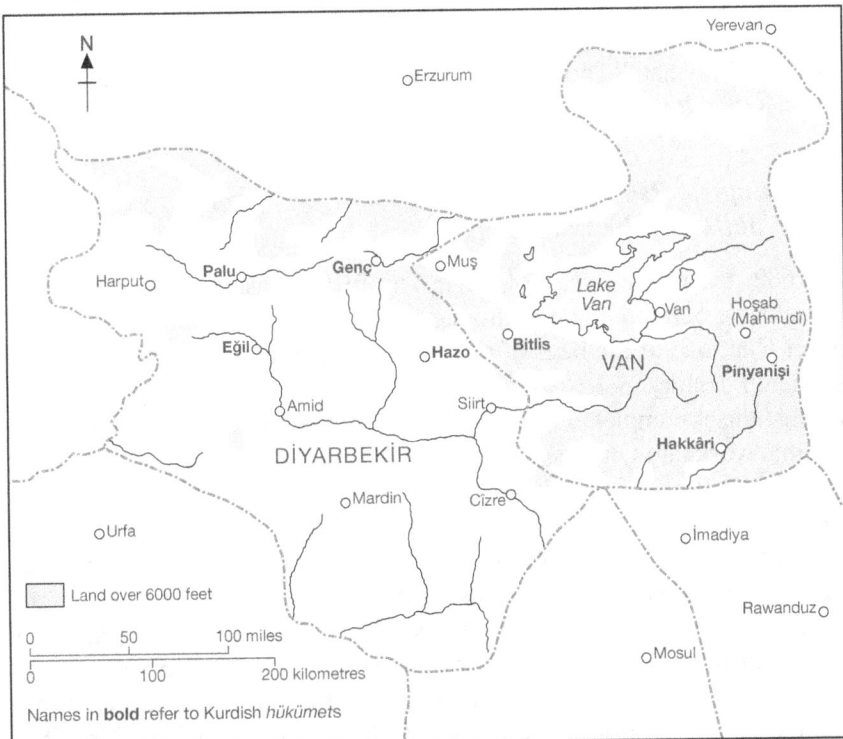

Map 1.1 Emirates that were granted *hükümet* status (c. 1520)[30]

The Kurdish Nobility in the Ottoman Empire

Within the Ottoman system, different regions had different fiscal responsibilities. The *timar* system was not implemented uniformly throughout the empire; for instance, the Arab-populated provinces paid tax revenues to tax farmers and the imperial centre received an annual tribute from the governors of these areas. Thus, what makes the *hükümet*s exceptional was not the non-existence of the *timar* system, but the *mefrûzü'l-kalem* and *maktû'ü'l-kadem* status, which indicated that the Ottoman state accepted the hereditary rule of the Kurdish begs. The *hükümet*s are a remarkable exception to the Ottoman imperial state's policy of not granting de jure legitimacy to ruling elites who claimed hereditary prerogatives. Thus, we see that, notwithstanding the widely held assumption in Ottoman historiography, hereditary nobility did exist in the Ottoman political system. The Ottoman acknowledgement of the hereditary rights of the Kurdish begs over their lands marked the transformation of the Kurdish begs into Ottoman-Kurdish nobility with specially defined exemptions and prerogatives. Once just the begs of a decentralised emirate, the Palu begs now had a new identity as a noble family with a recognised position in the Ottoman Empire. But what did nobility actually mean in Ottoman Kurdistan and for the Palu begs?

Genealogies, Pedigrees, Noble Titles: The Nobility of the Palu Begs

In 1682, the ruling *hâkim* of Palu, Yansûr Beg, asked his scribe Şem'i to translate *Şerefnâme* into Ottoman from Persian. The magnum opus of Şeref Hân, one of the begs of the Bitlis emirate in the second half of the sixteenth century, *Şerefnâme* was a history of the Kurdish dynasties and ruling houses completed in 1597. According to Şem'i, the idea of translating this work into Ottoman came when the guests of Yansûr Beg, many of whom were also Kurdish begs, began discussing their ancestors and their rule. As they shared what they knew about their noble past, they consulted *Şerefnâme* and realised that it was filled with information. Yansûr Beg then commissioned Şem'i to translate it.[31]

Yansûr Beg's patronage of the translation of *Şerefnâme* is an example of the Kurdish begs' interest in documenting the history of their noble ancestors. Around the same time period, Muhammed Beg of the Bitlis emirate, who was the great-great-grandson of Şeref Han, also had *Şerefnâme* translated into Turkish.[32] *Şerefnâme* was truly unique, not just because it provided a comprehensive history of Kurdish rulers, but because its author was a descendant of one of these Kurdish noble houses. Şeref Han presented detailed information about the lineages of the Kurdish rulers, classified according to the degree of their autonomy and the type of political authority they held.

The interest in genealogy is not unique to the Kurdish begs; in fact, it is a universal characteristic of nobilities. 'To speak of nobility', Marc Bloch wrote, 'is to speak of pedigrees.'[33] The way to justify hereditary rights over landed wealth in times of economic distress, or to protect existing fiscal or political privileges vis-à-vis a potentially hostile monarch, was often through genealogy. Another moment when genealogy becomes important is when nobility can be bought. Of course, genealogies can be faked, and the desire to be seen as pedigreed produced 'an industry of faked or doctored genealogies'.[34]

The Palu begs claimed descent from the Abbasids, a dynasty that claimed lineage from the Prophet Mohammad's uncle Abbas and ruled as second caliphate from 750 to 1258. This was mentioned cautiously in *Şerefnâme*, in phrases like 'according to the rumours', or 'reportedly'.[35] Several other Kurdish ruling families mentioned in *Şerefnâme* also claimed descent from the Abbasids, a prestige-boosting claim that was widespread among the ruling emirates in medieval Kurdistan.[36] This conviction continued throughout the centuries among the Kurdish begs: in the nineteenth century, a group of high-ranking *ulemâ* attested to the Abbasid origins of the Hakkâri rulers in a written document.[37] In the case of the Palu begs, this belief remained alive through the twentieth century. A family tree written in the twentieth century in Turkish traces the family's origins back to the Prophet Muhammad's uncle Abbas.[38]

Honorific titles are another symbolic component in the ideological underpinnings that legitimise the position of nobility. Whether an official title bestowed by the monarch or a traditional title used by nobles across generations, titles mark power, status and wealth and offer social distinction to their bearers. In the case of the Kurdish noble families, titles varied over time and included terms such as *pîr*, *beg/bey*, *emîr/mîr*. In *Şerefnâme*, one can see all these titles referring to the Kurdish rulers. Apparently, just before Cemşid Beg took power, the title 'beg' gained popularity, replacing emîr/mîr. In Ottoman imperial correspondence, three terms are used to refer to the Palu elites, with *beg* always accompanying the ruler's name. While this was a fairly common address for military and civilian notables in Ottoman administrative parlance, in the case of the Kurdish elites *beg* referred to the noble status of the addressee. Ottoman administrators also used *emîr/mîr* (pl. *ûmera*) when mentioning Kurdish nobility. The Ottoman imperial state carefully emphasised the distinction between *begs/emîr* and tribal chiefs (*aghas*), who never received these titles.[39]

The Ottoman state also addressed the Palu nobles as *hâkim*. While *emîr* or *beg* referred to the any male member of Kurdish noble families who had been given hereditary privileges, *hâkim* referred only to the ruling leader of the *hükümet*. In accordance with imperial decrees, this was originally a hereditary position. As discussed later, however, the appointment of one *beg* as the *hâkim* over others depended on power relations between the begs and their relationship with the imperial state.

The Noble Privilege of Palu Begs

Noble privilege refers to the rights granted to a specific group based on hereditary descent from a venerable ancestor.[40] Privilege, M. L. Bush argues, 'is European nobility's only indispensable characteristic'.[41] Although their wealth, political power and degree of authority varied according to region and context, 'there was no such thing as nobles without privilege'.[42] Historically, these privileges were bestowed by a monarch. European monarchs in the early modern era used the creation of new seigneurs through land grants as way of consolidating power and retaining control over their kingdoms.[43] Monarchs held the prerogative of assessing the veracity of noble claims and distributed noble titles to elite groups. The monarch's 'authority to issue letters of nobility became like minting gold coins, a measure of sovereignty'.[44]

Noble privileges included rights in political, juridical, fiscal and social realms.[45] These rights could be positive or, in the forms of exemptions, negative. Rights let nobles do things others could not; exemptions freed them from obligations others had to perform.[46] Due to the permutation of prerogatives and exemptions in various realms, noble privilege, like nobility itself, is a historically and contextually defined phenomenon. What, then, did noble privilege entail in the case of Kurdish begs, and, more specifically, the begs of Palu at the centre of this study? How were their rights, exceptions and prerogatives defined? The answers to these questions will help us conceptualise noble privilege in the Ottoman context, where the mere fact of nobility coupled with hereditary rights is a surprise.

The construction of noble privilege for the Kurdish begs began during their first encounter with İdris-i Bidlîsî, the Ottoman envoy dispatched to negotiate with them and enlist them as allies. But he did not start from scratch. İdris-i Bidlîsî built on the region's existing ruling practices to define the legitimacy of the begs and the rights and responsibilities conferred by their titles. Bidlîsî started from the conviction that the Kurdish begs had a legitimate right to rule over their territories, a rule accepted by the region's previous ruling dynasties from the Seljukids to Timur.⁴⁷ In Islamic states, İnalcik states, 'there existed a special kind of sultanic land grant (tamlik, temlik), bestowing absolute and hereditary immunities vis-à-vis the administration, making it a virtually autonomous enclave within the territory of the state'.⁴⁸ The aforementioned *hükümet*s and *yurtluk-ocaklık*s served as the administrative devices by which the scope of the Kurdish begs' privileges were defined in their autonomous realms in this manner. Throughout the sixteenth century, Ottoman lawbooks demonstrating the administrative organisation of the empire mentioned Palu using terms that highlighted the begs' rule over it and its different position from the classical Ottoman land regime. An early Ottoman register showing the administrative units of the empire after 1515 mentioned Palu as one of the 'Cemaat-i Kurdân', denoting its position as a part of the Kurdish collectivity.⁴⁹ According to another register dated 1522, Palu was one of the areas under the rule of *ûmera-ı Kürdistan*. Throughout the rest of the sixteenth century, Ottoman lawbooks used terminology such as *eyalet* or *hükümet*, indicating the continuing position of Palu as an area under the Kurdish begs' rule.⁵⁰

The earliest written document establishing the Palu begs as privileged nobility in the Ottoman realm dates from 1535, during the reign of Sultan Suleyman the Lawgiver, Sultan Selim I's son.⁵¹ The document is a *temlîknâme* or title deed granted to Cemşîd Beg by the Sultan during his eastern campaign. It begins with an account of the context in which these rights were given, that is, that the Grand Vizier İbrahim Pasha, who led the initial stages of the eastern campaign, consulted with the 'begs of Kurdistan' and moved on to Azerbaijan in alliance with them. Later, when the Sultan himself joined the campaign, the begs further proved their loyalty. Significantly, in this *temlîknâme*, Sultan Suleyman I also refers to military support that the Kurdistan begs provided during his father's time in the fight against the Kızılbaş.⁵²

Notwithstanding the top-down implications of the word 'privilege', the privileges decreed by the Sultan reflected the imperial state's recognition and acceptance of the begs' existing authority over these territories. The document is quite explicit about this: 'The aforementioned begs of Kurdistan ... had held and possessed [these] territories and the castles from the times immemorial which had been their *yurd*s and *ocak*s' [*kadîmü'l eyyamdan taht-ı yedlerinde ve kabza-i tasarruflarında olan eyâletleri ve kalâları, sevalif-i ezman yurdları ve ocakları idiğini*].⁵³ The *temlîknâme* further stated that the 'Kurdistan begs' aforementioned castles and territories [*ülkeler*] *that they inherited from their ancestors* [would stay] in their control'.⁵⁴

The Ottoman imperial state's non-intervention in the Palu begs' hereditary rights over their lands fundamentally defined the character of the privileges the begs were granted by the Sultan. It meant that they could transfer to their descendants not only their economic (proprietary) rights over land but also the politico-administrative prerogative to rule the territory, effectively reaffirming their noble status within the Ottoman realm.

In the *temlîknâme*, the bearers of the privilege of hereditary rule were defined as the 'begs of Kurdistan', indicating the imperial state's perception of them as a collective entity. Another indication of this comes through the way in which the question of appointment is discussed in the *temlîknâme*. The document explicitly highlights the hereditary character of rulership: in the absence of a legitimate heir, that is, a male descendant, the new ruler would be chosen by the 'consultation and consensus of all of the Kurdistan begs [*cümle Kürdistan begleri ile müşâveret ve ittifâk olunup ... ol diyârın begzâdelerinden her kime verilmek münâsib ve layık görürler ise ol kimse tevcih olunup*]'.[55] Thus, the Ottoman state not only acknowledged the Kurdish begs as a corporate group entitled to specific immunities and prerogatives, but also accepted their authority to decide on their ruler through their collective decision-making processes and established that the Ottoman state would not bring in someone from outside that collective.

While it laid out the privileges of all the begs of Kurdistan, the *temlîknâme* was specifically given to Cemşîd Beg, the *hâkim* of Palu. The castles, towns and fields and their yields were granted to him and his heirs [*cümle kal'aların ve şehirlerin ve mezra'aların kâffe mahsulatı ile*].[56] After his death, if he had multiple sons, his holdings would be apportioned to those sons. If he died without a male heir, the above-mentioned clause would take effect, authorising the other begs of Kurdistan to pick the next *hâkim*.

Overall, the Palu begs' privilege stood atop two pillars: the first was economic and concerned the proprietary rights of the begs over the land and its surplus; the second concerned their political/administrative authority over a delimited territory. The *temlîknâme* is explicit about both: '*Handing him this mülknâme, I decree that henceforth the said eyalet, with designated boundaries and explained borders, would be his property.*'[57] The *temlîknâme* (also known as *mülknâme-i hümayun*) granted to the Palu begs did not just spell out their privileges: in return for the noble privilege bestowed, the Kurdish begs were expected to remain loyal to Ottoman rule, collaborate with Ottoman administrators of different ranks and positions, and ally with the Ottomans against enemies. While the heart of the document's contractual character lay in the exchange of hereditary rights for Ottoman suzerainty, it also detailed specific ways in which the alliance would play out. The begs' most important responsibility was military – during military campaigns, they were required to be present with their men and weapons under the command of the governors (*beylerbeyi*) of Diyarbekir or Baghdad. The begs were also expected to provide labour and resources when called on to help construct a fort for the Ottomans. Last but not least, the Sultan sought to regulate the begs' rule, preventing over-exploitation and abuse of the people. In one clause, the begs were advised to treat their people fairly: 'destroy the tyrant; support the poor'.[58]

What makes these privileges the building block of a particular noble group is not the specific rights and exemptions, but that they were hereditary, recognised by the Sultan through legal means. The contract, however, required continuity from both ends. The imperial state wanted to maintain the loyalty of the Kurdish begs after the current Sultan's reign ended. This concern is evident in the *temlîknâme*: 'It is my *vasiyet* (will) and order to [my] children who are worthy of happiness that my blessed decree not to be altered or amended after me and they will obey my existing orders on this matter.'[59] Likewise, the begs were asked to submit to the rule of the Sultan's heirs and not support any potential external threats. In this way, the Palu begs were defined as a noble family with hereditary privileges within the Ottoman realm.

Conclusion

The Ottoman–Safavid rivalry in the early sixteenth century was a key historical moment for the formation of the Kurdish nobility in the Ottoman realm. For the Ottomans, negotiating with the existing ruling elites of an area they set out to conquer was not unusual. Neither was the recognition of the pre-existing laws, customs, and administrative and fiscal arrangements as main components of Ottoman rule in the newly-conquered areas. The special administrative organisation that Kurdistan held in the Ottoman system was an outcome of the Ottoman state's unequivocal recognition of the Kurdish begs' authority over the territories they had been ruling before the Ottoman arrival in the area. This chapter has demonstrated this pivotal moment at which the Ottoman state and the Kurdish elites sowed the seeds of a long-lasting relationship based on the former's recognition of the latter's hereditary privileges in an imperial setting. In this way, the Kurdish elites were effectively recognised as a noble group within the Ottoman system.

The scant writings that exist about Kurdistan's incorporation into the Ottoman Empire have focused almost exclusively on the administrative aspects of this process. This chapter examined the specific administrative system in Kurdistan in relation to the question of elite formation and its characteristics in this particular historical context. The *temliknâme*s granted by the Ottoman sultans to the Kurdish begs reveal that the Ottoman state had no qualms in accepting the Kurdish begs' hereditary claims over their wealth and authority. Through an analysis of the *temlîknâme* granted to Cemşîd Beg, the chapter demonstrated the terms of the formation of the Palu begs in the Ottoman context as a noble group.

Cemşîd Beg, who brought the Palu emirate under Ottoman rule, certainly had the skills needed to be a successful leader at the time. He proved his military valour by defending Palu from the Safavid invasion; he had diplomatic skills that he used to negotiate with the Ottomans for a settlement that recognised his hereditary privileges; and he successfully led the notable families of the area to his side and granted land and tax exemptions to those that fought with him against the Safavids.[60] Cemşîd Beg ruled the emirate for almost six decades. He performed pilgrimage three times during his lifetime.[61] He profited from a lucrative animal trade with ties to Aleppo. He invested in infrastructure and built charitable institutions. He founded a medrese in Palu, a *hamam* (public bath) in the Dağkapı neighbourhood of Diyarbekir and a *han* (inn) on the busy caravan road connecting Palu to Diyarbekir, Aleppo and Damascus in the south.[62]

Palu maintained its status as *hükümet* in the Ottoman administrative system for the next three centuries. While the de jure acceptance of the hereditary rights of the Palu begs remained intact from this time until the mid-nineteenth century, this striking continuity should not be misunderstood as meaning that the relationship between the begs and the imperial centre was static. It shifted continually according to changing military and fiscal exigencies and the unrelenting negotiation between the parties. Chapter 2 considers three realms in which the prerogatives and exemptions of the Palu nobility were defined and redefined: service in the military, service in mines, and land ownership.

Notes

1. Yavuz Bahadıroğlu, *Mısır'a Doğru* (Nesil Yayinlari, 2005), 53–4. 'Az sonra kapıda yine Kethüdabey belirdi: 'Palu Hâkimi Cemşit Bey' diye seslendi. Cemşit *ulemâ* girdi. Elli yaşlarında gösteriyordu. Çok uzun boylu ve esmerdi. Başında abani sarık, sırtında işlemeli bir hırka vardı. Belindeki kuşakta boş bir hançer kını duruyordu. İçeri girerken almışlardı hançerini, Padişahın huzuruna silâhla girmek yasaktı. Cemşit Beg Çaldıran Savaşı sırasında Padişaha

bağlılığını sunan Kürt beylerindendi. Osmanlı saflarında savaşa katılmış, önemli başarılar kazanmıştı. Zaferde emeği ve payı vardı. Tahta üç adım kala durdu. Elini göğsüne bastırıp selam verdi. 'Aleykümüsselâm, Cemşit Beg', diye selamını aldı Padişah, 'seni aramızda görmek bizi memnun etti. Hudut boylarındaki karındaşlarımız nasıl?'

2. A *kozak* is a rounded container with a lid used to transport sealed official documents securely. Selman Can, 'Osmanlı Diplomatikasında Kozalaklar', *Güzel Sanatlar Enstitüsü Dergisi*, no. 7 (2010).
3. Bahadıroğlu, *Mısır'a Doğru*, 54. 'Huzurunuzda Sünnî Kürt Beylerini temsil ediyorum. Aralarında beni seçtiler. Bağlılıklarını bildirmemi söylediler.' Elini kemerinin arasına soktu, bir kozak çıkardı. Padişaha uzattı: 'İşte bağlılık vesikası. Yirmi beş Kürt Beyi tarafından mühürlenmiştir.' Sultan Selim kozakı açtı. İçindeki kâğıdı çıkardı. Dikkatle okudu. Kürt Beyleri hiçbir ön şart koşmadan Osmanlıların yüksek ve âdil hâkimiyetini kabul ettiklerini bildiriyorlardı. Kağıdın alt tarafında yirmi beş mühür vardı. Bitlis Hâkimi Emir Şerefüddin, Hizan Meliki Emir Davud, Hısnıkeyfa Emiri Eyyübilerden Melik II. Halil, İmadi-ye Hâkimi Sultan Hüseyin ve diğerleri ... Padişahın yüzü pırıl pırıl aydınlanmıştı: 'Sağol', dedi, 'Allah hepinizden razı olsun. Şimdi bir menşur yazdırıp sana vereceğiz. Burada isimleri bulunan beyleri, bulundukları yerlere emir tayin ediyoruz. Mübarek ola.' Cemşit Bey uzandı. Padişahın elini öpecekti. Yavuz hızla kalktı, Cemşit Beyi iki omuzundan yakaladığı gibi kendine çekti: 'Biz karındaşlarımızla kucaklaşmayı severiz, Cemşit kardaş.'
4. Cemal Kafadar, *Between Two Worlds: The Construction of the Ottoman State* (Berkeley, CA: University of California Press, 1996), 1. I am alluding here to the analogy Kafadar makes in his seminal work on the establishment of the Ottoman Empire, 'Osman is to the Ottomans what Romulus is to the Romans'.
5. Şerefhan Bitlisi, *Şerefname*, trans. Abdullah Yegin, vol. Cilt: 1 (Nubihar Yayınları, 2018), 229–32.
6. Idris-i Bidlisi, *Selim Şah-Nâme*, trans. Hicabi Kırlangıç (Ankara: Hece Yayınları, 2016), 250.
7. Ünal, 'XVI. Yüzyılda Palu Hükümeti', 244.
8. Şerefhan Bitlisi, *Şerefname*, trans. Abdullah Yegin, Cilt: 1 (Nûbihar Yayınları, 2018), 230.
9. According to the legend, when sleeping in the house of Sheikh Edebali, Osman Beg had this dream: 'He saw that a moon arose from the holy man's breast and came to sink in his own breast. A tree then sprouted from his navel and its shade compassed the world. Beneath this shade there were mountains, and streams flowed forth from the foot of each mountain. Some people drank from these running waters, others watered gardens, while yet others caused fountains to flow. When Osman awoke he told the story to the holy man, who said "Osman, my son, congratulations, for God has given the imperial office to you and your descendants and my daughter Malhun shall be your wife".'

Rudi Paul Lindner, *Nomads and Ottomans in Medieval Anatolia*, illustrated edn (Bloomington: Sinor Research Institute of Inner Asian Studies, 1983), 37, cited in Caroline Finkel, *Osman's Dream: The History of the Ottoman Empire* (New York: Basic Books, 2007), 41–2. This became the founding myth of the Ottoman Empire.

10. Marshall G. S. Hodgson, *Rethinking World History: Essays on Europe, Islam and World History* (Cambridge: Cambridge University Press, 1993), 97.
11. Gábor Ágoston, 'Firearms and Military Adaptation: The Ottomans and the European Military Revolution, 1450–1800', *Journal of World History* 25, no. 1 (1 August 2014): 110.
12. See İnalcik, 'Ottoman Methods of Conquest'; Barkey, *Empire of Difference*.
13. Ebru Sönmez, 'An Acem Statesman in the Ottoman Court: İdris-i Bidlîsî and the Making of the Ottoman Polict on Iran' (MA thesis, Boğaziçi University, 2006), 13–22. The Sultan most likely wanted to benefit from Bidlîsî's knowledge of the region, and previous experience in the Akkoyunlu court. For more on this, see Vural Genç, '"Acem'den Ruma": İdris-i Bidlîsî'nin Hayatı, Tarihçiliği, ve Heşt Behişt'in II. Bayezid Kısmı (1481–1512)' (Ph.D. dissertation, Istanbul University, 2014), 255–7. He was tasked with winning hearts and minds of the Kurdish rulers by travelling around all the Kurdish areas. Vural, 261–78.
14. Sönmez, 37.
15. Ahmet Akgündüz, *Osmanlı Kanunnameleri ve Hukukî Tahlilleri: Yavuz Sultan Selim Devri Kanunnameleri*, vol. 3 (İstanbul: FEY Vakfı Yayınları, 1991), 208.
16. Sönmez, 'An Acem Statesman in the Ottoman Court: İdris-i Bidlîsî and the Making of the Ottoman Policy on Iran', 59–60.
17. Sönmez, 59–60, 65.
18. İdris-i Bidlîsî has a controversial legacy among contemporary Kurds. Given his Kurdish ethnic origin, the fact that he worked for the Ottoman state to incorporate the Kurdish begs under Ottoman authority is perceived by some as 'treachery'. For a critique of this perspective, see Şakir Epözdemir, *1514 Amasya Antlaşması Kürt-Osmanlı İttifakı ve Mevlana İdris-i* (Istanbul: Pêrî Yayınları, 2005). For a recent study which challenges the historicist accounts of İdris-i Bidlîsî's background, see Vural Genç, 'Rethinking Idris-i Bidlisi: An Iranian Bureaucrat and Historian between the Shah and the Sultan', *Iranian Studies* 52, nos 3–4 (4 July 2019): 425–47. Genç examines İdris-i Bidlîsî's intellectual life and career within the tumultuous political context of the Ottoman–Iranian borderland in the early sixteenth century.
19. Akgündüz, *Osmanlı Kanunnameleri ve Hukukî Tahlilleri: Yavuz Sultan Selim Devri Kanunnameleri*, 3: 205–6.
20. Akkoyunlu and Karakoyunlu were tribal confederations that emerged in the fourteenth century. Sönmez, 'An Acem Statesman in the Ottoman Court: İdris-i Bidlîsî and the Making of the Ottoman Policy on Iran', 64.

21. Sönmez, 53.
22. Vural Genc, *Acem'den Rum'a Bir Bürokrat ve Tarihci Idris-i Bidlîsî* (Ankara: Türk Tarih Kurumu, 2019), 335.
23. İnalcik, 'Ottoman Methods of Conquest'.
24. Agoston, 'A Flexible Empire', 16.
25. Nejat Göyünç, 'Diyarbekir Beylerbeyliği'nin İlk İdari Taksimatı', *Tarih Dergisi* 22 (1969): 24.
26. Agoston, 'A Flexible Empire'; Sönmez, 'An Acem Statesman in the Ottoman Court: İdris-i Bidlîsî and the Making of the Ottoman Polict on Iran'.
27. For the details of *timar* organisation, see Mehdi Ilhan, '1518 Tarihli Tapu Tahrir Defterine Göre Âmid Sancağında Timâr Dağılımı', *Tarih Enstitüsü Dergisi* XII (1982): 85–100.
28. Hakan Özoğlu, 'State–Tribe Relations: Kurdish Tribalism in the 16th- and 17th-Century Ottoman Empire', *British Journal of Middle Eastern Studies* 23, no. 1 (1996): 57.
29. See Halil İnalcık, 'Temlîks, Soyurghals, Yurdluk-Ocaklıks, Mâlikâne-Mukâta'a and Awqaf', in *History and Historiography of Post-Mongol Central Asia and the Middle East*, eds Judith Pfeiffer and Sholeh Alysia Quinn (Wiesbaden: Harrassowitz, 2006); Houston, '"Set Aside from the Pen and Cut off from the Foot"'; Nejat Göyünç, 'Yurtluk-Ocaklık Deyimleri Hakkında', in *Prof. Dr. Bekir Kütükoğlu'na Armağan* (İstanbul: İ.Ü. Edebiyat Fak, 1991), 269–78.
30. Donald Edgar Pitcher, *An Historical Geography of the Ottoman Empire: From Earliest Times to the End of the Sixteenth Century* (Leiden: Brill, 1973). Map XXXII. No page no.
31. Adnan Oktay, *Terceme-i Tevarih-i Şeref Han* (İstanbul: Nûbihar Yayinlari, 2016).
32. According to Sacha Alsancakli, these translations point to the increasing prestige of Turkish in Ottoman Kurdistan. Sacha Alsancakli, 'Historiography and Language in 17th-Century Ottoman Kurdistan: A Study of Two Turkish Translations of the Sharafnāma', *Kurdish Studies* 6, no. 2 (2018): 171–96.
33. Marc Bloch, *Feudal Society*, trans. L.A. Manyon, 1st edn (London: Routledge & Kegan Paul, 1961), 23.
34. Duggan, 'Introduction: Concepts, Origins, Transformations', 9.
35. Şerefhan Bitlisi, *Şerefname* (Nubihar Yayinlari, 2018), 222.
36. Mustafa Dehqan and Vural Genç, 'A Document on the Kurdish Hakkārī Claim to 'Abbāsid Descent', *Fritillaria Kurdca. Bulletin of Kurdish Studies*, no. 19–20 (2017): 6. For a study on the genealogies of the Eğil begs, Yunus Emre Gördük, 'Eğil Emirliği'nin Kısa Tarihçesi ve Eğil Emirlerine Ait Şecere Metninin Tercümesi', *OTAM* 35, no. Bahar (2014): 89–120.
37. Dehqan and Genç, 'A Document on the Kurdish Hakkārī Claim to 'Abbāsid Descent'.
38. The Palu begs' interest in genealogical trees continued across generations, even after the dissolution of the empire and the foundation of the Turkish

republic. The begs' descendants still hold on to two family trees – one in Ottoman Turkish, the other in modern Turkish; their creators are unknown. The trees are stored in a chest in the attic of the one of the descendants' homes along with other Ottoman documents and are not in particularly good condition. Interviews with the Palu begs' descendants reveal an identity that is still grounded in nobility even though their current wealth and status do not match that noble past.

39. Both *beg* and *emîr* had widespread usage in the pre-Ottoman context. Islamicate states including the Seljukids, the Akkoyunlu and the Karakoyunlu, as well as the Timurid state, used *beg* to refer to ruling elites. For example, when he was under the rule of the Akkoyunlu confederation, the title of beg was used to address Cemşîd Beg of Palu. The use of *beg* to address the Kurdish nobility in the Ottoman system continued this practice. Ömer Lütfi Barkan, 'Kanunnâme-i Boz Ulus', in *XV ve XVI Incı Asırlarda Osmanlı İmparatorluğunda Ziraı Ekonominin Esasları. Birinci Cilt: Kanunlar*, vol. 1 (Istanbul: Bürhaneddin Matbaası, 1943), 141.

40. For a comprehensive examination of noble privilege, see M. L. Bush, *Noble Privilege* (Manchester: Manchester University Press, 1983).

41. Bush, viii.

42. Bush, viii

43. Hugo G. Nutini, *The Wages of Conquest: The Mexican Aristocracy in the Context of Western Aristocracies*, 1st edn (Ann Arbor, MI: University of Michigan Press, 1995), 99–101.

44. Samuel Clark, *State and Status: The Rise of the State and Aristocratic Power in Western Europe*, 1st edn (Montreal ; Buffalo: Queen's School of Policy Studies, 1995), 162. Cited in Asch, *Nobilities in Transition 1550–1700*, 11.

45. Scott, *The European Nobilities in the Seventeenth and Eighteenth Centuries*, 9–11.

46. Lukowski, *The European Nobility in the Eighteenth Century*, 7.

47. Sönmez, 'An Acem Statesman in the Ottoman Court: İdris-i Bidlîsî and the Making of the Ottoman Policy on Iran', 54.

48. İnalcık, 'Temlîks, Soyurghals, Yurdluk-Ocaklıks, Mâlikâne-Mukâta'a and Awqaf', 112.

49. Orhan Kılıç, 'Klasik Dönem Osmanlı İdari Sisteminde Farklı Bir Unsur: Kürdistan Vilayeti/Eyaleti', in *CIEPO 22 Uluslararası Osmanlı Öncesi ve Osmanlı Çalışmaları Komitesi Bildiriler Kitabı* (CIEPO 22 Uluslararası Osmanlı Öncesi ve Osmanlı Çalışmaları Komitesi, Trabzon: Trabzon Büyükşehir Belediyesi, 2018), 550.

50. For an overview, see Kılıç, 'Klasik Dönem Osmanlı İdari Sisteminde Farklı Bir Unsur: Kürdistan Vilayeti/Eyaleti'.

51. Karacimşit Family Documents (henceforth KFD). The *temliknâme* granted to Cemşîd Beg by Sultan Suleyman I, dated 20 Cemâziyelâhir 942 [16 December 1535]. I will refer to this document as 'KFD-Temliknâme (1535)'. I am

grateful to the descendants of Cemşîd Bey, especially to Mehmet Karacimşit, for sharing the copies of the *temliknâme* with me.

52. According to Dehqan and Genç, Cemşîd Beg also served as a 'pro-Ottoman Kurdish spy' during Sultan Suleyman's eastern campaign. Mustafa Dehqan and Vural Genc, 'Kurds as Spies: Information-Gathering on the 16th-Century Ottoman–Safavid Frontier', *Acta Orientalia Academiae Scientiarum Hungaricae* 71, no. 2 (1 June 2018): 210.
53. KFD-Temliknâme (1535).
54. Ibid.
55. Ibid.
56. Ibid.
57. Ibid.
58. Ibid.
59. Ibid.
60. Serdar Karabulut, 'Şeyh Alâeddin İbn-i Şeyh Pir Vakfiyeyi Tarihiyesi Üzerine Bir İnceleme', *Bingöl Üniversitesi İlahiyat Fakültesi Dergisi* 5, no. 9 (2017): 265–6.
61. Ünal, 'XVI. Yüzyılda Palu Hükümeti', 246.
62. Serdar Karabulut, 'Palu'nun Siyasi/Ekonomik Tarihi (XIV–XVIII. Yüzyıllar Arası) ve Palu Çarşısı'na Dâir Vakıfname Belgesi'nin Tercümesi', *OTAM* 41, no. Bahar (2017): 151; Göyünç, 'Diyarbekir Beylerbeyliği'nin ilk idari taksimatı', 28.

Chapter 2

Noble Privilege on the Ground, from the 1720s to the 1830s

In July 1728, the Ottoman imperial state issued a laconic decree. It granted the ruler (*hâkim*) of Palu, İbrahim Beg, the title of *mîr-i mîrân*. Also known as the *beylerbeyi*, this was the highest military and administrative position in a locality, granting its bearer *pasha* status in the Ottoman administrative hierarchy.[1] While the title of *hâkim* referred to the bearer's position as the ruler of the autonomous *hükümet*, carrying the title of *mîr-i mîrân* meant that İbrahim Beg was part of the Ottoman provincial bureaucracy.

The title came with the requirement that İbrahim Beg dedicate his utmost power to the splendid service of the sultan and 'work for the securing of law and order, protection of the people, and expelling the malevolent'. *Beylerbeyi*s were the highest authority in their localities, and these requirements were made of all *pasha*s. Other clauses, however, were more specific to İbrahim Beg and his locality: he was required to provide grain and transport animals for the Iranian campaigns and to deliver charcoal and workers to the nearby Keban and Ergani mines.[2]

The Ottoman state did not expect İbrahim Beg to perform these services just because he had been given a new title. The Ottoman state had long relied on the begs' military power and on their provisioning of armies for long military campaigns in the east. What was new, however, was the clause making the Palu begs responsible for providing charcoal to the mines in their area. The Keban and Ergani mines served a vital function for the Ottoman treasury, providing precious metals for the Ottoman Imperial Mint (*Darbhâne-i Âmire*), and the imperial armory (*cebehane*) and foundry (*tophane*). The expectations of the Palu begs changed, becoming more about provisioning and supplies than about their hitherto critical task of providing military power to the Ottoman campaigns.

Noble Privilege on the Ground

In this chapter I analyse the relationship of the Palu nobility to the Ottoman imperial establishment throughout the eighteenth century prior to the Tanzimat reforms focusing on three realms – military, mining and land. In terms of their position with respect to the imperial state, the Kurdish nobility's military roles and mine service were essential. However, the Palu begs' main source of economic power was land and its surplus. Land also marked their identity and position as noble elites in the Ottoman realm. An examination of the prerogatives and exemptions of the Palu begs in these three realms – military, mining and land – provides a new perspective on the question of the Kurdish begs' autonomy vis-à-vis the central state. Existing historical narratives approach this question of autonomy by anachronistically projecting the nation-state paradigm backward onto the imperial context. All changes in the *hükümet* status of the emirates are interpreted as a sign of the increasing grip of the Ottoman state – without really looking at the ways in which things worked on the ground. They take the Ottoman state's power and the Kurdish nobles' autonomy as absolutes – with any increase in the Ottoman state's power causing a decrease in autonomy for the Kurdish nobles and vice versa. Not only does this view reflect a problematic nation-state bias, it is also a methodological fallacy, stemming from an exclusive focus on the status of the Kurdish emirates in the Ottoman administrative system.

Using comparative studies of nobility, I demonstrate that bestowal of noble privileges can be a marker of the imperial state's self-confident position in relatively relaxed military and fiscal circumstances, rather than a sign of frailty. And, similarly, threats or actual policies decreasing nobles' autonomy can be symptoms of the imperial state's vulnerability in the realms in which it relied on the Kurdish nobles. Notwithstanding the continuity of the Palu begs' noble identity, the actual content of noble privilege took shape within the context of constant negotiation between the Ottoman administration and the begs.

The Raison d'être *of Nobility: Palu Begs as Noble Warriors*

The definition of nobility in the European context relied on an 'idealized and somewhat theoretical, division of medieval society into three orders or Estates'.[3] In this system, nobility composed the 'second estate', the fighting class. In many European languages the term 'nobility' originated from this military function, such as *cavalieri* (Italian), *chevalerie* (French) and *riddarskapet* (Swedish).[4] The *raison d'être* of the nobility was to provide military service when a mass-conscript army did not yet exist; in exchange for their military service, nobles were granted immunities and privileges in other realms. The degree of their military might and the circumstances that rendered their service essential (or redundant) determined their power and leverage vis-à-vis the suzerain.

As discussed in the previous chapter, the context in which the seeds of the Kurdish nobility in the Ottoman realm were sown was defined by a fierce military rivalry between two empires. This military function continued in varying degrees for two centuries after this initial encounter, and was especially critical for the evolution of the Palu nobility. In fact, the practice of providing military service for a suzerain in return for material or political rights of hereditary character pre-dates Ottoman expansion in the region, starting as far back as the Abbasid, Seljukid and Ilkhanid Empires.[5] In the eleventh century during the Seljukid reign, this practice gained a new territorial character. Rulers began granting tribal chieftains (Turkish or Kurdish) whole regions as hereditary estates, resulting in decentralised rule by the powerful military-administrative rulers (*atabeg*s) of these chieftains.[6] This policy was a precedent for the later Ottoman practice of granting various degrees of autonomy to Kurdish rulers.

It is in the post-Seljukid context – a time of principalities – that the ancestors of the Palu begs in the Kurdish Buldukanî-Mırdasî principality captured the fortressed town of Eğil that became the centre of their rule. The Akkoyunlus had risen as a new force in the area, and the Buldukanî principality became one of fifty confederate clans that constituted the Akkoyunlu tribal confederation.[7] These tribes provided the majority of the confederation's military force and in return were rewarded with 'fiscal and administrative immunity over a specific territory'.[8] Under the Akkoyunlu ruler Uzun Hasan, tribal chieftains had to appear before him with their horses and men when summoned.[9] Although it was at the borders of the confederation, the Buldukanî-Mırdasî principality still participated in military operations. Their chiefs served as commanders in the Akkoyunlu army and tutored the children of the Akkoyunlu rulers.[10] It appears that, prior to Ottoman expansion in the area, these local begs maintained their own armed forces and had skirmishes with their neighbours, suggesting a long and engrained practice of begs having rule and fiscal privileges over land in exchange for military service, long before the first encounter between the Ottomans and the Kurdish principalities in the sixteenth century.

When the Ottomans arrived on the scene, their immediate military and political needs made this arrangement essential. Kurdistan was the major battle zone in the unfolding rivalry between the Safavids and the Ottomans. As discussed in the previous chapter, the Kurdish begs' acceptance of Ottoman suzerainty was shaped by a reciprocal military alliance against a common enemy. The Safavids captured the hereditary strongholds of numerous Kurdish begs, including Cemşîd Beg, and in response, the majority of the Kurdish begs formed an alliance with Ottoman forces in their anti-Safavid march.[11] In their efforts to defy the Safavid siege of Diyarbekir, the Kurdish begs demanded that the Ottoman sultan send additional soldiers.[12] Cemşîd Beg had assisted the Ottoman Empire militarily,[13] supporting İdris-i Bidlîsî by safeguarding the crucial safe passages from the dissident Kurdish chiefs who refused to co-operate with the Ottomans.[14]

The Kurdish begs' loyalty in this tumultuous area could not be taken for granted. The Ottoman state recognised the significance of maintaining their allegiance using incentives and prerogatives to channel their military might towards protecting this newly-Ottomanised frontier. The exigencies of war required the Ottoman state to be amenable to negotiation, and there were established political actors, structures and relations in the area that the Ottomans could not ignore or underestimate. It made sense for the Ottoman state to adapt the region's historic practice of granting a ruler near-to-total autonomy over territory in return for military service. The *temlîknâme* given to Cemşîd Beg by Selim I, and renewed by his father Kanunî Sultan Suleyman during his Iraqi campaign, praised the service of the Kurdish begs during the fight against the Kızılbaş.[15] This *temlîknâme* was renewed three times by successive sultans, and the agreement always stated that 'whenever there is a military campaign, they would participate in the campaigns gratis'.[16]

Sultan Suleyman I's Iraqi campaign (1533–5) to capture Baghdad from the Safavids was the first occasion to renew the original *temlîknâme* given to the Palu begs by his father Sultan Selim I. This campaign was particularly arduous for the Ottoman armies, who struggled with harsh topography, difficulties provisioning food, a shortage of water and adverse weather conditions.[17] The campaign's central battle resembled modern guerilla warfare, and halting the enemy's supply line became a key tactic.[18] Waging a long war in these challenging circumstances necessitated the loyalty and the military and logistical support of the local power holders, which came at a price.[19] Besides, it was not always clear that the chiefs' loyalty would be uninterrupted.[20] During the first year of the Iraqi campaign (1534), when grand vizier İbrahim Pasha led the Ottoman armies, he sought to win the loyalties of the Kurdish begs by granting them the revenues of particular districts.[21] He also consulted with them to develop campaign tactics and strategies. Indeed, he was pleased to have recruited 'the most skillful of the Kurdish men' to help him conduct reconnaissance in the Iranian lands.[22]

After this campaign, the Sultan sporadically dispatched decrees to the Kurdish begs, including Cemşîd Beg, asking them to remain ready and equipped for combat along with their tribal chiefs (*agha*s), tribal forces (*aşiret askeri*) and cavalrymen (*nöker*s).²³ They would gather under the command of the governor (*beglerbegi*) of Diyarbekir.²⁴ Each beg was also sent a *hil'at* (a special robe) and a sword, to formally honour their status as dignitaries.²⁵ Cemşîd Beg's name is included in narrative accounts as one of the Kurdish begs most willing to co-operate with Ottoman forces, which is perhaps why he was selected to represent the Kurdish begs before the sultan during the campaign.²⁶

Throughout the sixteenth century, the provincial cavalry of the *timar* system and the sultan's standing slave army (*kapıkulu*) were the Ottoman Empire's main military forces. They were supplemented, however, by auxiliary forces of vassals and other provincial elites, including the Kurdish begs.²⁷ Cemşîd Beg participated in all of the Iraqi campaigns during Sultan Suleyman's reign and also supported the Ottoman armies with men and ammunition during an attack by the Arab tribes around Basra.²⁸ After Cemşîd Beg died, his descendants continued to provide military service to the Ottomans in their protracted border disputes with Iran. For the rest of the sixteenth century, the Ottoman sultans frequently called on the Kurdish begs to fight against the Safavids. In 1578, the Ottomans organised a military campaign to seize Azerbaijan and Caucasus – a Safavid zone of influence at the time. Grand Vizier Lâlâ Mustafa Pasha led the campaign in the summer of 1578, acquiring Tblisi and Şirvan. Men and materials from the Kurdish begs again proved crucial – in terms both of military and logistical support. Two Palu begs – Rüstem Beg and Hasan Beg – fought and died during the Şirvan campaign.²⁹ A mere two years later, in 1580, Ferhâd Beg, the ruler of Palu, and his brother Alaaddin Beg, along with more than thirty other Kurdish begs, were summoned to bring provisions, rations and forces to Tabriz to join Cafer Pasha in repelling Abbas Mizra's Safavid military. ³⁰

The service of the Palu begs (or any Kurdish begs) during the Ottoman military campaigns was not guaranteed. Shortly after Cemşîd Beg died, tribal musketeers and infantry from the Palu emirate were summoned to serve in the Algerian campaign in 1568, but some fled after showing up at the front, reportedly at the provocation of Cemşîd Beg's son Hamza and his grandson Rüstem.³¹ At other times, the Palu begs used threats of withdrawing military support from the Ottomans, or promises to provide it, to gain leverage in their internal power struggles – mainly over who would lead the principality. The aforementioned Rüstem Beg, for example, agreed to join the ranks of Osman Pasha during the Şirvan campaign in exchange for being appointed ruler of the emirate.³²

In the sixteenth century, military service was a point of negotiation between Kurdish rulers and the Ottoman state. The Palu begs were frequently summoned to Ottoman campaigns in Iran and elsewhere, and as far away as Algeria. They complied at times, and resisted or deserted at other times. From the 1630s onward, however, the Kurdish begs' participation in Ottoman military campaigns began to change. In his analysis of the eastern campaigns of the Ottoman armies, which highlights the arduous circumstances of the eastern front, the historian Rhoads Murphey states that 'it is in the eastern theatre that we can see most clearly the limits of Ottoman warfare'.[33] Murad IV (r. 1623–40) mobilised sizeable troops for his Yerevan and Baghdad campaigns in 1635 and 1638, respectively. These did not come from the Kurdish begs, who could no longer marshal forces or resources at the levels they once had. Their participation in Ottoman campaigns became less important regarding their ties to the imperial state.

Kurdish Begs' Changing Military Roles in the Seventeenth Century

Writing circa 1632, Azîz Efendi, presumably an Ottoman court scribe, produced perhaps the most straightforward account of the Kurdish begs' changing military functions and their decreased military contribution during the Ottoman military campaigns in the seventeenth century. Azîz Efendi's treatise was in the genre of Advice to Kings, *nasihatnâme*, works in which the authors explicated the perceived problems in the Ottoman military and bureaucracy and presented ideas for reform.[34] Azîz Efendi juxtaposed the current decreased military potential of the Kurdish begs with their memorable service during the fights against *kızılbaş* and their guardianship of the frontier of Iran back in the sixteenth century. During the earlier Persian campaigns, the Kurdish commanders were like 'raging lions and wild tigers' with the ability to recruit '50,000 to 60,000 soldiers'.[35] In the most recent campaigns, however, they commanded forces as small as 600 or 700 men.

In the seventeenth-century *nasihatnâmes*, Ottoman 'decline' emerged as a leitmotif, with authors using Sultan Suleyman I's reign to highlight current problems.[36] Azîz Efendi's was one of many treatises of this kind, pointing to an idealised golden age prior to a period of 'decline'. As Rifa'at Abou-El-Haj points out, however, rather than seeing these problems cited in these works only as symptoms of an impending decline, we need to understand these writings as 'political tracts that represents a struggle within the ruling elites'.[37] This requires a careful eye on the specific historical contexts which produced each representative of this specific genre.

Azîz Efendi focused on transforming who was recruited into the Sultan's Janissary army and how. Non-military, tax-paying subjects began making their way into what had been an elite and selectively recruited group. He, along with other members of the Ottoman establishment, saw these admissions as a crisis. Along with changes in the military, seventeenth-century Ottomans also experienced drastic financial changes triggered by the economy's accelerated monetisation. The classical land-grant system (*timar*) that formed the backbone of the provincial cavalry army began to dissolve as tax farming on these lands became more and more widespread.[38]

While being a classical example of the *nasihatnâme* literature, the originality of Azîz Efendi's work stems from its special emphasis on the Kurdish begs and their changing positions within the Ottoman realm. As a result of the shifting of the military campaigns from Iran to Europe, Kurdish rulers lost the attention of the sultan and began to suffer under the oppression and corruption of provincial governors. In violation of the imperial decrees, the governors intervened in the begs' appointment processes, granting the begs' positions to their relatives or to outsiders, and even executing some of them.[39] According to Azîz Efendi, despite agreements that exempted the Kurdish rulers from paying taxes on land to the imperial state, the provincial governors extorted huge amounts of cash from them. Having consumed their cash reserves, the begs had to resort to usurers, became mired in debt, and fell into dire poverty. Thus, the avarice of the provincial governors was the root cause of the begs' decreased military might and inability to participate the campaigns.[40] For Azîz Efendi, curtailing the power of these provincial governors, protecting the begs from the abuses of the usurers and increasing the imperial state's purview over the appointment processes of the Kurdish rulers were paramount, because he believed that not benefiting from the Kurdish begs' military power was an important reason behind the Ottoman armies' lack of success during the Iranian campaigns from 1628 to 1630.[41]

Azîz Efendi also suggested that the Sultan try to revitalise the noble and respectable position of the Kurdish begs through appropriate etiquette and decorum. He wanted the Sultan to issue decrees that recounted the noble service the begs provided to the crown, by virtue of which they deserved to be treated with respect and care. He advised that 'whenever one of the Kurdish governors dies and it becomes necessary to assign his place to one of his sons or one of his brothers ... the candidates shall come in person to the Threshold of Felicity (i.e. Istanbul) and prostrate themselves at the foot of the imperial stirrup, and that all appointment to these governorships be made in the capital'.[42] This would both increase the imperial state's authority over the Kurdish rulers and honour them by hosting them at the imperial court. Furthermore, he suggested, 'documents of inducement (*istimaletnâme*) ... should be sent to all the Kurdish chiefs accompanied by ceremonial robes of honor, and to their relatives' land grants and benefices (*tiyul*)'.[43] Essentially, he was advising the Ottoman sultan to maintain the noble privileges granted to the begs during prior reigns and protect the hereditary succession of Kurdish nobility so that the imperial state could 'once again put to use the sharpest swords, the swiftest and most active Arabian horses, and the most valiant and blood-shedding Kurdish warriors accomplishing even greater services than in the past'.[44] We do not know whether the Sultan heard or considered Azîz Efendi's suggestions. We also do not know whether the Kurdish begs' plight was as bleak as he described. Did the state's expectation of military services from the Kurdish begs disappear altogether? – definitely not.

In Europe at this time, military services were gradually being concentrated in the hands of the central state, decreasing the martial responsibilities of the noble classes. But the state did not yet have a monopoly on violence, not in Europe or in the Ottoman Empire. In Europe, nobilities continued to serve the state by fighting for the crown.[45] And in this period and throughout the eighteenth century, the Ottoman state was still relying on 'fragmentary and not always reliable sources for military support' convened temporarily for particular military campaigns.[46]

The Ottoman state continued to turn to the Palu begs for military service throughout the late seventeenth and eighteenth centuries – albeit with little success. During this period, the Janissary army and the provincial fief-based cavalry army formed the core of the Ottoman fighting force. However, the Ottoman imperial state still had to 'mobilize effective fighting forces for the far-distant, seasonal and siege warfare characteristic of the age and maintain a series of fortresses along the northern border'.[47] During the eighteenth century, the Palu begs were summoned to serve in several military campaigns against Iran, Hungary, Habsburg and Russia, but compliance became even rarer than in the first Ottoman century of the Kurdish begs. Non-compliance came at a cost. After Yansûr Beg declined to serve in the Habsburg Wars, the Ottomans rescinded his rule over his emirate. In 1723, İbrahim Beg, along with the governor of Diyarbekir and some other Kurdish begs, were appointed to protect the Tiflis fortress from Russian and Iranian forces. Shortly thereafter, his name appeared in Ottoman correspondence as the ringleader of a desertion from the fortress.[48] The Ottoman state responded by putting a reservation (*şerh*) on the *'hükümet'* status of Palu in the Divan-ı Hümayûn registers that technically – but not necessarily actually – meant increased governmental purview of fiscal and administrative matters of the district.

Military support from the provincial nobles, including the Palu begs, became a vital, but also thorny, issue during the 1768–74 Russo-Ottoman War, as the Ottomans lacked the force or organisation for a large-scale military campaign. The core of the Ottoman military had already morphed from a professional army into a militia-based army.[49] Coupled with logistical problems, this structural transformation rendered the Ottoman state more dependent on local notables across the empire.[50] Local elites were crucial not only in mobilising troops for campaigns, but also in provisioning soldiers and financing the war.[51] In August 1769, in the face of an impending Russian attack on Özi, one of the two last Ottoman strongholds along the Russian border, the *hâkim* of Palu (along with other notables) was appointed to defend the fortress.[52] When he failed to respond, the Ottoman state intensified its call, ordering him to head to Özi immediately with his troops.[53] By late September, some of the Kurdish *hâkim*s at the front had already deserted, a widespread phenomenon on both sides. The unwillingness of Kurdish rulers to fight war prompted the Ottoman state to unleash its wrath. It promised to punish Kurdish rulers who deserted by taking away their *hükümet*s and *sanjak*s and granting them to those who served. As late as December 1769, the begs' absence from the military campaigns still preoccupied the Ottomans. Meanwhile, the state faced yet another threat, this time from the northernmost frontier of the empire in Kars and Çıldır. Erekli Han, the ruler of Tiflis, was collaborating with the Russians and attacked Ottoman lands. The ruler of Palu was summoned to serve under the command of the Erzurum governor Hâfız Mustafa Pasha, who was defending this front.[54] Apparently, the *hâkim* of Palu had finally headed to Bender, along the Russian border, but 1,200 miles away, to join the Ottoman forces there.[55] He received repeated orders asking him to join Hâfız Mustafa Pasha's ranks with his forces.[56]

The Ottoman Empire still expected military service from the *hâkim*s. Changes in the emirate's status from *hükümet* to *yurtluk-ocaklık* or vice versa were tied to military service. In retaliation against the begs' refusal to serve, their desertion, or their mere indifference to the state's calls to serve, the imperial state may have threatened to take away the *hükümet* status of Palu, which would mean increased state intervention in the emirate's fiscal and administrative matters. But sometimes the begs of Palu stepped in when other begs refused to serve in a military campaign. During the Ottoman–Habsburg wars, the *timar* holders in Çapakçur sent only fifty men to the campaigns, and failed to pay their dues to the treasury.

Therefore, Çapakçur was taken from them and granted to Yansûr Beg, the *hâkim* of Palu, who also received the title of *mîrimiran*.[57]

These negotiations over military service challenge the widely-held assumption that the changing administrative status of the Kurdish emirates resulted from a linear process of diminishing autonomy, presumably due to the imperial state's unilateral decision-making. In this pre-Tanzimat era, every time the Ottoman state intervened or threatened to intervene in the administrative status of the Kurdish emirates or the succession within them, the cause was an underlying need for military or fiscal service from these begs. These were not the moves of an increasingly dominant state, but rather indications of the state's increasing vulnerability. The degree of the Palu begs' autonomy was predicated less on the imperial state's unilateral decisions than on changing imperial and regional circumstances.

Nobility Undermined? The Palu Begs and Mine Service

THE KEBAN AND ERGANI MINES IN THE IMPERIAL ECONOMY

Throughout the eighteenth century, the main arena in which the Palu begs connected with the imperial state was the Keban-Ergani mines. The Palu begs, along with begs of other emirates in the vicinity, were charged with providing supplies for the mines, most importantly charcoal and wood from the surrounding forests, to be used in the mines' smelting furnaces. Providing these services involved the Palu begs in a complex new economy and a new constellation of power relations with local and imperial actors.

Extraction from the Ergani mines began in the late seventeenth century, and Keban likely started its operations in the first decade of the eighteenth century.[58] Both produced silver, gold and copper throughout the eighteenth century. The Ergani mine produced copper used mainly in the military industry, while for some part of the eighteenth century the Keban mine, reflecting a general pattern in Ottoman mines, had a mint attached to it.[59] Prior to that, the nearby city of Diyarbekir had housed a mint from the time of the Ottoman conquest in the 1500s.[60] Silver coins brought from Aleppo were cut in the Diyarbekir mint.[61] By the end of the seventeenth century, Ottoman coin minting slowed dramatically due to the influx of silver from the new world. Echoing the general eclipse of Ottoman mints, the Diyarbekir mint was defunct by the mid-seventeenth century.[62] The need for money and mints changed in the 1720s and 1730s when multi-front wars and greater commercialisation of the economy pushed demand. Technological innovations of the time made it possible to mint smoother coins more quickly.⁶³ As a result, a series of provincial mints were opened across the empire.⁶⁴ The Keban and Ergani mines gained crucial importance within this new context in which the Ottomans set out to mint coins more extensively.

Ottoman records indicate the presence of a mint in Keban before 1734, although it is not exactly clear how long it had operated.⁶⁵ By the early eighteenth century, the Ottoman state's policy of centralising monetary operations in the Imperial Mint meant that provincial mints were closed.⁶⁶ But Keban still provided necessary metals to the Imperial Mint. In 1788–9, the Keban mines produced more than 85 per cent of the silver used in the Imperial Mint and ranked first among all the other mines.⁶⁷ The Ergani mines provided much-needed copper to the Ottoman military industry, mainly to the Imperial Foundry in the capital.⁶⁸ In his study of the Ottoman weapons industry, Gabor Ágoston argues that in the eighteenth century, the Keban-Ergani mines became the 'foremost places for copper mining', overtaking the Black Sea mines.⁶⁹

Due to their fiscal and military significance, the Keban-Ergani mines received much of the state's attention. The Ottoman state needed the mines' output to remain consistent and their profits maximised. Initially, administrators appointed directly by the Imperial Treasury (*Hazine-i Âmire*) managed the mines. This changed in the 1730s when the empire decided to keep its valuables closer at hand. Mine oversight shifted to the Imperial Mint (*Darphane-i Âmire*), underscoring the mines' significance in monetary policy. To manage day-to-day operations, the Ottoman state used trusteeship (*emanet*). In this system, the imperial state directly appointed a superintendent (*emin*), who was given the necessary capital to invest in the mine and oversee all operations, from extraction and processing to transportation. This capital was sometimes granted in the form of the revenues from various sources in the mine area (*mukataa*).⁷⁰ Initially, these two mines were [assigned] to the Trustee of the Gümüşhane Mines in the north, who had the authority to appoint the trustees of the Keban-Ergani mines.⁷¹ In 1740 the Imperial Mint decided to increase its oversight, and it directly appointed two *emin*s to administer the mines.

The administration of these mines gained a new character with the establishment of the *Ma'adin-i Hümayûn Emaneti* in 1775. This special administrative and fiscal unit brought the two mines, along with other smaller mines nearby, under its purview. Typically, the Ottoman state assigned nearby towns and districts to provide for the specific needs of the mines in the vicinity. Instead of reporting to their provincial or district governors, area leaders now reported to the *Ma'adin-i Hümayûn Emaneti*. The list of districts tied to *Ma'adin-i Hümayûn Emaneti* changed from one year to the next depending on their responsibility to the mines.[72] The *emin* of the Emanet was appointed directly by the state. He was accorded what the government described as *istiklaliyet*, exempting him from the intervention of other administrators in the area, even the governors.[73] At some point, the *emin*s were required to reside near their mines, and many built special residences. Beyond his responsibilities for overseeing the extraction, processing and shipping of mine yields, with this special administrative unit the *emin* became the highest administrative authority in the region surrounding the mine. While overseeing mine-related fiscal and administrative matters, these *emin*s increased their power vis-à-vis the local power-holders such that they were significantly involved in appointing and dismissing the begs of the nearby Kurdish emirates, including Palu.

NOBILITY AND MINE SERVICE

Even before the Keban-Ergani mines were opened, Palu had a role in the local mining economy through its links to towns and cities further north and north-east. For example, in the sixteenth century, the *hâkim* of Palu sent local labourers to the Kiği mines in the north-east, where they helped produce iron for cannons going to the Erzurum fortress.[74] In the eighteenth century, however, this rather subsidiary role grew as the Keban-Ergani mines gained significance.

Palu was both an extraction site and a provisioner of materials needed for operations. Smaller-scale ore deposits were discovered around Palu throughout the eighteenth century. When ore was found in the Alaaddin village of the Sivan sub-district (*nahiye*) in Palu, the imperial state appointed the *emin* of the Ergani mines to oversee its extraction. However, Palu was a fifteen-hour trip from Ergani, and the metals extracted in Palu had to be transported and processed in the furnaces in Ergani. To get the metals to Ergani, *mekkari*s, porters who conveyed goods on animals, had to be imported from neighbouring Hani and Eğil districts and paid by the miners in cash.[75] At the same time, Palu had to provide the goods and services necessary to keep the mines operating in the Keban-Ergani area. From the 1720s on, what rendered Palu indispensable was not the ore in its vicinity, but its provision of charcoal and wood used in the smelting furnaces. Although they had no administrative authority for the mines, the Palu begs were responsible for maintaining the continuous flow of resources to them.[76]

The inhabitants of the villages under the rule of the Palu begs had to acquire and deliver a set amount of charcoal and wood annually to the mines. In this pre-industrial setting, mine work was remarkably specialised; villages and regions had their own crafts or vocations, and three different groups were involved in manufacturing charcoal: *baltacıs, kelekçis* and *kömürcübaşıs*. The *baltacıs* cut the trees, mostly oak, from surrounding forests and burnt them to create charcoal for the mines.[77] Some of the *baltacıs* came from Palu's villages but most came from outside, mostly Gümüşhane, and they did this work with the help of the inhabitants of these districts.[78] The charcoal was transported by *kelekçis* on *keleks*, special rafts made of animal skin, down the Euphrates river and its tributaries. The *kömürcübaşıs*, meanwhile, oversaw a variety of processes from cutting down the trees to delivering the charcoal to the mines to maintaining the security of the *baltacıs* and *kelekçis*. They were paid in cash at the time of delivery by miners under the command of the mine superintendent. Even though the amount of charcoal and wood required from Palu, and the price paid per its *yük*,[79] were specified by imperial decree, both the prices and the amount were subject to negotiation between the imperial state, the mine superintendent and the begs. From the 1760s to the 1790s, the amount of charcoal Palu provided fluctuated between 8,000 and 20,000 *yük*.[80] Perhaps this fluctuation was due to changes in the mines' production levels or to a diminishing supply of charcoal due to deforestation.[81] Between 1759 and 1785, the volume of silver produced in the Keban mines dropped drastically, with a partial recovery after 1787.[82] The need for charcoal remained high, however. Either due to greater production or because of increased furnace temperatures, the imperial state ordered the begs to supply more charcoal.[83]

In return for their service, local inhabitants received tax exemptions, specifically, from the lump sum taxes paid in times of war (*imdâd-ı seferiye*) and peace (*imdâd-ı hazariye*).[84] Notwithstanding these incentives, however, the work was challenging. Material difficulties made it difficult to maintain a stable supply of resources. *Keleks*, for example, required large amounts of animal skin, and thus large quantities of animals and animal feed, and so on. The provision of these skins constituted another chain in the local mining economy. When a scarcity emerged in one area, other villages and districts in the vicinity, including Palu, were ordered to fill the gap by providing skins to the *kelekçi* villages in return for monies from the mine superintendent.[85] When the inhabitants of Palu were responsible for providing these materials, the *hâkim* of Palu oversaw the process and made sure that animals from the named villages were slaughtered and the skins handed to the mine superintendent at the designated prices.[86]

The original agreement between the Ottoman state and the Kurdish nobles indicates no service other than participating in military campaigns

Noble Privilege on the Ground

and maintaining order and security in their spheres of authority. But by the eighteenth century, Palu's proximity to these mines transformed the relationship of the begs with the imperial state. Along with ensuring a continuous flow of charcoal and wood, the begs were also responsible for maintaining security in the areas around the mines. Typically, mine areas became economically and demographically vibrant hubs with high labour mobility. Labourers from around the empire came to work in the mines, and merchants made frequent trips to the mine area. Reports of banditry and attacks proliferated. While these were not uncommon throughout the empire, the imperial state paid more attention to security in this region because it was such a vital revenue source.[87] Though the Palu begs were charged with keeping the mine area safe, the threatening tone of orders from the imperial state gives the impression that the begs did not take these orders seriously, and attacks continued.[88]

Now, the Kurdish nobility's co-operation in this new realm became a major criterion for continuing Palu's *hükümet* status and its accompanying prerogatives. Moreover, the provision of charcoal to the mines became a precondition for government support in leadership squabbles between begs. The Palu begs received countless orders from the state asking them to perform their mine functions without negligence and threatening to seize the *hükümet* from a particular beg and give it to someone else.[89] When the aforementioned İbrahim Beg was granted the title of *beylerbeyi*, providing coal and workers to Keban-Ergani mines was cited as one of the reasons he deserved this title, with the grant calling the mines '[one of the] largest [sources of] revenue for the Imperial Treasury'.[90]

It was not the mine work, but the transformation of local power relations due to the emergence of this new mine bureaucracy that altered the Palu begs' noble privileges. Most of the area surrounding the Keban-Ergani mines had long been under the authority of the Kurdish nobles, including Palu, Çermik and Eğil. But after the establishment of the *Ma'âdin-i Hümayûn Emaneti*, its superintendents progressively increased their authority over the areas surrounding the mines. They struck deals with local begs, negotiating over the amount of charcoal each beg was responsible for providing, as well as other aspects of mine work. The superintendents frequently appealed to the imperial state on issues related to the provision of raw materials, mine security, or the defiance or collaboration of the Kurdish begs. They became increasingly powerful.

An example is the extraordinary career of El-Hâc Yusuf (also known as Yusuf Agha and later Yusuf Pasha after he was granted the *pasha* title), who began as the superintendent of the Ma'âdin-i Hümayûn Emaneti and rose to become grand vizier in Istanbul. He amassed enormous power through the careful appointment of local administrators and distribution of tax contracts, possessing such great power and wealth that he almost 'built his own sociopolitical infrastructure in the region'.[91] For the fifteen years he served as superintendent, El-Hâc Yusuf played a big role in shaping the local power configurations involving Kurdish nobility.

THE PALU BEGS VERSUS THE UNSTOPPABLE RISE OF A MINE SUPERINTENDENT: YUSUF ZIYA PASHA

Yusuf Agha began administrating the Keban mines in 1785 and served until 1799.[92] A decade later in 1809, he again became mine superintendent, until 1811.[93] In 1787, a year into his service, he was appointed Superintendent of the Imperial Mint (*Darbhane-i Âmire Nazırı or Emini*), serving until 1794, making his term the second longest of the approximately sixty people who held the position between 1717 and the 1840s.[94] Mine superintendents often seized the governorship of districts and provinces in the area. Yusuf Ziya's predecessor, Hafiz Mustafa Pasha, for instance, also served as governor of the Malatya sanjak and the *beglerbegi* of Islahiye.[95] Yusuf Ziya's accumulation of power, however, was unprecedented. Between 1793 and 1798, he served as the governor of Diyarbekir, Erzurum, Çıldır and Trabzon, and was given the title of *pasha*.[96] He consolidated his power in the region through aggressive military campaigns over the tribes around Harput and Dersim.[97] During the Ottoman campaign over southern Caucasia, he assembled a military force from among the surrounding tribes and emirates, including Palu.[98] In 1798, he reached the climax of his career when he was appointed Grand Vizier and came to the imperial capital. Shortly afterwards, he commanded the Ottoman forces in their fight against Napoleon Bonaparte in Egypt from 1799 to 1802.[99]

The increasing influence of the superintendent in the local economy was not based exclusively on the mine. Yusuf Ziya Pasha rushed to buy up life-term tax-farm (*malikâne*) contracts in and around Diyarbekir. While the imperial state sought to maintain an uninterrupted flow of provincial revenues to the imperial coffers through the *malikâne* contracts, along the way, the system became an instrument whereby private citizens could profit from these revenue sources.[100] His power provided him with the temerity to demand a contract for the stamp tax (*damga*) on clothes in the Çarsancak, Palu, Harput, Çemişgezek, Arapgir and Eğin districts.[101] At the time, the state was trying to tighten its control over the tax on these items, because, it claimed, *malikâne* contracts were costing the state money. The Ottoman administration wanted this tax to be collected via a trustee (*ber vech-i emanet*),[102] and ordered Yusuf Ziya to collect it and send the revenues and the tax registers to the capital. Yusuf Ziya was insistent, though, pointing out that the imperial state's refusal to give him his desired contract would damage his prestige. It is not clear if the cause was his insistence or the difficulties faced in the implementation of the trust system, but four years later, the stamp tax for these districts was still being collected through life-term tax farming.

The growing power of the mine superintendent affected the relationship between the Kurdish begs and the Ottoman state. Most importantly, the mine superintendent began to meddle in the appointment process of the *hâkim* leading the emirate, despite the original agreement granting the begs near-total autonomy in the appointment process. Although the Ottoman state had endorsed some begs over others from the same family, it had not otherwise interfered in the appointment process. The imperial state's appointment decrees left the section where the appointee's name was written blank, giving the begs absolute authority in naming their leader. Three key changes affected this appointment process and drastically transformed the character of the Palu nobility and its relationship with the Ottoman state.

First, mine superintendents gradually increased their power in the area and gained the authority to formally appoint the *hâkim* of the emirate, frequently writing letters to justify their dismissals or appointments. In a letter written to the Superintendent of the Imperial Mint in 1753, superintendent Numan Efendi sought authorisation to dismiss the current *hâkim*, İskender Beg, and appoint Abdulgafur Beg instead. Numan Efendi claimed that İskender Beg did not get along well with the inhabitants of Palu and failed to provide services to the mines. He requested Abdulgafur Beg's appointment on the condition that he would provide the needed charcoal, *kelek*, and grains to the mine.[103] Within a few months, the same Numan wrote to dismiss Abdulgafur Beg and re-appoint İskender Beg on the basis of the very same justifications. By the 1780s, the superintendents' authority in appointing the begs of Palu, Çermik and Eğil was established convention.

Power conflicts between the superintendents and the begs manifested in numerous ways. In 1780, Hüseyin Beg, for example, apparently refused to submit to the superintendent.[104] To make his dubious position in the eyes of the state even worse, Hüseyin Beg supported the Ömerganlu tribe, which the state had exiled from the district. More important to the superintendent, the local inhabitants stopped providing charcoal to the mines, halting the mining of gold and silver. For the imperial state, these offences required intervention – and Hüseyin Beg packed his figurative bags and Burhan Beg was appointed in his place. This decision was unpopular among the other begs, and when the newly-appointed Burhan Beg arrived, a coalition of begs and Çötelioğlu Mutaf Agha, a local notable from neighbouring Harput, along with a hundred cavalrymen, attacked him. He survived, but the judge (*kadı*) of Harput Es-Seyyid Hüseyin Efendi and his right-hand man Kapucuoğlu Osman died in the attack. The imperial state's response was harsh: it imprisoned Hüseyin Beg at Rumkale, around 400 miles from Palu.

Second, as mentioned before, though there were no references to material responsibilities in the original *temessük* given to the begs in the sixteenth century, by the end of the eighteenth century charcoal provision was a pre-condition for succession. According to an Ottoman archival document from 1780, 'it is a custom from old times (*mutad-i kadim*) to appoint someone, whose loyalty and integrity (*istikamet*) is evident, on the condition that [he] would [ensure] the provision and transport of three thousand *yük*s of charcoal annually from the mountains of Palu [to the mines]'.[105] For the imperial centre, mine production was a top priority, and mine supplies were the major consideration for the appointment of the Palu *hâkim*s.

Superintendents had concerns other than the mines, including power conflicts with the begs over the profits they derived from the appointments, which brings us to the third point. The incoming beg also paid a fee called *beylik câizesi* to the mine superintendent to have his name included on the appointment documents. This fee did not exist in the original agreement between the Ottoman sultans and the begs. More generally, *câize*, money paid by appointees to bureaucratic posts, a practice that had originated in the sixteenth century and become commonplace by the eighteenth century, represented vital revenue sources for the administrators.[106] To ensure prompt payment, a system in which appointees borrowed this amount from creditors (*sarraf*) was established as a widespread option. More often than not, having borrowed money from the *sarraf*s at high interest without the ability to pay it back, provincial notables intensified their exploitation of the agricultural population to recoup their losses.

The cycle laid a patina of venality upon the noble position of the beglik as well as ensnaring the Kurdish begs in a spiral of borrowing and debt. In 1788, Yusuf Ziya reported, or rather complained, to the imperial centre that the Palu *hükümet* was contracted to the *hâkim* of Palu for 60 thousand *guruş câize*, and 8 thousand *hamel* charcoal. After 11,000 guruş had been paid, an earthquake shook the region, and the *hâkim* had difficulty fulfilling his commitment. Yusuf Ziya gave him an extension and later forgave him the remaining part of the *câize* on condition that he bring an extra 4,000 *hamel* charcoal to the mines, which he failed to do.[107] While appealing to the state for the unpaid *câize* of the begs, in a striking move, Yusuf Pasha tried to convince the imperial state to exempt the begs of Palu, Eğil and Çermik from joining military campaigns. He argued that they would not be able to pay their *câize* if they served in the army, and that this would result in revenue losses for the mine administration. He added that even if he could collect this amount from the begs, the begs, in order to meet the costs of participating in the campaigns, would further burden the commoners by increasing their taxes. This would then cause the poor to flee, further damaging the mines since they were the labourers. The begs had not participated in a military campaign for nearly two decades, a fact that Yusuf Ziya used to support his argument:

> Even if they [the begs] were appointed [to serve in the campaigns] ... they would only cause loss for the Imperial Treasury ... Even though they served in previous military campaigns, nowadays, they cannot bring more than a hundred men, each accompanied by a lame horse, a broken pistol that will not fire, and a blunt *kurde*;[108] and most of them [would be] with an untrained ass (*tebeddünsüz zınbara*).[109]

Yusuf Ziya Pasha's unflattering description of the Kurdish nobles' military abilities reflects their changing roles in a new economic context where their service to the mines, and the *câize* they paid to claim office (even thought it was still a hereditary post), were cash cows for the mine superintendent. From the perspective of the Ottoman imperial government, however, the military responsibility of the Palu emirs was not obsolete or redundant. In 1810, the imperial state asked Yusuf Pasha to collect 100 cavalrymen from Pertek, along with 200 infantry soldiers from Palu, Çermik, Eğil and Ergani and 150 from Çarsancak. The state's order in the previous year had fallen on deaf ears, with Yusuf Ziya Pasha neither responding nor sending the soldiers.[110] There is no indication that he responded this time, either.

In the previous century, when court scribe Azîz Efendi lamented the lost military might of the Kurdish nobles, he was dismayed that the 'raging lions' of the past two centuries had been rendered 'abject' by the oppression of the provincial governors, who, he said, 'through their avarice dismissed some of them from office while executing others without reason'.[111] Azîz Efendi did not have prophetic powers, but he certainly had his finger on something: Ottoman provincial administrators' increasing attempts to undermine the hereditary privileges of the Kurdish beg. Nearly a hundred years later, Yusuf Ziya Pasha embodied the very processes Azîz Efendi had blamed for the 'despair' of the hereditary Kurdish begs. The mines challenged the begs' local authority because the mine superintendents were increasingly powerful and wealthy local administrators. However, the mines also gave a considerable degree of leverage to the begs in their dealings with the Ottoman centre. Keeping production uninterrupted at the mines was contingent upon the Kurdish begs' co-operation in providing for the mines' needs. This helped the begs continue to hold their noble privileges and the *hükümet* status of Palu to remain intact throughout the rest of the century.

Though the military and the mines served as important venues for the begs' interaction with the Ottoman administrators, they did not constitute the major source of the Palu begs' long-lived power and authority as a noble elite group *within* the locality. It lay elsewhere: land. In a pre-industrial, agrarian context, the begs' privileges were fundamentally defined by their control of land and its surplus, and analysis of the alterations in this realm will shed further light on the question of the Kurdish begs' noble privileges.

Land: The Palu Begs' Control over Land and the Changing Meanings of Fiscal Autonomy in the Eighteenth Century

Prior to Tanzimat, Palu nobility were exempt from paying annual agrarian taxes on land. The decree granted to Cemşîd Beg by Sultan Suleyman I in 1535 (which alluded to the one granted by his father Selim I) explicitly stated that the revenues of the castles, cities and *mezraa* (lit. sown land) belonged to the begs and their descendants.[112] In Ottoman administrative parlance, these exemptions were defined by the status of *mefrûzü'l-kalem* and *maktû'ü'l-kadem*, that is, the 'taxes were not entered in the imperial registers and there is no Ottoman state agent present; all the area is reserved (*tahsis*) to them [the emirs]'.[113] This formula, which granted a beg/emîr 'immunities and exemptions on land revenue and peasant labour within the borders of a well-defined area, freed from the control of the state and its agents', had, as mentioned, long precedents in the Islamic world.[114] The arrangement continued in Ottoman statecraft specifically within the context of the *hükümets*, where all sources of revenue remained in the begs' possession.[115]

The fiscal immunities granted to the Kurdish begs for their *hükümets* need to be considered at two levels. The first concerns the begs' fiscal responsibilities to the imperial centre. The *hükümets*' exemption from receiving surveyors, tax collectors or other Ottoman administrators appointed by the centre into their spheres of authority was a conspicuous recognition of the begs' fiscal privileges. The second – frequently overlooked – aspect of the Kurdish begs' autonomy concerns their control over land, labour and agrarian surplus. Fully understanding the begs' economic power requires consideration of both.

The begs' immunity from fiscal responsibility shows a significant degree of continuity from the original decrees accorded up to the Tanzimat era when Ottoman administrators began to question such de jure fiscal autonomy. During that time, since the begs were exempted from paying both *şer'i* (Islamic) and *örfi* (customary) taxes, the Ottoman state did not regularly claim the agrarian surplus from the *hükümet*s.[116] However, records indicate that while recognising their inalienable control over revenues on land, the state still expected the begs to pay a certain amount of annual tribute – for which they were often in arrears. This amount was not fixed, depending instead largely on the degree of leverage the begs had vis-à-vis the state at any given time. When the military responsibilities of the begs increased, the likelihood that government could acquire the annual tribute decreased. For example, during the 1580s Yusuf Beg participated in the Iranian campaigns for almost three years. He did not pay his annual dues. In other instances, the begs paid only a fraction of what they undertook to give.[117]

However, it is not accurate to assume that all the land under the Kurdish begs' control remained outside the Ottoman classical land regime given the complexity of land and tax regimes in different parts of Kurdistan and the Kurdish begs' varying degrees of power. During the sixteenth and seventeenth centuries, the *timar* system existed in some areas ruled by the Kurdish begs despite their *hükümet* status (one example being Bitlis).[118] There are cases of either the begs or their associates having fiefs (*dirliks*), typically outside, but sometimes within the *hükümet*. For instance, the begs of Eğil held *dirliks* in Harput, whereas the begs of Çermik held *dirliks* within Çermik. In this picture, Palu stands out in terms of its unhindered *dirlik*-free position. Throughout the sixteenth and seventeenth centuries, the Palu begs had no *dirliks* within Palu, even though they and their associates held some in neighbouring Harput (which was not a *hükümet*). This means that for two centuries after they accepted Ottoman suzerainty, the Palu begs effectively maintained their noble privilege of being exempt from the *timar* system within their hereditary territories.

Despite the Palu nobility's de jure exemption from agricultural dues and other taxes to the imperial treasury, the state tried to extract dues from the area, particularly when it was cash-poor. At those times, the state would levy dues on the population and appoint the begs to collect them for the imperial treasury. In the 1740s, records indicate that the inhabitants of Palu paid *avârız* taxes. Collected on a household basis, these taxes began as extraordinary wartime levies, but from the seventeenth century onwards they were used regularly to raise funds. İskender Beg, Seyfullah Beg and Mustafa Beg had been collecting *avârız* taxes from the population throughout the 1750s. Sporadic instances of complaints about over-taxation that reached the imperial state indicate that people recognised the difference between taxes the begs levied (a prerogative they had) and what they collected on behalf of the imperial state.[119] In some cases, the begs farmed out *avârız* collection to third parties, mostly from within Palu.[120]

Theoretically, the state's demand for taxes from Palu's population was a violation of Palu begs' hereditary fiscal privileges. which gave them the inalienable right to collect taxes. In reality, however, the state did not encroach upon the agrarian taxes, which were under the begs' domain, but rather demanded additional (new) taxes from the population. In this way, a fiscal burden was placed on the taxpaying population without causing a decrease in the begs' revenues from the agrarian surplus.

COMPETITION OVER AGRARIAN SURPLUS

In 1695, the Ottoman imperial state introduced a novel fiscal instrument for revenue extraction from its provincial periphery, the life-term tax farm (*malikâne*). Previously, tax farms (*iltizam*) had been granted only for three-year periods. Because of the need for cash and the countless technical, fiscal and social problems the tax-farming system created, the state established life-term grants to channel maximum revenues into the imperial treasury more sustainably. Ariel Salzmann argues that this new system of revenue contracts 'created diffused but interrelated loci of state power. It was this extensive network that sustained old-order power, knitting centre and periphery together over the eighteenth century.'[121] In other words, the life-term tax-farm system essentially privatised revenue collection. In this way, it gave the state access to revenues that hitherto were out of its reach. The administrative tool that made the *malikâne* work was a new institution called the *voyvodalık* that concentrated the various revenues from land, manufacturing, commerce, tribes, and so on, under the control of a *voyvoda*. He was a fiscal agent, a tax farmer himself, tasked with farming out these revenues to bidders, but he also discharged administrative authority in the areas under the scope of the *voyvodalık*.[122]

Thus, in the second half of the seventeenth century, imperial revenue sources (formerly administered by the provincial treasury [*defterdarlık*]) were funnelled into the newly-established *voyvodalık* of Diyarbekir.[123] Given that the begs' noble privileges exempting them in fiscal matters were still in effect at this time, it is imperative to understand whether revenue sources within the scope of the *voyvodalık* of Diyarbekir influenced the Kurdish begs' control over land and its surplus.

The *hükümet* status did not grant blanket immunity from the transformation of revenue sources under the begs' control into *malikânes* under the *voyvodalık*'s scope. A case in point was Tercil, a *hükümet* under rule of the the Zerkî begs located 120 miles south-east of Palu whose revenues technically belonged to its *hâkim*. Though it should have been shielded, the *voyvodalık* scooped up some of Tercil's agricultural lands. Palu, however, remained unfettered and retained its prerogatives over land and its surplus even as the *voyvodalık* and *malikanisation* process unfolded in Diyarbekir in the eighteenth century.[124] In one respect, this epitomised a broader pattern. In the second half of the eighteenth century, the number of autonomous units (i.e *hükümets*) in the region increased. According to Salzmann, this was an outcome of the Ottoman–Iranian wars that compromised the Ottoman state's authority in the region, but it was also part of an empire-wide process. Everywhere provincial elites increased their power in their spheres of authority and *ayan* dynasties began emerging across the empire.[125] There were also region-specific dynamics that helped the Kurdish begs maintain the *hükümet* status of their dominions. For instance, as Salzmann observes, in this period agricultural production shifted towards the fortified cities in the north of Diyarbekir ruled by the Kurdish hereditary elites, including Palu.[126] These dynamics increased the leverage of the Palu begs vis-à-vis the potential attempts to attach their revenue sources to the *voyvodalık*. But the superintendents of the special Mine Administration posed a challenge to the begs' fiscal autonomy, with the mine superintendent claiming many of the *malikâne* contracts taxing textiles manufactured in Palu. However, there is no indication that the superintendent acquired *malikâne* contracts on land revenues under the begs' authority. When superintendents or other local Ottoman administrators attempted to seize such revenue sources, the begs appealed to the imperial centre, referring to their *mefrûzü'l-kalem* and *maktû'ü'l-kadem* status, which they insisted meant their fiscal authority was free from all intervention.[127]

Whether because of its *hükümet* status or the leverage the begs had due to their mine service, Palu's agrarian revenues remained outside the scope of the *voyvodalık* of Diyarbekir and *largely* free from the encroachment of actors based *outside of* the Palu.[128] Nevertheless, through the second half of the eighteenth century – even though the de jure exemptions and prerogatives of the Palu begs remained intact – Palu's economic scene transformed dramatically, resulting in fierce competition over the agrarian surplus. The begs either farmed out or leased out the lands under their control to buyers with no noble background. They needed the money, because the mine administrators had gained enormous power over the appointment processes of the *hâkim*, and charging the *beylik caizesi* (the fee paid by the prospective *hâkim* to the superintendents) had become common practice, and so the begs' need for cash increased dramatically. Another factor was that the begs' mine service took place within credit networks. They borrowed cash from moneylenders to provide for the mines' needs. Echoing the processes mentioned by Azîz Efendi a century previously, their growing cash needs probably inclined them to farm out or lease out their lands. As a result, Palu witnessed the emergence of a new phenomenon of *çiftlik*s, the proliferation of private estates owned by actors other than the begs. These changes led to the fragmentation and diversification of the profile of those who sought to confiscate Palu's agrarian surplus in the eighteenth century.

TAX FARMING AND LEASING

Reflecting an empire-wide process, by the second half of the eighteenth century, tax farming had become the dominant fiscal instrument used to collect agrarian surplus within Palu. In much of their domain, the begs farmed out the collection of the agrarian dues. In this arrangement, the tax farmer bought the right to collect the tithe and other agrarian dues owed by the contracted areas from the begs. In one case in 1743, then *hâkim* of Palu, Mehmed, farmed out the tithe of the Kadem village in Karaçor *nahiye* to a certain Yusuf.[129] The inhabitants, however, were not happy with this arrangement, refusing to pay. Yusuf appealed to the imperial state for intervention when he faced large financial losses. In a similar case, in 1763, Palu nobility Abdullah Beg and his brother Hüseyin Beg farmed out the tithe of the Demirci village land to Seyyid el Hac Ibrahim, receiving 1,150 guruş as advance payment. But, as Seyyid el Hac Ibrahim found out, they had already farmed out the same land to others, and he had no way of collecting tithe revenues from the village.[130] By the second half of the eighteenth century, Palu begs had farmed out many of the lands under their control, albeit not without problems. In many cases, pre-existing claims clashed with the claims made by these new tax farmers. Unsurprisingly, the tax farmer's intrusion into long-standing relationships and established patterns of tax collection stirred the agrarian population of the farmed-out lands. By delegating the collection of agrarian dues to private parties through tax farming, the Palu begs violated the villagers' notion of the moral economy of surplus extraction.

Along with tax farming, there were other forms of land use and surplus extraction, including renting out land and collecting the tithe and other dues from the lessee. In these cases, the begs gave title deeds that granted the lessee use of the land, but the begs were still recognised as the land owner (*sahib-i arz*) by both the lessee and the imperial state.[131] As long as the lessee paid these dues, the begs were not allowed to intervene in his business.[132] Such dealings occasionally stirred conflict among the begs over the terms of the transactions. In one case, İbrahim Beg and Mehmed Beg leased out the land in Haşarig village to Kapıcızade el-Hâc Mehmed and levied the tithe from him. Later, Abdülgafur Beg, hoping, probably, for a share of the tithe revenues, challenged the transaction that the other two begs had initiated and prevented Mehmed from tilling the land.[133] In a similar case, a claimant got usage rights of lands in three villages but later complained that Halil Beg was demanding extra, illegal taxes from him even though he was paying the tithe and other dues on land.[134]

One reason for these contending claims was that the Palu begs had individualised their claims over land. They signed contracts for tax farming or leasing individually, even though the land was under the hereditary control of the noble family, as the imperial decrees that defined the noble family as a collective unit were still in effect. While making their noble claims over the Palu land at large, the begs were treating parcels of land as their private property – a tension stemming from the growing incompatibility of the Palu begs' familial rights over land with the privatisation of land ownership on the ground.

It was not only the begs who delegated their economic control over land and surplus through tax farming and leasing; non-nobles did so as well. Private parties acquired the use of land and then farmed it out or sub-leased it. In most cases, the lessee would till the land and pay the tithe to the owner of the land. Sometimes, the lessee subcontracted the usufruct rights to another lessee; such leases could last several decades. In one case, a certain Mollâ Ahmed from the Kabak village inherited land in this village from his father, land that had been in his family for almost five decades. He leased it out to a certain Mustafa, a distant cousin. What is noteworthy here is that, according to their contract, Mustafa paid the rent to Mollâ Ahmed, the leaser. But he paid the tithe to the 'owner of land', which means Mollâ Ahmed himself was not the land owner, but a long-term lessee.[135] Like tax farming, leasing out land often created clashes because of competing claims to the surplus. When a party leased a piece of land from the begs, the new possessor could face unexpected challenges from others using the land or claiming its surplus. In one case, Mollâ Muhyiddin, whose name appears a few times in the records, acquired the right to till the lands in Beydeve village, paying in return the tithe and other dues to the landowner. Despite having a *temessük* (title deed) granted by the landowner, he asked the imperial state for help, stating that other people were intervening in his use of land.[136] Instances of clashes between new claimants and existent claims over land abound in this period.[137]

It was common for the usufruct right to take on a hereditary character. In 1762, for example, a certain Sadık appealed to the state about his cousin, Salih, who encroached upon and seized the lands that Sadık had inherited from his father. Sadık had been tilling this land and paying the tithe to the landowner. Apparently, although he thought he owned the land, what he had inherited was just the usufruct.[138] In principle, usufruct rights were not sellable or transferable to other parties without the permission of the landowner, but this did happen. In one case, a certain Seyyit Diyab ceded (*ferağ*) the land he possessed to Abbas Agha and Ali Agha. This transaction was not considered *sahih* (lawful under Sharia) since he did not receive authorisation from the landowner.[139] But the significant point here is that this became an issue only after the original seller passed, and his sons, seeking to make a case for inheriting the land and annulling their father's transaction, disputed the transaction.[140] In rare instances, the begs sold *ownership* of inherited land to someone else, while the usufruct belonged to a third party. A certain Hüseyin purchased a *çiftlik* from Ismail Beg. The transaction was approved by the *kadı*, who confirmed the sale as final and guaranteed the rights of the parties.[141] Afterwards, however, Ismail Beg encroached upon the sold land, saying that he regretted selling it and wanted the deal annulled. One aspect of this case needs special emphasis here. Unlike the cases of leasing discussed earlier, in this instance the terminology of *bey'* (lit. to 'sell') was used – referring to a transfer of ownership. Reflecting the de facto privatisation of *mîrî* (state) land as an empire-wide trend, the term *bey'* became more common for the sale of agricultural land from the seventeenth century onwards.[142] In eighteenth-century Palu, the sale of land ownership in this way represented only a small minority of the land transactions. The great majority entailed the transfer of use through leasing out land in return for agrarian dues (mainly the tithe) on land rather than the ownership of the land itself. This allowed the Palu begs to maintain their hereditary ownership of the land while transferring the usufruct rights through leasing and delegating rights to surplus extraction to third parties through tax farming.

The conflicts discussed here arose from the transformation in how the Palu begs approached and used their hereditary lands, which they now saw as a profit-making commodity. Happening as it did at a time of accelerated monetisation and commercialisation, the commodification of land should not come as a surprise. Begs retained hereditary control of their land; it was this that allowed them to sell or lease the surplus extraction to private parties. What changed was how the land was used and how surplus was extracted.

We also see the loosening of the tie between noble status and landed wealth, as the begs began to engage in economic transactions outside their fellow nobles. This did not necessarily mean a deterioration of the begs' overall well-being or a decrease of their power. Comparative studies of nobility have long challenged the 'decline of the nobility' thesis, arguing that neither the transformation of the nobility's attachment to land nor their increasing economic engagements necessarily eroded their wealth and power. Portraying nobility as an ideal type representing tradition in the face of the transformative forces of modernity feeds into this decline narrative – suggesting that the nobility is a group incapable of adaptation and reactionary by nature. However, in his study of late imperial Russia, Becker observes changes in land ownership patterns by nobility characterised by a decrease in the amount of land the nobles owned from the second half of the nineteenth century on. But he argues that while noble acreage did contract, it was nobles themselves who sold the land, and mostly to other nobles.[143] He argues that the nobles' divestiture of land, after the emancipation of the serfs, 'was a sign of a healthy ability to adjust to a radically changed social and economic environment'.[144]

An analysis of the Palu begs' economic activities in the eighteenth century echoes this revisionist perspective. It is true that the begs' control over land changed as tax farming became the major source of surplus extraction. And as we have seen, the Palu nobility also transferred land use through leasing agreements and sometimes outright sale. Despite the lack of systematic statistical data on the Palu begs' land ownership, these processes point to an adaptation to changing economic realities similar to that of the Russian nobles. Needing cash, the begs resorted to their hereditary land, which they now saw as an economic asset. One result of these transformations was the emergence of rivals who accumulated land, which the last part of this chapter examines in more detail. But even a century later, the begs still held the inalienable ownership of the great majority of the Palu land – which is why the state attempted to confiscate it during the Tanzimat era.

The Emergence of *Çİftlİks*

One of the outcomes of the begs' loosening control over land and its surplus was the emergence of *çiftlik*s, large landed estates, in Palu's countryside in the second half of the eighteenth century. In the Ottoman world, the concept of *çiftlik* never had a standard meaning across time and space. As Çağlar Keyder points out, its 'protean nature and diversity of historical incarnations make it difficult to define or identify'.[145] Nonetheless, Keyder offers a provisional definition for *çiftlik*, at the core of which is 'private control over landed property which tends to reduce the autonomy of the peasantry'.[146] In this definition, the emergence of the *çiftlik*s refers both to a process of land accumulation by private persons who engaged in market-oriented agriculture and the resultant alterations in the way that production is organised. Historians working on the Balkans, Anatolia and the Arab provinces added nuance to this general definition by showing variants of *çiftlik* throughout Ottoman lands. Ariel Salzmann's study on Diyarbekir and its surroundings hints at the existence of a similar process of 'private landholdings in the form of fields (*mülk çiftlik*) and gardens (*mülk bağçe*), often in the area of old tribal *hükümet*'.[147]

The case of Palu corroborates Salzmann's suggestion about private landholdings emerging in the *hükümet*s in and around Diyarbekir. In the second half of the eighteenth century, the term *çiftlik* appears frequently in archival records to refer to the land accumulated by people outside the Palu nobility. In the previously mentioned case of İsmail Beg's sale (*bey'*) in 1757, the item sold was called *Tepe çiftliği*.[148] In a similar case, a man named Seyfullah sold two *çiftlik*s called Abdibeg and Yamak to a certain Mansur (but later changed his mind and wanted them back).[149] Sometimes a group of partners combined resources to buy several *çiftlik*s collectively. In one such case, Mehmed Emin and Murtaza claimed to have hereditary ownership over several *mülk çiftlik*s in the Palu countryside and appealed to the imperial centre for protection from a group of people who had a competing claim over these.[150] Similarly, Mir İsmail and Seyid jointly held a series of *çiftlik*s called Halidan, Kelhüseyin, Feşan and Elburun in the late 1760s. The record specifically states that these were *mülk çiftlik*s owned as freehold property (*mülkiyet üzere*) and sold with a title deed.[151]

The records relating to these *çiftlik*s use a nascent grammar of legal private property and ownership rights. The term *bey'*, which refers to a legally valid sale, denoted their transfer, and parties emphasised their *mülkiyet* (property) rights, rather than usufruct (*tasarruf*). The owners of these *çiftlik*s saw their rights over these holdings as inalienable, and whenever they perceived a threat they sought the state's help, usually by referring to the *mülk* status of these *çiftlik*s.[152] In disputes, what the complainants sought to ensure was not just their right to till the land or confiscate the surplus, but the land itself, described as *mülk*. While the begs sometimes sold their land to these *çiftlik* owners, the begs generally resented the accumulation of large chunks of land in the hands of private parties outside the nobility. The owners of the *çiftlik*s, however, resented their continuous claims being treated as irrelevant, and when the begs disputed their ownership rights, the owners frequently appealed to Istanbul.

In all the examples from Palu from the 1750s and 1760s, *çiftlik*s have specific names, although they were neither villages nor other administrative units. And in all these cases, the buyers, either individually or as shareholders, owned several *çiftlik*s, typically in one area such as a *nahiye* or a village. These facts indicate that these *çiftlik*s were estates owned by private parties in the Palu countryside. Since Palu operated largely outside the imperial state's fiscal record by virtue of its *hükümet* status, it is impossible to get a systematic picture of the size of these *çiftlik*s. Often, however, the owners appear to have had several units under their control, suggesting that *çiftlik*s were far from small peasant units. There is not enough evidence to establish whether the owners of these *çiftlik*s were from within or outside of Palu. The available records do show, however, that the owners of these *çiftlik*s were, almost without exception, Muslim.

What was being produced in these *çiftlik*s? Commercial agriculture on large estates varied regionally. Dina Khoury's study of Mosul demonstrated that one of the major catalysts for the growth of commercial agriculture there was the development of regional trade. Mosul's major agrarian trading partner was Baghdad, and along with the development of regional markets, the emergence of one powerful family, the Jalilis, who invested in land and commercialised agrarian production, created an important dynamic that set the groundwork for the commercialisation of agriculture in the province.[153]

In Palu, the major catalyst for commercialised agriculture in these *çiftlik*s was the provisioning of the military troops. The biggest recipient of Palu's agrarian products was the governor of Baghdad, who needed them for his armies. The process was complex: the *voyvoda* of Diyarbekir purchased the grain from Diyarbekir's hinterland and then sent it on *kelek*s over the Tigris and Euphrates rivers to Baghdad.[154] Palu provided 5,800 *keyl* [kile] of the 40,000 *kile* wheat and 9,300 kile of the 60,000 kile barley purchased from nineteen districts in Diyarbekir, including the areas ruled by the other Kurdish begs (the *hükümet*s), or 14.5 per cent of the wheat and 15.5 per cent of the barley sent to Baghdad.[155] The imperial centre also ordered the governor of Diyarbekir to collect grain that was stored in Diyarbekir castle and shipped to Baghdad later. Palu contributed 2,000 kiles of wheat, the highest amount (along with Çarsancak) of the nineteen districts contributing, to this batch. Thus, Palu provided 15 per cent of all the grains destined for Baghdad. Palu's position by the Murad River, one of the major tributaries of the Euphrates, facilitated its entrance into the market-place by giving it a connection to the towns and cities in the south along the river. Unlike in Mosul, where the concentration of land in the hands of one powerful family shaped agricultural commercialisation, in Palu the commercialisation came in the context of the erosion of the nobility's monopoly over land.

Finally, the private ownership of *çiftlik*s and their focus on market-oriented production also altered labour relations. While there is not enough evidence for a concrete account of the labour force in these new Palu *çiftlik*s, in the early decades of the nineteenth century sharecropping (*ortakçılık*) appeared as the major labour form, not just in the *çiftlik*s, but also (and more so) in the still-large chunks of land under the control of the Palu nobility. Below, I elaborate on the anxieties this system created in the Palu countryside, particularly among the Armenians who made up the great majority of the sharecropping population. For the moment, suffice it to say that the second half of the eighteenth century was a transformative moment in terms of land ownership and labour organisation in the Palu countryside.

An Alternative Discourse of Nobility? Seyyids versus the Begs

Change creates opportunity, and as the nature of the Palu begs' control over land and agrarian surplus shifted, one may wonder who emerged to benefit. The signatures on tax-farming contracts and the owners of the *çiftlik*s increasingly use the title '*seyyid*'. *Seyyid* refers to those claiming descent from the Prophet Mohammad, and the title is used as an indication of social prestige and status, not to mention tax exemptions. Various historians, particularly from the Arab world, observed that in the eighteenth century claims to this status increased, along with a greater overlap between socio-economic status and these claims.[156]

In the later part of the eighteenth century, people bearing the *seyyid* title became more visible on Palu's economic scene and featured in local power conflicts involving Palu nobility. In some cases, the conflicts stemmed from the begs' demands for tax payments from the *seyyids*, even though their title accorded them exemptions. But conflicts around taxation were the tip of the iceberg. The *seyyids* of Palu were mostly economically active individuals in the process of climbing up local socio-economic hierarchies and they appear in governmental records primarily through their complaints about the begs.

As mentioned, being a *seyyid* afforded tax privileges, one reason many tax-paying subjects sought the title. The title appealed to claimants for social reasons as well: as several historians have pointed out, *seyyid* status amplified the social prestige of notables who already held wealth and power. Hülya Canbakal argues that the title 'turned notability into nobility as legally recognized status', as it accorded rights based on descent through blood.[157] This seems to be the case in Palu, with people bearing the *seyyid* title becoming active players in its economic scene. They acquired tax-farming contracts, leased and sub-leased usufruct rights on land owned primarily by the begs, and engaged in financial dealings with the begs as creditors. Ariel Salzmann observes a similar process in Diyarbekir where the *seyyid*s had the upper hand in buying the rights to tax farms.[158] In Palu, people who accumulated wealth through these types of economic activities could finally crown their wealth with an acquired noble title, granting them the esteem that wealth along could not offer. *Seyyid*s were among the many rivals for Palu's agrarian surplus when the begs' control over land was loosening. In a way, the *seyyid* title marked the members of Palu's *nouveau riche* – new economic rivals competing for the sources of the begs' long-lived economic superiority. For example, a certain Seyyid İbrahim petitioned the Porte complaining about Halil Beg, from whom he had rented the lands of three villages in the Palu countryside. The conflict stemmed from the beg's demand for additional taxes after Seyyid İbrahim paid the land's agrarian dues.[159] Similarly, in 1757, a certain Süleyman from Palu farmed out revenues of several villages to Seyyid Muhyiddin. This brought the latter into conflict with others who had pre-existing claims to the agrarian surplus, and his attempt to collect the dues was prevented by more powerful and influential groups in the area. He went to court to ask Süleyman to return the payment he had made.[160]

In this period, the *seyyid*s were also important as financiers. As they expanded into *vakıf* lands, tax-farming contracts and money-lending, they became increasingly visible creditors and the local begs were their primary clients. Seyyid Osman, for instance, loaned 1,080 guruş to Ömer Beg and Mehmed Beg. When he could not collect his debt, he appealed to the imperial state, which sent an order to the local court for the collection of his debt from the begs.[161] Similarly, Seyyid Mehmed loaned 1,150 guruş to Cemşid, Ahmed and Seyfullah Begs. The first two died before paying, so Seyyid Mehmed sought the state's help to claim all the debt from the remaining borrower, Seyfullah.[162] A certain Seyyid Hacı Hüseyin was in the same situation, as Ismail Beg died without paying back his debt of 3,250 guruş. The former demanded it be taken from the beg's inheritance which now was in his sons' hands, and the case was sent to the local court.[163]

Salzmann interprets the increasing share of the *seyyid*s' tax-farm contracts in Diyarbekir as an indication of the *ulemâ*'s rising economic influence.[164] While this may be true, the adoption of the *seyyid* title was not the exclusive right of the *ulemâ*. People from different backgrounds and socio-economic statuses claimed descent from the Prophet Muhammad, including local prominent families at different times and in different areas, particularly in the Arab provinces of the empire.[165] In Palu, there were cases of *seyyid*s appealing to the state to demand tax exemptions and explicitly stating that they were not holders of any wealth or land. This hints at their attempt to differentiate themselves from *seyyid*s with wealth and land. But there was a growing overlap between the adoption of the *seyyid* title and socio-economic status, a result of Muslim notables' increasing economic power and growing interest in acquiring the title. The wealthy with *seyyid* title also established charitable endowments in the town. Significantly, it was not the begs, but two *seyyid*s, Seyyid el-Hac Mustafa and Seyyid el-Hac Abdurrahman, who founded Ulu Cami, the largest mosque at the time. They also endowed the revenues of five shops to this mosque. The patina of nobility that accompanied the *seyyid* title was useful in challenging the Palu nobility's long-standing social capital. It provided an alternative version of nobility – one deemed equally legitimate by the imperial state. Having secured landed wealth and a noble title, the *seyyid*s lacked one thing: political influence. Later we will see how, in the nineteenth century, the town-based Muslim elites, the majority of whom had the *seyyid* title, became important players in local politics and frequently challenged the begs.

Conclusion

In Ottoman historical writing, there has long been a consensus on the eighteenth century being 'the 'age of the *ayan*' – a period of rising power and authority of the provincial notables.[166] By acquiring offices and contracts from the state, local magnates accumulated wealth and established regional zones of influence in different parts of the empire.[167] The rule of these magnates has been one of the most widely examined aspects of the eighteenth-century history of the Ottoman Empire.[168] By demonstrating the mutually-constitutive relationship between the imperial centre and the provincial notables, recent scholarship on the *ayan* dynasties challenged the meta-narrative of decline and state–society dichotomy in Ottoman historiography.[169]

While presenting a more complex picture of the profile of the provincial elites in different parts of the empire, the revisionist studies still assume a certain degree of uniformity in terms of the elite formation in the eighteenth century throughout the empire (i.e. notwithstanding regional differences, the eighteenth century is taken as a period of rising power and wealth on the part of the provincial notables). Isa Blumi rightfully states that 'as Ottoman history is often constructed along thematic time frames that experientially, temporally, and spatially condense the entire empire, it is assumed that the many different peoples living in, for example, the Western Balkans, experience the same "decline", "crisis", "reforms", and "transformations" as those in Syria, Eastern Anatolia, or Cyprus'.[170]

Blumi's critique is relevant from the perspective of the study of Kurdistan. As shown in the first chapter, the Kurdish nobility was incorporated into the Ottoman realm with de jure hereditary privileges, which makes it a different case from the *ayan* dynasties mentioned above. The analytical and conceptual frameworks derived from this overarching theme of the age of the *ayan* do not suffice to explain the changes that the Kurdish nobility was undergoing in the eighteenth century. The de jure hereditary character of the begs' rule meant that there were no Ottoman military troops and Ottoman administrators present in the nobles' sphere of authority, and the state would not have a claim over the wealth produced in these lands. Contrary to many of the magnates in other parts of the empire, prior to the Tanzimat era, the Palu begs never sought to acquire governmental positions, such as governorships. By the eighteenth century, their wealth and position had long been recognised by the Ottoman state. Thus the Kurdish nobility's experience of the eighteenth-century transformations needs to be considered within the specific context of its incorporation into the Ottoman realm in the sixteenth century, what the hereditary character of their rule entailed, and how it changed as a corollary of the military, fiscal and political exigencies of the time.

Keeping the specificity of the Kurdish nobility in mind, this chapter showed that the Kurdish begs entered the Ottoman authority as an elite group with a primarily military function and served in Ottoman military campaigns. The initial military role the begs performed diminished progressively after the seventeenth century, together with their military prowess. Among other things, this was a result of the new roles and responsibilities that the begs took over with the revitalisation of the mining activities in the Keban and Ergani region. The chapter showed that the presence of these mines affected the Palu begs' position and fortune in numerous ways. The ever-increasing energy needs of the mines rendered the begs' role critical in the provision of charcoal. As the mines gained a special autonomous administrative position, the mine superintendent increasingly emerged as a figure challenging the economic, military and administrative authority of the Palu nobility. Nevertheless, the begs retained their hereditary privileges in the face of the mine superintendents' ongoing challenge.

The Kurdish Nobility in the Ottoman Empire

The eighteenth century was a critical period in the emergence of a modern fiscal regime in the Ottoman Empire. In this period, the life-term tax farm (*malikâne*) system emerged as the key fiscal instrument used by the imperial state to increase the revenues flowing into the central treasury. In essence, life-term tax farms referred to a process of the privatisation of tax collection in various sectors. Salzmann argues that *mâlikanisation* 'provided special political immunities for contractors while associating them in a long-term and formal fashion with the provincial state apparatus'.[171] In this sense, the outcome of this process was far from the absolute devolution of state authority to the provincial actors.

Nonetheless, it is also true that various *ayan* families accumulated wealth and power thanks to the economic opportunities opened to them with the life-term tax farm system. This chapter demonstrated that notwithstanding these drastic changes in the Ottoman fiscal regime and their impact on the provinces, the lands of the Palu nobility remained outside of the larger process of *mâlikanisation* in and around Diyarbekir. The hereditary character of the begs' control over the Palu land, together with the leverage they had due to mine service, shielded the begs from the potential encroachments of the state and the private contractors outside of Palu. However, the eighteenth century *was* a period of drastic change for the begs' economic position in the locality and vis-à-vis the state. The chapter demonstrated economic changes of this period affected the begs in significant ways. Ever-growing indebtedness resulted in the commodification of land. From the 1750s through the 1760s, the begs lost control over parts of Palu land through economic processes which resulted in the emergence of private landholdings – *çiftlik*s – in Palu's countryside. But the begs' de jure hereditary control over land was still in place.

Finally, by examining the Kurdish nobility's changing position vis-à-vis the Ottoman state from the sixteenth through the eighteenth century, this chapter debunked a widely-accepted periodisation in the history of the Kurdish emirates. According to this, Kurdish emirates came under Ottoman rule in the sixteenth century with privileges that gave them autonomy. And then, the narrative shifts to the mid-nineteenth-century Tanzimat era, during which the autonomy of the emirates was terminated by an ever-recalcitrant Ottoman state. This chapter demonstrated that before the changes of the nineteenth century, even though the emirates' official position remained largely unchanged, the relationship between the begs and the Ottoman state was subject to change in line with the military, fiscal and political exigencies of the time. By examining these two processes, the chapter pushed the literature on the Kurdish emirates beyond the nineteenth century and showed that, from the 1720s onwards, the

Noble Privilege on the Ground

Palu begs' position as a landed elite group underwent significant changes. Notwithstanding these economic changes, however, the Palu begs maintained their de jure hereditary control over land. Starting from the 1840s, this would change as a result of the Ottoman state's conscious policy. Indeed, the official position of the Kurdish emirates within the Ottoman political system underwent a drastic transformation during the Tanzimat era – as this book will show in the following chapters.

Notes

1. Mehmet İpşirli, 'Beylerbeyi', in *TDV İslâm Ansiklopedisi* (Istanbul: Türkiye Diyanet Vakfı, 1992), https://islamansiklopedisi.org.tr/beylerbeyi (last accessed 15 February 2020).
2. BOA. IE.TCT 19/2116, 24 Zilkade 1140 [2 July 1728].
3. H. M. Scott and Christopher Storrs, 'The Consolidation of Noble Power in Europe, c. 1600–1800', in *The European Nobilities in the Seventeenth and Eighteenth Centuries, Vol. 1: Western and Southern Europe*, ed. H.M. Scott (New York: Palgrave Macmillan, 2007), 7. As Burke states, this tripartite image was normative rather than purely descriptive. Peter Burke, 'The Language of Orders in Early Modern Europe', in *Social Orders and Social Classes in Europe since 1500: Studies in Social Stratification*, ed. Michael L. Bush (London and New York: Routledge, 2014), 5.
4. Scott and Storrs, 'The Consolidation of Noble Power in Europe, c. 1600–1800', 7.
5. Halil Inalcik, 'Temlîks, Soyurghals, Yurdluk-Ocaklıks, Mâlikâne-Mukâta'a and Awqaf', in *History and Historiography of Post-Mongol Central Asia and the Middle East*, eds Judith Pfeiffer and Sholeh Alysia Quinn (Wiesbaden: Harrassowitz, 2006). Inalcik's discussion of these autonomous enclaves of various types in the Islamic Middle East focused on the type of the exemptions and the nature of the grantees' control over land as inalienable hereditary property. Curiously, he does not mention the service aspect of this arrangement, usually military service required of the person who was granted these immunities.
6. Inalcik, 115–16.
7. John E. Woods, *The Aqquyunlu: Clan, Confederation, Empire*, revised, expanded edn (Salt Lake City: University of Utah Press, 1999), 13.
8. Woods, 12.
9. Woods, 11.
10. Şerefhan, *Şerefname: Kürt Tarihi* (trans. Mehmed Emin Bozarslan) 3. Baskı (Istanbul: Hasat Yayınları, 1990), 208.
11. Hoca Saadettin Efendi, *Tacü't-Tevârih* Volume IV (ed.). İsmet Parmaksızoğlu (Ankara: Kültür Bakanlığı Yayınları, 1992), 250; Ömer Lütfi Barkan, 'Timar', *İslâm Ansiklopedisi* 123–4 (1972): 814–15. In Turkish nationalist historical accounts, one can see a deliberate effort to prove that

the Kurdish begs did not offer much service to Ottomans in their fight against the Safavids. Even these accounts, however, mention Cemşîd Beg as the only beg who participated in the Çaldiran War.
12. Idris-i Bidlisi, *Selim Şah-nâme*, 303–13, 323–7.
13. Idris-i Bidlisi, *Selim Şah-nâme*, 318.
14. Hoca Sadettin Efendi, *Tacü't-Tevarih*, vol. 4. İsmet Parmaksızoğlu (ed.) (Ankara: Kültür Bakanlığı, 1999), 257.
15. The *temlîknâme* I am referring to here is the one given to Cemşid Beg in 1535 by Sultan Suleyman I presented in the previous chapter. In it, Sultan Suleyman refers to his father Selim I's rule as the period during which Kurdistan's begs declared their allegiance to the Ottoman sultan and fought against the Kızılbaş. KFD-Temliknâme (1535).
16. BOA.İ.MVL 237/8388, 1 Şevval 1257 (16 November 1841). 'The copy of the imperial decrees granted to the Palu begs during the reigns of Sultan Suleyman Han, Sultan Murad III and Sultan Ahmed I and under their possession at the present.' The *temlîknâme* granted by Sultan Ahmed I in 1611 is very close to the wording of the original one granted by Sultan Suleyman in 1535, albeit not verbatim. For a comparison, see Mehmet Ali Ünal, 'XVI. Yüzyılda Palu Hükümeti', *Ondokuz Mayıs Üniversitesi Eğitim Fakültesi Dergisi* 7, no. 1 (1992): n. 12, 245.
17. Rhoads Murphey, 'Süleyman's Eastern Policy', in *Süleymân the Second and His Time*, edited by Halil Inalcik and Cemal Kafadar (Istanbul: Isis Press, 1993), 232.
18. Murphey, 232.
19. Rhoads Murphey, *Ottoman Warfare, 1500–1700* (London: Routledge, 2006), 32.
20. For example, the ruler of the Bitlis principality Şerefhan defected to the Persian side, then returned to the Ottomans. See also Feridun M. Emecen, *Osmanli Klasik Çağında Savaş* (İstanbul: Timas Yayinlari, 2010).
21. M. Tayyip Gökbilgin, 'Arz ve Raporlarına Göre Ibrahim Paşa'nin Irakyen Seferindeki İlk Tedbirleri ve Futuhati' 21, no. 83 (1957): 452–3, 466.
22. M. Tayyip Gökbilgin, 'Arz ve Raporlarına Göre İbrahim Paşa'nin Irakeyn Seferindeki İlk Tedbirleri ve Futuhati' 21, no. 83 (1957): 452–3, 466.
23. 3 Numaralı Mühimme Defteri, *966–968/1558–1560* (Ankara: T.C. Başbakanlık Devlet Arşivleri Genel Müdürlüğü, 1993), #770 and # 770-c, 15 Cemâziyelevvel 967 (12 February 1560), 340–1.
24. 3 numaralı mühimme defteri, 966–968/1558–1560, #234, 18 Zilkade 966 (22 August 1559), 110.
25. For the definition of *hil'at*, see Korkut Bugday, *An Introduction to Literary Ottoman* (Routledge, 2014), 102.
26. Şerefhan, *Şerefname: Kürt Tarihi*, 212. The nineteenth-century version of the original *temlîknâme* corroborates this account, listing him as one of the Kurdish begs who visited the sultan in his encampment to declare his allegiance. BOA.İ.MVL 237/8388, 1 Şevval 1257 (16 November 1841).

27. Murphey, *Ottoman Warfare, 1500–1700*, 43.
28. 5 Numarali Mühimme Defteri (Ankara: T. C. Başbakanlık Devlet Arsivleri, 1994), # 1029, 28 Receb 973 [18 February 1566], 389.
29. Şerefhan, *Şerefname: Kürt Tarihi*, 214; Also see Ünal, 'XVI. Yüzyılda Palu Hükümeti', 247–8.
30. Serdar Kar, '63 Numaralı Mühimme Defteri (995–996/1587–1588)' (MA thesis, Marmara University, 2002), 36.
31. 7 Numaralı Mühimme Defteri, *975–976/1567–1569 Tıpkıbasım I, Özet ve Transkripsiyon Ve Indeks Ii–iii–iv* (Ankara: T.C. Başbakanlık Devlet Arşivleri Genel Müdürlüğü, 1999), #2378, 6 Cemâziyelevvel 976 (27 October 1568).
32. Şerefhan, *Şerefname: Kürt Tarihi*, 214.
33. Murphey, *Ottoman Warfare, 1500–1700*, 5.
34. Rhoads Murphey, *Kanun-Name-i Sultani Li'Aziz Efendi: Aziz Efendi's Book of Sultanic Laws and Regulations : An Agenda for Reform by a Seventeenth-Century Ottoman Statesman* (Cambridge, MA: Harvard University Press, 1985), pp.vii–viii.
35. Murphey, 14.
36. Lowry, *The Nature of the Early Ottoman State*; Abou-El-Haj, *Formation of the Modern State*; Cornell H. Fleischer, *Bureaucrat and Intellectual in the Ottoman Empire: The Historian Mustafa Ali (1541–1600)* (Princeton, NJ: Princeton University Press, 2014).
37. Rifa 'at Abou-El-Haj, *Formation of the Modern State: The Ottoman Empire Sixteenth to Eighteenth Centuries*, 2nd edn (Syracuse, NY: Syracuse University Press, 2005), 22.
38. Baki Tezcan interprets this as a transformation from a feudal socio-economic organisation into a monetary one which set in motion the transformation in military recruitment – the change bemoaned by Azîz Efendi and his like. Baki Tezcan, *The Second Ottoman Empire: Political and Social Transformation in the Early Modern World*, Reprint edn (Cambridge: Cambridge University Press, 2012).
39. Murphey, *Kanun-Name-i Sultani Li'Aziz Efendi*, 14–15.
40. Murphey, 14–15.
41. Rezan Ekinci, 'Azîz Efendi'nin Islahatnâmesi Üzerine', *Kürt Tarihi* Sayı 2, Ağustos-Eylül 2012, 17.
42. Murphey, *Kanun-Name-i Sultani Li'Aziz Efendi*, 16.
43. Murphey, 16.
44. Murphey, 17.
45. Scott and Storrs, 'The Consolidation of Noble Power in Europe, c. 1600–1800', 40.
46. Rhoads Murphey, *Ottoman Warfare 1500–1700* (New Brunswick, NJ: Rutgers University Press, 1999), 32.
47. Virginia Aksan, *Ottoman Wars, 1700–1870: An Empire Besieged* (Routledge, 2014), 50.

48. BOA.C.DH 210/10496 Evâsıt-ı Muharrem 1136 (15 October 1723).
49. Aksan, *Ottoman Wars, 1700–1870*, 134.
50. Aksan, 130.
51. Aksan, 130–4.
52. Ersin Kırca, 'Başbakanlık Osmanlı Arşivi 168 Numaralı Mühimme Defteri (S.1–200) (1183–1185/1769–1771)' (MA thesis, Marmara University, 2007), 4. Hüküm no. 2, Evâhir-i Rebîülâhir 1183 [August 1769] This study is a transliteration of the parts of an *ordu mühimme defteri* recording Ottoman official correspondence during the 1768–74 Russo-Ottoman War.
53. Kırca 32–3. Hüküm # 51, Evâ'il-i Cemâziyelevvel 1183 [September 1769].
54. Kırca, 263, Hüküm # 401, Evâsıt-ı Şevval 1183 [December 1769].
55. Kırca, 297, Hüküm # 467, Evâhir-i Ramazan 1183 [January 1770].
56. Kırca, 297, Hüküm # 467, Evâsıt-ı Şevval 1183 [February 1770].
57. BOA.IE.DH 14/1262 10 Rebîülâhir 1107 [19 October 1695].
58. Fahrettin Tızlak, 'Keban-Ergani Yöresinde Madencilik (1775–1850)' (Ph.D. dissertation, Fırat University, 1991), 4–5.
59. Tızlak, 5.
60. İbrahim Yılmazçelik, 'Osmanlı Hakimiyeti Süresince Diyarbakır Eyaleti Valileri (1516–1838)' 10, no. 1 (2000): 239.
61. Yunus Eren, '34 Numaralı ve H.986/1578 Tarihli Mühimme Defteri' (MA thesis, Istanbul, Marmara University, 2011), 25. Hüküm # 42, 14 Muharrem 986 [23 March 1578].
62. Yılmazçelik, 'Osmanlı Hakimiyeti Süresince Diyarbakır Eyaleti Valileri (1516–1838)', 241.
63. Ömerül Faruk Bölükbaşı, 'XVIII. Yüzyılın İkinci Yarısında Darbhâne-i Âmire' (Ph.D. dissertation Istanbul, 2010), 54–5.
64. Ömerül Faruk Bölükbaşı, 'Osmanlı Taşra Darphaneleri (1697–1758)', *Türk Kültürü İncelemeleri Dergisi* 29 (2013): 29–31.
65. Fahrettin Tızlak, 'XVIII. Yüzyıl Sonu İşe XIX. Yüzyılın İlk Yarısında Harput Çevresinde Madencilik Faaliyetleri' in *Geçmişten Geleceğe Harput Sempozyumu* (Elazığ: Fırat Üniversitesi Harput Uygulama ve Araştırma Merkezi, 2013), 352.
66. Bölükbaşı, 'XVIII. Yüzyılın İkinci Yarısında Darbhâne-i Âmire', 10–11.
67. Ömerül Faruk Bölükbaşı, '1788–1825 (Hicrî 1203–1240) Dönemine Ait Bir İcmâl Defterine Göre Darphanenin Maden Temin ve Sikke Darp Faaliyeti', *VAKANÜVİS- Uluslararası Tarih Araştırmaları Dergisi* 1, no. 1 (March 2016): 98.
68. Gábor Ágoston, *Guns for the Sultan: Military Power and the Weapons Industry in the Ottoman Empire* (New York: Cambridge University Press, 2008), 172.
69. Ágoston, 171.
70. Tızlak, 'Keban-Ergani Yöresinde Madencilik (1775–1850)', 97.
71. Tızlak, 22.
72. Tızlak, 21–4.

73. Tızlak, 62–4.
74. Gülay Kahveci, '29 Numaralı Mühimme Defteri' (MA thesis, Istanbul, Istanbul University, 1998), 173–4.
75. BOA.C.DRB 55/2743 7 Safer 1148 (29 June 1735).
76. BOA.IE.TCT 19/2116 23 Zilkade 1140 (2 July 1728).
77. On the details of the mine work and for more information on the '*baltacıs*' see Tızlak, '*Keban-Ergani Yöresinde Madencilik* (1775–1850)' (Ph.D. dissertation, Fırat University), 191–3.
78. Tızlak, 192.
79. 1 *yük* equalled 162.144 kilograms in Diyarbekir. Ünal Taşkın, 'Osmanlı Devletinde Kullanılan Ölçü ve Tartı Birimleri' (MA Thesis, Fırat University, 2005), 121.
80. BOA.C.DRB 4/179, 14 Ramazan 1175 [29 March1763]; BOA.C.DRB 48/2395, Belge #3 5 Zilhicce 1194 [2 December 1780]; BOA. C.DRB 29/1416, 6 Cemâziyelevvel 1201 [24 February 1787]; BOA.C.DRB 32/1597, 23 Rebîülâhir 1202 [6 February 1788]; BOA.C.DRB 19/906 10 Rebîülâhir 1212 [2 October 1797].
81. BOA.C.DRB 19/906 10 Rebîülâhir 1212 [2 October 1797].
82. Tızlak, 'Keban-Ergani Yöresinde Madencilik (1775–1850)', 198.
83. BOA.C.DRB 13/646 22 Rebîülevvel 1211 [25 September 1796].
84. BOA. C.DRB 4/179, 14 Ramazan 1175 [29 March 1763].
85. BOA.C.DRB 19/906 10 Rebîülâhir 1212 [2 October 1797].
86. BOA.C.DRB 59/2912 17 Şevval 1180 [18 March 1767].
87. BOA.C.DH 62/3088 Evail-i Zilkade 1167 [August 1754].
88. BOA.C.DRB 55/2743 7 Safer 1148 [29 June 1735].
89. BOA.C.DRB 36/1767 6 Rebîülâhir 1200 [7 January 1786]; C.DRB 62/3075 1 Muharrem 1185 [1 May 1771].
90. BOA. IE.TCT 19/2116, 24 Zilkade 1140 [2 July 1728].
91. Ariel Salzmann, *Tocqueville in the Ottoman Empire: Rival Paths to the Modern State* (Boston: Brill, 2003), 138.
92. BOA.C.DRB 36/1767 6 Rebîülâhir 1200 [7 January 1786].
93. Fahrettin Tızlak, *Osmanlı döneminde Keban-Ergani yöresinde madencilik, 1775–1850* (Ankara: Türk Tarih Kurumu Basımevi, 1997), 58.
94. BOA.C.DRB 32/1597 Document # 2 28 Rebîülâhir 1202 [6 February 1768]; Bölükbaşı, 'XVIII. Yüzyılın İkinci Yarısında Darbhâne-i Âmire', 24–5.
95. BOA.C.DRB 3/124 10 Şevval 1182 [17 February 1769]; C.ML 25/1174 2 Zilhicce 1181 [20 April 1768].
96. BOA.C.DRB 10/474 26 Cemâziyelâhir 1208 [29 January 1794]. Yılmazçelik, 'Osmanlı Hakimiyeti Süresince Diyarbakır Eyaleti Valileri (1516–1838)', 250.
97. Mehmet İlkin Erkutun, 'Darendeli İzzet Hasan: Ziyânâme (Sadrazam Yusuf Ziya Paşa ve Fransızların İşgali Üzerine Yapılan Osmanlı Devleti'nin Mısır Seferi 1798–1802)' (Ph.D. dissertation, Istanbul University, 2004), 108–21.
98. Erkutun, 120.

99. Aksan, *Ottoman Wars, 1700–1870*, 238; Juan Cole, *Napoleon's Egypt: Invading the Middle East*, 1st edn (New York (NY: St Martin's Griffin, 2008), 255–6. For a detailed account of Yusuf Ziya Pasha's campaign in Egypt, see Erkutun, 'Darendeli İzzet Hasan: Ziyânâme (Sadrazam Yusuf Ziya Paşa ve Fransızların İşgali Üzerine Yapılan Osmanlı Devleti'nin Mısır Seferi 1798–1802)'.
100. For the *malikâne* system in Diyarbekir, see Salzmann, *Tocqueville in the Ottoman Empire*.
101. BOA.C.İKT 26/1296 n.d.
102. BOA.C.İKT 26/1296 17 Zilhicce 1207 [26 July 1793].
103. BOA.C.DRB 22/1056 5 Rebîülevvel 1166 [10 January 1753]. The date on which the appointment was approved by the imperial centre is 3 Muharrem 1167 [31 October 1753].
104. C.DRB 22/1080, 29 Zilhicce 1255 (26 February 1840).
105. BOA.C.DRB 55/2748 Date 29 Zilkade 1194 [26 November 1780].
106. Muzaffer Doğan, 'Osmanlı İmparatorluğu'nda Makam Vergisi: Câize', *Türk Kültürü İncelemeleri Dergisi* 7 (2002): 58–9.
107. BOA.C.DRB 32/1596 28 Rebîülâhir 1202 [6 February 1788].
108. A Kurdish war-knife (Redhouse dictionary).
109. BOA.C.AS 999/43682 19 Rebîülâhir 1788 [28 January 1788].
110. BOA.HAT 1511/1 20 Cemâziyelâhir 1225 [23 July 1810].
111. Murphey, *Kanun-Name-i Sultani Li'Aziz Efendi*, 14–15.
112. KFD-Temliknâme (1535). 'cümle kal'aların ve şehirlerin ve mezra'ların ile kaffe-i mahsulat-ı âbidesi ile kendüye oğul oğlu neslen ba'de neslin temlîk ve ihsân eyleyüp …'.
113. İnalcık, 'Temlîks, Soyurghals, Yurdluk-Ocaklıks, Mâlikâne-Mukâta'a and Awqaf', 128.
114. See Inalcik, 'Temlîks, Soyurghals, Yurdluk-Ocaklıks, Mâlikâne-Mukâta'a and Awqaf'.
115. İnalcık, 128.
116. As late as 1844, Palu was mentioned as *hükümet* in governmental accounts. See, for example, BOA.A.MKT 16/82, 8 Ramazan 1260 [21 September 1844].
117. Ünal, 'XVI. Yüzyılda Palu Hükümeti', 254.
118. Kumiko Saíto, '16. ve 17. Yüzyıllar Doğu ve Güneydoğu Anadolusu'nda Timarların Çeşitli Biçimleri: Farklı Uygulamalara Tek İsim Koymak', *Osmanlı Araştırmaları* 51, no. 51 (20 April 2018): 70.
119. See, for example, Diyarbekir Ahkâm Defterleri, 1 Numaralı Defter, Hüküm #584, Evâsıt-ı Muharrem 1161 [c. 16 January 1748].
120. Diyarbekir Ahkâm Defterleri, 1 Numaralı Defter Hüküm# 730, 422. Evâil-i Ramazan 1162 [19 August 1749].
121. Salzmann, 'An Ancien Régime Revisited', 395.
122. Özlem Başarır, 'XVIII. Yüzyılda Diyarbekir Voyvodalığı'nın Mekânsal Örgütlenmesi', *The Journal of International Social Research* 4, no. 18 (2009): 196–229.

123. Özlem Başarır, 'Diyarbekir Voyvodalığı Aklâmı Malikânecileri Örneğinde XIII. Yüzyılda Yatırımcıların Kimlikleri Üzerine Bir Değerlendirme', *Hacettepe Üniversitesi Türkiyat Araştırmaları Dergisi* 15 (2011.): 39–61. Ariel Salzmann, 'Measures of Empire: Tax Farmers and the Ottoman Ancien Regime, 1695–1807' (Ph.D. dissertation, New York University, 1996), 287–9.
124. Fahameddin Başar, *Osmanlı Eyalet Tevcihatı (1717–1730)* (Ankara: TTK Yayınları, 1997); Orhan Kılıç, *18. yüzyılın ilk yarısında Osmanlı Devleti'nin idari taksimatı. Eyalet ve sancak tevcihatı* (Elazığ: Şark Pazarlama, 1997).
125. The literature on the rise of the provincial notables in the eighteenth century is extensive. For a classical work, see Yücel Özkaya, *Osmanlı İmparatorluğu'nda Ayanlık* (Ankara Üniversitesi Basimevi, 1977). For a general overview, see Bruce McGowan, 'The Age of the Ayans, 1699–1812', in *An Economic and Social History of the Ottoman Empire*, vol. 2 (Cambridge: Cambridge University Press, 1994), 1600–1914. For a comparative work, see Anastasopoulos ed., *Provincial Elites in the Ottoman Empire: Halcyon Days in Crete V: A Symposium Held in Rethymnon 10–12 January 2003*. For a more recent study on the *ayan* dynasties that complicates the classical decentralisation perspective, see Yaycioglu, *Partners of the Empire*.
126. Salzmann, 'Measures of Empire', 251.
127. Diyarbekir Ahkâm Defterleri, 3 Numaralı Defter, Hüküm #522, 331, Evâil-i Ramazan 1180 [c. 1 February 1767].
128. The privatisation of the provincial revenue sources through the life-term tax farms was not totally unforeseen in the areas ruled by the Kurdish Begs. In 1796, Çarsancak, Palu, Harput, Çemişgezek, Arapgir and Eğin districts were contracted to two court-based individuals, El-Hâc Ibrahim Reşid, the Chief Treasurer (*Defterdâr-ı Şıkk-ı Evvel*) and Ahmed Aziz, Overseer of the Imperial Kitchen (*Matbah-ı Âmire Emini*) as life-term tax farms (*malikane*). The two then subcontracted the tax farms of stamp tax (*damga*) on clothes such as *alaca* and *kirpa*s of the said districts to Yusuf Ziya Pasha. These cases, however, did remain as exceptions. C.İKT 9/432 13 Safer 1212 [7 August 1797].
129. The decree sent by the centre mentions not only Mehmed's position as *hâkim*, but also the status of his lands as *yurtluk-ocaklık*, attesting to the ongoing relevance of the hereditary position of the Palu nobility in the imperial state's eyes. While their administrative roles continued, however, the begs' fiscal roles vis-à-vis the imperial state and within the locality were changing with the growing prevalence of the farming out of the agrarian dues on land. Diyarbekir Ahkâm Defterleri, 1 Numaralı Defter, Hüküm #169, p. 89, Evâhir-ı Cemâziyelâhir 1156 [c. 11 August 1745].
130. Diyarbekir Ahkâm Defterleri, 3 Numaralı Defter, Hüküm #591, 368 Evâil-ı Safer 1181 [c. 29 June 1767].
131. See, for example, Diyarbekir Ahkâm Defterleri, 2 Numaralı Defter, Hüküm # 14, p.13, Evâil-i Safer 1168 [c. 17 November 1754].

132. Diyarbekir Ahkâm Defterleri, 2 Numaralı Defter, Hüküm # 14, p. 13, Evâil-i Safer 1168 [c. 17 November 1754].
133. Diyarbekir Ahkâm Defterleri, 2 Numaralı Defter, Hüküm # 14, p. 13 Evâil-i Safer 1168 [c. 17 November 1754].
134. Diyarbekir Ahkâm Defterleri, 3 Numaralı Defter, Hüküm # 593, p. 369 Evâil-i Safer 1181 [c. 29 June 1767].
135. Diyarbekir Ahkâm Defterleri, 2 Numaralı Defter, Hüküm # 534, p. 333, Evâsıt-ı Muharrem 1170 [c. 18 September 1758].
136. Diyarbekir Ahkâm Defterleri, 1 Numaralı Defter, Hüküm # 175, 92, Evâhir-i Cemâziyelevvel 1156 [c. 13 July 1743]; also Diyarbekir Ahkâm Defterleri, 1 Numaralı Defter, Hüküm # 173, p. 91, Evâsıt- ı Cemâziyelevvel 1156 [c. 2 July 1743].
137. In a similar case, a certain Emin had been tilling lands from Sivan and Arzumak villages and paying the tithe to the landowner. He also complained about interventions from others despite having a *temessük*. Diyarbekir Ahkâm Defterleri, 2 Numaralı Defter, Hüküm # 392, p. 244, Evâil-i Zilkade 1170 [c. 18 July 1757]. In another case, Yusuf from Palu got the usufruct rights of the Kârur village with a title-deed from the landowner and paid the tithe to him in return. He complained about Osman from the same village, who did not let him use the land. Diyarbekir Ahkâm Defterleri, 2 Numaralı Defter, Hüküm # 328, Evâil-i Receb 1170 [c. 22 March 1757].
138. Diyarbekir Ahkâm Defterleri, 2 Numaralı Defter, Hüküm # 944, p. 13, Evâsıt- ı Zilkade 1175 [c. 7 June 1762].
139. Diyarbekir Ahkâm Defterleri, 3 Numaralı Defter, Hüküm # 1006, p. 645, Evâil-i Cemâziyelevvel 1176 [c. 18 November 1762].
140. While not being a common occurrence, it was not impossible for women to acquire the usufruct right to land, which brought them into conflict with the begs. Emetullah Hanım, the daughter of a Sheikh Mehmed, was tilling the land she inherited within the Isabeg village and held with a title deed. She went to court complaining about Ismail Beg (from the Palu begs), who, she said, had confiscated the harvest unlawfully. Diyarbekir Ahkâm Defterleri, 3 Numaralı Defter, Hüküm # 527, p. 333, Evâhir-i Ramazan 1180 [c. 19 February 1767]; Diyarbekir Ahkâm Defterleri, 3 Numaralı Defter, Hüküm # 572, p. 358, Evâsıt-ı Muharrem 1180 [c. 18 June 1766].
141. Diyarbekir Ahkâm Defterleri, 2 Numaralı Defter, Hüküm # 406, 252, Evâil-i Zilhicce 1170 [c. 17 August 1757].
142. Bedirhan Laçin, 'New Inclinations towards Land Usufruct in the 18th Century Anatolia' (MA thesis, Ankara, Bilkent University, 2017), 39.
143. Becker, *Nobility and Privilege in Late Imperial Russia*, 32–3.
144. Becker, 172.
145. Çağlar Keyder and Faruk Tabak eds, *Landholding and Commercial Agriculture in the Middle East* (Albany, NY: State University of New York Press, 1991), 1.

146. Keyder and Tabak, 1.
147. Salzmann, 'An Ancien Régime Revisited', 143.
148. Diyarbekir Ahkâm Defterleri, 2 Numaralı Defter, Hüküm # 406, p. 252, Evâil-i Zilhicce 1170 [c. 17 August 1757].
149. Diyarbekir Ahkâm Defterleri, 3 Numaralı Defter, Hüküm # 591 p. 371, Evâsıt-ı Safer 1181 [c. 8 July 1767].
150. Diyarbekir Ahkâm Defterleri, 3 Numaralı Defter, Hüküm # 620 p. 385, Evâil-i Rebîülâhir 1181 [c. 27 August 1767].
151. Diyarbekir Ahkâm Defterleri, 3 Numaralı Defter, Hüküm # 601, p. 373, Evâsıt-ı Safer 1181 [c. 8 July 1767].
152. See, among others, Diyarbekir Ahkâm Defterleri, 3 Numaralı Defter, Hüküm # 609 p. 379, Evâhir-i Rebîülevvel 1181 [c. 28 July 1767].
153. Dina Rizk Khoury, 'The Introduction of Commercial Agriculture in the Province of Mosul and Its Effects on the Peasantry, 1750–1850', in *Landholding and Commercial Agriculture in the Middle East: Globalization, Revolution, and Popular Culture*, eds Çağlar Keyder and Faruk Tabak (Albany, NY: State University of New York Press, 1991), 157.
154. Ahmet Zeki İzgöer, *Diyarbekir Şer'iyye Sicilleri: Âmid Mahkemesi. Cilt 3 3754 Numaralı Sicil (H.1151–1154/1738–1741)* (Diyarbakır: Dicle Üniversitesi İlahiyat Fakültesi Yayınları, 2014), 148.
155. Ahmet Zeki İzgöer, *Diyarbekir Şer'iyye Sicilleri: Âmid Mahkemesi. Cilt 3 3754 Numaralı Sicil (H.1151–1154/1738–1741)* (Diyarbakır: Dicle Üniversitesi İlahiyat Fakültesi Yayınları, 2014), 151 and 266. Kile (keyle/ keyl) was a unit used to measure grain. Its actual value changed regionally. One kile was around 368 *okka* in Palu. Taşkın, 'Osmanlı Devletinde Kullanılan Ölçü ve Tartı Birimleri', 66–7. The standard Ottoman *okka* was approximately 1.28 kilograms. Halil Inalcik, 'Weights and Measures', in *An Economic and Social History of the Ottoman Empire 1300–1914* (Cambridge: Cambridge University Press, 1994), 990.
156. Hülya Canbakal, 'On the Nobility of Urban Notables', in *Provincial Elites in the Ottoman Empire: Halcyon Days in Crete V: A Symposium Held in Rethymnon 10–12 January 2003*, 39–40.
157. Canbakal, 49. For more on the fictive claims of Muhammadan nobility, Hülya Canbakal, 'The Ottoman State and Descendants of the Prophet in Anatolia and the Balkans (c. 1500–1700)', *Journal of the Economic and Social History of the Orient* 52, no. 3 (2009): 542–78.
158. Salzmann, *Tocqueville in the Ottoman Empire*, 124.
159. Diyarbekir Ahkâm Defterleri, 3 Numaralı Defter, Hüküm # 593, 369, Evâil-i Safer 1181 [c. 3 July 1767].
160. Diyarbekir Ahkâm Defterleri, 2 Numaralı Defter, Hüküm # 801, 502, Evâsıt-ı Şevval 1174 [c. 22 May 1761].
161. Diyarbekir Ahkâm Defterleri, 2 Numaralı Defter, Hüküm # 58, 42, Evâil-i Şevval 1168 [c. 15 July 1755].
162. Diyarbekir Ahkâm Defterleri, 2 Numaralı Defter, Hüküm # 343, 214.

163. Diyarbekir Ahkâm Defterleri, 2 Numaralı Defter, Hüküm # 387, 241, Evâil-i Zilkade 1170 [c. 21 August 1757].
164. Salzmann, *Tocqueville in the Ottoman Empire*, 149. In the Ottoman Empire, *ulemâ* refers to the 'those who were trained in the Islamic religious sciences (such as the Quran, the traditions of the Prophet Muhammad and Islamic jurisprudence), and were members of the Ottoman religious establishment'. Gabor Agoston, 'Ulema', in *Encyclopedia of the Ottoman Empire* (Infobase Publishing, 21 May 2010), 577.
165. Canbakal, 'On the Nobility of Urban Notables', 40.
166. Bruce McGowan, 'The Age of the Ayans, 1699–1812', in *An Economic and Social History of the Ottoman Empire, 1300–1914* (Cambridge: Cambridge University Press, 1994), 637–742. See also Bruce Masters, *The Arabs of the Ottoman Empire, 1516–1918: A Social and Cultural History* (Cambridge: Cambridge University Press, 2013), 83–8.
167. Yaycioglu, *Partners of the Empire*, 67.
168. For classical works on the subject, see Yücel Özkaya, *Osmanlı İmparatorluğu'nda Ayanlık* (Ankara Üniversitesi Basimevi, 1977); Yücel Özkaya, 'Anadolu'daki Büyük Hanedanlıklar', *Belleten* 56, no. 217 (1992): 809–46; Yuzo Nagata, *Tarihte Âyânlar. Karaosmanoğulları Üzerinde Bir İnceleme* (Ankara: Türk Tarih Kurumu Yayınları, 1997).
169. Examples include Salzmann, *Tocqueville in the Ottoman Empire*; Dina Rizk Khoury, *State and Provincial Society in the Ottoman Empire: Mosul, 1540–1834* (Cambridge: Cambridge University Press, 2002); Yaycioglu, *Partners of the Empire*.
170. Isa Blumi, *Foundations of Modernity: Human Agency and the Imperial State* (London: Routledge, 2017), 16.
171. Salzmann, 'An Ancien Régime Revisited', 405.

PART II
A QUASI-RIFT

Chapter 3

The Kurdish Nobility and the Making of Modern State Power in Kurdistan

Around the year 1838, one year before the promulgation of the Tanzimat (Re-organisation) Decree, and seven years before the provinces of Diyarbekir, Van and Maden-i Hümayûn were brought under the Tanzimat programme, the Finance Ministry produced a register showing the recent revenue accounts of different provinces. Along with presenting data about the values of tax farms, and *timar* revenues, the register offered a brief report about the general situation in Diyarbekir province in terms of the prevalent land-holding and taxation systems:

> The vacant tax resources in Diyarbekir province [such as] those fiefs (*timars*) and tax units (*mukataa*s) that remained [vacant] after the Zirkî begs'[1] [exile] along with the fiefs granted to the male slaves (*gılman*) of the Amid fortress, have been seized by the Mansure treasury and converted to tax-farms. However, the Diyarbekir province has long been under the control of the Kurds (*ekrad*). As a result, it has not been possible to accurately determine what regulations are needed, and [what] the various vacant [holdings] are ... Should one wish to seize and tithe each of these tax-farms, since the inhabitants of this area are like animals (*hayvana benzer adamlar*) unaccustomed to being governed, they would not take easily such an arrangement. For instance, if there are a few tax units in a district, and if each unit is granted to a tax farmer, he would set out to tithe [the inhabitants] separately and their [demand for] food and fodder would be a burden on the poor [commoners]. Thus, these ungovernable people would not be able to tolerate too many officers. [In this way], [even if] part of the province is brought under control, another part will be in disorder, and there will not be a time without disorderliness.[2]

The report reveals an Ottoman official's unadulterated frustration with the diversity of landholding and tax-collection arrangements in Kurdistan. To the contemporary eye, too, this description seems befuddling, given that none of the land/tax-collection arrangements mentioned – *iltizam*, *malikâne* or *timar* – survives today. Lacking any information about this official's background and position, we can be sure of one thing: his report was very much in line with the Ottoman administrators' overarching agenda at that moment in the imperial capital.

In 1839, the Ottoman state embarked upon a massive re-organisation in its fiscal and military institutions under the scope of the Tanzimat (Re-organisation). Protecting the 'life, honor, and property' of all Ottoman subjects was the first of the three fundamental goals of the Gülhane Decree, the document that announced the beginning of this reform process. The other goals addressed two other pressing issues: the establishment of regular tax collection and a conscription system. Regular tax collection was to address what reformers called 'the harmful practice of tax-farming' and conscription was intended to redefine military service as 'the inescapable duty of all the people to provide soldiers for the defense of the fatherland [vatan]'.[3] The decree was in line with the Ottoman imperial administration's goal of consolidating its authority in the realms deemed vital to surviving in an age of European encroachment, continuing wars with Russia and Iran, a rising tide of nationalisms in the Balkans, and the increased power of the provincial notables throughout the empire.[4]

This was the context in which the state began to see the diversity of fiscal instruments in the periphery of the empire as a problem. The effort to bring legibility to its conduct in the provincial periphery was a major goal of the Ottoman central administration during the early Tanzimat era from the 1830s through the 1850s.[5] The Ottoman state already had a strong tradition of surveying its population and their incomes for tax and record keeping purposes. Now it wanted to extend that to the provincial periphery (including but not limited to Kurdistan), and censuses, conscription, local councils and new taxation methods were its tools.[6]

What bothered the Ottoman official who penned the above report, however, was not just the lack of uniformity in landholding and revenue extraction methods. His concern about the *ekrad*'s long-lived control over the revenue sources echoes the sentiment of the central administration in this period. In the context of modern state-making, exemptions and prerogatives that the Kurdish nobility had enjoyed since the sixteenth century were increasingly seen as obsolete.

The Kurdish nobility's hereditary privileges were problematic from an economic/fiscal standpoint. Not only did the nobles control the land and its revenues, but they also received tax exemptions. More broadly, their political and administrative authority, the opposite of a modern, centralised bureaucracy, was a concern. But along with these material considerations came an even more fundamental question: legitimacy. How could an imperial dynasty annul the contracts, institutions and relations built by previous sultans without endangering its own legitimacy? To complicate matters more, Kurdistan's geo-strategic position on the Iranian border compromised the Ottoman centre's leverage vis-à-vis the local power holders at the time of a renewed Ottoman–Iranian war between 1820 and 1823.[7] In the two decades between the 1830s and the 1850s, the Kurdish hereditary nobility's presence in this critical zone shaped Ottoman administrative strategies and its ability to assert *stateness* in this region. This chapter focuses on this transformative moment in the Sublime Porte's approach to the Kurdish nobility and analyses the making of the governmental rationalities pertaining to the abolition of the hereditary privileges of the Kurdish begs. This analysis demonstrates that Palu's geo-strategic position away from the Ottoman–Iranian borderlands brought it onto the Ottoman state's radar as a place where it could abolish hereditary nobility without having to compromise the security of the critical border with Iran.

Modern State Formation as a Global Phenomenon

'From the vantage point of post-World War I Europe, the nineteenth century must have appeared as the veritable *golden age of the state*', writes Jürgen Osterhammel in his *magnum opus*.[8] In Osterhammel's account, the modern state entails a set of institutional, administrative and ideological changes that together created a novel political form. Military restructuring, a 'modern' bureaucracy, taxation by the central state, constitutional rule of law and a new idea of citizenship are the major tenets of this new political organisation.[9] While acknowledging these institutional components of the modern state as differentiating it as a new political entity, scholars in different disciplines sought for a key moment that paved the way for its making. Be it the emergence of a modern bureaucracy *à la* Weber, the monopoly of violence *à la* Tilly, or its appearance as the repressive arm of the bourgeoisie from conventional Marxian perspectives, scholars sought for ways to explain the state's origins, character and function.[10] However, recent historical-anthropological theories of the state take issue with the bellicist, economic reductionist and functionalist theories that treat 'the state' as an a priori empirical object.[11] They suggest *state formation* as an alternative framework to the characterisation of the state as a reified, 'distinct, fixed, and unitary entity'.[12] This approach also avoids the teleological underpinnings of older approaches' references to institutional, economic and cultural practices through which 'the state' 'comes to assume' its position as the highest authority in modern societies.[13]

Rather than manifesting at a 'mythical moment' of the monopolisation of violence, or of the emergent capitalist economy, state formation refers to an open-ended *process* of institutional, legal and cultural transformation. Unlike the study of its frequently ahistorical predecessor, the study of state formation is essentially historical.[14]

And unlike classical state theories that were unabashedly Euro-centric, state formation perspectives create space for non-European contexts. Questioning the 'the bifurcation of world history into two irreconcilable trajectories, European and non-European', and challenging 'ideal-type' perspectives derived from Orientalist and modernisation approaches, revisionist works suggest looking at modern state formation as a global phenomenon with local interpretations rather than a derivative process outside of Europe.[15] The primarily land-based, old empires of Eurasia experienced their own journey into modern statehood. Significant transformations took place in the political formations, ruling ideologies and administrative practices of China, Russia and the Ottoman Empire in the long nineteenth century.

In the Ottoman Empire, the Tanzimat era was such a transformative period for modern state making, offering a jump-start for key state markers including the monopolisation of violence, a modern bureaucracy, a centralised tax system and the standardisation of administrative practices throughout the imperial geography.[16] As such, it is one of the most extensively studied periods in Ottoman historiography. Recently, conventional accounts that saw the Tanzimat period from a top-down, success–failure standpoint have been challenged by societal perspectives that complicate this zero-sum-game approach by showing co-optation, alliances, and interdependencies between the state and social actors.[17] In these revisionist works, the study of the Tanzimat policies in the provinces takes up significant space.[18]

State formation as a global phenomenon with local trajectories is a useful perspective for exploring the Ottoman experience of modern statehood in Kurdistan, particularly in areas where the Kurdish nobility had long been influential. However, there is no equivalent of revisionist provincial histories of Ottoman state making for Ottoman Kurdistan in the Tanzimat era. The dominant accounts of Kurdistan in the long nineteenth century are based on the Ottoman state's massive military campaigns from the 1830s onward. Yet the narrative of military operations opening the way for centralisation and a linear increase in the Ottoman state's power overlooks the intricacies of politics that involved a diverse array of local and imperial actors and the gamut of strategies and discourses they deployed. The result has been that the relationship between the Kurdish elites and the Ottoman state has been portrayed mostly through the lens of military confrontation, with politics reduced to violent encounters and local actors stripped of their agency.[19] Such a perspective not only blurs the dynamics of politics in Kurdistan, but takes a simplistic approach to state power, reducing its complexity to the use of force to impose its will. Certainly, the powerful leaders of the Kurdish emirates, particularly Bedirkhan Beg of Cîzre, were the target of these military campaigns and of Ottoman state tactics of exile and resettlement of the emîrs/mîrs and their families, but they were more than that. There is a much more complex version of Kurdistan on the eve of Tanzimat that reveals a shifting interplay of local, regional and imperial actors and political strategies as integral constituents of Ottoman state formation.

Kurdistan on the Eve of the Tanzimat

In his excellent analysis of the making of the Iranian–Ottoman boundary in the nineteenth century, Sabri Ateş argues that processes of centralisation/state-making and the drawing of the boundary went hand in hand in Kurdistan. The demarcating of the border between the two empires reflected an expression of territoriality. This process of territorialisation reflected the state's efforts to assume power through its consolidation of infrastructural capacity in a specific geographical area. It ran parallel to the state's attempt to increase its grip over the populations inhabiting the borderlands and to bring the autonomous rulers of the area under its control. For the imperial state, Ateş argues, 'the elimination of the lords of the marches, who hitherto held power at the borderland, facilitated the making of the boundary even as the making of the boundary facilitated their elimination'.[20] The Ottoman state's effort to consolidate its sway over the Kurdish emirates in this manner signified a transformation of its position vis-à-vis the Kurdish begs from a suzerain that maintained its legitimacy through the granting of privileges to a sovereign that sought to subdue potential threats to its authority over a territory.[21]

From the Ottoman side, Erzurum and Van provinces were strategically located on the borderland, aptly described as *serhad* – frontier cities – in the Ottoman bureaucratic parlance.[22] Meanwhile, the Iranian side of the borderland had also long been under the rule of the Kurdish emirates: the Baban emirate centred on Suleimania and the Soran emirate in Rawanduz were both on the border. In these frontier provinces, the Ottoman state mainly engaged with tribal chiefs and the mîrs of the emirates, with areas in the south and south-east of Lake Van, mainly Müküs, Hoşap and Hakkâri, all under the control of Kurdish mîrs. Politics in this frontier zone required the ability to manoeuvre between two powerful empires, and survival usually involved playing them off against each other.[23] The begs' loyalties to the two empires fluctuated. Around 1825, Iran invaded Hakkâri and Hoşap areas and forced the begs to submit to its authority. Using a military force that consisted mainly of Kurdish tribesmen, the Ottoman forces re-took the area. Beyond their critical location on the Iranian border, these areas also contained important resources. For example, Nurullah Beg of Hakkâri was in control of the valuable *zırnık* (arsenic sulphide) mines, a fact that the Ottoman administrators saw as requiring military intervention to conquer the space.[24]

Along with begs/mîrs, the other key actors in the area were tribes. Powerful Kurdish tribes such as the Hayderan, Şıkak and Ertoşi lived on both sides of the border and moved in large numbers back and forth, which both the Ottoman and Qajar administrations perceived as a threat. Kurdish tribes were also critical as a military force in the conflicts between Iran and the Ottomans, as both sides used the tribesmen as cavalrymen against the other.[25] From the Ottoman point of view, the 'subjecthood' of the frontier-based tribes was 'debatable'.[26] Both empires gave concessions to the tribal chiefs to keep their loyalty, and at times went further, attempting to prove their 'Ottoman' or 'Iranian' identity by finding relevant written records in their archives or even interviewing elderly tribe members for evidence about their identities.[27] The begs' and tribes' fluid loyalties, the tribes' physical mobility and the accommodationist policy of the Ottoman imperial state towards the borderland populations characterised Ottoman–Kurdish relations through the first three decades of the nineteenth century.

With the Treaty of Erzurum in 1823, active military conflict with Iran ceased and Ottoman–Iranian relations entered an era of diplomacy and negotiations over fixing the border. The increasing threat from Russia was one important factor behind this improved relationship.[28] By the 1820s, Russia had made inroads into the eastern part of the Ottoman Empire, and during the Russo-Ottoman War of 1828, frontier cities of Erzurum, Bayezid and Kars were under Russian occupation for over a year before the 1829 Edirne Treaty brought them back to the Ottomans.

From the 1830s on, the Ottoman administration turned its attention to the Kurdish rulers of the frontier areas. Given the threat to their eastern frontiers, the Ottomans could not adopt an antagonistic approach to the Kurdish tribes and emirates as a blanket policy. But whenever a Kurdish ruler's power increased to a level that could disturb the delicate balance of power, the Ottoman state policy got stricter. A case in point was the ruler of the Soran emirate, Mîr Muhammad. His power and authority had initially been recognised by the Ottoman state and he was honoured with a ceremonial robe (*hilat*). Later in the 1830s, when he started to expand his sphere of authority, the Ottoman governor of Sivas, Reşid Pasha, sought to prevent him from expanding his power.[29]

Reşid Pasha was soon seen as the embodiment of an intractable Ottoman governor by the Kurdish ruling elites and the tribal groups, especially in those isolated parts of Kurdistan. In 1835, he organised a military operation over Garzan – a tribal area inhabited predominantly by the Yezidi population. Continuing his uncompromising approach towards the Kurdish elites, he marched on the Zırkî Begs based around Hazro and Lice in Diyarbekir and then over the chiefs of the Millî tribes.[30] As the 1830s came to a close, ambitious Ottoman governors had made significant inroads into Kurdistan through sporadic military operations that shifted the balance of power among the different Kurdish ruling houses. When Mîr Muhammad of Rawanduz disappeared from the scene, the rulers of Cîzre in the north became more influential. And as the Ottoman state had to contend with İbrahim Pasha of Egypt at Nizib (which ended in an embarrassing defeat) it paid less attention to the Kurdish rulers. By the 1840s, Bedirkhan Beg of Cîzre had emerged as a powerful leader. The previously exiled Han Mahmud and his household returned to their homeland and allied with Bedirkhan Beg against the Ottoman state's increased attempts to consolidate its infrastructural power in the area through conscription, censuses and taxation policies. Other Kurdish rulers joined this alliance later, which worried the Ottoman governors. By the end of 1846, the Ottoman state's approach to the Kurdish rulers hardened. At the same time, the Ottoman administration was attempting to dissolve real or potential alliances between the Kurdish begs by honouring them with medals or giving them positions within the provincial bureaucracy. Finally, in 1847, the Ottoman troops, armed with heavy artillery, marched on Bedirkhan Beg. Bedirkhan Beg and Han Mahmud were exiled; the former to Crete, the latter to Russia. In 1847, the Ottoman state restructured provincial organisation by establishing the *Kurdistan Eyaleti* (the province of Kurdistan), consisting of Diyarbekir, Van, Cîzre, Botan, Hakkâri and Mardin. At the core of this administrative change was the question of sovereignty: According to the related governmental decree, the reason behind naming this new province Kurdistan was to remind everyone that the sultan was the true conqueror of this region.[31] This re-conquest was not based solely on military force: for decades, even as it tried to appease, co-opt or suppress the Kurdish rulers, Ottoman administrators had also been trying to institute the infrastructure of a modern state throughout Kurdistan.

The Making of the Modern State's Power in Kurdistan: Institutional Infrastructure

When the Tanzimat programme was promulgated in 1839, it was initially only in provinces near the capital such as Edirne, Hüdâvendigar, Ankara, Aydın and İzmir.[32] Later, its scope was broadened, and in March 1845, Diyarbekir and Erzurum provinces, and the districts of the Ma'âdin-i Hümâyun Emâneti, were incorporated into the programme. Since the majority of the population was Kurdish-speaking, the state considered the need to employ a translator in Diyarbekir to facilitate the government's operations. Up until that time, the district governorship of Diyarbekir had intermittently hired a local, Fetullah Agha, as the translator. With the Tanzimat he was turned into a permanent, salaried official.[33]

But even before the Tanzimat came to Kurdistan, the Ottoman administration had been trying to reform the administrative organisation there. A new military-administrative post called *müşirlik* was created in 1836, with *müşir*s (upper-level military commanders) charged with performing both military and administrative functions. The Diyarbekir Müşirliği was established in 1838.[34] The government envisioned it as being above the convoluted local power relations that involved the governor, local elites and provincial population at large. *Müşir*s were expected to curtail the power of the governors.[35] One of the goals of the Tanzimat reforms was to remove the fiscal component of the governors' role and make the position purely administrative.[36] In the absence of a salaried bureaucracy, prior to the Tanzimat the governors' income came primarily from taxes and gifts received in return for granting tax farms to the notables. The Tanzimat policies aimed to curtail this, and in order to further limit the governors' influence in financial matters treasurers (*defterdar*s) were appointed as salaried officials at the provincial level.

These changes were related to the Ottoman administration's goal of establishing a functioning tax-collection system in the provinces. Tax farming was defined as a harmful practice that allowed imperial revenues to be siphoned off by intermediaries, and the initial years of Tanzimat reflected an ongoing effort to eliminate the intermediaries from tax collection. There were two objectives: establishing equity in taxation and instituting direct taxation by eliminating intermediaries. For the former, regulating the tithe (*öşür*) was the most important step. The tithe was collected as a ratio of the agricultural output, and the actual ratio collected varied between 1:2 and 1:10. An 1840 government order fixed the tithe at 1/10.[37] Achieving the second goal required annulling the tax immunities of various religious, military and landowning notables. In the same vein, the government sought to abolish the tax immunities of the *vakıf*s and tax-collection rights of the supervisors (*mütevelli*), and settle the nomadic groups so they would engage in agriculture and pay taxes.[38] The tax-farming system was abolished in 1840 and a centrally-appointed, salaried tax collector (*muhassıl-ı emvâl*) was established in its place. The goal was to establish an unmediated tax-collection process, but this quickly failed, and tax farming remained the dominant instrument of surplus extraction. Along with the tithe, there was also an effort to restructure the *örfi* (customary) taxes.[39] A number of customary taxes were abolished, and in their stead 'a single type of tax was put into practice, based on ability to pay, that is according to proportion of each individual's real estate (*emlak*), agricultural land (*arazi*) and income (*temettü*)'.[40] The amount a district would pay would be calculated on the basis of the previous year's *örfi* taxes it paid, and this amount would be divided among heads of households according to their incomes. These policies also involved an effort to shift the tax burden from the rural producers to the urban wealthy.[41]

With the failure of the *muhassıllık* system, the provincial governors once again oversaw tax collection, largely by controlling tax farm auctions.[42] In the re-organisation of provincial bureaucracy, one of the most important changes was the establishment of the local councils in the provinces (*eyalet*), sanjaks and districts (*kaza*). The origins of these local councils go back to the *muhassıllık*, as these tax collectors formed local councils (*muhassıllık meclisleri*) that consisted of 'ex-officio members including the tax collector, two scribes, the judge, the müfti, the security chief (*umur-ı zabtiye me'muru*), and four elected members elected from among the local notables'.[43] In areas with Christian populations, they would be represented in the council's meeting by the metropolitan and two notables (*kocabaş*). One lasting impact of the *muhassıllık* system was the establishment of local councils at the provincial, sanjak and district (*kaza*) levels through the end of the empire.[44] These councils consisted of local Ottoman administrators (e.g. governor, *kaymakam* or *müdür*), local notables and the representatives of the non-Muslim communities. Tanzimat councils were formed in various sanjaks and districts in Kurdistan, including Diyarbekir, Malatya and Arabgir in 1845. There was a provincial council in Harput from 1846 on,[45] and a well-functioning district council in Palu from 1848. In a strikingly short time period, these local councils gained visible influence in decision-making processes pertaining to land and taxation disputes.

Another key element of the Tanzimat programme was the institution of conscription. Ottoman efforts to establish a regular, mass-conscript army took off during the era of Mahmud II (r. 1808–39) and continued with the Tanzimat. The Tanzimat Decree emphasised the 'obligatory nature of military service' and promised a 'fair, codified system of military recruitment'.[46] Subsequent reform programmes in 1843 and 1846 institutionalised the draft lottery system (*kur'a-i şeriyye*) as an annual event administered by a council consisting of the judge of the local Islamic court, local notables and religious dignitaries.[47] Males between the ages of twenty and twenty-five would gather at the administrative centre of each district for the lottery. But despite its promise of fairness, the *kur'a* system aroused serious resistance from potential conscripts across the empire, not least in Kurdistan.[48]

In Palu, *kur'a* was implemented first in 1849. In June, the governor of Harput, Mustafa Sabri, informed the chief commander (*serasker*) of the Anatolian Army that the Palu *kur'a* had been successfully completed.[49] The next year, however, things did not go smoothly. As was the case elsewhere, there was resistance, or at the least indifference, to conscription. People did not show up, or else those names that were called in the lottery fled.[50] In face of this resistance, governor Mustafa Sabri advocated a stringent policy of finding and locating the men whose names came up in the lottery, whether they were located in Harput or elsewhere. In a year, resistance to the lottery from the inhabitants of Palu and neighbouring Şiro grew.[51] The *müşir* of the Anatolian Army got involved, informing the Sublime Porte that things had calmed down, the lottery was completed, and even the taxes (most likely the tithe) were collected.[52] Throughout the rest of the nineteenth century, conscription was one of the most conflicted areas of imperial reform in Kurdistan. In Palu, however, the rate of success in implementing the *kur'a* was much higher than in many other places in Kurdistan. It is important to note that in the areas that had historically been ruled by the Kurdish begs, the *kur'a* was a key step in the state's monopolisation of violence. As mentioned previously, from the sixteenth century onwards, the Kurdish begs held standing armies which consisted of armed tribal groups. Starting from the late seventeenth century, the Palu begs' military power diminished, and by the second half of the eighteenth century their military roles in the Ottoman campaigns had become obsolete. But other Kurdish begs continued to hold armed retinues and join Ottoman campaigns against Iran well into the mid-nineteenth century. At any rate, with *kur'a*, the Ottoman administration, regardless of its actual infrastructural ability to achieve this, was trying to exclude the Kurdish nobles from the process of military recruitment. *Kur'a* meant that, for the Ottoman state, the military *raison d'être* of the Kurdish nobility no longer existed.

Modern State Power in Kurdistan

Making modern state infrastructure in the provincial periphery entailed new processes of enumeration and quantification. The counting of males for conscription and of wealth for taxation purposes were two essential components of modern census making in the Ottoman Empire. Indeed, all of the Empire's administrators had to grapple with the lack of systematic data about these key matters, and provincial administrators mentioned it frequently as one of their biggest challenges. It was especially problematic in the areas where the Kurdish begs' hereditary rule prevailed – including Palu – since they had been exempt from the land and population surveys (*tahrir*) emblematic of the Ottoman state's conquest of an area in its early centuries. Despite this exemption, however, the Ottoman state tried to conduct *tahrir* in these areas whenever it could. For the most part, however, it failed, and the principle stayed in effect. Thus, well into the nineteenth century, the imperial state lacked systematic records about the population and economy of many of these areas.

The first modern Ottoman census, which was essentially related to military reform, started in 1830 and was conducted nearer the imperial centre. In the eastern provinces, Erzurum had the first modern census, in 1836. Throughout the 1830s and 1840s, however, the question of a population census in Kurdistan was on the state's agenda. In 1845, the Meclis-i Vâlâ decided to conduct a census of the male population in accordance with the Tanzimat programme in Diyarbekir, Sivas and Erzurum provinces along with the districts administratively attached to the Ma'âdin-i Hümâyun Emâneti.[53] This gap between the first census and this one was not unusual, given that the implementation of the first census was an uneven process throughout the empire. The first modern census in Palu was conducted in 1841.[54] In 1846, another census was taken in Palu, along with the surrounding Ergani and Çermik districts.[55] Denoting the wider goal of bureaucratisation, a census clerk, Ali Efendi, was dispatched to Palu around 1849.[56] After 1846, the next record of a population census in Palu comes in 1856.[57]

As with the lottery, people's reaction to population census was less than welcoming – and not just in Kurdistan. People associated the census with conscription or increased taxes and tried to evade it. Censuses took place within the context of local politics that involved local actors and Ottoman administrators and involved a great degree of negotiation and co-optation, along with resistance and evasion. This became more evident with the census of property and wealth that constituted the other pillar of the emerging modern enumerative practices within the Tanzimat context.

The counting of wealth and property was related to the goal of restructuring the tax system. The implementation of the new tax policies required the imperial government to have a clear view of the population's tax-paying potential, that is, of its wealth and income. The state set out to conduct income surveys (*tahrir-i temettüât*) throughout the empire. After failing in 1840, the Porte dispatched special instructions in 1845 to the provinces on how to conduct the surveys, and thousands of income registers were sent to Istanbul within a year.[58] Despite being incorporated into the Tanzimat regime in 1845, the province of Diyarbekir – and the surrounding districts attached to Ma'âdin-i Hümâyun Emâneti – did not send any registers. Nonetheless, the issue of conducting the surveys and the related question of tax ratios on the rural and urban population were hotly debated among the local population. In 1845, the government conducted a census of the movable (*emvâl*) and immovable (*emlak*) property in Diyarbekir and fixed the tax at 15 per cent. In response, notables from Diyarbekir and its surrounding districts, including Palu, sent a petition to the imperial centre with 152 signatories that said that the provincial council had discussed tax ratios and had reached a resolution on an alternative to the government's tax plan.[59] Eleven of the signatories were from Palu, including the *müfti* and the deputy judge (*na'ib*). Armenian clergy (*kocabaş*) and Muslim notables (*vücuh*) were also among the signatories. Significantly, three of the Palu nobility also signed, including Mîr Abdullah (who was the *müdür* of Palu at the time), Mîr Ahmed and Mîr Mehmed. Their participation attests to their anxiety over the imperial state's latest attempt to record their wealth and property and tax them accordingly.

Instead of the government's proportional taxation of 15 per cent on the non-agricultural populations (merchants and craftsmen), the petitioners suggested a fixed amount of 50 guruş. They also called for agricultural producers to pay a 1/10 tithe and 2/10 tax (*vergi*) over the annual harvest.[60] This represented an effort by the notables on the provincial council to halt proportional representation and shift the tax burden to the rural producers. They knew that the income surveys were the harbingers of proportional taxation, which is why they resisted them, and why the income registers of the Diyarbekir province went unsent. These demands of the petitioners were approved at the Meclis-i Vâlâ, so the income survey was postponed and the proposed tax ratios were accepted by the imperial council: the wealthy in and around the province, including the Palu begs, stopped the wealth census. An account register from 1845 demonstrates that the tax arrangement they proposed was implemented in some parts of the province, including Malatya, Harput and Siverek.[61] These resolutions of the wealthy coalition did not go unchallenged. In at least one case, the inhabitants of Palu reacted to the tax ratios by allying with neighbouring Çarsancak in what official correspondence described as an uprising (*ihtilal*).[62]

The census of population and wealth was related to the multitude of diverse tax systems and the prevalence of indirect forms of taxation, which was especially acute in the periphery of the empire. This diversity, in turn, resulted from the many different forms of land ownership in the empire. The Tanzimat wanted to standardise and register land ownership, but less is known about this restructuring and codification of the land system than about taxation and military re-organisation. Studies of the land policies of the modernising Ottoman state have mainly focused on the Land Code of 1858, considered the 'central piece of legislation on landed property in the nineteenth century'.[63] An extensive literature on the Code has examined its preparation, goals and effects and its significance in terms of the privatisation of land in the empire.[64] However, the question of standardising and registering landed property preoccupied the Ottoman ruling elites almost two decades prior to the Land Code of 1858, with a series of laws, decrees and regulations issued in the 1840s. An official decree in April 1847 regulated the distribution of title deeds (*tapu temessükatı*) from the Imperial Registry (*Defterhane*). The same year, another set of regulations (*tapu nizamnamesi*) worked to centralise the use, sale and inheritance of *mîrî* lands by issuing detailed legal procedures pertaining to these processes.[65]

These efforts to restructure land registration extended into Kurdistan. In February 1848, shortly after the above regulations were issued, the Porte dispatched an order to the governor of Kurdistan about unregistered lands that needed title deeds. Unregistered lands were especially prevalent in Harput, Diyarbekir, Mardin, Cîzre and the Botan, Bitlis, and Muş areas, where the majority of land ownership was undocumented, in part because much of the population was nomadic (*haymenişin*).[66] The prevalence of hereditary estates of the Kurdish begs' (*yurtluk-ocaklık*) lands and those held with title deeds bestowed on them by the sultan (*mülkname-i hümayûn*) was especially mentioned.[67] Beyond the lands of the Kurdish nobility, there was also a general problem of undocumented landowning. In some cases, the current owners of the land still held the title deeds of the previous owners. The other issue that concerned the Ottoman administration was the *vakıf* lands that over time had de facto become the property of individuals who did not hold a valid title deed. Some had built a masjid, a madrasah or a dervish lodge (*tekke*), or turned state lands into a *vakıf*. According to the imperial correspondence, this was especially common in the Cîzre, Botan and Hacı Behram districts. The unregistered *vakıf* lands were also related to the state's anxiety over the begs' control over land and its surplus. To undercut the begs' influence over the process of land registration, the Meclis-i Vâlâ entrusted the *kaymakam*s with the task of granting valid title deeds for land and appointed a director of pious foundations (*evkaf müdürü*) to the region.[68]

The governmental order asked the provincial administrators to update land registration in Kurdistan by granting landowners title deeds, either for a fee or free. The local administrators – the governor and the treasurer – responded positively because they thought that title deeds that originated from the imperial centre would increase government revenues and end local land disputes. They requested copies of the new land regulations, as well as 3,000 title deeds. Their request for the former was approved, but not their request for the latter. The new regulations stated that the old title deeds were to be sent to Istanbul where they would be replaced by the new ones. If a property had no title deed, its borders would be marked and then it would be assigned a new title deed. The state did not want to give authority to the local administrators for the distribution of new title deeds, preferring to centralise the process.[69] Considering the imperial state's lack of capacity to administer a cadaster, this goal was utterly unrealistic, but the point here is that as early as the 1840s, Ottoman administration wanted to bring legibility to its administration of land in Kurdistan, regardless of its capacity to do so. For the Ottoman administrators, hereditary land control of the Kurdish begs over lands was a big obstacle to the success of land registration. Among various echelons of Ottoman bureaucracy, this issue was discussed at great length.

The Question of Hereditary Ownership of Land by the Kurdish Begs

The imperial decrees which granted the Kurdish begs hereditary ownership over land were revised several times by successive sultans – in the case of Palu begs the latest renewal was in 1841, shortly before Kurdistan came under the scope of the Tanzimat programme implemented by Sultan Abdulmecid I (r. 1839–61).[70] Notwithstanding this recent renewal, however, at around the same time Ottoman administrators were reconsidering the legitimacy or relevancy of the hereditary privileges of the Kurdish nobility over land. In the areas where Kurdish nobility were influential, their hereditary privileges and exemptions essentially rendered the Ottoman central administration's authority nominal. These privileges had to be dealt with if the Ottoman state was to assume full power in the region. Curiously, Palu had a central place in these discussions.

In the early Tanzimat era, the question of the Kurdish nobility's privileges preoccupied both provincial administrators based in Kurdistan and the central elites at the Meclis-i Vâlâ in Istanbul. These discussions revolved around two axes. First, there were the concerns over the material implications of the exemptions and about how noble prerogatives compromised the state's authority. Taxes not flowing into the central treasury, problems with instituting conscription, and difficulties conducting population and wealth censuses all worked against the Ottoman administration's attempts to assume stateness in these areas. Second was the idea of 'change'. As we will see, for the Ottoman administrators, these privileges were remnants of a past that was so distant and different from the present as to be irrelevant. The problem was that annulling the Kurdish nobility's sultan-given hereditary rights could be seen as denying the imperial legacy. Overall, however, the Ottoman administrators were more concerned with the tangible problems caused by the Kurdish nobles' privilege, including protection of the border, local balance of power between elite groups, tax revenues, and the potential costs of compensating the begs if their privileges were abolished. Rather than coming up with a grand plan, the Ottoman administrators considered these points individually for each part of Kurdistan and used that information to decide on continuing or abolishing hereditary rights. To put it differently, instead of abolishing the Kurdish begs' hereditary privileges all around Kurdistan at once, the state granted each noble family a different arrangement.

In the 1840s, while ambitious Ottoman administrators were seeking ways to co-opt, pacify and subdue the Kurdish nobility in the frontier areas using negotiation, accommodation and aggressive military campaigns, the de jure hereditary character of the Kurdish begs' rule was still in effect. Both the Ottoman state and the Kurdish nobles accepted the Kurdish nobility's long-standing prerogatives, specifically, the hereditary character of the *hâkim*s and the begs' control over land. For instance, the surviving register of the first census in Palu conducted in 1841 was prefaced by a statement that the land of the Palu district was in the hands of the Palu *ûmera* with titled deeds (*temlîk*) which granted them hereditary ownership.[71] In this period, the begs could still transfer their land to their heirs without any obstruction from the government. The transference of the begs' shares to their sons and grandson had been approved in the Meclis-i Vâlâ, which stated that the Tanzimat had not yet been implemented in this region.[72] But from the perspective of the state, things were starting to change, as Ottoman administrators began thinking that this practice was antithetical to the Tanzimat programme.

But what did the hereditary privileges of the Kurdish nobility entail at this time? From the perspective of the Ottoman state, what, specifically, were the problems caused by having a noble class when the Tanzimat policies were making inroads into more remote corners of the empire? In the 1840s, the begs' hereditary rights as the rulers (*hâkim*) of Palu, defined in age-old imperial decrees, meant that they had inalienable authority over their dominions, immunity from the Ottoman surveyors and the right to bear armed forces, and were exempt from various taxes. As we saw, over the course of the eighteenth century, the administrative aspect of their authority was challenged by the mine superintendent. Nonetheless, the Palu begs were still recognised as the *hâkim* of Palu in the Ottoman administrative hierarchy.

But the administrative aspect of the begs' hereditary rule was just one piece of a bigger problem for the Ottoman authorities – namely, the fiscal and economic aspect. As of the 1840s, the begs had control over big chunks of agricultural land that was tilled by sharecroppers, land that the state could not confiscate unless a beg died without a primary heir. Due to the economic transformations of the second half of the eighteenth century, more and different people had a claim to the agrarian revenues of the Palu land. Yet it was still the begs who decided to whom they would farm or lease out the land, and no matter what, they did not share their revenues with the Ottoman state. Agrarian surplus was now shared among multiple claimants, but it remained within Palu. All in all, in the 1840s, when the Ottoman state talked about the hereditary rights of the Palu nobility, it was referring to all facets of their hereditary rights over land as *territory*, *property*, and to their rights to the *surplus* produced by that land depending on the context.[73]

Besides, the question of hereditary nobility in Palu was part of a problem that, in the eyes of the state, plagued all of Kurdistan, where begs with varying degrees of power, authority, land and wealth abounded. Although some of the begs had *hükümet* powers and others had *yurtluk-ocaklık* status (and thus, different degrees of privilege and autonomy), central and provincial administrators referred to the *yurtluk-ocaklık* status of these areas. This speaks to the fact that for the state, the underlying problem was the begs' hereditary ownership of the land in any form.

Government correspondence demonstrates that there was no blueprint on how to change the hereditary character of the Kurdish nobility accompanying the Tanzimat decree. Neither the administrators at the imperial centre nor the newly-appointed Tanzimat officials in the region saw Kurdistan as a uniform, homogeneous body in which they could implement standardised policies. In the lead-up to the abolition of hereditary rights, provincial administrators had a key role in shaping the ideas of Tanzimat reformers by conveying their observations, impressions and judgements. These gained momentum when the region was officially brought under the Tanzimat programme in 1845. In a detailed report, the *müşir* and the treasurer (*defterdar*) of the Diyarbekir province discussed the situation of hereditary lands in different parts of the province. Despite not being the largest or the most powerful Kurdish emirates, Palu and Eğil constituted the starting points for the calculations about what to do with the hereditary landholdings in the region. They stood out because of the abundance of agriculturally fertile lands that would make it profitable to eliminate the begs and channel the revenues from the land directly into the imperial treasury. According to Ottoman administrators, confiscating the lands of the Kurdish begs of Palu and Eğil would increase the tithe revenues from these places threefold. The reports highlighted the two areas to demonstrate the potential benefits of bringing the hereditary lands of Kurdish begs under state control in areas further east and north in and around the Erzurum, Çıldır and Van provinces. For each area, the Ottoman administrators carefully weighed economic costs and benefits, politico-strategic risks, local power configurations and alliances, as well as topography and geography, in order to determine whether hereditary land ownership should be abolished or left intact.[74]

The majority of *yurtluk-ocaklık* lands were in Erzurum. However, because of the province's geo-strategic position on the delicate border with Iran, the decision was made not to abolish the hereditary lands for the time being. In other places, economic calculations carried more weight, as annulling the *yurtluk-ocaklık* lands came with a set of costs. In these calculations, there was a conscious effort to mitigate the reaction of the begs through material rewards and incorporate them into the new system as shareholders. In order to prevent the begs from reacting negatively, the government considered appointing them as salaried district governors (*müdür*). This raised the question of whether the revenues these lands would bring would exceed the total cost of salaries paid to the begs and the gendarmerie sent to the region. In Çıldır, the answer to this question was negative. The begs controlled the thirteen districts of the province as *yurtluk-ocaklık*, collecting the tithe revenues of these districts, which was one fifth of the harvest. After bringing these lands under government control, the tithe ratio would be reduced to 1:10 in line with the government regulations. However, the situation was challenging, since 'most areas of the province were rocky (*sengistan*) and barren (*bîhasıl*)'. One way to economise on the administrative costs of abolishing the hereditary lands was to merge two or three smaller districts into bigger ones and appoint one beg as *müdür* to administer these bigger districts. In the end, the Meclis-i Vâlâ decided to abolish the hereditary landholding of the begs in Çıldır.

There were also cases in which the begs negotiated with the state and preferred to surrender their hereditary rights in return for a salary. Behlül Pasha, the hereditary ruler of the Bayezid sanjak, was brought to Erzurum to receive the imperial order to confiscate the begs' lands. To the consternation of the *müşir* and the *defterdar*, Behlül Pasha was not averse to the idea, given the scantiness of the revenues accruing from these lands. From 1845 on, Behlül Beg's lands belonged to the imperial treasury, and he was granted a lifetime salary in return.

In some places, alliances between begs dissuaded the Ottoman state from initiating a drastic policy. The Hakkâri sanjak had been brought under the Tanzimat programme because, although it was a flourishing area, its ruler, Turan Beg, had not paid any tax revenues to the imperial state despite repeated requests. For the Ottoman imperial state, the real complication stemmed from Turan Beg's close relations with Bedirkhan Beg of the Botan Emirate – one of the most formidable Kurdish rulers of the time. Worried about a potential concerted action from the two and not wanting to risk the security of this border area with Iran, the Meclis-i Vâlâ decided to postpone implementing the Tanzimat and the confiscation. Even in places from which the state expected to derive considerable economic gains through abolishing the begs' hereditary rights, it was cautious, mainly because of concerns about Bedirkhan Beg. A case in point was Hizan district in Muş, which contained approximately sixty fertile villages. Despite the potential economic benefits, the state decided to leave the hereditary rights of Şerif Beg, the ruler of Hizan, who was on good terms with Bedirkhan Beg.

In all these calculations, the biggest factor in the state's decision to opt for the status quo or gradual change rather than an abrupt transformation was its lack of capacity. The Kurdish begs had fiscal, administrative and military authority in places where, despite regional variations, the state's power was nominal at best. Financial calculations had to be balanced against the realities of dealing with border areas in the context of a protracted geo-strategic rivalry with a neighbouring empire. If the state undermined the Kurdish begs' power, it would have to be responsible for the security (*muhafaza*) and administration (*idare*) of the area. These discussions on the Erzurum, Van and Çıldır provinces demonstrate that for the border areas, the Ottoman state was more willing to maintain the hereditary rights of the Kurdish begs. At the same time, however, coercion was an ever-present option for the imperial state. From the 1820s through the 1840s, these negotiations, or what Sabri Ateş describes as 'strategic co-optation', went hand in hand with military operations specifically targeting the most powerful and influential Kurdish begs.[75]

Where did Palu stand in the spectrum of coercion versus negotiation/ co-optation? It was far from the Iranian border. In the sixteenth century, before the Ottoman entry into the region, Kurdish emirates in the north of Diyarbekir, including Palu, Eğil and Çermik, were a part of a frontier zone between the rival Ottoman and Safavid Empires. As discussed in the first chapter, after the Çaldıran battle, Diyarbekir and Van came under the Ottoman rule. Thenceforth, despite their unique status with hereditary privileges and regardless of their actual submission to the military, fiscal and other demands of the Ottoman centre, the Palu begs' loyalty to the Ottomans as their suzerain was never in jeopardy. Palu was far away from the Ottoman border, the tribes based in and around it did not cross the Iranian border, and the Palu emirs' loyalty did not fluctuate between the two empires. Palu had long lost whatever frontier status it had once had, and when justifying the need to abolish the hereditary land rights of the Palu begs Ottoman administrators claimed that the rights had been given because of their role in the protecting the frontier (*serhad*) and for their service in the holy war (*hidemat-i cihadiye*).[76] With the emergence of a regular army, the argument went, the begs had lost their former military function, and thus should also lose those rights.

In the calculations of the Ottoman administrators, Palu stood out as a potentially more profitable place in terms of the tithe revenues it could pay. Local administrators repeatedly emphasised that removing the begs' hereditary control would significantly increase the tithe revenues. All things considered, being agriculturally productive, not on the frontier, and not on the radar of or in co-operation with the formidable Bedirkhan Beg of Cîzre, Palu seemed to the Ottoman administrators to be a low-risk place in which to experiment with abolishing the hereditary prerogatives of the Kurdish nobility.

Conclusion

The making of the modern Ottoman state did not start with the Tanzimat period. As several historians have emphasised, the early modern origins of the Ottoman state lie in the transformations of the previous centuries. Nevertheless, the changes envisioned by the Ottoman administration in the Tanzimat context evince a discernible effort to bureaucratise, monopolise violence by establishing a regular army, and territorialise – key aspects of building the institutional background for a modern state. Economically, this was a significant period for the emergence of the Ottoman fiscal state. The economic historian Şevket Pamuk states that '[f]rom the 1770s until the 1840s the Ottoman state finances frequently experienced large budget deficits. These deficits reached their peak during the 1820s and 1830s.'[77] The economic reforms of the Tanzimat era were a response to this.

It was within this context that the Ottoman central administration set out to reconfigure its relationship with the provincial periphery in a way that would reassert its authority. Echoing its efforts in other parts of the empire, the Ottoman administration developed policies and practices to extend its administrative, military and fiscal authority to Kurdistan. The Sublime Porte tried to institute conscription, establish new administrative posts, and appoint new cadres to these posts. It established local councils to enable the participation and integration of provincial elites in the process of modern state-making. As the next few chapters will demonstrate, these councils played a critical role not only in implementing the Tanzimat's institutional changes, but also in resolving local conflicts about agrarian relations of production.

The question of the Kurdish nobility's hereditary privileges stood as the major issue that the Ottoman state needed to deal with to achieve these goals. This chapter has demonstrated that the discussions around this among the Ottoman administrators revolved mainly around fiscal, geo-strategic and power balance considerations.

But the position of the Kurdish nobility did not only preoccupy governmental actors. Local actors from different socio-economic and ethno-religious backgrounds fiercely contested the begs' hereditary prerogatives and position. It is imperative to comprehend the local discourses, conflicts, and negotiations over the position of the Kurdish nobility in order to fully grasp the historical processes leading up to the abolishment of the begs' de jure hereditary rights.

Notes

1. Zirki begs ruled around Lice, Hazro and Baykan area in Siirt. They were another group of Kurdish begs who held their hereditary privileges from the sixteenth century onwards and whose properties were confiscated in the Tanzimat period. See Fatih Pekol, 'Zirki Beylikleri ve Beyleri Tarihi' (MA thesis, Mardin Artuklu University, 2017). See also Uğur Bahadır Bayraktar, ''Periphery's Centre: Reform, Taxation, and Local Notables in Diyarbakir, 1845–1855' (Ph.D. dissertation, Boğaziçi University, 2015).
2. BOA.ML.VRD 7, 1254 (1838–1839), 5.
3. J. C. Hurewitz, *The Middle East and North Africa in World Politics: A Documentary Record: European Expansion, 1535–1914.*, 2nd rev. and enlarged edn (New Haven, CT: Yale University Press, 1975), 315–18. Cited in James Gelvin, *The Modern Middle East*, 3rd edn (New York; Oxford: Oxford University Press, 2011), 159–61.

4. For an overview of political developments in the long nineteenth century, see Donald Quataert, 'Overview of the Nineteenth Century', in *An Economic and Social History of the Ottoman Empire, 1300–1914*, eds Halil İnalcık and Donald Quataert (Cambridge: Cambridge University Press, 1994), 761–76.
5. James C. Scott, *Seeing Like a State: How Certain Schemes to Improve the Human Condition Have Failed* (Yale University Press, 1998).
6. For a similar discussion on the Ottoman state's policy of consolidating its infrastructural power in the provinces, see Eugene L. Rogan, *Frontiers of the State in the Late Ottoman Empire: Transjordan, 1850–1921* (Cambridge; New York: Cambridge University Press, 2002). For Anatolia, see Yonca Köksal, *The Ottoman Empire in the Tanzimat Era: Provincial Perspectives from Ankara to Edirne* (London; New York: Routledge, 2019) and John Bragg, *Ottoman Notables and Participatory Politics: Tanzimat Reform in Tokat, 1839–1876*, 1st edn (New York: Routledge, 2014); For Cyprus, see Marc Aymes, *A Provincial History of the Ottoman Empire: Cyprus and the Eastern Mediterranean in the Nineteenth Century*, 1st edn (London: Routledge, 2013). For Arab provinces, see Jens Hanssen, Thomas Philipp and Stefan Weber eds, *The Empire in the City: Arab Provincial Capitals in the Late Ottoman Empire* (Beirut and Würzburg: Ergon in Kommission, 2002).
7. Ateş, *Ottoman–Iranian Borderlands*, 52–7.
8. Jürgen Osterhammel, *The Transformation of the World: A Global History of the Nineteenth Century* (Princeton University Press, 2015), 573. Emphasis added.
9. Osterhammel, 573–4.
10. Literature on the classical theories of the state is extensive. For a useful overview, see John L. Brooke and Julia C. Strauss eds, 'Introduction', in *State Formations: Global Histories and Cultures of Statehood* (New York: Cambridge University Press, 2018), 1–20.
11. Aradhana Sharma and Akhil Gupta, 'Introduction: Rethinking the Theories of the State in an Age of Globalization', in *The Anthropology of the State: A Reader*, eds Aradhana Sharma and Akhil Gupta (Oxford: Blackwell, 2009), 8. For this revisionist approach to the state, also see George Steinmetz ed., *State/Culture: State-Formation after the Cultural Turn* (Cornell University Press, 2018); Benoît de L'Estoile, Federico Neiburg and Lygia Maria Sigaud eds, *Empires, Nations, and Natives: Anthropology and State-Making* (Duke University Press, 2005); Gilbert Michael Joseph and Daniel Nugent eds, *Everyday Forms of State Formation: Revolution and the Negotiation of Rule in Modern Mexico* (Duke University Press, 1994).
12. Sharma and Gupta, 'Introduction: Rethinking the Theories of the State in An Age of Globalization', 9.
13. Sharma and Gupta, 7.
14. For a study that aims to demystify the state by looking at its everyday practices in the Ottoman context, see Nadir Özbek, 'The Politics of Taxation and

the "Armenian Question" during the Late Ottoman Empire, 1876–1908', *Comparative Studies in Society and History* 54, no. 04 (October 2012): 770–97.
15. Islamoglu and Perdue, 'Introduction', 274–5.
16. I do not mean that modernity took off with the Tanzimat decree. My emphasis here is on the significance of the Tanzimat era in terms of the acceleration of policies that built up the state's infrastructural power. For an illuminating discussion of the early modern origins of eighteenth-century modern state formation, see the excellent contributions to Huri Islamoglu and Peter C. Perdue, eds *Shared Histories of Modernity: China, India and the Ottoman Empire*, 1st edn (New Delhi: Routledge India, 2009).
17. For a critique of the conventional approaches and overview of the revisionist works, see Yonca Köksal, 'Tanzimat ve Tarih Yazımı', *Doğu Batı* 51 (2010): 193–216. See also Yonca Köksal, *The Ottoman Empire in the Tanzimat Era: Provincial Perspectives from Ankara to Edirne* (London; New York: Routledge, 2019), 1–19.
18. For these provincial histories, see Donald Quataert, 'Recent Writings in Late Ottoman History', *International Journal of Middle East Studies* 35, no. 01 (2003): 133–9.
19. This perspective is a product of methodological nationalism prevalent in historical accounts of Kurds and Kurdistan. The protracted conflict between contemporary nation-states and the Kurdish populations made historians project concepts, theories andframeworks useful for understanding nation-state contexts onto an imperial setting in an anachronistic fashion.
20. Ateş, *Ottoman–Iranian Borderlands*, 32.
21. Ateş, 37.
22. Ateş, 27.
23. For example, in 1825, Han Mahmud, the ruling beg of the Müküs area, sent a letter written in Persian to the Ottoman governor of Van, Galip Pasha, asking for help in the face of the unrelenting Iranian forces. Sinan Hakan, *Osmanlı Arşiv Belgelerinde: Kürtler ve Kürt Direnişleri, 1817–1867* (Doz Yayıncılık, 2007), 47–8.
24. Hakan, 55.
25. Hakan, 44; Erdal Çiftçi, 'Migration, Memory and Mythification: Relocation of Suleymani Tribes on the Northern Ottoman–Iranian Frontier', *Middle Eastern Studies* 54, no. 2 (4 March 2018): 72.
26. Ateş, *Ottoman–Iranian Borderlands*, 49.
27. Çiftçi, 'Migration, Memory and Mythification', 72.
28. Ateş, *Ottoman–Iranian Borderlands*, 54.
29. Hakan, *Osmanlı Arşiv Belgelerinde*, 69–70.
30. Hakan, 75–80.
31. Hakan, 256–7; Hakan Özoğlu, *Kurdish Notables and the Ottoman State: Evolving Identities, Competing Loyalties, and Shifting Boundaries* (Albany, NY: State University of New York Press, 2004), 37.

32. Musa Çadırcı, *Tanzimat Döneminde Anadolu Kentlerinin Sosyal ve Ekonomik Yapıları* (Ankara: TTK, 1991), 190.
33. BOA.C.DH. 276/13764, 11 Receb 1261 (16 July 1845).
34. İbrahim Yılmazçelik, *XIX. Yüzyılın İlk Yarısında Diyarbakır: (1790–1840); (Fizikî, İdarî ve Sosyo-Ekonomik Yapı)* (Ankara: Türk Tarih Kurumu Basımevi, 1995), 181–4.
35. Halil İnalcık, *Application of the Tanzimat and Its Social Effects* (Lisse: Peter de Ridder Press, 1976), 5.
36. For a detailed analysis of these conflicts in the locality revolving around the first Ottoman censuses in the 1840s and 1850s, see Nilay Özok-Gündoğan, 'Counting the Population and the Wealth in an "Unruly" Land: Census Making as a Social Process in Ottoman Kurdistan, 1830–50', *Journal of Social History*, vol. 3, issue 3, Spring 2020: 763–91.
37. Ömer Lütfi Barkan, 'Türk Toprak Hukuku Tarihinde Tanzimat ve 1274 (1858) Tarihli Arazi Kanunnamesi', in *Türkiye'de Toprak Meselesi* (İstanbul: Gözlem Yayınları, 1980), 319–20.
38. Ömer Lütfi Barkan, 'Türk Toprak Hukuku Tarihinde Tanzimat ve 1274 (1858) Tarihli Arazi Kanunnamesi', in *Türkiye'de Toprak Meselesi* (İstanbul: Gözlem Yayınları, 1980), 318–19.
39. In the Ottoman Empire there were two general categories of state revenues: religious (*şer'i*) taxes and customary (*örfi*) taxes. The former referred to the tithe (*öşr*) and the poll tax (*cizye*). The latter referred to 'sovereign right taxes' and consisted of various land dues, pastures dues andcustom dues imposed by the sovereign. John Haldon, 'The Ottoman State and the Question of State Autonomy: Comparative Perspectives', *Journal of Peasant Studies* 18, nos 3–4 (1991): 56.
40. Tevfik Güran, 'Temettüat Registers as a Resource about Ottoman Social and Economic Life', in *The Ottoman State and Societies in Change: A Study of the Nineteenth Century Temettüat Registers*, eds Hayashi Kayoko and Mahir Aydın (London: Kegan Paul, 2004), 5.
41. Köksal, *The Ottoman Empire in the Tanzimat Era*, 10.
42. Jun Akiba, 'The Local Councils as the Origin of the Parliamentary System in the Ottoman Empire', in *Development of Parliamentarism in the Modern Islamic World*, ed. Tsugitaka Satō (Tokyo, Japan: Toyo Bunko, 2009), 180. Revisionist approaches to tax farming have revisited the idea that it was inherently incongruent with a centralised administrative system. These studies suggest that the persistent use of tax farming did not necessarily indicate the weakness of the Ottoman state, since there was a visible increase in the extractive capacity of the state that was reflected in the amount of tax revenues collected. Özbek argues that treasury revenues as a ratio of gross domestic product increased between 1850 and 1914. See Nadir Özbek, 'Tax Farming in the Nineteenth-Century Ottoman Empire: Institutional Backwardness or the Emergence of Modern Public Finance?', *The Journal of Interdisciplinary History* 49, no. 2 (1 August 2018): 227–8.

43. Akiba, 'The Local Councils as the Origin of the Parliamentary System in the Ottoman Empire', 178.
44. Akiba, 178.
45. Ahmet Aksın, *19. Yüzyılda Harput* (Elazığ Turkey: Ceren Ofset, 1999), 82.
46. Veysel Şimşek, 'The Grand Strategy of the Ottoman Empire, 1826–1841' (Ph.D. dissertation, McMaster University, 2015), 137.
47. Şimşek, 176–7.
48. For resistance to conscription, see Gültekin Yıldız, *Neferin Adı Yok* (Istanbul: Kitabevi Yayinlari, 2015); Edip Gölbaşı, 'The Yezidis and the Ottoman State: Modern Power, Military Conscription, and Conversion Policies, 1830–1909' (MA thesis, Istanbul, Boğaziçi University, 2008).
49. BOA.A.MKT.MHM 14/13 20 Receb 1265 [11 June 1849].
50. BOA.A.MKT 212/25 17 Şaban 1265 [8 July 1849].
51. BOA.A.MKT.MHM 22/35 8 Şaban 1266 [19 June 1859]; BOA.İ.DH 216/12700 19 Şaban 1266 [30 June 1850].
52. BOA.A.AMD 19/25 21 Şaban 1266 [2 July 1850].
53. BOA.I.DH 97/4852 14 Muharrem 1261 [23 January 1845].
54. Süleyman Yapıcı, *Palu 1841 Nüfus ve Toplum Yapısı*, Birinci baskı (Elazığ: Süleyman Yapıcı, 2016.), 23.
55. Yılmazçelik, *XIX. Yüzyılın İlk Yarısında Diyarbakır*, 101.
56. BOA.A.MKT 236/77 29 Zilhicce 1265 [15 November 1849]. The date is an estimate.
57. BOA.NFS.d 7427, A register of the Muslim population of Palu. 29 Zilhicce 1272 [31 August 1856].
58. Güran, 'Temettüat Registers as a Resource about Ottoman Social and Economic Life', 6.
59. BOA.İ.MSM 68/1990 document # 3, n.d.
60. BOA.İ.MSM 68/1990, document #5, 17 Rebîülevvel 1261 [26 March 1845].
61. BOA.İ.MSM. 68/1993, n.m. 1261 (c. 1845).
62. BOA.A.MKT 21/8 29 Zilhicce 1260 [21 January 1845] The date is an estimate.
63. Huricihan İslamoğlu, 'Property as a Contested Domain: A Reevaluation of the Ottoman Land Code of 1858'. In *New Perspectives on Property and Land in the Middle East*, ed. Roger Owen (London: Harvard University Press, 2000), 26.
64. For an examination of the extensive literatures on the Ottoman Land Code of 1858, see E. Attila Aytekin, 'Agrarian Relations, Property and Law: An Analysis of the Land Code of 1858 in the Ottoman Empire', *Middle Eastern Studies* 45, no. 6 (1 November 2009): 935–51.
65. For the details of these regulations, see Barkan, 'Türk Toprak Hukuku Tarihinde Tanzimat ve 1274 (1858) Tarihli Arazi Kanunnamesi', 324–28. In their study on Ajlun in Ottoman Syria, Mundy and Smith present a detailed account of the genealogy of land legislation in the Ottoman Empire prior to the Land Code of 1858. Martha Mundy and Richard Saumarez Smith,

Governing Property, Making the Modern State: Law, Administration and Production in Ottoman Syria (London: I. B. Tauris, 2007).

66. BOA.İ.MSM 23/576, 16 Cemâziyelevvel 1264 [20 April 1848].
67. BOA.İ.MSM 23/576, 16 Cemâziyelevvel 1264 [20 April 1848].
68. BOA.İ.MSM 23/577, 28 Şevval Cemâziyelâhir 1264 [27 September 1848].
69. BOA.İ.MSM 23/576, 10 Cemâziyelâhir 1264 [20 May 1848].
70. BOA.İ.MVL 237/8388 Document #1 Şevval 1257 [14 November 1841].
71. Yapıcı, '1841 Nüfus Defterlerinde Palu', 233.'*Kasaba-ı Palu mezkûre arazisi dahi ba o emr-i âlî-yi şan ber-vech-i temlik Palu ümeraları ahidlerinde olmakla şerh verildi*'.
72. BOA.C.ML 338/13891, 12 Muharrem 1258 [23 February 1842].
73. The next two chapters will elaborate on the nature of the Palu begs' economic control over land.
74. BOA. İ.MVL 66/1254, 11 Rebîülevvel 1261 (20 March 1845).
75. Ateş, *Ottoman–Iranian Borderlands*, 82.
76. BOA.A.MKT.MVL 53/68, 2 Ramazan 1268 (20 June 1852).
77. Şevket Pamuk, 'The Evolution of Fiscal Institutions in the Ottoman Empire, 1500–1914', in *The Rise of Fiscal States: A Global History, 1500–1914* eds Bartolomé Yun-Casalilla, Patrick K. O'Brien and Francisco Comín Comín (Cambridge: Cambridge University Press, 2012), 325.

Chapter 4

A System in Transition: Negotiating Nobility in the Locality

One evening in 1840, a group of notables from Diyarbekir and Harput were visiting İsmail, the Diyarbekir governor Sadullah Pasha's official deputy (*kapı kethüdası*), at his residence. The guests were Şeyhoğlu İbrahim Pashazade Mehmed Beg, from one of the notable families of Diyarbekir, and his *müfti* friend, Colonel (*miralay*) Süleyman Beg of the reserve troops (*redif*) from the Çötelizade family of Harput, along with his friend, *müfti* Ömer Naîmi Efendi. Sadullah Pasha had invited them on the pretext of discussing Tanzimat-ı Hayriye. In reality, however, the governor and his deputy were trying to sound them out about the Palu begs and investigate the complaints raised about them in a recent collective petition sent from Palu.[1] With the advent of Tanzimat, the governors often got involved in local clashes of this type, especially when the begs were involved.

The need for such a meeting speaks to the local politics of negotiating the Palu begs' position, actions, and, ultimately, their noble privileges. While it is true that the imperial capital had increasing qualms about the necessity or legitimacy of the fiscal and administrative privileges of the Kurdish nobility, and only a few years after this meeting the Ottoman state organised a massive military operation to subdue Bedirkhan Beg of Cîzre, locals also had concerns about the Kurdish begs. During the early Tanzimat era, their privileges were fiercely discussed and contested among various local actors, both implicitly and explicitly. Local concerns were not based on the categorical rejection of the notion of the privilege per se, and local actors, including rival notable families, Ottoman provincial administrators, tribes, agrarian producers and Armenian *sarraf*s, considered the Kurdish nobility's position through the prism of their own interests and in a context of changing economic structures. Their discontent with the nobility's privileged position was expressed through negotiations over aspects of the local economy, including mine work, landownership, and agrarian production, surplus extraction and labour organisation. This chapter will zoom in on the locality and show how a Kurdish *hükümet*, ruled by the Kurdish nobles for three centuries, met the economic, administrative and political changes of the Ottoman Empire's long nineteenth century.

The Anxieties of Mine Work

In Ottoman official correspondence, the villagers tasked with providing charcoal to the mines were described as the *kömürkeş ahali*, which literally meant the carrier of coal, but was also a description that evoked the burdensome nature of the job and the heavy weight the bearers carried.[2] Throughout the eighteenth century and into the nineteenth, the inhabitants of Palu struggled under pressures of living so near the precious Keban and Ergani mines, with each group impacted in different ways. For the begs, the biggest concern was the mine superintendents gaining the authority to appoint the *hâkim*, which the begs saw as a violation of their established hereditary rights: 'These districts were granted to our ancestors as their hereditary estates; what do the mine superintendents have to do with these districts? We shall not let [them] appoint the *hâkim* to these sanjaks. Being a *hükümet*, henceforth we will not submit or be in the service of these mines.'[3]

The mine superintendents' extraordinary degree of power also created conflicts with other Ottoman administrators, particularly the governors. In 1802, Palu was administratively removed from the Diyarbekir province and attached to the Mine Administration in an effort to curtail the provincial governors' authority in mining areas.[4] This clash of interests between different echelons of Ottoman provincial bureaucracy and the resulting change benefited neither the Palu nobility nor the mining villages. Even as they provided mine service, the begs also had to pay cash tributes to the Diyarbekir governor, and the humbler inhabitants were doubly exploited by heavy mine work and the Diyarbekir governors' tax demands.[5] Meanwhile, even though the Ottoman state had demanded little military service from the Kurdish nobility over the course of the eighteenth century, it still occasionally asked for military support. During the Russo-Ottoman War of 1808, for example, Sultan Mustafa IV (r. 1807–8) sent an imperial decree (*ferman*) urging the *hâkim* of Palu to join the Chief Commander of Erzurum, Osman Pasha, with his military forces, stating that although there was a ceasefire, there was not yet a treaty in place.[6] A few years later, the Ottoman state wanted the Palu begs to recruit military forces to march to Baghdad to deal with a conflict.[7] In these cases, the begs, the urban elite and sometimes even the local Ottoman administrators brought up the mine responsibilities of the Palu inhabitants to demand exemption from military service.[8] The military roles of the Palu nobility had long since become obsolete, but the Porte, which needed every bit of military support against Russia, its insurmountable enemy to the east, did not see it that way.

A lucrative business for the mine superintendents and a repository of minerals that the state needed, the Keban and Ergani mines were locally and imperially significant, and the mining responsibilities of the villagers in Palu (and elsewhere near the mines) remained well into the early 1840s. Then the Ottoman state embarked upon modernising its mining technology via what it described as 'European style smelters'. These new smelters would boost copper production, but demanded sizeable amounts of charcoal from Palu.[9] However, the local population was ever more resistant to the mine-related responsibilities. The Palu begs' provision of charcoal to the mines had become more and more difficult over time and the voices of opposition were rising. In 1809, mine superintendent Ahmed Pasha appealed to the imperial state because Mehmed Tahir Beg had refused to provide all the charcoal demanded from him. He provided some, then increased the price of the as-yet-undelivered coal. This bargaining was by no means unusual, but agreement on the terms of coal provision was becoming harder to obtain. Violence was an ever-present option for the provincial Ottoman administrators, and at Ahmed Pasha's request, the centre dispatched orders threatening to imprison the beg at Diyarbekir castle if he failed to provide coal.[10]

The Palu begs' increasing qualms about providing coal was partly because of the difficulty of the work. The biggest problem was the availability of wood: almost a century of charcoal provision had been destructive to local forests, with choppers (*baltaciyan*s) having to go further outside the district's borders.[11] The need to maintain their safety in remote mountain areas had become increasingly costly, which meant more indebtedness for the Palu begs.[12] The mine work was becoming less and less profitable for the Palu nobility. Another issue was that the villagers who did the actual work resisted the begs' requests, refusing to provide coal.[13] Nonetheless, the superintendents kept hounding them for more charcoal.

By the 1820s the Palu begs' discontent with the mounting demands and diminishing profits of the mine work brought them head to head with the superintendent, and the district practically turned into a battle zone. Hacı Bekirzâde Ahmed Beg, İskender Beg, Selim Beg and Feyzullah Beg acted in concert with both the nearby İzoli tribe and the begs of the neighbouring Çarsancak area in their revolt against superintendent Salih Pasha. From the superintendent's view, what he faced was nothing less than a rebellion (*isyan*). The begs constructed twenty redoubts (*tabya*s) around the district, supported by armed tribesmen. These redoubts were the ultimate expression of the begs' reaction to the economic burden of mines, the challenge that came from the mine administrators and the growing presence of the state through ongoing correspondence, record keeping, and regulations to keep mines open and operational.

This moment also highlighted the fault lines between local elites and the Ottoman administrators. The latter were alarmed not only by the resistance to mine work but by the alliance between the Palu and Çarsancak begs and the İzoli tribe. The *müfti* of neighbouring Harput issued a *fetva* authorising the burning down of nine villages with the pretext that the villages housed 'bandits and thieves (*hayâdid and lüsûs*)' in support of the Ottoman administrators against the begs. The town was besieged by the superintendent's military forces, with clashes continuing for more than two days until superintendent Salih Pasha's forces regained complete control of the town. The redoubts were demolished, Iskender Beg and Selim Begs were arrested and Feyzullah Beg fled, aiming, according to the superintendent's report, to recruit armed forces from among the *ekrad* (the Kurds).[14] When Salih Pasha wrote the report, the begs were imprisoned in the mines, and he wanted the centre to tell him how to proceed.

The superintendent's report can be read as an effort to convince his superiors of the necessity for violent intervention. While Salih Pasha detailed the begs' actions (e.g. building the redoubts, the alliance between the *ûmera* and the tribes, etc.), he gives absolutely no indication about their motivations. The detailed report gives a clear sense of the severity of the conflict between the Ottoman officials (the superintendent, the military and even the mufti) and the local actors (the begs and the tribes); however, by portraying the begs and the Kurdish tribes as unruly bandits (by no means uncommon in Ottoman records), the superintendent pushed the local actors and their actions outside the realm of politics and towards the territory of a primordial economy of senseless violence that would justify his intervention. The imperial centre gave the superintendent complete authority. 'Since you are the governor and the ruler of that vicinity', the imperial decree said, 'instituting order in the areas under your rule whether through punishment, discipline, or accommodation (*istimalet*) is up to you.'[15]

These were signs of a system in transition. For more than half a century, mine work had restructured the area's economy and destroyed its ecology, while also exacerbating tensions between the begs and the mining villagers on the one hand, and the begs and Ottoman administrators on the other. Production was decreasing due to lack of technology, the superintendents' involvement in other economic activities, and the ongoing problems with the begs and the villagers over the provision of wood and charcoal. This coincided with the transformations taking place at the imperial centre as the Ottoman state embarked upon the centralisation of the Tanzimat programme. Together, these created a context in which to further reconsider the Kurdish nobility's place in the imperial system. Mine work had served as a shield for the Palu begs and accorded them exemptions from participating in Ottoman military campaigns, but as it became riskier and less profitable, the conflicts between the Ottoman provincial administrators and the begs intensified.

From Noble Begs to Tax Collectors

Tezyid-i vâridat, that is, increasing governmental revenues, was a fundamental pillar of the Tanzimat era.[16] The question was how to achieve this in the absence of a centralised fiscal bureaucracy that could channel the tax revenues to the central treasury without over-reliance on intermediaries. Throughout the seventeenth and eighteenth centuries, 'a large part, more than half according to most observers, of the gross tax receipts were retained by various intermediaries, most importantly the urban elites in the provinces'.[17] The Tanzimat statesmen blamed the decentralised fiscal organisation based on the delegation of tax collection to the private parties through tax farming (and life-term tax farming) for the difficulties in increasing imperial treasury revenues. Nonetheless, tax farming continued to be the main mode of collecting the tithe (*öşr*), albeit with some variations in implementation. However, recent studies show that its continuation did not mean that the system was the same as before the nineteenth century. Rather, the Ottoman state revised the tax farming system to increase its tithe revenues throughout the rest of the century.[18]

An imperial state's success in collecting taxes rested on the country's size, urban versus rural differences, the degree of monetisation and the general economic well-being of the population.[19] In addition to these material factors, there is also a societal factor. Tax collection took place in the context of relations between the state and social actors and depended on 'the bargains reached between the central administrations and various social groups, and the institutions that emerged during that process'.[20] During the Tanzimat era, the Ottoman administrators' efforts to increase tax revenues went hand in hand with state formation in the provincial periphery, that is, with policies intended to increase state capacity. The effect of these policies varied across regions depending on the type of

A System in Transition

fiscal institutions and power configurations in a given area. From its earliest days, Ottoman conquest was based less on imposing a standardised fiscal institution in newly-conquered areas than on a flexible approach that incorporated different regions at different degrees of fiscal autonomy. The *timar* system, the backbone of Ottoman fiscal-military institution in the early centuries, was not implemented uniformly across the empire. In her comparative study of the implementation of the Tanzimat programme in two provinces, Yonca Köksal emphasises 'path dependency', by which she means the way in which established administrative practices conditioned the state's approach to the reform process.[21] Thus, the question is how the Ottoman state would try to establish a viable tax-collection system in areas ruled by the Kurdish begs, given that these places had long been outside its fiscal reach.

The re-organisation of provincial bureaucracy was a key component of efforts to increase tax revenues. This involved redefining the position and role of the provincial governors (*vali*) in an effort to decrease their role in collecting tax revenues by turning them into salaried agents. There was a conscious attempt to appoint governors from the centre, as opposed to from the local areas. The establishment of the *müşirlik*s in Kurdistan was a corollary of this effort to move the governorates from being heavily entrenched in the local power structure to being a bureaucratised role with military, administrative and fiscal responsibilities. This approach, however, would prove to be futile, as we will see, with the governors remaining involved in local politics.

The Diyarbekir *Müşirliği* was established in 1838, and its governors received the title of *müşir*. Prior to this arrangement, governors had usually been appointed from among the local elites. The two previous governors of Diyarbekir, Çötelizade Hacı İbrahim Pasha and Çötelizade İshak Pasha, were from the Çötelizade dynasty from the neighbouring Harput area.[22] From the 1830s on, even before the official beginning of Tanzimat, the Ottoman administration started the practice of appointing governors from the centre. In 1834, Mehmed Reşid Pasha, who was also the superintendent of the Ma'âdin-i Hümâyun Emâneti, was appointed governor. Unlike his predecessors, he did not have local roots. He had served in high-ranking posts in different parts of the empire and was then appointed to the governorates of Sivas (1833) and Diyarbekir (1834). His successor Hafız Mehmed Pasha was also a high-ranking Ottoman statesman with no local ties.[23]

Provincial governors of Diyarbekir and Harput had a key role in the lead-up to the stripping of the Kurdish begs of their noble privileges. An important transformation took place in the long-standing tax-exempt status of the Palu begs when Hafız Pasha was governor of Diyarbekir. During his short tenure, he took issue with the existing fiscal arrangement based on the Palu begs' provision of charcoal and payment of a very small tribute that they rarely paid. The major beneficiary of this arrangement was the Mine Administration, as the begs' mining responsibilities prevailed over all other tasks the imperial state asked of them. Hafız Pasha initiated two changes. First, he dramatically increased the annual dues that the begs had to pay to the imperial centre. Second, he appointed İbrahim Beg of the Palu nobility as *voyvoda*.[24] The former targeted the Palu begs' long-lived fiscal exemptions. The latter designated the Palu begs as the proxies of the governors to collect the agrarian dues – which meant that the tax-exempt status of the begs would be compromised.

As discussed in Chapter 2, in the second half of the eighteenth century the Palu begs farmed out or leased out their hereditary lands. Despite the growing prevalence of tax farming, up until the Tanzimat the begs maintained their hereditary rights over land and their fiscal immunities vis-à-vis the imperial state. The change initiated by Hafız Pasha needs to be considered against this background. Before this, while the begs farmed out or leased out the land to clients, the imperial treasury had no claim to tithe monies because of the begs' prerogatives and exemptions. The appointment of the Palu nobles as *voyvoda* points to Hafız Pasha's desire to consolidate his grip over agrarian surplus in an area that had largely been outside the Ottoman administrators' reach. The rationale for appointing the Palu begs as tax collectors responsible for sending a portion of the agricultural dues to the central treasury was making the nobility, potentially the most recalcitrant group, into allies. By the 1830s and, especially, the 1840s, the Palu begs had acquired the titles (varyingly named *voyvoda*, tax farmer [*mültezim*] or *mütesellim*, depending on the collection system in place) used to describe tax collectors.

At this time, the de jure hereditary character of the begs was still in effect, expressed in the idea that the *hâkim* would be from the lineage of the Palu nobility. Signifying the Tanzimat state's growing concern for channelling the maximum tax revenues to the treasury, tax collection gained more significance in the appointment of the Palu begs as the *hâkim*. Their commitment to collecting the annual dues became the most important parameter for their appointment, with mine work declining in significance. This related partly to Palu's decreasing role in providing charcoal for the mines, but more to the fact that the mine superintendent's role in appointing the Palu begs was decreasing in face of the changes in provincial administration. Provincial Ottoman administrators, mainly the governors (*vali*) and the *müşir*, gained more say in the appointment processes, often by shaping, or even manipulating, the imperial centre's views of the Palu nobility.

From the perspective of the Palu nobles, these alterations did not mean an abrupt change in their fiscal exemptions and prerogatives. Even several decades after the Tanzimat changes, the begs continued to refer to the immunities granted to them in the past, emphasising the hereditary tax-exempt status of Palu in their interactions with the government. But the begs' perception of their rights notwithstanding, the tax-collector position assigned by Hafiz Pasha reconfigured the *hâkim* role in a way that made it ever more contested, particularly in rural areas. After they undertook the role of tax collector, the begs' names started to appear increasingly in petitions or cases related to tensions about this role, including over-taxation, double taxation and deepened exploitation. The Tanzimat turned the begs into the centre of gravity for the rural conflicts around the appropriation of agrarian surplus. This was the context for the emergence of Abdullah Beg, who had growing wealth from the agrarian sector, as a powerful, even quintessential Palu noble and tax collector in the early Tanzimat years.

Abdullah Beg: The Rise of a Beg as a Tax Collector

Abdullah Beg, or Abdullah Rüşdü as he signed his name, inherited his lands from his father Hacı Ali Beg around 1841.[25] In 1843, he was appointed as the *hâkim* of the emirate, remaining in this capacity until 1848.[26] His tenure occurred in a period when the Palu begs adopted the government's tax-collector role, developed closer connections with local Ottoman administrators, and served in various capacities in provincial bureaucracy.[27] He was also granted the military title of *asakir-i redif binbaşısı* (major of the reserve troops), referring to the provincial troops instituted after the establishment of the Janissary Army.[28] In 1848, Abdullah Beg was in the retinue of the *mirliva* (major-general) and *kaymakam* Veli Pasha during his visit around Mazgirt and Ovacık in the neighbouring Dersim area.[29] Abdullah Beg also held positions in the newly-established provincial Tanzimat bureaucracy. In 1845, he was appointed *müdür* of Palu,[30] and he also held the governorship (*kaymakam*) of the Hüsnümansur district.[31]

As Abdullah Beg was becoming more entrenched in the provincial bureaucracy, conflicts with the local population started emerging; not unexpectedly, villages providing for the needs of the mines were the first to complain. At the heart of the conflict was the arrangement, already mentioned, that increased the tax responsibility of Palu. The begs in turn demanded more from the tax-paying population. The mining villagers were used to being exempt from paying taxes as an incentive to maintain the provisioning of charcoal and wood, but this disappeared under the new system. In March 1843, the villagers stopped providing coal and submitted a petition to the *müşir* when he was visiting, complaining about the oppressive rule of Abdullah Beg and asking for him to be replaced.[32] Their demand fell on deaf ears, and Abdullah Beg remained *hâkim*.[33] The discontented gathered to protest this news, but the Ottoman administration had sent the *hâkim* troops. They dispersed the crowd at the cost of the lives of thirty people, an incident that the *müşir* described as an uprising (*ihtilal*), alluding to the scale of resistance.[34] Having to rely on the beg's local authority for the provision of charcoal for the mines, the Ottoman administration sided with him.

Meanwhile, there were ongoing conflicts between the Ottoman administrations to exploit the land revenues from Palu. At the heart of the conflict between the governor and mine superintendents was their competition to exploit the rural population in line with their agendas. By imposing high taxes on Palu and taking away the fiscal immunities of the mining villages, Hafiz Pasha's policies put the rural population under great pressure, even as the mine superintendent continued demanding wood and charcoal. Now that the begs were tax collectors, the rural populace saw them as the face of this new economic exploitation, even though the machinery of extraction also included the governor and the superintendent. Meanwhile, wary of coming into direct conflict with the governors, the superintendent put Abdullah Beg under the spotlight. In a letter to the Sublime Porte he blamed Abdullah Beg's treatment of the villagers for their defiance and warned the government of the potential dangers to mine production. He also implicitly criticised the provincial government for protecting Abdullah Beg and not paying attention to the people's complaints.[35]

This encounter is symptomatic of the complexities of local bargaining over the legitimacy of the begs' economic power as the Ottoman provincial administrators made increasing claims on agrarian surplus. Contrary to the ethnocentric reconstructions of the region found in many historical accounts, conflicts and alliances between different local groups were not necessarily defined by the ethnic and/or religious identification of the parties. In this case, for example, Abdullah Beg was supported by twelve Armenians who penned a petition to refute the mine superintendent's claims. They blamed a group of Muslim villagers for refusing to perform their mine duties and stated that neither the begs nor the soldiers accompanying them did any harm to the people.[36] Their support for

Abdullah Beg was most likely related to financial and economic relations they had with the begs related to tax farming and mining businesses detailed below. The support that Abdullah Beg received and the violence that resulted in deaths that came in front of the Meclis-i Vâlâ in Istanbul dissuaded the villagers from pursuing their case. The Muslim notables of the area, who described themselves as the *'ulemâ* and *suleha* and *eimme* and *hutebâ'*, penned a letter in which they promised to be guarantors for one another for the provision of coal and the payment of their taxes, and asked for forgiveness.[37]

The position of the begs was contested. We can trace the increasing discontent with the begs back to Hafiz Pasha's tax reform, both the increase in taxes and the involvement of the begs as tax collectors. This was a transitional era, from the days when mine administrators had the upper hand in local power configurations to the Tanzimat administrators' increasing power, represented in this case by the *müşir*. The villagers' refusal to provide coal to the mines was also related to the new Tanzimat arrangements.

The Palu nobles' role as tax collectors for the imperial state brought them into conflict with local tribes as well. In the past, the tribes had participated in military campaigns led by the begs. The transformation of relations between the tribes and the begs needs more research. For nineteenth-century Palu, archival records clearly show that the Tanzimat state's goal of taxing the tribes brought the begs into conflict with them. In one instance, the begs were in the countryside when a violent encounter took place with the İzoli tribe.[38] According to the begs' account, tribesmen attacked three of the begs' villages, plundered their belongings, stole their animals and burnt down one of their houses. The begs appealed to the governor of the surrounding Arapkir district, stating that they had had a long conflict with the tribe and demanding the deployment of two battalions and two cannons to punish the tribe. In his letter to the centre, the governor backed the begs, emphasising their hereditary control over Palu in the form of ownership (*ber vech-i mülkiyet*) as well as their rank of *kaymakam* (lieutenant colonel) and reserve army major. He also referred to the perceived threat from the nearby Dersim Kurds and suggested keeping the hereditary appointment process intact and not bringing anyone outside the Palu begs' descendants to be ruler of the emirate. Honouring the begs' request, the imperial state decided to deploy one battalion against what it called the 'Kurds' – by which it meant the tribes.[39] The annual dues (*emvâl-i mîrî*) of Palu were granted to Abdullah Beg with the condition that he would ensure order and security in the area.[40]

The Begs, the Sarrafs *and the Credit Nexus*

As the position of the begs was negotiated among local and imperial actors, another group becomes increasingly visible in the governmental records through their disputes with the begs: the *sarraf*s (a term translated variously as 'money-lenders', 'financiers', 'bankers' or 'creditors'). The *sarraf*s' role as guarantors and financiers made them one of the pillars of the Ottoman tax-farming system.[41] In the system of tax farming, the highest bidder won the right to collect the taxes of a defined unit of revenues (*mukataa*) for a defined time period. Would-be tax farmers had to have a credible guarantor (*kefil*) for the tax farmer's debt to the treasury. Tax farmers also had to make a down-payment, which they typically borrowed from the *sarraf*s.[42] With the transformation of term-limited tax farming into life-term tax farming (*malikâne*) in 1695, the *sarraf*s' role became even more important as the bidders had to make several other payments in addition to the initial down-payment. *Sarraf*s, who were mainly Armenian, were key players in the tax-farming system; indeed, given the lack of a banking system and the ongoing cash shortage, the *sarraf*s financed tax farming through the eighteenth century and up to the mid-nineteenth century, usually at a 20 per cent rate of interest.[43]

By the 1820s, the *sarraf*s operated in Palu, loaning money to the begs, governmental functionaries and the rural peasantry, and the names of begs start turning up in letters written by Armenian *sarraf*s, mostly based in Istanbul, seeking the state's help in collecting their debts. But the begs' borrowing pre-dated this period, as they had relied on loans from a variety of financiers, Muslim and non-Muslim, locally based or operating in the capital, going back to the late eighteenth century. In 1761, Mehmed Beg died without paying off his 420 guruş debt to Yazıcıoğlu Hüdaverdi, an Istanbul draper. In cases like this, the *sarraf* would demand payment from the debtor's estate.[44] In another instance, the former superintendent of the Keban mine, Abdüllatif, appealed to the imperial state asking for help collecting 7,500 guruş that Abdülgafur Beg from the Palu nobility had borrowed from him almost a decade earlier.[45] Prior to the nineteenth century, however, these debt–credit relations involved a variety of creditors, both Armenian and Muslim, including even Ottoman administrators from whom the begs borrowed considerable amounts of cash. The growing cash needs of the begs in face of the increasing tribute demands of the mine superintendents was the main reason for their ever-increasing indebtedness.

Mine work was one sector in which Palu begs engaged in financial transactions with the *sarraf*s. Ottoman mines generally had their own private *sarraf*s, and this was the case for the Keban and Ergani mines.⁴⁶ The provision of charcoal and other resources to the mines involved multiple groups. While the begs were intermediaries in terms of overseeing the villages responsible for provisioning the mines, they worked with other intermediaries, typically Armenian *sarraf*s who loaned money that the begs used to buy supplies;⁴⁷ occasionally the *sarraf*s provided the charcoal and other needs directly. In 1840 and 1841, Abdullah Beg and his brother İbrahim Beg worked with Mardiros, an Armenian *sarraf* from Khoşmat village in Palu, who provided charcoal, butter and other needs of the mine.⁴⁸

From the 1830s on, however, the credit relation between the begs and the *sarraf*s stemmed mainly from tax farming. During the Tanzimat period, provincial governors increasingly sought to bring the Palu begs' tithes under their grip. After Hafız Pasha's reforms, the begs were increasingly involved in the economy of tax farming, which put them into more intense contact with the Armenian *sarraf*s, who were the main financiers in this system. When the Harput governorship auctioned the tithe, the begs were the most likely bidders. But their bid was financed by Istanbul-based Armenian *sarraf*s with proxies from among the Palu based in the locality. By the 1840s, the Kurdish nobility of Palu and surrounding districts were deeply in debt. Said Beg and Necib Beg of the Palu dynasty owed 12,000 guruş to two sarrafs, Kevork and Artin.⁴⁹ In 1848, Abdullah Beg owed 3,515 guruş to a certain Hekim Yanaki.⁵⁰ The Palu begs' indebtedness to the *sarraf*s grew at unprecedented rates over the course of the next few decades; by the 1860s, Mehmed Beg and Mustafa Beg owed 176,212 guruş to *sarraf*s Boğos and Oseb.⁵¹ Mardiros, whose name will appear more frequently in the next chapters, loaned a great deal of money to the Palu begs. According to his accounts, as of 1859, Abdullah, İbrahim, Ahmed and Mehmed Begs together owed him over 400,000 guruş.⁵²

When the begs borrowed from the *sarraf*s, they put up collateral – either immovable property or revenues from other sources. For example, *sarraf* Bogos demanded that Mehmed Tahir Beg sell his *han* (inn) in Palu city centre to pay the 88,000 guruş the beg owed him. Bogos's account suggests that the sale of the *han* would not raise enough money, and he also demanded the sale of the beg's lands.⁵³ Generally, when land was put up as collateral, complications arose. In the 1820s, Yansûr Beg, Hacı Ali Beg, Hacı Devlet Şah Beg and Mehmed Tahir Beg borrowed money from a group of Armenian *sarraf*s of the Ma'âdin-i Hümâyun Emâneti, putting up the revenues from their hereditary lands as collateral.⁵⁴ Similarly, the begs put up the revenues of various villages in Palu as collateral for Mardiros's services to the mines, amounting to 102,310 guruş – which remained in arrears with Abdullah Beg's death.[55] These arrangements meant that credit–debt relations between the begs and the *sarraf*s were interconnected with land ownership and surplus extraction in the rural sector, which created conflicts between the *sarraf*s and pre-existing claims on land and its revenue. In one case, *sarraf* Kigork found himself in conflict with a certain Osman Agha, likely a leasee of the land, who refused to let him collect the revenues of the land in the Kuşçu village which Tahir and Necib Begs had put up as collateral.[56] The begs' indebtedness put not only their revenues from land but the land itself at risk – an indication of the growing commodification of land in a context of continuing hereditary claims. In cases of non-payment, the *sarraf*s would appeal the government, asking for collection of their debts through the sale of the begs' lands. When Mustafa and Mehmed Begs could not pay the 176,236 guruş back to *sarraf* Bogos, he demanded the sale of their lands and other property so he could collect his debt.[57]

The economic repercussions of the begs' indebtedness are obvious. Their control over land and other property, revenues from the agrarian sector and salaries from the government were all at risk, although we do not have systematic information about the actual extent of property loss. Beyond the economic impact, however, the begs' indebtedness to the *sarraf*s had significant implications for their hereditary privileged position. The *sarraf*s frequently appealed to the imperial state to collect their debts from the begs, and these efforts to collect their debts would bring them into conflict with the begs before government authorities. Before Tanzimat, the imperial state mainly maintained a non-interventionist approach to relations between creditors and debtors (e.g. tax farmers). When a dispute about debt payment was presented to it, the state ordered local administrators to hear the case in the local *şer'i* courts.[58] With Tanzimat, however, the Porte started to intervene more directly and to take a stricter approach to make sure the *sarraf*s' debts were collected and local administrators held responsible. After all, glitches in the tax farming system meant potential decreases in the imperial treasury's revenues. From the 1820s through the 1850s, the begs' conflicts with *sarraf*s increasingly brought them under the scrutiny of local and central Ottoman administrations, jeopardising the most important aspect of the hereditary privileges of the Palu begs: land. They were frequently asked to sell their land to pay their debts, and since their power and privileged position rested on land ownership, this would have been a major blow, both economically and symbolically. By the 1850s, the *sarraf*s and their proxies based in the locality had the economic upper hand vis-à-vis the begs. We will see later that this class of Armenian financiers would want

A System in Transition

to crown this superiority with the land ownership themselves, becoming potential buyers for the Palu begs' lands after they were confiscated by the imperial treasury.

Mounting Pressure in the Agrarian Sector

The nobility of the Palu begs was negotiated by different sectors of the local society from a variety of perspectives. At the centre of these negotiations stood land ownership and the relations of production in the agrarian sector – more specifically the confiscation of rural surplus. Under the Tanzimat, once the imperial state put its claim on the rural taxes, the relations between the begs and the central state was transformed, with serious repercussions for the production relations between the begs and the cultivators, who along with Armenian creditors, Ottoman administrators and local notables also took part in contesting the begs' position.

Before the Tanzimat changes, the begs collected a 1/5 tithe. On top of the tithe, there were also cases of begs imposing additional payments, variously called '*harmancalık*', '*sakalık*' or '*seyislik*', as cash levies.[59] While the peasantry appealed to the state to complain about such overcharging, the begs sought the imperial state's intervention when peasants failed to pay the tithe or other dues.[60] Before the Tanzimat era, these disputes between the begs and the agricultural producers do not show a systematic pattern. This might be because agrarian disputes did not regularly come before the Ottoman authorities but were instead resolved (or not) locally. For the agrarian poor, it was not easy to bring injustices to the court or seek redress from the imperial state. However, the least-known aspect of the Kurdish nobility's rule concerns their legal authority. We know that the Ottoman imperial state did appoint a judge in the *hükümet*s. Yet without information on the begs' role in administering justice, it is hard to gauge to what extent disputes between the begs and the agrarian population were solved in situ and what percentage of cases were heard at *şer'i* courts by the Ottoman-appointed *qadı*.

This caveat notwithstanding, one can observe an increase from the pre-Tanzimat era to the post-Tanzimat in terms of how many agrarian disputes were brought to the capital at the newly-established Meclis-i Vâlâ. This was partly because the new provincial Tanzimat bureaucracy increased the likelihood of local actors' looking to Ottoman administrators for justice. Agrarian producers found new institutional venues like the provincial councils where they could voice these issues. But the proliferation of cases was also related to an aggravated burden on the cultivators stemming from the Ottoman state's increased demand for agrarian dues from the begs.

Not only did Hafız Pasha increase the tax burden on the agrarian population, but also the begs reflected this increase back on them by raising the annual taxes (*varidât-ı seniyye*) up to seven times.⁶¹ In addition, the begs raised additional dues (both in kind and in cash) such as levying grains for the armed troops or charging fees to marry and the like.⁶² According to the accounts of the agrarian producers, tax farmers literally 'invented' (*bid'at*) new dues that the tax paying rural population considered unlawful (*memnu'*). The new position of the tax collector also created conflicts among the begs. When the beg appointed as the *voyvoda* went ahead and levied taxes from an area, other begs with existing claims on the same area protested, and these clashes rendered cultivators vulnerable to double- and over-taxation.

In reconfiguring its relationship with the Palu begs in this way, the Ottoman state opened the way for intensified exploitation in the rural sector. It is important to emphasise that the agrarian producers protested these new or higher taxes because they disturbed the accepted notion of the moral economy of surplus extraction which was based on the notion that anything they paid beyond the tithe was unlawful. When they said they were paying their tithe 'in accordance with the Tanzimat' in their petitions, they meant that they had the legal and moral right to make a claim about the illegitimacy of extra dues. Producers frequently complained about tax farmers (*deruhteciler*) who violated the terms of conventional conduct by imposing extra dues, showing up unexpectedly, and asking for food for themselves and fodder for their animals.⁶³ Another issue was multiple begs, beyond the *hâkim*, demanding dues. The *hâkim* had that authority, but the producers (reasonably) protested demands from other begs' that came in many guises and affected everyday practices such as authorisation for marriages or for going out of town.⁶⁴

The first episode of rural discontent related to these issues erupted only a few years after Hafız Pasha's reforms took effect. In 1840, the Porte received a group petition (*mahzar*) signed by seventy Armenian and fifteen Muslim inhabitants of Palu. The petitioners complained that İbrahim Beg, the *voyvoda*, and Hamdullah Beg, El Hâc Ali Beg, Abdullah Beg, Es-Seyyid Ahmed Beg and Ömer Beg had imposed heavy and double taxation and additional cash levies. The dispute was not minor; according to government accounts, the agrarian population had opened fire on the begs, and to suppress them the government dispatched two battalions that ended up staying for months because of the harsh winter.⁶⁵ Ironically, this increased the burden on the agrarian population, since the cost of provisioning the troops was farmed out to the *voyvoda*, who in turn levied it from the local producers.

The petitioners claimed that the exploitation and oppression were so grave that some of them had been forced to leave their homes for Istanbul to work as ship labourers. Threatening to leave their towns or villages is a common theme in petitions sent to the Ottoman administrators, a strategy to prove the severity of their situation. In this case, however, this was more than a discursive tool in the petition: when the case came before the governor of Diyarbekir and his deputy, emigration from Palu by producers was described as a genuine concern that warranted intervention. During the next few decades, the agrarian population of this area migrated not only to big cities in the west of the Empire, but all the way to the United States, a fact that should be read in the context of rural exploitation in and around Palu.[66]

Palu Begs and Sharecroppers

The transformation of how surplus is extracted is intrinsically related to the question of how labour is organised. Unfortunately, we know little about labour organisation in Ottoman Kurdistan. As a transformative period in terms of the government's approach to surplus extraction in the countryside, the Tanzimat changes offer a glimpse into alterations in labour organisation in the area, and thus into how negotiations over labour organisation were a way of contesting the legitimacy of the begs' proprietary rights over land, and by implication their noble privilege.

In 1845, when Kurdistan was incorporated into the Tanzimat programme, the government order that fixed the tithe at 1/10 came to Palu.[67] A decrease from the old tithe of 1/5, this new rule was not in the begs' best interests. Although it is not entirely possible to determine when sharecropping became the dominant labour organisation in the rural sector in Palu, it had happened by this time. Sharecropping meant that the begs provided producers with seeds, and after the tithe was paid the cultivators and the begs shared the harvest equally. In its essence, sharecropping is a surplus extraction system based on the 'leasing of land on the basis of product-sharing rents reinforced by peasant indebtedness'.[68] Beyond this, however, it is impossible to talk about one single context that led to the rise or demise of sharecropping. Different modalities of sharecropping emerged in different parts of the world in response to varying circumstances. For instance, in the post-Civil War United States, sharecropping appeared to meet the labour shortage created by the abolition of slavery, whereas in twentieth-century Spain it was a response to the shortage of cheap labour as a result of organised action by wage labourers.[69] In her comparative work on Syria and France, Sabrina Joseph points to the increasing dispossession of small land holders as the main reason for the emergence of sharecropping.[70] While in France the culprit was the rising urban merchant class and the nobility's growing encroachment over land, in Ottoman Syria it was the central Ottoman state's efforts to bring arable lands under its control to increase its revenues.[71] In both cases, however, the outcome was the stripping of small landholders from land and the growing prevalence of sharecropping and tenancy.

In Palu, the origins of sharecropping as the dominant labour form went back to changes in landholding patterns in the second half of the eighteenth century. As discussed, there was a growing fragmentation in landholding and surplus extraction patterns in this period, as the cash-strapped begs increasingly farmed out or leased out land to non-nobles. In a context defined by the monetisation of the economy, commodification of land and the increased volume of grain cultivation, tax farming and leasing contracts proliferated and the formation of *çiftlik*s – that is, the accumulation of large chunks of land by people producing grains mostly to provision the Ottoman troops during the wars with Iran also took a toll. Sharecropping's roots in Palu lie in this time, when cultivators were increasingly exploited by profit-seeking tax farmers and land holders and stripped of land.

Even though the begs relinquished surplus extraction to outside parties in the mid-nineteenth century, they maintained control over the majority of the agrarian land in Palu. The district, according to official records, 'was in the hands of the *ûmera* [emirs] in accordance with the imperial decrees', and these lands were tilled by sharecroppers [*maraba*]. A majority-Armenian sharecropping population tilled the fertile lands spreading north of the Aradzani/Murad River, to the north and north-west of town. Even before Tanzimat, the tithes changed: the 1/5 tithe shifted, as, instead of receiving seeds from the begs, the cultivators started to sow their own seeds and pay a 2/10 tithe and 1.5/10 rent.[72] This shows that producers had already been negotiating the terms of sharecropping, and hints at a relative empowerment vis-à-vis the landowning begs. While the producers wanted to sow their own seeds, the begs wanted to bring back the custom of providing seeds and appropriating half the produce in addition to the tithe. On the eve of the Tanzimat, the cultivators refused to accept seeds from the landowners, which reduced the previous 50 per cent extraction to 15 per cent. Nevertheless, the problem of forced sharecropping still loomed over the Palu countryside as the major axis of conflict between the begs and the agrarian population.

In 1845, the state fixed the tithe at 1/10 and outlawed any other extractions. Naturally, this new arrangement triggered new conflicts, and it was not long before the begs took action. In 1846, they petitioned the Harput provincial council for its annulment, stating that decreasing the tithe ratio to 1:10 would hurt them. The begs were brought for a hearing at the council – established in 1846,[73] Harput provincial council consisted of two representatives of the Armenian community, four Muslim members, the governor of the Harput province, the treasurer, the deputy judge (*naib*) and two scribes.

At this time, the begs' hereditary rights over the land were still in place. Hence, the council responded positively to the begs' appeal. Referring to their ownership of these villages and lands (*kura ve mezaraa-ı mezbure ûmera-ı mumaileyhin mülkü olduğundan*) and stating the Tanzimat's new tax regulation harmed their interests, the council authorised a reversion to the status quo ante in the following year. The council defined the old system as the one in which the begs provided seeds and the produce was split between the begs and the producers after the tithe. This meant the annulment of the cultivators' hard-won position decreasing the extraction to 15 per cent.

This, however, was not the final round. Determined to take advantage of the legal context launched by the Tanzimat programme, the producers appealed to the imperial centre, disputing the council's decision and insisting on compliance with the new tax arrangement. The imperial centre referred the case back to the provincial council to be heard again. This time, both parties were brought to the council. The cultivators came themselves along with clergy representatives including the Armenian bishop [*piskopos*], a priest [*karabaş*], and the local informants (*karye muhbirleri*) of each village. The representatives of the discontented were Armenians, laymen, and also clergy (*murahhasa*) from the Havav, Sekrat, Sığam and Kapıaçmaz [Tset] villages. The begs brought the imperial edicts, title deeds and other documents from the Ottoman state to prove their ownership rights.

The cultivators conceded that the lands, in accordance with age-old imperial decrees, were the property of the begs and agreed on the continuation of the system in which the begs provided seeds and extracted half of the harvest in addition to the 1/10 tithe. However, they demanded something in return: for every ten *kile*s of seeds that they sowed for the begs, they would sow two *kile*s for themselves on which they would pay only the tithe.[74] The resolution also affected other contested issues. Sharecropping's continuation was predicated upon the chronic indebtedness of the cultivators. In Palu, it was a widespread practice for sharecroppers to borrow cash from the begs to acquire the means of production, primarily oxen and wagons, at high interest rates. At the council, the parties agreed that the begs would waive interest on these loans. Finally, there was the issue of *noksan-ı arz*, the soil rent, usually 0.5–1.5/10, that the sharecroppers paid to the begs. It was agreed that the begs would no longer ask for this rent.

At the end, both parties consented to the terms by signing the council's minutes. While this would by no means guarantee compliance by the landowners, the encounter and the resulting agreement had an impact on the resolution or lack thereof of similar cases, becoming a reference point for similar disputes in Palu. Four years later, when other producers appealed to the Sublime Porte about over-taxation and disputes with begs, the state brought up this agreement and ordered the begs to comply with their past commitments.[75] But twenty years after this initial encounter, producers were still complaining about the begs' insistence on sharecropping. In the words of Bedros, Avadis and Toros, who petitioned the imperial centre in 1861, the begs 'were giving seeds and turning them virtually into [their] sharecroppers [*ahaliye tohum verip adeta kendilerine ortakçılık ettirmek dâiyesinde bulundukları*]'.[76] Likewise, the *noksan-ı arz* remained at the centre of rural discontent in Palu for several decades and preoccupied the imperial state, because its scale attested to the amount of surplus still in the begs' hands.

Local councils like the provincial council of Harput were the main arena for these types of negotiation over agrarian production and noble privileges. In addition to having ex officio members from the provincial bureaucracy, these councils also had representatives of the Armenian community and elected Muslim notables. Historians of the Ottoman Empire have spilled much ink on the role of local councils and state–society relations on the provincial periphery. As Safa Saracoğlu aptly states, the councils epitomised the 'emergence of a judiciary administrative sphere at the local level' in the late-nineteenth-century Ottoman Empire.[77] Similarly, Jun Akiba emphasises the function of these councils as places for the local resolution of disputes before the establishment of the civil (*nizamiye*) courts in the 1860s.[78] Beyond that function, Akiba also considers these councils in the context of the long-term history of Ottoman constitutionalism, demonstrating that the 'the experiences of the local councils prepared the ground for the Ottoman constitutional system'.[79] However, other scholars have criticised what they portray as an 'optimistic' reading, arguing that the local councils were simply the embodiment of the class interests of provincial Ottoman administrators and local notables.[80]

But this argument does not refute the fact that these councils were arenas where clashing class interests could be negotiated. Both the district council of Palu and the provincial council of Harput served as spaces of dispute resolution from as early as 1848 and in the processes leading up to the abolition of the Palu begs' propriety rights in the coming years. Underscoring the councils' roles as new spaces of conflict resolution does not suggest that they were neutral spaces of presumed legal equality. Of course, the local judiciary reflected class alliances and interests – and we will see more examples of this in the following chapters – but the cultivators sought to use this space to get the result they wanted.

In essence, what was being negotiated in this specific case was more than the terms of agrarian production. The parties also represented opposing positions on the legitimacy of the Palu begs' hereditary rights over land and whether those rights justified their claim to agrarian surplus. By negotiating the terms of sharecropping at the council, the cultivators implicitly challenged the hereditary privileges of the nobility. Their insistence on sowing their own seeds and paying only the tithe would mean eliminating the begs' entitlement to surplus appropriation, as the tithe technically went into the central coffers. Moreover, it would effectively reduce the begs' position to that of tax collectors rather than landowners – in line with the Tanzimat-era Ottoman policy towards provincial elites. The council's decision to go back to the conventional sharecropping arrangement on the grounds that the begs owned the Palu land no doubt reflected its elite composition, but this is not the end of the story. Despite the intra-elite alliance, only a few years later this same council played a key role in stripping the begs of landowning rights.

Conclusion

From the sixteenth century on, the Kurdish nobility's position, the extent of their privileges and the nature of their relationship with the Ottoman imperial state went through several phases. Their military power and role fluctuated. Their administrative authority was challenged by rival provincial elites and Ottoman administrators. At the mid-nineteenth century, the material basis of their nobility, their landownership, was challenged from top and bottom. While the Ottoman administration was taking determined steps to move hitherto untapped revenues from the Kurdish begs' control to its own grip, the Armenian financial bourgeoisie was demanding that the begs sell their lands to pay their debts. Meanwhile, the cultivators were contesting the terms of sharecropping as the Ottoman state tried to enforce a new fiscal regime that benefited the cultivators by lowering the tithe.

Channelling as much revenue as possible into the imperial treasury through new tax-collection methods was the Ottoman administration's major economic motive. Increasing agrarian tax revenues required reconfiguring relations with the provincial notables: since they could not be eliminated from the revenue extraction system, a strategic alliance had to be made. At the same time, restructuring the provincial bureaucracies created new institutional venues, mainly the local councils that became an arena in which the Kurdish begs' hereditary rights over land and surplus extraction were contested and negotiated. Sharecroppers suffering under excessive taxation and indebtedness, villagers looking to be paid by the begs and *sarraf*s who sought the imperial state's help to collect the begs' debts came to the councils seeking solutions.[81]

The decisions that came out of these councils reflected their elite composition, but that composition does not mean that other local actors were entirely powerless. Nor was the local power bloc static. As relations between the Kurdish nobility and the local Ottoman administrators – mainly the governor – soured, the latter used complaints from the agrarian population to argue for abolishing the begs' noble privileges. Of course, the councils were not rose gardens of negotiation, deliberation and accommodation, and the use of force and violent encounters increased also intensified. The Ottoman administration's new role as a claimant in surplus extraction aggravated the burden on the cultivators, while the begs becoming tax collectors damaged their relations with the local population.

The complaints of the petitioners attest to the intensification of violence at other levels. For example, when the begs found out that they had reached out to the state, they bastinadoed them to death. There were cases of the local population resisting the outrageous tax demands by opening fire. Furthermore, the Ottoman provincial administrators became more and more involved in local affairs and took sides in local conflicts. Administrators were increasingly willing to dispatch military force to support the begs in their attempts to extract surplus, which meant not only that violence increased, but also that provincial society was increasingly militarised, with the Ottoman troops often deployed for extended periods. Not only was this potentially dangerous, it was also costly, as the local population had to contribute to their provisioning.

These local conflicts over the terms of agrarian surplus brought the Palu begs, specifically Abdullah Beg, more and more to the attention of the imperial state. One key incident occurred at Weşin, where a violent encounter between him and the villagers led to him being brought before the Meclis-i Vâlâ' by the villagers and the governors – who were on bad terms with Abdullah Beg. This, as we will see, opened the door for the Ottoman administration to intervene in the Palu nobility's hereditary rights.

Notes

1. BOA.İ.MVL 9/133 Document #4, c. 1839.
2. I thank my colleague Hadi Hosainy for his help in understanding the meaning of the suffix *-keş* in Persian.
3. BOA.AE.SABH I 23/1902 29 Zilhicce 1199 [2 November 1785]. 'Bu kazalar ecdadımıza yurtluk ve ocaklık ihsan olunmuştur. Maden emininin bu kazalarda ne alâkası vardır. Elviye-i mezkureye hâkim nasb ettirmeyiz. Bizler dahi hükümet kabulüyle Ma'âdin-i Hümâyun Emâneti tarafında fimaba'd hizmet ve itaat etmeyiz.'
4. BOA.C.DRB 14/6929 Şaban 1222 [12 October 1807].
5. BOA.C.DRB 14/692 9 Şaban 1222 [12 October 1807].
6. BOA.TS.MA.e 444/33 29 Muharrem 1223 [27 March 1808].
7. BOA.TA.MA.e 312/60 13 Muharrem 1228 [16 January 1813].
8. BOA.TA.MA.e 498/29 11 Safer 1222 [20 April 1807]; BOA.HAT 1511/10 20 Cemâziyelâhir 1223 [13 August 1808]; BOA.TS.MA.e 478/1 29 Zilhicce 1226 [14 January 1812]; BOA.TS.MA.e 312/60 13 Muharrem 1328 [16 January 1813].
9. BOA.TS.MA.e 1213/58 14 Receb 1260 [30 July 1844].
10. BOA.C.DRB 33/1617, 19 Rebîülevvel 1224 [4 May 1809].
11. In the 1830s the nearest forest which could provide wood to the Ergani mine was at a twelve-hour distance. Selçuk Dursun, 'Forest and the State: History of Forestry and Forest Administration in the Ottoman Empire' (Ph.D. dissertation, Sabancı University, 2007), 175.
12. BOA.C.DRB 28/1385 18 Şevval 1249 [28 February 1834]. More than a century of mining had devastating effects on the ecology of the region, chiefly upon deforestation. In his study of Ottoman forestry, Dursun notes that by the 1830s, most of the areas around the mines either completely lacked wood or had overcut forests with no efforts towards regeneration. Dursun, 175–6.
13. BOA.C.DH 254/12658 29 Cemâziyelâhir 1259 [27 July 1848].
14. BOA.HAT 508/24975 2 Zilhicce 1240 [18 July 1825].
15. BOA.HAT 508/24975 2 Zilhicce 1240 [18 July 1825].
16. Abdullatif Şener, *Tanzimat Dönemi Osmanlı Vergi Sistemi* (Istanbul: İşaret Yayınları, 1990), 201.
17. Şevket Pamuk, 'Fiscal Centralisation and the Rise of the Modern State in the Ottoman Empire', *The Medieval History Journal* 17, no. 1 (1 April 2014): 5.
18. Özbek, 'Tax Farming in the Nineteenth-Century Ottoman Empire'.
19. Pamuk, 'Fiscal Centralisation and the Rise of the Modern State in the Ottoman Empire', 4.
20. Pamuk, 4.
21. Köksal, *The Ottoman Empire in the Tanzimat Era*, 14.
22. Yılmazçelik, 'Osmanlı Hakimiyeti Süresince Diyarbakır Eyaleti Valileri (1516–1838)', 251.
23. Hafız Mehmed Pasha served as the governor of the Diyarbekir province between 1836 and 1839. Yılmazçelik, 266.

24. BOA.İ.MVL 9/133 Document # 4, 1256 [1840].
25. BOA.İ.MVL 237/8388 1 Şevvâl 1257 [14 November 1841].
26. BOA.MVL 1/7 Document # 6, 27 Rebîülâhir 1259 [28 May 1843].
27. He enjoyed official titles and recognition given by the Ottoman imperial state, including that of the *rikâb-ı hümayun kapıcıbaşısı*. In Ottoman palace bureaucracy, this position originally referred to the person who accompanied the sultan on foot as he rode his horse. Its holders seem to have accompanied military and civilian Ottoman officials during their visits, making sure their logistical needs were met. The title became widely distributed over the eighteenth century and was even given to the provincial notables. Abdülkadir Özcan, 'Kapıcı', in *TDV İslâm Ansiklopedisi* (İstanbul: Türkiye Diyanet Vakfı, 2001). https://islamansiklopedisi.org.tr/kapici (Last accessed 1 March 2021).
28. Abdülkadir Özcan, 'Redif', in *TDV İslâm Ansiklopedisi* (İstanbul: Türkiye Diyanet Vakfı, 2007). https://islamansiklopedisi.org.tr/redif--ordu (Last accessed 20 January 2021).
29. BOA.C.AS 990/43287 Document # 7 5 Zilkade 1264 (3 October 1848). He signed his letter 'serbevâbbin-i rikâb-ı şâhâne'.
30. BOA.İ.MVL 2/60, 9 Şaban 1264 [13 Ağustos 1848].
31. BOA.MVL 131/3491, 9 Şevval 1264 [8 September 1845].
32. BOA.MVL 1/7 Document # 6, 27 Rebîülâhir 1259 [28 May 1843].
33. BOA.MVL 1/7 Document # 6, 25 Rebîülâhir 1259 [25 May 1843].
34. BOA.MVL 1/7 Document # 6, 25 Rebîülâhir 1259 [25 May 1843].
35. BOA.MVL 1/7 Document # 7, 27 Rebîülâhir 1259 [28 May 1843].
36. BOA.MVL 1/7 Document # 3, n.d.
37. BOA.MVL 1/7 Document # 5, n.d.
38. Izol/Izoli was a sizeable nomadic tribe spread across a large area from the south of Diyarbekir to the north of the eastern Euphrates.
39. BOA.A.MKT 16/82, 8 Ramazan 1260 [21 September 1844].
40. BOA.A.MKT 16/82, 8 Ramazan 1260 [21 September 1844].
41. For a study on *sarraf*s and their roles as money lenders, see Onnik Jamgocyan, *Osmanlı İmparatorluğu'nda Sarraflık – Rumlar, Museviler, Frenkler, Ermeniler* (İstanbul: Yapi Kredi Yayinlari, 2017), 80–91. One of the wealthiest Armenian *sarraf*s of the late Ottoman Empire was Mıgırdiç Cezayirliyan. His career ended with the Ottoman state's confiscation of his wealth. Mustafa Erdem Kabadayı, 'Mkrdich Cezayirliyan or the Sharp Rise and Sudden Fall of an Ottoman Entrepreneur', in *Merchants in the Ottoman Empire*, 2008, 281–99.
42. Nuran Koyuncu, 'Osmanlı Devleti'nde Sarrafların Mültezimlere Kefilliği', *İnönü Üniversitesi Hukuk Fakültesi Dergisi* 5, no. 1 (2014): 308.
43. Araks Sahiner, 'The Sarrafs of Istanbul: Financiers of the Empire' (MA thesis, Istanbul: Boğaziçi University, 1995), 40–4. In the Ottoman Empire, Greeks, Jews and Armenians constituted the majority of the *sarraf*s. As Ali Yaycıoğlı states, rather than ethnic or religious factors, this was related to these groups' active connections with the trade and financial networks in the Mediterranean basin, Europe and Asia. Ali Yaycıoğlu, 'Perdenin Arkasındakiler: Osmanlı

İmparatorluğunda Sarraflar ve Finans Ağları Üzerine Bir Deneme', *Journal of Turkish Studies* (Türklük Bilgisi Araştırmaları): Özer Ergenç Armağanı: *Festschrift in Honor of Özer Ergenç*, vol. 51 (December), 375–96.

44. Diyarbekir Ahkâm Defterleri, 1 Numaralı Defter, Hüküm# 766: 484, Evâsit-i Receb 1174 [c. 19 February 1761].
45. Diyarbekir Ahkâm Defterleri, 1 Numaralı Defter, Hüküm# 104: 66, Evâil-i Zilkade 1168 [c. 15 August 1755].
46. Sahiner, 'The Sarrafs of Istanbul', 25.
47. BOA.C.DRB 36/1758 2 Rebîülâhir 1272 [15 April 1812].
48. BOA.A.MKT 368/9 7 Safer 1276 [9 Ağustos 1859].
49. Examples are abundant. In 1845, Said Beg of the Eğil dynasty owed 45,000 guruş and Mehmet Beg 46,000. Abdürrahim Beg of the Çemişgezek dynasty owed 45,000 guruş. BOA.A.MKT 9/48 29 Zilhicce 1260 [9 January 1845] (date estimated). These *sarraf*s belonged to Anadolu Kumpanyası, the official professional association of *sarraf*s established in 1842. Hagop Barsoumian, 'The Dual Role of the Armenian Amira Class within the Ottoman Government and the Armenian Millet (1750–1850)', in *Christians and Jews in the Ottoman Empire: The Functioning of a Plural Society*, eds Braude Benjamin and Bernard Lewis. (Teaneck: Holmes & Meier, 1982), 174.
50. These *sarraf*s based in Istanbul usually would use local conduits in their dealings and Hekim Yanaki (?) was asking for this amount to be paid to a certain Bizo (Pizo?), a tailor in Palu who represented him. BOA.A.DVN 161/14 1 Safer 1265 [27 November 1848] The date is an estimate.
51. BAO.A.MKT.DV 185/1 14 Ramazan 1277 [26 March 1865].
52. BOA.A.MKT 146/24 16 Rebîülâhir 1276 [12 November 1859]. In 1845, the salary of the Diyarbekir *müşir* was 75,000 *kuruş*. BOA.İ.DH 97/4852, 14 Muharrem 1261 (23 January 1845). Between 1840 and 1847, the average price of bread in Diyarbekir was c. 17–46 *para*s (1 kuruş = 40 *para*s). Yılmazçelik (1995), 326.
53. BOA.MVL 430/159 5 Cemâziyelevvel 1280 [18 October 1853]. In the 1840s, the sale price of one shop in the Ali Pasha Han was around 1,000 guruş. Again in Diyarbekir, a fairly large house was sold for 8,000 guruş. Put in a comparative perspective with these two examples, it becomes clear that the begs owed outrageous amounts of money to the *sarraf*s. İbrahim Yılmazçelik, 332–3.
54. BOA.TS.MA.e 1221/2 9 Şaban 1236 [12 May 1821].
55. BOA.A.MKT 368/9 7 Safer 1276 [9 Ağustos 1859].
56. BOA.A.MKT.DV 108/88 26 Şaban 1273 [21 April 1857].
57. BOA.A.MKT.DV 145/41 26 Rebîülâhir 1276 [22 November 1859].
58. These records are found in *ahkâm* registers that contain the responses of the imperial centre to the petitions sent from the provinces.
59. Diyarbekir Ahkâm Defterleri, 1 Numaralı Defter, Hüküm# 189: 100, Evâhir-i Receb 1174 [c. 12 August 1743].
60. For the former, see *Diyarbekir Ahkâm Defterleri*, 1 Numaralı Defter, Hüküm# 189: 100, Evâhir-i Receb 1174 [c. 12 August 1743]; for the latter, see, for

example, *Diyarbekir Ahkâm Defterleri*, 1 Numaralı Defter, Hüküm# 170: 89–90, Evâsıt-ı Receb 1156 [c. 7 July 1743].
61. BOA.İ.MVL 9/133 Document # 2, no date.
62. BOA.İ.MVL 9/133 Document # 1, 15 Receb 1256 [12 September 1840] (date estimated).
63. BOA.A.MKT.DV 29/64, 26 Rebîülevvel 1266, [9 February 1850].
64. BOA.C.ADL 78/4675, 29 Zilhicce 1255 [4 March 1840]. The date is an estimate.
65. BOA.İ.MVL 9/133 Document # 4, 1256 [1840]. The date is an estimate.
66. For a study of the Armenian migration from the neighbouring Harput area, see David Gutman, *The Politics of Armenian Migration to North America, 1885–1915: Migrants, Smugglers and Dubious Citizens* (Edinburgh: Edinburgh University Press, 2019).
67. BOA.İ.MVL 237/8388 Document # 3 9 Rebîülevvel 1264 [14 February 1848].
68. R. Pearce, 'Sharecropping: Towards a Marxist View', *The Journal of Peasant Studies* 10, nos 2–3 (1January 1983): 41.
69. Pearce, 41–3.
70. Sabrina Joseph, 'The Legal Status of Tenants and Sharecroppers in Seventeenth- and Eighteenth-Century France and Ottoman Syria', *Rural History* 18, no. 1 (April 2007): 24.
71. Joseph, 24.
72. BOA.İ.MVL 237/8388 9 Rebîülevvel 1264 [14 February 1848].
73. Aksın, *19. yüzyılda Harput*, 59.
74. A unit of measurement used for grains, it had different values in different parts of the empire. In Palu, one *kile* equalled 368 *okka*s. One *okka* equalled 1.282 grams. See Taşkın, 'Osmanlı Devletinde Kullanılan Ölçü ve Tartı Birimleri', 67.
75. BOA.İ.MVL 237/8388, 9 Rebîülevvel 1264 [14 February 1848].
76. BOA.A.MKT.UM 463/6 2 Ramazan 1277 [14 March 1861].
77. M. Safa Saraçoğlu, 'Some Aspects of Ottoman Governmentality at the Local Level: The Judicio-Administrative Sphere of the Vidin County in the 1860s and 1870s', *Ab Imperio 2008*, no. 2 (2008): 224.
78. Akiba, 'The Local Councils as the Origin of the Parliamentary System in the Ottoman Empire', 179.
79. Akiba, 177.
80. Nadir Özbek, *İmparatorluğun bedeli: Osmanlı'da vergi, siyaset ve toplumsal adalet (1839–1908)* (Istanbul: Boğaziçi Üniversitesi Yayınevi, 2015), 34.
81. In one such case, complaining about the unpaid labour that the begs imposed on them, the discontented specifically demanded to confront the begs at Harput council in their petition, BOA.MVL 83/37 13 Rebîülevvel 1266 [27 January 1850]. The date is an estimate.

Chapter 5

The Weşin Incident: the Spark that Burnt a Village ... and the Arsonist

In the winter of 1848, an architect named Agop, an appraiser (*muhammin*) named Hacı Mehmed Agha and an official named Ali Agha were sent by the Palu district council to Weşin village. Along with another official sent by the Harput provincial council, they were tasked with determining the damage caused by the violent encounter between Abdullah Beg and village inhabitants in the late summer.[1] It was a tedious job. They had to examine the destruction caused by an apparently mysterious fire that had burnt down houses, granaries, trees, orchards and vineyards. The crew came up with a detailed list of who had lost what, together with the monetary value of each item, with the total loss amounting to 58,180 guruş.[2] Around this time, Abdullah Beg was writing to the imperial centre from his prison room in the Harput council to complain about the conditions in which he was being held and to request a transfer to the imperial capital.[3] How did Abdullah Beg, the descendant of the Palu nobility and holder of several positions in the provincial bureaucracy, end up in a cell? It was all connected to what happened in Weşin on that hot summer day of Eid el Fitr in 1848.

Located eighteen miles south-east of Palu's centre, Weşin was one of the exclusively Muslim settlements of the emirate. The population was (and is) Zaza-speaking and of Sunni orientation. The 1841 population register designated it as a *nahiye* (sub-district) consisting of twenty-seven villages. Notwithstanding this designation, however, both locals and the Ottoman bureaucracy called it a village. Either way, it was a sizeable settlement of around 140 households mostly living in adobe houses scattered in and around hills studded with tall poplar trees.[4] Weşin's inhabitants subsisted primarily on animal husbandry and produced substantial amounts of dairy – as seen from the sizeable amount of clarified butter they were expected to pay as taxes to Abdullah Beg. The poplar trees were another

The Kurdish Nobility in the Ottoman Empire

source of economic value; the wood's soft texture and straight shape made it suitable for construction and furniture.[5] As an observer stated, 'poplar trees [were] to be found in all the stands of timber in the Palu district, and the villagers [took] great care of their growth'.[6] Poplar wood was also used to produce charcoal, a vital energy source for the mining industry. Additionally, due to its position on the mountain slopes, Weşin, like many other parts of Palu, was abundant in vineyards.

All this made Weşin wealthy, which explains why Abdullah Beg journeyed for miles on the morning of Eid-el Fitr in 1848 to collect three years of back taxes. Little did he know that this encounter would result in his exile to Tekirdağ, almost 900 miles away from his dominions, followed by his death and then the death of the Kurdish nobility's hereditary rights over Palu. This violent moment between Abdullah Beg and the inhabitants of the Weşin village led to the annulling of the de jure prerogatives of the Palu nobility that they had held for three centuries, across vastly changed economic, military and political conditions.

This chapter focuses on the Weşin incident as a moment of the villagers' refusal to comply with the tax demands of the Tanzimat regime and recognise Abdullah Beg's authority to extract taxes from them. Their efforts, coupled with those of the governor, made their case the subject of first a local legal process and then another one in the imperial capital. The chapter will look at the strategies, discourses and actions of the Weşin inhabitants in their legal struggle, particularly the ways in which they were able to present their accounts of that tragic day in Weşin and how

Figure 5.1 A contemporary view from Weşin – now called Erimli – a sub-district (belde) of the Elazığ province. Photo by Yaşar Gündoğan, 2019

this became a contest between competing discourses about the legitimacy of the Kurdish nobility's administrative and fiscal authority and land ownership and the nature and limits of the Ottoman state's power. This analysis adds a complex social history perspective to the historiography of Kurdistan, which has tended to centre on the elite.[7]

The Incident: What Really Happened in Weşin?

In his seminal work on the implementation of the Tanzimat policies in Bulgaria, Halil İnalcik makes a seemingly obvious but critical remark: the Gülhane Decree launching the Tanzimat was, he says, not a dead document. To the contrary: it triggered large-scale movements across the empire. Once the *ferman* was announced in the provinces, 'every group started to give the reforms its own interpretation'.[8] The Tanzimat's clauses about the abolition of tax farming, the establishment of tax equity and the abolition of corvée emboldened the cultivators against their local landlords. There were peasant uprisings in the Balkans, Anatolia and the Arab provinces. Yet in the vast Ottoman imperial geography, the impact of the Tanzimat's fiscal policies on the rural areas varied widely. The peasants might have been exploited across the Empire, but their motivations and demands were not identical. And even where there were no rural uprisings, the Tanzimat's policies on land and taxation still affected the perceptions, responses and actions of the rural population. A more nuanced understanding of these influences requires an eye on small-scale, seemingly more mundane encounters between a variety of local actors as new terms of surplus extraction made inroads into the locality. The question that emerges from such an inquiry is, what do these more mundane, small-scale and potentially less inconsequential moments in rural settings mean for understanding the impact of the Tanzimat on rural populations in the Ottoman periphery?

Recent studies on the Tanzimat era have complicated older approaches to rural populations that see them either as passive recipients of external forces or irrational reactionaries.[9] Nuanced readings let us see that resistance to Tanzimat in various forms and scales, on the one hand, and compliance with it and adoption of its institutional structures, discourses and ideological tenets on the other, are not mutually exclusive processes. Resistance and compliance both took shape in a context defined by the rural populations' perceptions of the Tanzimat changes and their re-interpretation of its discourses and institutional channels in strategic ways. Rural responses to institutional and fiscal re-organisation at the provincial level did not necessarily oscillate between outright reaction and passive submission, and the Weşin incident reveals how resistance to the Tanzimat policies can be concurrent with the strategic deployment of its institutional structures.

The violent encounter in Weşin triggered a long and convoluted legal case that was eventually transferred to the capital, where it came in front of the *Meclis-i Vâlâ-i Ahkâm-i Adliye* (Ottoman Supreme Council of Judiciary Ordinances). Before this, however, local actors including the begs, the villagers and provincial Ottoman administrators sought to settle the case at the local level. Immediately after the incident, the Harput provincial council ordered Abdullah Beg jailed. The villagers sent a petition to the Harput governor – which Abdullah Beg called slanderous.[10] It is worth highlighting here that the villagers did not appeal first to the district council of Palu or the local court, but to the governor of the Harput province. Wittingly or not, the inhabitants of Weşin were trying to avoid being ensnared in local power relations by appealing to what they considered a higher authority. Abdullah Beg and the representatives of the village, Mullah İsmail and Mehmed, were brought to the council for investigation,[11] and the local council became a judiciary platform with a tacit claim to impartiality. The confrontation at the council was a spectacular moment that symbolically shattered hierarchies between the begs and the villagers. A descendant of the Palu nobility, who for three centuries had held the legal right to rule the district, had to defend himself in a courtroom. Even as the legitimacy of the Palu nobility's authority was being contested, this moment stood as testimony to its ongoing diminishment.

Throughout the investigative process, Abdullah Beg, having given up on any help from local channels, wrote to the Sultan, the Grand Vizier and the Meclis-i Vâlâ to defend himself. In his account, Weşin and the surrounding villages owed 15,000 guruş in back taxes. Despite his orders and those of the district council, the villagers had refused to fulfil their tax obligations. Finally, they promised to pay their taxes to an official sent there: it was then that, after having received authorisation from the provincial council of Harput, Abdullah Beg took off on the twenty-seventh day of Ramazan with twenty cavalrymen and 150 infantrymen. At the neighbouring Bağın village, he picked up Mehmed Beg, a Bağın notable, and they arrived in Weşin on the first day of Eid. As they approached, villagers opened fire, killing one man from Abdullah Beg's group. Hesitant to retaliate, Abdullah Beg sent Tahir Agha of Karaçor, Boz Agha of Weşin and other aghas to calm the villagers down, to no avail. Even before they had retreated, Abdulllah Beg said, the villagers opened fire again from rooftops and inside houses, killing four people and wounding eight. In the mayhem, one horse was killed and two wounded. By 1:00 a.m., Abdullah Beg and his forces had retreated to the neighbouring Srin village.

Abdullah Beg's account was corroborated by the Palu district council, which was actively involved in the investigative process. The council had an Armenian member, two Muslim members, the governor of the district (*müdür*), the *müfti* and the deputy judge (*naib*). The council got involved fairly early: in early September, soon after the incident, it issued a report describing what had happened (or what it thought had happened) in Weşin. In its tone and overall narration, the report echoed Abdullah Beg's statements, blaming what had happened in Weşin on its inhabitants' opposition (*muhalefet*) to and obstruction of (*mümanaat*) the collection of the back taxes. The report insisted that Abdullah Beg had gone to the village that day because the villagers had promised to pay their dues and that the villagers had opened fire when Abdullah Beg approached the village – because, it said, of their natural malignancy (*habaset*) and treachery (*hıyanet*). The council's pro-Abdullah Beg position was not a surprise. After all, it was based in Palu, which, as the report mentioned, 'had been the livelihood [*nanpare*] of the begs from time immemorial [*min el kadim*] with an imperial title deed [*mülkname-i hümayûn*]'.[12] The council also functioned as a conduit for procedural details of the investigation, such as corresponding with the Harput council and appointing and confirming the village representatives.[13]

In the villagers' account, things did not happen in quite the way Abdullah Beg recounted:

> [We] the poor inhabitants of the Weşin village … have had no fault and showed no carelessness in paying our taxes in good time. However, this past month of Ramadan, when we gathered at the village mosque to perform Eid el Fitr prayer, one of the Palu begs, named Abdullah Beg, attacked our village with his nine hundred men, unlawfully demanding five thousand *vukiyye*[14] of purified butter from your slaves. They burnt down our houses, stole our goods, and killed three people. As we scattered in horror, some women and kids were crushed and badly injured … The value of our properties and goods which were destroyed amounts to 369,000 guruş.[15]

Not only were the big pictures different, the accounts had different details. For example, Abdullah Beg stated that the villagers owed him 15,000 guruş, while the villagers repeatedly mentioned that he planned to collect a sizeable amount of clarified butter. In Abdullah Beg's account, he had come to the village with about 150 men, whereas in different accounts the villagers gave at different times the number varied from 600 to 900.

Notwithstanding the inconsistent, at times conflicting, narratives, there were essentially three issues that needed to be investigated and resolved. The first concerned the casualties and who the culprit was. From the Ottoman state's perspective, this was at the heart of the issue. The second concerned the fire that caused immense damage to the village – who set it, and how (or if) the villagers would be compensated. Last was the question of back taxes, Abdullah Beg's right to collect them, and the villagers' refusal to pay their debt.

In their letters and testimonies, both the villagers and Abdullah Beg tried to prove they had not fired the first bullet. Abdullah Beg insisted that he had not used violence, had sought to negotiate with the villagers by sending respectable notables, and had avoided retaliation even when the villagers opened fire. He even claimed that all the casualties were on his side, since the villagers used rifles while remaining safe inside their houses. As he minimised his role in the violence, Abdullah Beg sought to portray the villagers as irrational and inherently prone to violence. Significantly, he used the term '*ekrad*' (plural for Kurd) to describe them – the same language Ottoman administrators used to describe the Kurdish tribes in the region, a term replete with negative stereotypes.[16]

While Abdullah Beg's detailed description sounded more carefully crafted, the villagers' account was more concise. They basically stated that Abdullah Beg and his men attacked them while the community was at the mosque and that, in the resultant commotion, they had fled to the surrounding mountains to save their lives.[17] Nowhere did they mention anything about firing on Abdullah Beg and no one in the investigative process ever confirmed or denied it. The villagers totally avoided the question of whether they fired bullets on Abdullah Beg and his men.

The second issue concerned the burning down of houses – who did it, what was the extent of the damage, and how (or if) reparations would be made. The villagers consistently stated that the day after the shooting, Abdullah Beg and his men came to the abandoned village, plundered the villagers' belongings and set the houses on fire,[18] all of which Abdullah Beg denied. He stated that after the incident, he retreated to the neighbouring Srin village, and six days after this the villagers repented and withdrew to Eğil, fifty miles south-east of Palu. According to Abdullah Beg, the fire had been set by the Karabegan tribe, who had a long-standing enmity with Weşin. Abdullah Beg added that, having heard news of fire, he had taken the two-hour journey from Srin to Weşin to put it out.[19]

The last issue was the taxes. According to Abdullah Beg, the villagers had refused to pay their tithe and other taxes for the past three years. He had been unable to deal with the matter earlier because his tenure

The Weşin Incident

as the governor of the Hüsnumansur sanjak meant he was away from Palu and had no one to take care of his business.[20] Upon his return, he investigated the records, determined the amount the village owed and sought to convince the villagers to pay. As we have seen, Abdullah Beg stated that only after receiving an affirmative answer from the villagers did he set out to collect the dues.[21] The villagers' narrative said only that they had paid their taxes in a timely manner and that Abdullah Beg 'unfairly demanded five thousand *vukiyye* of purified butter' from them.[22]

It is not surprising that the plaintiff and the defendant provided contradictory accounts. What is more noteworthy is that the incident became the subject of a comprehensive investigative process. Local (district and provincial) councils of the Tanzimat became key legal arenas in which the parties sought justice. Understanding their roles provides insights into newly-established Tanzimat institutions and new administrators (mainly the governor) in Kurdistan in a case involving a beg.

As mentioned, in 1848, there was a provincial council in Harput. As we saw in the dispute between the begs and the Armenian sharecroppers a few years back, the council functioned like a court. It heard both parties, then reached a decision that recognised the Palu begs' hereditary land rights, while also making some concessions to the sharecroppers. In the Weşin case, however, the council was more antagonistic towards Abdullah Beg. Under the leadership of the governor, in fact, it played a key role in pushing the administrators in the capital towards abolishing the begs' hereditary privileges altogether. When the villagers petitioned for an investigation two months after the incident, the council called Abdullah Beg and the representative of the village, Molla İsmail, before it for *muvacehe* (confrontation). At that time, eleven members were present: the governor, treasurer (*defterdar*), chief scribe (*katib-i mal*), judge, deputy judge, four Muslim members, and two Armenian ones.[23]

While the Council agreed that Abdullah Beg had the right to collect the unpaid taxes of Weşin villagers, it wanted to investigate the attack further. The governor and the Harput council knew that Abdullah Beg was planning to go to the village prior to the incident, as he had appealed to them about the unpaid tithe. In this way, Abdullah Beg sought official approval for his acts. In response, the Harput provincial council dispatched a decree (*buyruldu*) to the district council of Palu regarding the village's unpaid taxes and assigned an official to accompany Abdullah Beg.[24] Thus, the Harput governor had, he contended, entrusted the Palu council with overseeing Abdullah Beg's tax collection. The governor also said that Abdullah Beg took action immediately; instead of waiting for the council to discuss the issue, he went to the village with his armed men. In what seems like an attempt to absolve himself of any responsibility, the governor repeatedly emphasised that Abdullah Beg had gone to Weşin on his own accord (*hôd be hôd*).[25] The issue of whether Abdullah Beg had sought the governor's approval before going to Weşin and the fact that the governor had issued a decree transformed the latter's position from being just that of an arbitrator to having a role in the dispute. In his testimony, Abdullah Beg stated that an earlier dispute between himself and the governor had prompted this 'slander' about burning the village.[26] The dispute was over two Circassian slaves, one male and one female, whom the governor attempted to purchase but, in the end, they were bought by Abdullah Beg. Abdullah Beg claimed that if he had agreed to give the slaves to the governor, then the governor would not have accused him of the Weşin village attack. This added another controversy to the issue. The question of why the governor demanded these slaves from Abdullah Beg, either as a gift or for some other reason, was also considered a problem to be interrogated by the Supreme Council.[27]

Abdullah Beg admitted that he had gone to Weşin, but consistently denied burning the village.[28] According to the Harput council's account, two men outside the village had testified that Abdullah Beg had burnt the village down and killed three people.[29] This was when the council sought expert opinion on the matter and dispatched appraiser Hacı Mehmed Agha and architect Agop to the village to conduct an on-site investigation.[30] The experts attested to the burning down of sixty-five houses. Throughout the investigation, the two councils, Harput (province) and Palu (district), interrogated the parties, investigated the crime scene, imprisoned Abdullah Beg, communicated their findings to higher authorities and demanded further investigation. They were not just neutral extensions of the central state's authority or passive observers of imperial policies; rather, they played a key role in addressing the local politics of villagers battling a beg.

At the same time, it is evident from the councils' discourses that while the Palu district council sided with Abdullah Beg, the provincial council in Harput reflected the governor's position. Harput governor Mustafa Sabri was determined to bring the issue to the central authorities in Istanbul. While the case was being discussed locally in the provincial and district councils, the governor and the district treasurer sent the Ottoman Meclis-i Vâlâ in Istanbul a detailed account of the case. In this way, the case entered the sphere of the central Ottoman state and the parties were summoned to the capital to be interrogated in the Meclis-i Vâlâ, which meant that the Weşin case would be discussed in the context of the broader question of what to do with the hereditary estates (*yurtluk-ocaklık*) of the Kurdish begs.

The Weşin Incident

Mustafa Sabri Pasha: The Governor, the Nobility and the Tanzimat State

The governor, as stated, had a complicated position in the Weşin incident. Not surprisingly, in the letter he wrote to the Meclis-i Vâlâ, Mustafa Sabri Pasha was trying to prove that Abdullah Beg had acted on his own initiative. Abdullah Beg, the governor claimed, did not pay attention and remained indifferent to his warnings to approach the issue 'sensibly' (*üslûb-ı hâkimane*) and solve it through consultation.[31] Throughout the letter, the governor used negative, even derogatory, adjectives to describe Abdullah Beg. Referring to Abdullah Beg's 'misdeed' (*isâet*) and 'disgrace' (*fazahat*), the governor suggested that exile was the appropriate punishment. He stressed the parts of Abdullah Beg's acts that violated the new Tanzimat regulations, claiming that Abdullah Beg had disobeyed Tanzimat orders, specifically the imperial order (*irade*) that prohibited tax collectors from demanding anything from agricultural producers other than the tithe. Moreover, he claimed that Abdullah Beg had previously committed fraud by concealing some of his property during a property survey.

Regardless of the truth of these charges, what is notable here is the governor's effort to convince the imperial state to destroy the material and political basis of the Palu nobility's authority. He wanted to dismiss the begs from the post of *müdür* (district governor); however, he knew that it would be difficult to make dramatic changes in the socio-economic structure. Referring to the 'largeness' (*cesamet*) of the (Palu) district, and the prevalence of 'Kurds and tribes' (*ekrad* and *aşair*), the governor asked the state to dispatch a battalion of regular (*nizamiye*) soldiers, or 700–800 irregular troops, to the district.[32] Later, we will see that the *müdür* appointment was highly contentious in the locality, standing at the centre of discussions about how to curtail the Palu begs' authority.[33] The other main focus of the governor's plan concerned the begs' access to Palu's agrarian dues on land in the form of taxes, mainly the tithe. Since the begs had Palu as *yurtluk-ocaklık*, that is, as their hereditary property, the tax revenues (tithes) of the Palu lands were under the begs' control, and Mustafa Sabri claimed that the begs oppressed the inhabitants both overtly and covertly. Bringing the lands under the control of the central treasury would not only 'rescue the inhabitants from oppression and offense', it would benefit the treasury by increasing tax revenues. He proposed that the current year's tithe be collected by the central treasury through trusteeship (*emanet*), and then that it go to the highest bidder. That is, the governor proposed taking away the tax-collection privileges of the Palu begs and farming out the collection of Palu's tithe to others.[34]

The Weşin attack provided the governor, the highest-ranking Ottoman administrator in the locality, with an opportunity to negotiate and possibly change the terms of Palu's land holding and taxation structure. The underlying reason for his eagerness to undermine the material and political basis of the Palu begs' authority was his desire to bring tax collection in Palu under his grip. As mentioned before, the Tanzimat state was ambivalent about the governor's role. Before the Tanzimat, governors were key actors in overseeing the fiscal business of the provinces because they distributed the tax farm contracts. In the early years of the Tanzimat era, the imperial state tried to reduce the governor's role to an administrative one, a salaried position with no fiscal role, as that aspect would be filled by a centrally-appointed tax collector (*muhassıl*). The system did not succeed, and soon the governors regained their fiscal responsibilities and, together with the provincial treasurer (*defterdar*), played key roles in the politics of local tax collection. In Palu (and elsewhere in Kurdistan), no *muhassıl*s were sent from the centre – presumably because of the begs' fiscal prerogatives. Instead, from the 1830s onward, governors delegated the authority of collecting the tithe to the Palu begs. Mustafa Sabri wanted to reverse this by eliminating the begs from the process of revenue extraction. And since the lands the begs owned were exempt from taxation, abolishing their hereditary rights would make a lot of revenues available, something that the governor was very interested in.

The governor brought these seemingly local anxieties to the central state, broadening their scale. Once the issue was on the agenda of the Meclis-i Vâlâ, Abdullah Beg and the two representatives of Weşin village were brought to Istanbul.[35]

Abdullah Beg versus the Weşin Village in the Imperial Capital: Confrontation at the Meclis-i Vâlâ

Established in 1838, the main duty of the Meclis-i Vâlâ was the 'implementation of the *Tanzimat-i Hayriye* [Beneficial Reforms]'.[36] More specifically, the Council had advisory, legislative and court of appeal functions.[37] Council members were selected from among viziers, the military, *ulama* (clergy) and upper-level bureaucrats. Initially, there was a chair and five members, but the number of members kept increasing and by the 1850s it had twenty-five members.[38] The Weşin case was transferred to the Meclis-i Vâlâ because of its function as a court of appeal for cases seen by the local councils – specifically cases involving manslaughter or theft.[39] As we have seen, the case was brought to the Council's attention by a letter penned by the Harput governor and the treasurer. In its response, the

Council expressed concern that the case would not be treated fairly in the locality due to personal enmity (presumably between Abdullah Beg and the governor) and ordered the parties to come before the council.

At the Meclis-i Vâlâ, Abdullah Beg mainly reiterated what he had told the Harput council. The villagers did the same.[40] Abdullah Beg claimed that if he had agreed to give the aforementioned Circassian slaves to the governor, the governor would not have accused him of the Weşin attack.[41] This added another element to the case, as the Meclis-i Vâlâ now wanted to investigate the question of why the governor had demanded these slaves from Abdullah Beg, but only after the main question of the 'killing of people' and the destruction of the villagers' property was resolved. Nonetheless, after Abdullah Beg raised the issue of his personal quarrel with Governor Mustafa Sabri, the governor's position as the highest local authority to address the Weşin case was rendered dubious in the eyes of the Meclis-i Vâlâ.

According to the Meclis-i Vâlâ, there were three significant issues concerning the Weşin case. First, there was no question that the governor gave an order to Abdullah Beg authorising the collection of taxes from the village.[42] Second, although Abdullah Beg was right in seeking to collect the tithe, he had no right to attack the village. The third issue concerned the villagers' opposition to Abdullah Beg and their refusal to pay their tithes. Three parties involved in the issue, Abdullah Beg, the Weşin village and the governor Mustafa Sabri, were all seen as having played roles in the incident. The final decision of the Meclis-i Vâlâ concerned all parties and engaged with the governor's suggestions for the case's resolution.

According to the Meclis-i Vâlâ's verdict, although Abdullah Beg was guilty of attacking the Weşin village, it was not certain who had burnt the village. Therefore, the council decided that the question of who had done so – Abdullah Beg and his men, or the Karabegan tribe (as Abdullah Beg asserted) – needed further investigation. Moreover, the governor, whose position was more dubious after Abdullah Beg's accusations, was deemed at fault for he showed sluggishness and negligence. To ensure an impartial investigation, the Meclis-i Vâlâ moved the case out of the governor's jurisdiction and into that of Ahmed Pasha, the governor (*kaymakam*) of the neighbouring Dersim sanjak (sub-district). The emphasis on the investigation process's impartiality was also reflected in the Meclis-i Vâlâ's decision about appointing a new *müdür* to the Palu district. As mentioned, the governor had replaced the Palu *müdür* with one from the notable families of neighbouring Harput. The Meclis-i Vâlâ, however, objected to this decision because it meant that the area was still ruled by powerful local households, which could hamper the investigation. The Meclis-i Vâlâ sent a new *müdür* from Istanbul, but adopted the same terms as those the governor had suggested in making the appointment. That is, the inhabitants of the Palu district, in addition to their tax responsibilities, were responsible for paying the salary of this central state official.[43]

The Meclis-i Vâlâ's judgement casts light on how the central state approached and perceived Kurdistan and its inhabitants. The Council stated that Abdullah Beg was right in demanding the back taxes from the villagers, and therefore the villagers' resistance to him was unacceptable. Additionally, reflecting the prevalent sense in government circles at that time, the inhabitants were described in stereotyped ways; for instance, they were called inherently 'crude' (*huşunet*) and 'spoiled' because they had long remained undisciplined.[44] The assumption was that these characteristics kept them from properly understanding the Tanzimat's beneficence. These descriptions also included some paternalistic compassion: though the villagers' actions were deemed unacceptable, there was no mention of punishment. As they were 'crude', 'undisciplined' and 'spoiled', their mistakes were understandable – and correctable – but only by the implementation of the new Tanzimat policies.

The Meclis-i Vâlâ's take on the broader question of how to break the power of the Kurdish emirs and dissolve their *yurtluk-ocaklık* lands is also interesting. As mentioned, the governor's letters to the Meclis-i Vâlâ were adamant about abolishing this type of landholding pattern and immediately bringing the lands under central treasury control. The Meclis-i Vâlâ was equally sceptical about the holders of these *yurtluk-ocaklık* lands, saying that 'they had long been accustomed to [using] oppressive and cruel manners'.[45] However, it did not enact the governor's suggestion to dissolve the system immediately. Instead, it ruled that before these *yurtluk-ocaklık* lands could be re-organised, the region would have to be stabilised and disciplined. Essentially, the central state did not want to take steps that might destabilise the region. Furthermore, the *yurtluk-ocaklık* question in Palu needed to be considered within a broader plan that applied all the *yurtluk-ocaklık* lands in the Kurdish region. In a previous report, the Meclis-i Vâlâ had decided to postpone addressing the issue until it could implement the solution in all the affected lands.[46] In this later verdict, the Council did not offer a plan to address the situation. Instead, the Meclis-i Vâlâ found Abdullah Beg guilty of attacking the village with armed men and exiled him to Tekfurdağı (Tekirdağ) in Rumelia, 900 miles away from Palu. The broader investigation continued, however, since it was still not clear who had burnt the village.

At the end of the final investigation by impartial officials, Abdullah Beg was found guilty of burning the houses, too. The damage from the attack amounted to 55,381 guruş, and he was ordered to pay that to the villagers.[47] However, Abdullah Beg died in exile in Tekfurdağı before the villagers could collect the money.

Conclusion

When Abdullah Beg entered Weşin on that Eid al Fitr day in August, he probably did not think that it would be his last visit to the Palu countryside. He could not have imagined that this encounter would result in his uprooting to a distant, unknown place. Even less imaginable, however, was that this violent encounter would result in the destruction of a landholding pattern, the *yurtluk-ocaklık*, that had remained intact since the 1500s. Before the Tanzimat, regardless of the ups and downs in the relationship between the Kurdish nobility and the imperial Ottoman state, the de facto prerogatives of the Kurdish begs in Palu had never been questioned.

If it had not been for the Harput governor Mustafa Sabri, Weşin might not have brought such a drastic transformation. Mustafa Sabri saw the horrific events there as a convenient occasion to make a case against the Palu begs' right to expropriate agrarian surplus. In his letters, he framed the issue in a way that extended beyond Abdullah Beg and the Weşin village and problematised the long-standing arrangement between the Kurdish nobles and the Ottoman state. Obviously, rather than just being an independent representative of the central state's authority in the province, the governor was also part of a power matrix in the locality. Through his letters and reports, he sought to construct the central state's perception about the region, the *yurtluk-ocaklık* system and the Palu begs.

What makes Weşin important from the perspective of a historian, however, is not just the changes that it triggered in the socio-political organisation in Palu. Equally significant are the ways in which various echelons of local and imperial bureaucracy handled the case. Local Tanzimat councils at the district (Palu) and provincial (Harput) level were instrumental in the investigation. While they both represented the agendas of main players, with the district council siding with Abdullah Beg and the provincial council in Harput reflecting governor Mustafa Sabri's agenda, what is essential is that the councils listened to testimony, judged its truthfulness, and appointed experts to conduct an on-site assessment of the damage in the village. In a very short time after they were established, these councils became important legal platforms for conflict resolution.

There is a widespread but unsubstantiated and rather anachronistic assumption in historical writings on Kurdistan that there was a power vacuum in the region after the Kurdish emirates were abolished, a vacuum that – or so the argument goes – was filled by religious sheikhs. According to this narrative, with the disappearance of the mîrs' roles as the leaders of Kurdish society who held the authority for conflict resolution, petty tribal chieftains emerged as the most important actors in Kurdistan, vying for power, wealth and authority. Rural society became ensnared in lawlessness, chaos and violence. It was within this context, the argument goes, that religious chiefs appeared as powerful new actors to mediate conflicts in the vacuum left after the demise of the emirates.[48]

This narrative is built upon a set of methodological problems. First of all, the argument about this so-called power vacuum is not based on empirical evidence. It lacks regional and temporal specificity. Also, the suggestion that the religious sheikhs rose to become the new leaders of the Kurdish community rests primarily on the nationalist rebellions led by Naqshbandi sheikhs, mainly Sheikh Ubeydullah of Nehri and Sheikh Said of Palu (1925). This ostensibly smooth narrative of the decline of the emirates and rise of the religious sheikhs with new political roles in Kurdish society projects what appear to be late nineteenth- and early twentieth-century phenomena back to the period between the 1830s and the 1880s – the half-century period from the demise of the emirates to the rise of the religious sheikhs as influential leaders in Kurdistan. In addition to being anachronistic, this narrative also presents a problematic, largely essentialising, portrayal of the Kurdish commoners as docile followers of its leadership, be it mîrs or religious sheikhs, and Kurdish tribal structures as prone to violence, chaos and lawlessness when left to their own devices. This misrepresentation goes hand in hand with the assumption that the modernising changes of the mid-nineteenth century had absolutely no resonance among the larger segments of Kurdish society in terms of creating new political strategies, motivations and subjectivities. Wadie Jwadieh, the scholar who first formulated the power vacuum argument, articulated this essentialising view of the Kurdish society in the following manner:

> Since Bedir Khan's surrender to the Ottomans in 1847, absence of a paramount figure embodying all the virile ideals of a tribal society was both unnatural and incomprehensible to the Kurds. It did violence to their system of values and left unfulfilled one of their most deeply felt psychological needs. The Kurds, like most primitive and warlike people, are inveterate hero worshippers. This

intensely parochial people, still largely in their heroic age, yearned for one of their own kith and kin to wield supreme authority among them.[49]

But a thorough analysis of the Weşin case contests this narrative at all levels. For one thing, the abolition of the hereditary privileges of the Kurdish nobility, despite being on the agenda of Tanzimat statesmen, was not a foregone conclusion. Just as important as the imperial state's plans were the contingencies, the local actors, and their encounters, conflicts and negotiations with other local and imperial actors. Furthermore, the ways in which the Weşin incident was handled reveal that while the begs' local authority diminished vis-à-vis other local actors, there was also a process of law and legality in the making. The local councils of the Tanzimat became legal spaces that local actors of all ranks used to pursue their own agendas. Rather than passively accepting the violence, the Kurdish villagers appealed to the authorities and demanded reparations for their losses. They sent their representatives to the provincial council in Harput and then to the Meclis-i Vâlâ in Istanbul. Thus, analysis of the Weşin case shows that the power vacuum argument does not take into consideration that various local actors had their own interests, agendas and agencies which they sought to realise using modern institutions, relations and political discourses in this locality in this period of drastic transformations in Kurdistan. The idea that the rise of the sheikhs was an inevitable outcome of the demise of the emirates is based on a similar perspective that overlooks the complexity of political structures and relations within the Kurdish society in the second half of the nineteenth century.

The Weşin incident provided the central state with a concrete case that let it impose a new vocabulary of economic domination in the district, one that emphasised state control over the *yurtluk-ocaklık* lands, the significance of direct taxation and the need to end the Kurdish nobility's economic power. The next chapter will elaborate on the steps the Ottoman state took to implement these policies and look at its attempts to dissolve Palu's *yurtluk-ocaklık* lands after Abdullah Beg died in exile. This will shed further light on the complexities of local power configurations in Kurdistan within the Tanzimat context.

Notes

1. BOA.MVL 30/13 Document # 3 20 Muharrem 1265 [16 December 1848].
2. BOA.MVL 30/13 Document # 4 17 Muharrem 1265 [13 December 1848].
3. BOA.MVL 30/13 Document # 2 17 5 Zilhicce 1264 [2 November 1848].
4. BOA.İ.MVL 131/3491 Document # 12 1 Zilkade 1264 [29 September 1848].

5. Dikran S. Papazian, *History of Havav Village in Palu*, published by Mshag, Beirut, 1960, pp. 134–6 (in Armenian). English translation cited at https://www.houshamadyan.org/tur/haritalar/diyarbakir-vilayeti/palu/ekonomi/agriculture-trees.html (last accessed 31 July 2020).
6. Ibid.
7. For a discussion on the elite-centredness of Kurdish historical writings, see Nilay Özok-Gündoğan, 'Can One Save the Voices of the Ordinary Kurds Fom the Enormous Condescension of Posterity? An Agenda for Social History in Kurdish Historical Writings', in *Armenians and Kurds in the Late Ottoman Empire*, eds Ümit Kurt and Ara Sarafian; (Fresno, CA: California State University Press, 2020), 95–114.
8. Halil İnalcık, 'Tanzimat'ın Uygulanması ve Sosyal Tepkiler', *Belleten* 112 (Ekim 1964): 624.
9. Milen V. Petrov, 'Everyday Forms of Compliance: Subaltern Commentaries on Ottoman Reform, 1864–1868', *Comparative Studies in Society and History* 46, no. 4 (2004): 730–59; E. Attila Aytekin, 'Tax Revolts during the Tanzimat Period (1839–1876) and before the Young Turk Revolution (1904–1908): Popular Protest and State Formation in the Late Ottoman Empire', *Journal of Policy History* 25, no. 3 (July 2013): 330. Here, Aytekin criticises İnalcık's approach as it reduces these revolts to 'conservative reaction to reform'.
10. BOA.A.DVN 30/13, Document # 2. 5 Zilhicce 1264 [2 November 1848].
11. BOA.İ.MVL, 139/3859 Document # 3. No date.
12. BOA.İ.MVL 131/3491 Document # 7, 29 Şevval 1264 [8 September 1848].
13. BOA.İ.MVL 139/3859 Document # 3, 15 Rebîülevvel 1265 [8 February 1849].
14. One *vukıyye* (or *okka*) equalled 1.282945 kg; 5,000 vukiyye of butter equalled approximately 6.5 tons. In different accounts, the amount of butter that Abdullah Beg demanded varied.
15. BOA.İ.MVL 139/3859 Document # 4 15 Rebîülâhir 1265 [10 March 1849].
16. BOA.İ.MVL 131/3491 Document # 5 and # 6. No date.
17. BOA.İ.MVL 139/3859 Document #4 15 Rebîülâhir 1265 [10 March 1849], no date, and Document #5, 20 Rebîülevvel 1265 [13 February 1849].
18. BOA.İ.MVL 139/3859 Document #5, 20 Rebîülevvel 1265 [13 February 1849].
19. BOA.İ.MVL 139/3859 Document #5, 20 Rebîülevvel 1265 [13 February 1849].
20. BOA.İ.MVL 131/3491 Document #7, 9 Şevval 1264 [8 September 1848].
21. BOA.İ.MVL 131/3491 Document #5, no date.
22. BOA.İ.MVL 139/3859 Document #4, 15 Zilhicce 1265 [1 November 1849].
23. BOA.İ.MVL 131/3491 Document # 8 29 Zilkade 1264 [27 October 1848].
24. BOA.İ.MVL 131/3491, Document #5, no date.
25. BOA.İ.MVL 131/3491, Document # 11 1 Zilhicce 1264 [29 October 1848].
26. BOA.İ.MVL 139/3859, Document #6 24 Cemâziyelevvel 1265 [17 April 1849].

27. BOA.İ.MVL 139/3859, Document #6 24 Cemâziyelevvel 1265 [17 April 1849].
28. BOA.İ.MVL 131/3491, Document # 5, no date.
29. BOA.İ.MVL 131/3491, Document # 5, no date.
30. BOA.A.DVN 30/13, Document # 5, 17 Muharrem 1265 [13 December 1848].
31. BOA.İ.MVL 131/3491, Document # 11, 1 Zilkade 1264 [29 September 1848].
32. BOA.İ.MVL 131/3491, Document # 11, 1 Zilhicce 1264 [29 October 1848].
33. BOA.MVL 2/60, Document #1, 7 Receb 1261 [12 July 1845].
34. BOA.İ.MVL 131/3491, Document # 11, 1 Zilhicce 1264 [29 October 1848].
35. BOA.İ.MVL 139/3859, Document # 5, 20 Rebîülâhir 1265 [15 March 1849].
36. Seyitdanlıoğlu, *Tanzimat devrinde Meclis-i Vâlâ, 1838–1868*, 37.
37. Ibid., 41. See also Sedat Bingöl, *Tanzimat devrinde Osmanlı'da yargı reformu: (Nizamiyye mahkemelerinin kuruluşu ve işleyişi 1840–1876)* (Anadolu Üniversitesi, 2004), 103–8.
38. Seyitdanlıoğlu, *Tanzimat devrinde Meclis-i Vâlâ, 1838–1868*, 83.
39. Bingöl, *Tanzimat devrinde Osmanlı'da yargı reformu*, 104–5.
40. BOA.İ.MVL 139/3859, Document # 5, 20 Rebîülâhir 1265 [15 March 1849].
41. BOA.İ.MVL 139/3859, Document # 6, 24 Cemâziyelevvel 1265 [17 April 1849].
42. See BOA.İ.MVL 139/3859, Document # 6 24 Cemâziyelevvel 1265 [17 April 1849] for the Meclis-i Vâlâ's decision that is being discussed here.
43. BOA.A.MKT.MVL 12/33, 6 Safer 1265 [1 January 1849].
44. BOA.İ.MVL 139/3859, 24 Cemâziyelevvel 1265 [17 April 1849].
45. BOA.İ.MVL 139/3859, Document # 6, 24 Cemâziyelevvel 1265 [17 April 1849].
46. BOA.İ.MVL 131/3491, Document #15, 26 Muharrem 1265 [22 December 1848].
47. BOA.İ.MVL 150/4258, Document # 1, 7 Receb 1265 [29 May 1849].
48. This narrative of the demise of the emirates, the resultant power vacuum and lawlessness and the rise of the sheikhs as new political leaders within the Kurdish community in this new context was first raised by Wadie Jwadieh in his dissertation in 1960. Jwadieh's dissertation was published posthumously, first in Turkish (1999) and later in English (2006). But before Jwadieh's work reached a larger readership with the book, this narrative became influential mainly through Bruinessen's dissertation (1978), which was published in English in 1992 and translated into Turkish in the 1990s. Around the same time, David McDowall's sizeable survey of Kurdish history, which also found a large audience among the Kurdish studies scholars, reiterated this schematic narrative of the dissolution of the Kurdish emirates and its impact on the Kurdish society. In this way, the thesis became one of the meta-narratives of Kurdish history in the past five decades or so. Wadie

Jwaideh, *The Kurdish National Movement: Its Origins and Development* (Syracuse: Syracuse University Press, 2006), 75–6; Martin van Bruinessen, *Agha, Shaikh and State: The Social and Political Structures of Kurdistan* (London and New Jersey: Zed Books, 1992), 181–2; David McDowall, *A Modern History of the Kurds* (Bloomsbury Academic, 2007), 49–50.
49. Jwaideh, *The Kurdish National Movement*, 76.

PART III
RESTRUCTURING AND VIOLENCE

Chapter 6

After Abdullah Beg: The Politics of Dividing the Kurdish Nobles' Lands

Rural conflicts stemming from the extraction of agrarian surplus such as over-taxation and cultivators' resistance, as well as landowners' violent retaliation, are normal aspects of rural politics in agrarian empires. Thus, there was nothing extraordinary about the violent encounter in Weşin in August 1848. Nevertheless, the incident triggered a long legal case that came under the eye of newly-established Tanzimat institutions. While the material and physical destruction Abdullah Beg wreaked on the village was the obvious issue, the broader question of the Palu begs' hereditary rule also loomed. From the perspective of the Ottoman imperial state, however, confiscating Abdullah Beg's lands and attempting to dissolve the *yurtluk-ocaklık* lands was premature. A year earlier, in 1847, the Ottoman armies had organised the Kurdistan campaign against the formidable Bedirkhan Beg of Cîzre, destroying the emirate and exiling him to Crete. It is telling that despite plunging a dagger into the heart of the Kurdish emirate system, the imperial state was not overly enthusiastic about a sudden change for Palu. At least, this was the sentiment voiced by the Meclis-i Vâlâ in response to the insistent calls of Mustafa Sabri, the Harput governor, to confiscate Abdullah Beg's lands. Pointing out the region's lack of security and discipline, the council decided to postpone the re-organisation of these lands. Advising a gradual strategy in the implementation of the Tanzimat policies, it stopped at exiling Abdullah Beg.[1]

At the discursive level, the council justified its gradual strategy by what it called the unruly character of the population in Kurdistan. This perspective dominated Ottoman ruling elites at the time – not just towards Kurdistan or the Kurds, but towards nomadic or semi-nomadic tribal groups across the empire.[2] In reality, however, this emphasis on gradual change was less to do with how the imperial state perceived these groups than with its elites' still extant recognition of the hereditary privileges of the Kurdish nobility. Despite including an assault on the various types of hereditary exemptions and privileges various groups maintained, the Tanzimat was a work-in-progress involving interplay between old and new, rather than a total rejection of the imperial legacy. As such, it involved the elements of both worlds, setbacks and occasional jump-starts.

The question of the Kurdish nobility's hereditary rights was a textbook example. In a year, the imperial state's emphasis on gradual change would be replaced by a more radical approach. Abdullah Beg's exile, followed by his death a year later, allowed the Ottoman state to experiment with transforming landholding patterns in Palu. It decided to confiscate Abdullah Beg's lands and sell them to people unrelated to the begs. This triggered a complex set of conflicts in the region, starting with Abdullah Beg's heirs, then expanding to other potential buyers and the Ottoman state. This chapter explores this thorny process of confiscation and the politics of land purchases in Palu – a process that reflected the state's attempt to dissolve the long-established hereditary estates (*yurtluk-ocaklık*) of the begs' lands and annul their privileges. This discussion shows that the Tanzimat state's policies in land and taxation resulted in drastic changes in land ownership patterns and power configurations in the locality. The begs, the tribal chiefs, Armenian and Kurdish cultivators and the Armenian financial bourgeois constituted the major actors in the scramble for land in this new context. Land sales were slow, uneven and rife with conflicts. Nevertheless, there *were* land sales; hence it was a time of drastic change in the local power structures and relations. A budding Armenian financial bourgeois constituted the main group of potential buyers. Meanwhile, a middle peasantry seeking to completely discard the begs' claim to agrarian surplus was in the making through claiming lands. At the bottom of the rural hierarchy were the Armenian and Kurdish sharecroppers whose main agenda was getting relief from the outrageous extractions in the rural sector while the imperial state was seeking to render itself a legitimate party in surplus extraction. In this way, by confiscating the begs' lands and opening them up for purchase, the Tanzimat state up-ended the social hierarchies within the locality. This chapter demonstrates the anxieties of this process.

What To Do with Abdullah Beg's Land after his Death?

Four months after Abdullah Beg was exiled, the district governor (*kaymakam*) of Tekfurdağı sent a letter to the grand vizierate that claimed that Abdullah Beg was 'shedding tears with sorrow and regret (*tevbe*) because of his previous mistake'.[3] Moreover, he was sick and frail and the

After Abdullah Beg

kaymakam was requesting permission for Abdullah Beg to go to Istanbul for treatment. Since his case with the Weşin village was still ongoing, the letter said, allowing Abdullah Beg to return would make it possible to institute justice.[4] But in a month, news of his death reached the capital.[5]

The case about the burning down of the village was still open. While he was in exile, investigators had concluded that he did burn the village, causing damages of 55,000 guruş (or 58,000, according to some documents), which the villagers demanded in reparations. After his death, however, the village representatives in Istanbul were sent back and the case was transferred back to the local Sharia court – now between the village and Abdullah Beg's heirs.[6] This brought his wife, Kadre Hanım (also his cousin through Ismail Beg), and his half-sister Asiye Hanım to the scene. They designated a certain İbrahim Agha as their deputy.[7] The other heir was Necib Beg, Abdullah Beg's brother. After two years, the court reached a solution with a reference to Prophet Muhammed's famous saying, '*Es sulhu seyyidûl ahkâm*' ('peace is the master of all verdicts'): both parties relinquished their material demands. In return for giving up their demand for reparations, the villagers were forgiven their back taxes (which amounted to 7,500 guruş) by Necib Beg.[8]

Abdullah Beg's legacy was complicated. What he left behind was not just the protracted case, but also fertile lands that earned good revenues for whoever controlled them. A few months after his death, the governor of Harput, Mustafa Sabri, wrote to the centre announcing that order and security had been restored. The major problem he raised was that the district was still under the control of *ûmera* (pl. of *emîr*) and *agavat* (plural of *agha*, or tribal chief) just as it had been. He urged the imperial treasury to seize Abdullah Beg's lands.[9]

Deliberations within the Ottoman bureaucracy about what to do with Abdullah Beg's lands focused mostly on economic aspects. This was particularly so with Palu, as opposed to other areas with the same type of land system. For instance, Eğil, a nearby *yurtluk-ocaklık* area, was also under consideration for confiscation, but 'Eğil was not comparable to Palu [in terms of the revenues it generated] as [its land] was mostly rocky'.[10] Palu's fertile land made it a particularly desirable choice for a comprehensive re-organisation of land ownership.

The Supreme Council's statement about what to do with the hereditary lands of the Kurdish begs reveals the specifics of this new government approach.[11] First, it was necessary to learn who had received the revenues since Abdullah Beg's death. The council emphasised the significance of a reliable property census, as previous attempts had been compromised by owners hiding property from the surveyors. The question of legibility pertaining to property, revenue and population in the areas ruled by the Kurdish nobility haunted the imperial state for the rest of the century. The *mefrûzü'l-kalem* status had kept Palu mostly out of government records, including the *Defterhane-i Âmire* (Imperial Registry), and the Court mentioned this as a problem to be addressed.[12] Re-organising the land system went hand in hand with efforts to count wealth and population in Palu – and throughout Kurdistan.[13]

As for the actual land system, the government's plan involved four components, namely: abolishing the hereditary character of their control by confiscating their lands; undermining large land ownership by selling their land to claimants outside of the Palu nobility; bringing cadaster (*mesaha*) and assigning title deeds centrally from the Imperial Registry (*Defterhâne*); and consequently, claiming the agrarian surplus accruing from the Palu land to the imperial treasury.

LAND

In order to better understand the nature, scope and significance of these changes, we need to consider the nature of the begs' land ownership at two interrelated levels: first, with regard to the de jure definition of the Kurdish nobility's prerogatives as defined in the *temlîk* given to Cemşîd Beg by Sultan Suleyman I (r. 1520–66) in 1535 and renewed three times by the successive sultans, Murad III (r. 1575–95), Ahmed I (r. 1603–17) and Sultan Abdülmecid I (r. 1839–61);[14] and second, in terms of what this change meant regarding the status of land as *mîrî* (state) or *mülk* (private) within Ottoman legal-administrative parlance.

The original *temlîk* granted to Cemşîd Beg in 1535 defined the hereditary character of the begs' control over Palu land clearly and fully. It said that Cemşîd Beg's heirs would own all castles, towns, fields and produce of Palu, and could pass all of it on (neslen *ba'de* neslin *mülkiyet üzere*). If the beg died without a rightful heir, the decree stated that the territory would still go to a beg or the son of a beg (*begzade*) from the area, in consultation and consensus with all the begs of Kurdistan.[15] This clause suggests that the Ottoman state recognised the Kurdistan begs as a corporate entity with authority to issue collective decisions about succession. In the most recent *temlîk* from 1841 (before Tanzimat), however, this clause was replaced with one stating that when a beg died without a son, the sublime sultanate (*saltanat-i seniyye*) would grant it to another suitable person.[16] The state no longer recognised the begs of Kurdistan as a collective body that could issue authoritative decisions about succession. Such a change clearly suggests a transformation within the power configuration in Kurdistan and the resultant alterations in the begs' relations with the imperial centre. Nevertheless, the de jure recognition of the hereditary rights of the begs over the Palu land remained.[17] Only when a beg died without a son could the state step in and give the land to someone else (*bila-veled olduğu halde taraf-ı saltanat-ı seniyyeden ahar münasibine tevcih kılınmak*).[18]

Prior to the Tanzimat, in accordance with the original *temlîk*, the Ottoman administration did not aim to confiscate the lands of a deceased beg. Even the most recent *temlîk* limited its authority to granting the land to another *beg*. As mentioned, the changes the state envisioned after Abdullah Beg would transform the legal status of the *yurtluk-ocaklık* lands by bringing them under the central treasury, then selling them and granting the buyers title deeds. To understand this proposed transformation better, we need to consider the status of the Kurdish nobility's land within the Ottoman land system at large.

In the classical Ottoman land system, 'all agricultural land, or more specifically, grain producing land in the state was declared *mîrî*, "that is belonging formally to the state"'.[19] While the state maintained the ownership of all agricultural land, the cultivator had usufruct rights, 'which could not be taken away from him so long as he paid the tax due on the lot'.[20] As Gerber states, however, 'the question of the separation between *mîrî* and *mülk* land was an extremely complex one'.[21] Despite being the underlying principle of the Ottoman land system, state ownership of land – which was not actually ownership but the monopoly on distributing the usufruct and collecting the surplus – was not static or standard across time and space.[22] Regardless of the legal definition of state ownership of land, from the eighteenth century on there was a move to transform *mîrî* lands into de facto private property, although this was not codified until the Land Code of 1858. In his discussion of peasant land tenure in lower Egypt, Cuno argues that the 'doctrine of state ownership of land' did not reflect the situation in terms of actual land ownership patterns, since 'in the eighteenth century, judicial and administrative authority was decentralised, allowing custom and local interests great influence in disposition of land. Peasants regarded the land they farmed as their own and tended to treat it as such.'[23] By the mid-nineteenth century, Sluglett and Farouk-Sluglett argue, the 'distinction between *mülk* and *mîrî* lands in Syria had become considerably blurred in practice if not in law'.[24] In similar vein, Owen posits that the 'two tiers of rights [pertaining to land] – the right of access to the land and the right to its surplus – collapsed into one another to create a single right to both land and surplus that came to be regarded as much the same as the right to individual private property'.[25] In this sense, usufruct right was akin to private property, as it was protected by the state.[26]

The question is where the hereditary lands of the Kurdish nobility stood in the *mîrî* versus *mülk* distinction. For historians writing from a state-centred and Turkish nationalist viewpoint, this question has implications for the related question of the Kurdish begs' autonomy. For these historians, this historical debate about the Kurdish begs' autonomy has far-reaching implications about the present, because accepting the *mülk* status of the Kurdish begs' lands would not only jeopardise the all-powerful Ottoman state mythology, but would also potentially provide a discursive justification for the contemporary Kurdish political claims for autonomous rule. Therefore, taking the dictum that all agricultural land in the Ottoman Empire is state land at face value, these historians seek to prove the *mîrî* status of the Kurdish nobility's lands – since the contrary would strengthen the idea that the begs actually had a certain degree of autonomy vis-à-vis the Ottoman state.[27]

The assumption here is that what was actually granted to Palu begs was not absolute ownership of the land (*rakabe*), but only the right to the revenues the land generated.[28] To prove this point, these historians argue that the Palu begs had to receive a separate *temlîkname* from the state in order to exercise some of their rights to the land, such as converting it into *vakıf*.

Looking at the genealogy of the autonomous enclaves in the Islamic world, Halil İnalcik argues otherwise:

> In Islamic states, there existed a special kind of sultanic land grant (tamlīk, temlîk) bestowing absolute and hereditary immunities vis-à-vis administrations, making it a virtually autonomous enclave within the territory of the state. Such enclaves, originally in the form of private properties (milk/mulk/mülk; pl. amlak/emlâk) were converted in most cases to pious foundations (waqf/vaqf/vakf. pl. awqāf/evkâf).[29]

İnalcik also adds that in Islamic jurisprudence, 'in the case of tamlīk', contrary to variants of *timar* and its historical antecedents in the Islamic world, 'the land assumed the full qualities of *mulk*, i.e., the proprietor could sell, donate, pawn or make a *vaqf* out of it. These points were always made expressly clear in the document of a *tamlīk*.'[30] Significantly, İnalcik situates the *yurtluk-ocaklık* and the *hükümet*s in the Ottoman context within the long genealogy of the hereditary and autonomous ownership of land via the granting of a *temlîkâme*.[31] He argues that in terms of the autonomy they enjoyed, the Kurdish *hükümet*s were 'comparable to the areas under the *temlîkâme* regime'.[32]

These points are given credence by the wording of the original *temlîkâme* granted to Cemşid Beg back in the sixteenth century. The document unequivocally stated that he was granted all castles, towns and fields, together with the entire revenues, in 'a hereditary way as freehold property (*neslen ba'de neslin mülkiyet üzere*)'.[33] The imperial lawbooks and treatises of jurists from the seventeenth century indicate the continuation of the *mülk* status of the *hükümet* in this period in the Ottoman politico-administrative system.[34] They state that the rulers held the *hükümet* as property (*hâkimleri mülkiyet tarikiyle tasarruf ederler*)[35] in a hereditary way (*mülk-ü mevrus*) with a certificate given by the sultan.[36]

All this discussion refers to the status of the Palu begs' land in Ottoman politico-administrative classification, that is, de jure definitions, and it was this type of land ownership that the Ottoman administration sought to abolish after Abdullah Beg's death.

TAX

From the perspective of the Ottoman state, the issue was the actual use of land, the method of surplus expropriation and who was entitled to it. All this made the reality much more complex than legal *mülk* versus *mîrî* designations indicate. As discussed, on the eve of Tanzimat, landowner-ship patterns in Palu showed noticeable fragmentation and diversity. In the 1850s, there were around 360 villages in Palu. Eighty-eight of these were the Palu begs' hereditary property, including the *vakıf* lands. The aghas held thirty-six villages. In the approximately 150 villages not owned by the begs or the aghas, land belonged to the *ahali* (commoners), either with or without title deeds. Seemingly, almost half of the Palu land was already in the hands of people outside the Palu nobility.[37] Because of its *mefrûzü'l-kalem* status, the Ottoman state did not conduct land and population surveys (*tahrir*s) in Palu in the sixteenth century. Therefore, it is not possible to know the exact number of villages that the Palu begs held in their first century under the Ottoman rule. The wording of the *temlîknâme* suggests that the entire Palu (which was a larger area than what it became in the nineteenth century) was under the Palu begs' rule. However, as discussed in Chapter 2, the Palu begs had already surrendered their monopoly over the control of land by leasing or selling land outside the family by the end of the eighteenth century. Significantly, this ability to profit from the land itself, even to dispose of it, corroborates the idea that they had full ownership rights.

The discussions about what to do with Abdullah Beg's lands – and by implication, the Palu begs' hereditary land ownership in general – were also aimed at bringing agrarian dues under the imperial state's purview. The post-confiscation process entailed two pillars: the land would be sold out and the district tithe would be auctioned off by the treasury. In 1845, the governor of the Arabgir district, İsmail, claimed that confiscating the lands of the Palu begs would increase the tithe and other miscellaneous revenues threefold.[38] Tanzimat meant that the imperial state was an ever more determined claimant to agrarian surplus, trying out methods, including the appointment of the begs as the overseer of the tax-farming contracts, sending a trustee from the centre (*emanet sistemi*), bringing parts and parcels of Palu land under the imperial state's control, or administering tax-farm contracts. For example, in 1841, the state appointed İsmail Agha of Çötelizades, a notable family based in neighbouring Harput, to collect the tithe arrears. But to the imperial state's consternation, despite staying three and a half months in Palu, İsmail Agha was unable to collect even one piaster. Tied hand and foot, İsmail Agha gave up and the tithe was again auctioned and entrusted to Tahir Beg, from the Palu nobles.[39]

After Abdullah Beg's death, the imperial state – with considerable pressure from provincial administrators – moved towards a comprehensive transformation in land ownership and methods of surplus extraction in Palu. To the begs' dismay, the Ottoman administration decreed that starting in 1850, the treasury would administer the agrarian dues from the lands (mainly the tithe) controlled by the Palu begs.[40] But these two issues, land ownership and methods of surplus extraction, while tied, were not the same thing. The former aimed at abolishing the Kurdish nobility's hereditary land ownership as a category, while the latter was a corollary of the Tanzimat state's goal of channelling more monies to imperial coffers. This second aspect concerned the begs' roles as tax collectors, which they had only received a few years back. Yet in governmental discussions, land ownership and tax collection were discussed together – as if they referred to one and the same phenomenon.

Competing Claims on Palu Land

THE BEGS AND THE AGHAS

Shortly after Abdullah Beg's lands were confiscated by the central treasury, his brother Mehmed Necib petitioned the government demanding he be given his late brother's land as his legitimate heir. Referring to the imperial decrees, Mehmed Necib argued that in the absence of a child, the deceased beg's brother was to inherit his land.[41] To prove his case, he presented a copy of the imperial certificate (*temessük*) granted to Abdullah Beg in 1841.[42]

After Abdullah Beg

This document corroborated Mehmed Necib's point; it explicitly mentioned brothers as legal inheritors of the lands of a deceased beg and stated that the central treasury could seize the lands only when the deceased had neither sons nor brothers.[43] The Meclis-i Vâlâ agreed, indicating its acceptance of the *temessük* that had been given to the Necib Beg's ancestors, and Mehmed Necib was given half (around eight villages) of his brother's land.[44]

But the Porte's plan was aimed at abolishing hereditary landownership as a whole, and as soon as the the Meclis-i Vâlâ's decision on the division and sale of noble lands was approved with a sultanic decree, the begs and aghas acted to stop it. They dispatched Şerif, Mehmed, Necib and Tahir Begs to Istanbul to pursue the case and protect their rights. They were representing seventeen begs and seventeen aghas.[45] But staying in Istanbul was not cheap and the case was unlikely to be solved overnight. The begs committed to share the representatives' expenses during their stay in the capital, but they lacked cash.[46] Thus, once they were in Istanbul, the begs knocked on the door of Sarraf Hoca Nişan, a *sarraf* based in Yeni Han. By the end of their sixth year in Istanbul, they had borrowed 195,000 guruş in cash plus interest. Hoca Nişan wanted his money, but the other begs had paid nothing towards their expenses. Desperate, the quartet appealed the governor of Harput to push the begs in Palu to pay.

For the begs, this state's policy of confiscating their lands was a violation of their four-century-old rule over not only 'the tithe but also the land of Palu' granted to them with an imperial title deed (*mülknâme-i hümayun*).[47] They might or might not have done this purposefully, but the mention of 'four centuries' let the begs underscore the fact that they had held the lands before the Ottomans took over. Relatedly, when the Ottoman administrators discussed the problem of the Kurdish begs' non-payment of taxes, they emphasised that this had been an issue for three centuries, meaning from the moment the begs had recognised Ottoman rule.

Ever since the central treasury had decided to take hold of Palu's tithe revenues, the begs complained, 'some *reaya*, who are farmers (*çiftçi*) and sharecroppers (*maraba*) have been fancying to seize (*zabt etme arzusunda oldukları*) villages which had been under our humble possession'.[48] The begs sought to halt the implementation of the imperial decrees and to pursue the issue of the salary that they were to be given as compensation for their lands. Even as the begs tried to keep their lands, they recognised that things had already changed. Adopting a more realistic perspective meant asking for compensation from the imperial state for their losses, painting a desolate picture of 'four hundred households and two thousand people' in their extended family living in misery and poverty due to the loss of their major means of subsistence.[49]

As seen in the above-mentioned petition and throughout the entire process of appealing the state, the begs and aghas acted collectively in search of the return of their land or appropriate compensation. *Agha* is a term usually used generically to refer to a tribal chief in the Kurdish society. Behind this generality, however, the term carries a great degree of variation across time and space. The concept of agha reflects the protean nature of the tribe as a socio-economic form in the Kurdish society.[50]

In the Kurdish emirates, the tribes historically constituted the begs' fighting forces – a role that was most likely obsolete by the nineteenth century. The aghas also acted as proxies for begs in terms of collecting agrarian taxes on behalf of the begs from the agrarian population. Typically, the begs would grant title deeds to aghas in return for providing military forces for the begs or accompanying them 'at both war and peace [*sefer ve hazarda*.]'[51] In the 1850s the aghas owned thirty-six villages in Palu. It seems that the lands that the aghas had been granted by the begs in return for their services had long been under the former's control and had gained a de facto property character, and these lands were also included in the Ottoman state's land confiscation scheme. This is why the aghas also signed the petition that assigned the role of representative to the begs when the latter went to the capital to seek redress from the government for their lost lands.

Interestingly, when the issue of the Palu begs' hereditary lands was discussed at various levels of central and local bureaucracy, no one ever mentioned the aghas. They apparently were not considered a separate category, something that changed once they were trying to regain their lost lands. For now, though, the two acted collectively, bound by their shared status as landowners. At the same time, however, the begs emphasised the difference by signing the letters separately as begs and aghas with their titles. Later, this affected the imperial state's approach to land re-organisation as it came up with different offers for each group.

CULTIVATORS

The begs were discontented with the Tanzimat changes not just because of the risk of losing their land, but also because of their ramifications for changing relations of production and surplus extraction. Sharecropping was the dominant labour organisation in the area at the time, but when this system did not work, mostly because the begs did not have enough seeds, they leased the land out (*icare*) and collected rent (*icare-i zemin*).[52] In 1850, shortly after the land confiscation, the Ottoman administration removed the begs' tax-collection prerogatives and brought the tithe collection under the purview of the imperial treasury. This move was received enthusiastically by the majority Armenian cultivators, who saw it as an opportunity to claim ownership of lands they had been tilling as sharecroppers for the Palu begs. The cultivators openly resisted the dominant sharecropping arrangement by refusing to accept seeds from the begs and share the harvest with them.

Behind the cultivators' refusal to sharecrop was their desire to acquire land via the government's new land programme. The state's decision to confiscate the begs' lands was a convenient moment for the cultivators to claim ownership. In the begs' appeal to the state, they complained that the farmers (which the begs specified as mostly '*reaya*', meaning non-Muslim producers) started sowing their own seeds and stopped giving anything from the harvest to them.[53] The begs referred to the prior court case that had sustained sharecropping and their hereditary rights to prevent the cultivators from claiming these lands. But for the sharecroppers, the begs' hereditary rights were no longer relevant. They requested that they should keep a sufficient amount of land for their subsistence and promised to pay their tithe and other taxes to the imperial treasury.

For the begs, the cultivators' refusal of sharecropping was illegitimate since they did not have any official documentation proving their rights over the land. To counter this, the sharecroppers felt the need to explain why they lacked relevant official documents, even saying at one point that they had imperial orders (*irade*), but never presenting them.[54] Another time, they said they had had title deeds but had lost them when their houses were burnt to the ground by the begs.[55] Written documents helped in a court, and these the cultivators did not have, which helped the Palu begs to continue insisting on their rights to the land. However, with the cultivators' refusal to accept sharecropping, the begs started to levy a type of rent – later described generically as *noksan-ı arz*, a term that essentially referred to the fee paid to cover the loss of the soil's fertility after cultivation.[56] Meanwhile, the cultivators continued their effort to acquire land. As the Ottoman administration was working on giving the land sale schema its final shape, the cultivators tried to make the state hear their voices.

Something Resembling a Resolution

The decision on the confiscation of Abdullah Beg's lands and the abolition of the hereditary prerogatives of the Palu begs was taken at the Meclis-i Vâlâ, the highest council authorised to make binding decisions on the implementation of Tanzimat policies. But rights claims based on traditional contracts were still pertinent. The begs' effort to stop the confiscation and the cultivators' unwillingness to give up brought the case – and the parties – to the capital city and the Meclis-i Vâlâ. After having received a detailed report on the case from the Council of Financial Accounting (*Meclis-i Muhasabe*), the Meclis-i Vâlâ came up with a resolution. A product of the overarching goals of the Tanzimat programme, it also reflected the government's response to the claims of three parties (the begs, the aghas and sharecroppers) as well as the council's attempt to reconcile existing contracts, historical claims, material exigencies and ongoing practices with the new land programme.

When the begs appealed the council, they stated their wish to keep their lands in hand so that 'the light of their dynasty would not fade out'.[57] The Meclis-i Vâlâ's approach focused instead on financial matters, stating 'It is obvious that the aforementioned emirs are in need of lands' which 'provided living for two thousand [emirs and aghas] population for four hundred years as their hereditary private properties (*mülkiyet ve evladiyet vechle*)'.[58] Moreover, it was 'necessary to maintain their well-being and security'. It did not however, consider it appropriate to leave all the lands in the begs' possession, because this would contravene the relevant Tanzimat regulations.

The imperial state's rationale reflected its view that things had changed since the time when the begs were given these rights. They were granted the lands in return for service in the holy war (*hidemat-i cihadiye*), which was no longer relevant.[59] The only reason Meclis-i Vâlâ found a modicum of right in the begs' demand was their economic needs. 'The protection of the safety and wellbeing of the *ûmera*, and safeguarding them from poverty', was a mark of the sultan's compassion.[60] Previously, Meclis-i Vâlâ had granted the begs salaries as a compensation, but considering the size of their extended family, salary would not meet their needs. Therefore, it decided that, instead, the begs would be granted one-third of the lands that they had traditionally held – on condition that they paid their tithe and other taxes directly to the imperial treasury.

What was at stake here for both parties was more than just the material value of the lands. The Meclis-i Vâlâ and the begs were in essence negotiating the legitimacy of the Kurdish nobility's hereditary prerogatives. Yet the case was fraught with ambiguities, including the lack of a definitive blueprint about the relevance of the erstwhile sultanic orders and decrees granting exemptions and privileges to particular interest groups. In taking away their hereditary rights, the council was ripping away the begs' recognition by the Ottoman sultans. In turn, evoking imperial certificates, the begs were asking the council to remember the imperial legacy. By leaving one-third of the lands in the begs' hands, the imperial state displayed its benevolence while reminding all parties of their place.

The Meclis-i Vâlâ also evaluated the aghas' demands. While most aghas received the title deeds for their lands from the Palu begs in return for military service,[61] some were given land by the state with *berat*s (a letter showing their rights to the revenues of these lands). From the perspective of the Meclis-i Vâlâ, however, neither the title deeds from the begs nor the *berat*s granted the aghas ownership. Begs and aghas were different, and the decision about the aghas' lands reflected this: the aghas kept one-fifth of their lands in hand and were given free title deeds. Like the begs, aghas were not granted salaries. The state, thus, maintained the existing hierarchy between the two groups.

After it had been determined how much land would be taken from the begs and the aghas, the next question was what to do with the confiscated land. The state was unsympathetic to the idea of giving land to the cultivators free as they did not have any relevant title deeds.[62] Nonetheless, the Meclis-i Vâlâ addressed the cultivators' wish to keep the lands in their hands, albeit vaguely compared to its in-depth deliberations about the issues that pertained to begs and aghas. It decreed that the remaining land (after the 1/3 and 1/5 given to the begs and aghas) would be opened up to sale (*füruht*) to both Muslim and non-Muslim (*reaya*) claimants. That land was now *mîrî* (state) land, and thus its use and sale would be handled in accordance with the treasury's title deed regulations.[63]

This designation of Muslim and non-Muslim in the council's decision is noteworthy. The conflict between begs and cultivators had gone on for quite a while in Palu, but up to this point, the religious difference had never been brought up as a parameter. Armenians constituted the majority of the sharecroppers who tilled the Palu begs' lands, but the petitions sent to the imperial state show that Muslims also complained about sharecropping, over-taxation or corvée. Almost all the petitions sent by sharecroppers were signed as 'Muslim and non-Muslim inhabitants' of such and such village – the formulation most likely to render their claims legitimate in the eyes of the state. Yet it is also true that the Armenians were more vocal, and, for lack of a better word, more resourceful in conveying these issues to the imperial state. We will see later that Armenians based in Istanbul took it upon themselves to push the state towards completing the confiscation of the begs' lands by undermining their economic power to acquire land. For the moment, it is worth noticing that the imperial state specified that both Muslims and non-Muslims could purchase the confiscated lands of the Palu begs.

Apart from the local actors and their demands, what stood between the imperial state and its desired goal of tapping into the agrarian dues of Palu through land restructuring was Palu's *mefrûzü'l-kalem* status. That is, its *hükümet* status had largely kept it outside the Ottoman fiscal recording system, and the state therefore lacked systematic and reliable information on the area's potential for agrarian revenues. Cadaster was non-existent in the area, and the lack of reliable data about land tenure posed problems for land sales since it appeared, for example, that some of the saleable lands were *vakıf* lands exempted from state confiscation. The council decided to send an expert (*mütefennin*) from the Imperial Registry (*Defterhane-i Âmire*) to perform cadastral surveying of land (*mesaha*).[64] Finally, as a corollary of the council's decision to sell the land to both Muslim and non-Muslims, the need for a population census was reiterated. After one had been conducted, the population of each group would be recorded separately in registers – the usual way of registering the population in Ottoman censuses, as their military and tax responsibilities varied.

For the council, that was it. This was the resolution. Now it was time for action. It sent a governmental order to the governors of Harput and Kurdistan and the commander of the Anatolian Army (*müşir*) in the area, detailing the new regulations. But the council's land scheme satisfied none of the discontented groups; not the begs, nor the aghas, nor the sharecroppers. The decision was not finalised; it would be re-drawn again.

The aghas protested the council's decision to give them only one-fifth of the land, stating that this amount was insufficient for their livelihood. The imperial state was bothered by the aghas' lack of title deeds for their lands (the council did not consider the documents given to them by the begs valid), but given that the aghas were no different from the begs in terms of needing land to maintain their extended families, the council revisited its decision. The aghas were now allowed to keep one-third of their land in hand (the remaining two-thirds would still be confiscated).[65]

The commoners (*reaya*) also wanted the government's land allocation scheme revised. Their concern related to the council's decision to sell the confiscated lands to clients while the aghas and begs got to keep some portion of their lands without payment. Their petition was clear: 'The emirs and aghas', they said, 'have wealth and riches, [while] we have no power but we spent labor [*emek*] and [provided] service to make these lands flourish.'[66] And, they added, if the state sells these lands, 'the emirs and the aghas will again purchase them and this will mean the continuation of [our] dependent condition under their oppression'.[67] Their final point was close to a threat: if they were not given any land, they would not be able to pay their yearly taxes to the state and would have to leave their homeland, leaving the land uncultivated.[68]

Their discontent also apparently stemmed from another plan being cooked up in Palu regarding the land allocations between Muslim and non-Muslim commoners. At some point, there was a plan to sell two-thirds of the confiscated land to Muslims, and the other to non-Muslims. The latter voiced their opposition to this plan to Reşid Pasha, the governor of Baghdad, who prevented it from being included in the government's plan.[69] The final decision was to open half the land to sale for Muslim claimants and the other half to non-Muslim claimants, which also meant that half the land was kept outside the begs' reach. Receiving an official guarantee that they would be able to purchase land was no small victory for the Armenians. The council also decreed that, Muslim or non-Muslim, those who already held land with relevant title deeds could keep their lands and would be given new title deeds.

Beyond the official decision about who was allowed to purchase land, however, was the question of who could actually buy land once it had been opened up for sale. The council's final decision specified that the commoners would make a moderate down-payment (*muaccele*) to purchase land, and a not so insignificant group could afford to make the down-payment. This, coupled with the council's decision to let the commoners keep their lands with new title deeds, suggests that by the mid-nineteenth century there was a sizeable class of small landowners who could and did buy land from the begs' confiscated lands, and the proceeds of these sales would go to the imperial treasury. Of the circa 360 villages of Palu, nearly 157 were owned by commoners (*ahali*), some with title deeds and others without.[70] Since the Armenians had been vocal in seeking to purchase land from the Palu begs, it is plausible that the majority of this new class of small landowners were Armenians. Even though the begs and aghas still controlled almost half of the land in the area (88 and 36 villages respectively), this group of small landowners was sizeable enough to push for change – to work to abolish sharecropping and give an official character to their land purchases. The council's final decision to reserve half of the land exclusively for the non-Muslim claimants indicated their strength.

This new final resolution was far from being a top-down process; rather, it was a 'negotiated settlement' between the parties – the begs, the aghas and the cultivators.[71] The decision to confiscate the begs' lands came from the Tanzimat context, but it was the provincial governor of Harput and the Armenian clients who pushed the imperial state to take such a definitive step. After the decision had been approved by a sultanic order, a clerk from the Imperial Treasury, Sadık Efendi, was sent to Palu to conduct land surveys.[72] Hoping to build the necessary institutional infrastructure to survey Palu's lands, the Sublime Porte also entrusted the Harput governor with oversight of the new land programme.[73]

The government's land scheme gained its final shape amid multiple claimants, competing rights claims, and the structural challenges of operating in an area outside the Ottoman state record system. These factors continued to delay the Ottoman administration's efforts to implement the land programme. From the decision to confiscate the begs' lands in the 1850s through the 1870s, the district was the scene for ever-intensifying disputes over how to put the plan into practice. The begs, the cultivators, and members of the Armenian financial bourgeois struggled over Palu's agricultural lands. These issues will be discussed in the rest of this chapter in terms of the local politics of land sales and the extent to which the state achieved its goals and in terms of surplus extraction and the alterations in agrarian relations of production as the land programme was put into practice.

Plans versus Reality: Dividing Lands on the Ground

THE BUYERS OF LAND

In the decades following the decision to confiscate the begs' lands, Palu was embroiled in a fierce struggle between parties seeking shares of this newly-available land. Around 1860, nearly a decade after the Council's decision to divide the land, information about the implementation of the land programme started flowing to the imperial centre. The impression that emerges is that land sales were not functioning as planned. One problem noted repeatedly was that the begs continued to buy the land apportioned for the purchase of the *ahali*. Another problem was that the cash accrued from land sold had not arrived in the imperial treasury. And those who bought the land were not given title deeds.

The provincial administrators wanted military deployments to address these problems, but the Ottoman administration said that it would be inappropriate to send military force to resolve the issue.[74] But it was not just reports from the provincial administrators that kept the land allocations on the centre's agenda for so long, including several meetings of the Meclis-i Vâlâ. The council's decision to sell land to Muslim and non-Muslim *ahali* with a moderate down-payment had energised certain sectors of the Armenian population of Palu, and it was largely those Armenians, mostly based in the imperial capital, who helped keep the issue alive through regular petitions.

From the second half of the eighteenth century on, Armenian society in Palu's countryside was noticeably stratified.[75] In the discussions around the sales of the confiscated land, one group was generically defined as sharecroppers (*maraba* or *ortakçı*), but this group was not homogeneous. In the Ottoman archival documents, the term *maraba/ortakçı* was used in a way that concealed the differences between groups that had different relations to land ownership and labour organisation. Careful reading of archival documentation shows that sharecroppers actually consisted of two very different groups: landless cultivators and a group akin to middle peasantry.[76] The latter group were those who either had already acquired land through lease or sale and were seeking an official imprint for these sales or who had enough capital to buy land through the new land programme. It is not a coincidence that when the begs talked about those who sought to buy their lands, they referred to 'some *reaya*, who are farmers (*çiftçi*) and sharecroppers (*maraba*)'.[77] The former wanted to buy land, acquire the deeds for land they already owned, and prevent the begs from buying land from the market allocated to the *reaya*. The latter mostly raised questions about agrarian relations of production, including over-taxation, double taxation and sharecropping. Even after the land changed hands, cultivators complained that the new owners continued the oppressive practice of sharecropping.

And there was another group as well that wanted to purchase the newly-available land: these were wealthy Armenian notables sometimes described as *çorbacı*s who took it upon themselves to bring issues related to the land purchases to the Ottoman state's attention. They had accumulated wealth through trade, moneylending, or doing artisanal work like barbering, or carpentry. They were based in *han*s (urban inns) known for hosting the activities of money-lenders (*sarraf*s), such as Çukurçeşme Han or Yeni Han in Istanbul's economically vibrant Laleli or Fatih districts.[78] This group comprised people who had served as financiers and guarantors for the Palu begs and other notables for the tax-farming leases of the 1820s through the late 1830s, and their land claims dated from the early years of the Tanzimat, when they were financiers for tax farmers. As mentioned, the begs frequently used their property, including their land, as collateral when borrowing money. In the face of the begs' inability to pay their debts, the *sarraf*s demanded they sell their property.

These *çorbacı*s also acquired tax-farm contracts from Palu villages. Before the Tanzimat era, the begs had the upper hand in leasing or farming out Palu lands, but the arrival of provincial governors committed to breaking the power of the Kurdish elites made it an opportune time for the wealthy Armenians to acquire tax-farm contracts. In 1849, before Abdullah Beg's death, the Armenians, in alliance with the Diyarbekir governor Esat Pasha and the Harput governor Yusuf Pasha, moved towards acquiring the tithe revenues of significant chunks of land from the begs.[79] Reportedly, Esat Pasha and Yusuf Pasha gathered Abdullah, İbrahim, Ahmed, Mehmed and Hamdullah Begs and paid each 5,000 guruş for promising that they would not intervene in the tithe revenues of lands in Palu and Eğin.[80] The goal was to eliminate the begs from the collection of the tithe. Subsequently, the lands under question were appraised (*keşf*) and their value put at 30,000 guruş. To this amount, the buyers added the tithe and paid 32,000 guruş in the auction in an effort to collect the tithe revenues of the two areas. Despite numerous appeals to the imperial centre, however, the buyers never got hold of the tithe revenues of the areas, nor did the money they paid reach the imperial treasury. These efforts to eliminate the begs from tax farming proved futile.[81]

Throughout the 1850s and the 1860s, these Palu Armenians based in Istanbul sent the Meclis-i Vâlâ detailed accounts of the land sales and agrarian relations of production in Palu. In most cases, they described themselves as the representatives of certain villages and raised specific questions about land sales or the problems of the sharecroppers in those places. Along with this role of representation, it is also clear that they had a vested interest in land sales. For the next few decades, they acted as a conduit conveying issues of a local nature to the imperial centre while voicing their personal agendas about land acquisition.

One name in this group particularly stands out for the next few decades. Mardiros – or Mardiros Kalfa[82] – from Palu sent countless letters to the imperial state claiming to be the representative (*vekil*) of the Muslim and non-Muslim inhabitants of Palu. The Meclis-i Vâlâ carefully reviewed the letters and, on at least a few occasions, called the begs and these claimants in to discuss the issue. The appeals of these men, together with the resultant Meclis-i Vâlâ reports, provide fascinating information about the complexity of land claims in this period.

LAND SALES

The begs used their local influence and connections with local administrators to re-purchase the land that had been opened up for the *ahali*'s purchase.[83] They were on good terms with the members of the Harput provincial council; the letters claimed that the men were seen eating together, which surely meant that justice was not being served.[84] The letters mentioned instances of begs and aghas dividing the lands among each other or registering land with their family members to avoid confiscation. For instance, Çötelioğlu Abdüllatif Efendi had registered the lands of the Tepe village in his brother-in-law's name.[85] Similarly, Tahir Beg had registered the Abrank village in his brother's name.[86]

But the begs' encroachment over land in contravention of the new land programme was only one side of the coin. In reality, land sales and the resulting changes in property and land relations were much more complex. The picture that emerges from these complaints indicates that even though the begs sought to maintain their historical rights over land and prevent land sales, sales were under way and the begs' hereditary proprietorship was being eroded by land purchases.

Kapıaçmaz/Tset, located north of the Murad/Aradzani River, was one of the villages that had historically been the property of the Palu begs. A mixed, Muslim-Armenian settlement, it was originally owned by Necib Beg, Abdullah Beg's brother, then, after the government's land plan was put into effect, the village lands were divided into three in accordance with the imperial order. One-third stayed with Necib Beg; the remaining two-thirds were confiscated by the imperial treasury. A quarter of those was sold to Necib Beg, who paid 7,300 guruş as a down-payment. The value of the remaining three-quarters of confiscated land was determined at 22,050 guruş and sold to village inhabitants who were given title deeds. From one perspective, one can see cases like this one as examples of the begs' ability to shape land sales in their favour, as they were able to buy parcels of the land confiscated by the treasury. However, what is more noteworthy is that three-quarters of the land was sold to people other than the begs – creating a veritable transformation in land ownership in the village.[87]

As we have seen, even before the government came up with its plan to confiscate and sell the begs' lands, the begs had already been farming out, leasing or selling their lands. From the second half of the eighteenth century on, the begs had transferred the right to extract surplus (through farming out), usufruct (through lease) and ownership (through sale). What the imperial state was targeting was the begs' absolute authority over land. When the land plan was put into effect, however, the Ottoman administration found that it had to deal with past land transfers made by the begs. The question was what to do with these lands, which, despite officially being *yurtluk-ocaklık*, had been transferred to people other than begs. In its final decision, the council exempted lands of this sort from confiscation. But at the local level, controversial cases between the begs and those who had purchased land from them previously came to the fore after the reallocation plan was put into practice. One case concerned Abrank village, located north of the Murad/Aradzani River.[88] Tahir and Cemşid Beg held 418 *kıt'a* (plot., pl. *kıt'aât*) of this village, including

Table 6.1 Latif Efendi's account of the lands sold by the Treasury (in guruş) in Abrank village (c. 1860)[89]

Total amount of down-payment paid for the lands sold.	448,888
Total amount of instalments paid.	160,700
Total amount of instalments having reached the imperial treasury.	153,000
Total amount of instalments not having reached the imperial treasury.	7,700
Part of the instalments not paid yet.	280,000

fields, vineyards and orchards which, according to the accounts of the villagers, had previously been either sold or farmed out to villagers. After the government issued the order to divide the lands, the begs took action and, claiming the ownership of these lands, appealed to the Imperial Registry. Their lands were registered and they were given new title deeds, which the inhabitants of the village quickly disputed. From the perspective of the imperial centre, the lack of a definitive solution to the problems stemming from land allocation was because of 'corruption and malice' in local operations, but beyond this it had little information. The Council of Accounting appointed Latif Efendi, a Palu-based provincial official, to investigate. His elaborate response revealed the intricacies of land sales, the parties' positions, and the shifts in agrarian production relations. He provided the council with a fairly detailed account of the finances related to the land sales (Table 6.1).

Latif Efendi's attention was focused more on the unsold lands and the reason for the slowness of land sales in the area. A decade had passed since the state had issued its resolution about the sale of the *yurtluk-ocaklık* lands, but there had been no significant progress. According to Latif Efendi, village inhabitants were trying to manipulate land sales in various ways. They were trying to hold back sales so the prices would fall and they could buy the lands for themselves. Reportedly, they also deterred potential customers from outside the village by hassling them about soil rent and other taxes.[90]

The imperial government was concerned not just about the unsold lands, but also about monies paid for sold lands that had not been sent to the central treasury. As Table 6.1 shows, even though local records indicate that 160,700 guruş were paid as instalments, the Imperial Treasury only received 153,000 guruş – an investigation was needed to determine the whereabouts of the 7,700 guruş. Apparently, local politics were preventing the uninterrupted flow of money to the centre. But reading the report from the perspective of the Ottoman administration can be misleading. Latif Efendi's account also shows that even with these problems, things were changing in terms of land ownership.

After Abdullah Beg

The report clearly shows that as of 1860 – nearly a decade after the initial land allocation plan was issued – land sales were under way. The slowness of the sales or problems associated with the begs' re-acquiring land is only one facet of the process. In the absence of systematic records, it is not clear how much land was actually sold, and at what prices, at a given time in a particular village. However, judging from the down-payments made for the land, as indicated in Table 6.1, the government's land programme was working and buyers unrelated to the begs invested significant amounts of money buying land from the Treasury. Regardless of the begs' ongoing claims to the land and their efforts to re-buy it, other people also bought lands and demanded title deeds for lands they were already tilling.

The continuation of land sales is also shown by the types of disputes brought to the imperial centre. Most stemmed from clashes between pre-existing claims and new claimants. An example is the Khoşmat village – a sizeable village an hour's ride north-east from Palu's centre.[91] Seven Armenians based in Çukurçeşme Han in Istanbul appealed to the Ottoman state,[92] complaining that Necib Beg unlawfully seized the lands that they said had been in the possession of village inhabitants for generations. When Necib Beg, Abdullah Beg's brother, claimed inheritance of his lands, he listed Khoşmat as having been owned in its entirety by his brother. The Meclis-i Vâlâ gave half (around eight villages) of his brother's land to Necib Beg without specifying specific villages.[93] Evidently, half of the village's land was opened up for sale and most likely either bought by the petitioners or by other villagers connected to them. But as an earlier Meclis-i Vâlâ report attested, even though there was a title deed official in the area, the buyers were not given title deeds and the money accrued was not sent to the imperial treasury.[94] While demonstrating that land sales were under way in the village, the case also reveals the clash of historical claims over land with the new situations created with land sales.

Some convoluted cases involved multiple layers of pre-existing claims – even after the begs relinquished their propriety rights over land. In one such case, Tahir and Cemşîd Beg sold land to a certain Serkiz from Harput who then sold a quarter of the land to Agop and Avedis, who brought a complaint against Hacadur, who represented the inhabitants of the village. Hacadur claimed that the land had been bought by the village inhabitants after the land confiscation and that they had title deeds, whereas the begs and Serkiz did not.[95] After checking the records, the Imperial Registry confirmed the village's ownership of the land. Despite this, the land had changed hands three times!

By 1866, because of the insistent calls of Armenian notables of Palu in Istanbul, the issue once again appeared on the agenda of the imperial state, which sent the Harput-based land surveyor Osman Nuri Efendi to Palu. He was charged with investigating the sale of the Palu lands and overseeing the land sales to be performed by the Harput provincial council. He was also to determine the condition, location and value of the lands to be sold. While far from thorough, Osman Nuri's account provides a glimpse into the land sales in Palu a decade and a half after the land programme went into effect.

Osman Nuri Efendi found out that a considerable percentage of the begs' land (sixty-three *kıt'aât*) had already been sold (eleven *kıt'aât* were unsold). He also demonstrated that 185 *kıt'aât*, of land were owned by the *ahali* with title deeds. This means that by 1866, the begs had relinquished the ownership of a sizeable portion of Palu's agrarian land. Questions remained about land that was classified as *vakıf* but whose classification was hazy.

Osman Nuri Efendi's account revealed that the total value of land sold was 1,048,419 guruş. Except for 44,000 guruş, this entire amount shown had been submitted to the Imperial Treasury. However, further investigation revealed that in the accounts of the central treasury, the value of sold land was registered as 527,945.5 guruş, confirming that there was a large (520,473.5 guruş) discrepancy between the actual amounts paid by the purchasers and the amounts submitted to the central treasury.[96] From the Ottoman state's point of view, this discrepancy that Osman Nuri detected was at the heart of the issue – that land was being sold but that the revenues from these sales did not entirely flow into the imperial treasury. Throughout this process, the Ottoman administration's major challenge was lack of reliable information on the types and amount of land sold, as well as total revenues. The need to reform record keeping was obvious to all. Even though officials in the Tanzimat period tried to address record keeping, the prior *mefrûzü'l kalem* status still posed challenges. The population censuses conducted in the 1840s had yielded an unforeseen amount of quantitative information on Palu's population,[97] but the same was not true for information about land and revenues. Previous attempts to conduct the empire-wide property and revenue surveys (*temettuat*) of 1840–1 in Palu (and in fact throughout Kurdistan) were ensnared in local conflicts and largely failed.[98] Osman Nuri Efendi's records, while nowhere near a systematic land survey, provided fairly detailed information. His records not only showed the size of the land sold in both *dönüm* and *kıt'aât*, but also presented measures such as *ölçek*, *habbe*, *kot* or *keyl* (kile) – all units used to measure grains – that showed its productive capacity.

The major complaint of the *ahali* was that they were not shown any lands that they could purchase. In 1867, the *murahhasa* of the Palu Armenians, together with the community representative, petitioned the local council asking that the 1/3 share apportioned to the begs be left with the village inhabitants as well – it appears that they had already acquired the 2/3 that the original governmental decision had opened up for their purchase and were asking to buy the remaining portion held by the begs. They protested that the begs got to keep 1/3 land without payment, while they had to pay to buy the land.[99]

For the potential buyers, the underlying problem was the alliance between the provincial administrators and the local notables. Ever since the decision to open the land to purchase by commoners, the provincial council of Harput and the district council of Palu had tried to obstruct sales.[100] They asked for a new surveyor – but they also wanted him to be sent to Diyarbekir, which would disempower the local councils and thus lessen the influence of the local notables and provincial Ottoman administrators ensnared in local politics. The Meclis-i Vâlâ addressed their complaint by granting Osman Nuri, the current surveyor, a salary of 2,000 guruş. Previously, he had been appointed without a salary, which presumably rendered him more liable to take bribes. The council decided to dispatch a neutral officer to the district. Muhtar Efendi, a scribe of the Meclis-i Vâlâ, was sent from Istanbul to investigate in greater detail.[101]

The representatives of the villages also claimed that the eleven plots of unsold land that had previously been described as having 'low value since they were [located] among the Kurds' were actually land that had not been given to the *ahali*, even when they made the down-payment. They claimed that some of this land was instead given to the 'notables of the area' (*rueasa-i memleket*). This claim might or might not be true; we can say that the point about some land not being sold because it was located within the Kurdish population is plausible, given the geographical pattern of the land sales. This was reiterated by Muhtar Efendi, who stated that twenty-two of the villages were not sold due to their location in the Kurdish-populated areas of Palu. It is no coincidence that the issues and complaints about land sales throughout this period came mostly from the villages north-west of the Murad/Aradzani River where the Armenian population concentrated. In contrast, the villages in the south and south-east of Palu where the Kurdish tribal population lived had few disputes because they had few land sales. The majority of land sales took place mostly in the Armenian-populated villages in the north and north-west of Palu. The buyers were either village inhabitants or wealthy Armenians who might have ties with the village, but were not necessarily residents. Among these were the Istanbul-based Armenian *sarraf*s who pursued their business, like land purchases, through local proxies in the villages.

The register that Osman Nuri prepared during his stay in Palu did not survive, but his summaries offer invaluable information. The amount of land sold by the Imperial Treasury to *ahali* equalled 5,141 *kıt'aât* the number of the cultivators who purchased land was 200. This was slightly higher than the amount of land given to the emirs and aghas for free, which equalled 4,932 *kıt'aat*. Significantly, 4,694 additional *kıt'aât* of land were already in the possession (with title deeds) of the *ahali*. Muhtar Efendi, the scribe sent to accompany Osman Nuri, formed a commission to investigate the land sales. In a year, he presented his findings, which provided a clearer account of land sales.

Both Osman Nuri's earlier accounts and the new figures provided by Muhtar Efendi indicate that, notwithstanding the problems raised in countless petitions sent to the imperial centre, land sales were well under way. The total amount of cash derived from land sales (1,059,419 guruş) also indicates that land sales were occurring. Granted, a fraction of this amount (527,945.5) was actually channelled to the Imperial Treasury, but the amount of land sold indicates that the Palu begs' unhindered control over land and its revenues was being challenged. The begs still held a substantial portion of the land inherited from their ancestors, but they no longer had a legitimate claim to hereditary ownership over the entire Palu land and its produce. From Abdullah Beg's death in 1849 to the 1870s, the Palu nobility's control over Palu's agrarian land came under attack on two fronts, from the Armenians from Palu, mainly the financial bourgeoise who pushed for the sale of the lands, and the imperial state, whose major preoccupation was maximising the amount of tithes and other monies that accrued to the imperial treasury.

As the land tenure changed, it inevitably affected the relations of production. At the heart of the issue is how alterations in land ownership

Table 6.2 Muhtar Efendi's account of land sales[102]

	# of Villages
Total number of villages	313
Lands in the hands of *ahali* with title deed (i.e. not to be opened for sale)	184
vakıf land	48
Those within Kurdish [areas] (*yirmi iki para karye de ekrad içinde bulunarak ...*)	22
Land sold	59

changed the methods of surplus extraction and labour organisation. Did the loosening of the begs' control over land along with the Ottoman state's attempts at centralising the tithe collection alleviate the tax burden on cultivators? Did the new landowners change the established patterns of surplus extraction? Did exploitation lessen? Let us see.

Anxieties around the Collection of Agrarian Surplus

From the early years of the Tanzimat, the Ottoman imperial state wanted to collect agrarian dues on land efficiently and maximise state revenue. Although it wanted to undermine the power of the tax farmers who claimed a big chunk of agrarian surplus, the state lacked the necessary infrastructural capacity to bypass them altogether. As we have seen, after briefly trying a new system of sending tax collectors (*muhassıl*) to collect the tithe, the state abandoned the system. For the rest of the century, tax farming remained the major method of collecting dues on land.

In 1850, shortly after Abdullah Beg's exile, the tithes of Palu were brought under the imperial treasury's control (*canib-i miriden zabt edildi*) and auctioned. But the process was fraught with complications, as the tithes were simultaneously farmed out to multiple people at different prices, including: a certain Dimitri, who was a foreman at the Ma'âdin-i Hümâyun; Ahmed Agha, the *müdür* of neighbouring Mazgird district; a certain Yahya Agha; and someone named Artin from Ankara.[103] There was no standard profile of the emergent tax farmers after the Palu begs' lands were confiscated: they included merchants, artisans and provincial administrators, and both Muslims and non-Muslims. In 1851, the imperial state set out to implement the 'new method' (*usul-u cedide*), which meant auctioning the tithe in lump sum (*maktu'en ihale*) for a period of five years.[104]

The Ottoman state's experimentation with new ways of tax collection disturbed the established socio-economic arrangements in the areas that had remained outside its fiscal sway. In Palu, the reception of the Tanzimat's land and tax policies showed a regional pattern. Where the population was primarily Kurdish, that is, the south and south-east of Palu and further north-west, there was a larger reaction to the imperial state's attempt to claim agrarian surplus. A letter sent by the *müdür* of Palu in 1861 specifically named the *nahiye*s (sub-districts) of Weşin, Karabegân, Sivan, Hûn and Gökdere as resistant to paying annual dues.[105] We can also add Karaçor in the north-west. From the earliest days of the Tanzimat, local and central Ottoman administrators frequently deployed military force to collect taxes from the Kurdish tribes. Karaçor entered the imperial state's radar back in 1845, the year Kurdistan was brought under the Tanzimat programme. The Kurdish tribes of Karaçor, in alliance with the neighbouring Çarsancak, had paid no dues to the imperial treasury.[106] Abdullah Beg was policing the tribes at the time, and he reached out to the centre asking for military deployments. The Ottoman administrators described what was happening as 'turmoil and insurrection [*şuriş ve ihtilal*]'.[107] The imperial state deployed six cannons, six battalions of infantry and one regiment of imperial troops to the area, ready to take action if attempts to convince the tribes failed. In 1857, local administrators again complained that the Kurdish population of Palu and Eğil were refusing to pay taxes. After dispatching a battalion to the area, the governor of Harput collected about 20,000 guruş in annual tax.[108] Two decades later in 1876, in one land register it was reported that the village of Weşin did not complete the land survey and it was impossible to determine the value of its tithe revenues.[109]

The sheer size of the district and the amount of taxes to be collected made collection challenging. 'Despite sending a coterie of tax-collectors', the *müdür* complained, 'the inhabitants of Weşin, Karabegân, Sivan, Hûn, and Gökdere showed resistance to paying their dues in a timely manner.'[110] Whenever they discussed the difficulties of tax collection in this region, Ottoman administrators pointed out that 'the majority of its inhabitants [were] Kurds and tribes [*ahâlinin ekserisi ekrad ve aşâyirden ibaret bulunmasıyla*]'. *Kurdishness* in this sense meant a set of socio-economic characteristics that included nomadism, warriorship and tribalism – which were equivalent for the Ottoman administrators to lawlessness and tax evasion. In other words, tax payment was considered the major sign of accepting the state's authority and refusal to do so was perceived as a sign of lawlessness. For the Tanzimat state, taxation was *the* entry into a new world of law and legality whose contours were still being defined. Taxation became the major arena for the state's aspirations of consolidating its symbolic capital, the arena that reflected its level of *stateness*.[111] The way the Harput council described the situation pertaining to taxes is indicative: one report stated that the majority of the inhabitants of Palu (and neighbouring Eğil), 'let alone paying their dues, did not even appeal to the government in any condition [*değil zimmetlerini vermek hiçbir sûretle cânib-i hükûmete mürâca'at etmemekde olduklarından*]'.[112]

Refusal to pay taxes became the major characteristics of Kurdishness for the Ottoman administrators. When they talked about the '*ekrad*', the language of Ottoman administrators frequently entailed descriptions like *huşunet* (harshness), being spoiled (*şımarmış*) by the absence of state authority, or even resembling animals (*hayvana benzer adamlar*). Equating *stateness* to being able to tax, the Ottoman administrators relegated *Kurdishness* to a world of primitiveness, backwardness and unruliness. As law and legality were redefined, Kurdishness was constructed in ways that rendered it almost anathema to law and legality.

For the Kurdish rural population, the state's attempts to institute conscription, direct taxation and legibility in record keeping were not readily accepted practices. But one also needs to remember that the making of the modern state was nowhere a smooth process. In Kurdistan, as elsewhere, the population's perception of the modern state was more complex than an acceptance versus resistance dichotomy can potentially reveal. As will be shown below, the Kurdish population did continue to pay agrarian dues to the begs and aghas. So while claiming a share from the agrarian surplus, the state was only deepening the exploitation in the rural sector. Societal reactions to the state in the Kurdish areas need to be understood within this economic context.

The Curious Case of Noksan-ı Arz

Tanzimat tax policies in Palu were bifurcated along regional lines. While in the Kurdish areas the major issue for the state was tax resistance, on the northern bank of the Murad/Aradzani River where Armenians constituted the sharecropping population, the imperial state emerged as a rival claimant for the agrarian surplus, competing with the begs who insisted on their historical land rights. After the confiscation of the begs' lands, these conflicts over the rural surplus were embodied in *noksan-ı arz*, a type of agrarian dues the begs collected from Palu's rural population.

In Ottoman land legislation, *noksan-ı arz* refers to the difference between land's pre-harvest and post-harvest value.[113] It was based on the assumption that land was worth less after harvest due to decreased fertility. *Noksan-ı arz* was also used to refer to a landowner's financial losses when his land was seized by someone else – in which case the seizer had to pay a fee, called *noksan-ı arz*, to the landowner to compensate him for his losses.[114] In the aftermath of the land confiscation, *noksan-ı arz* became a blanket term used to describe any surplus levied from the agrarian producers that the producers deemed illegitimate. Interestingly, right after the confiscation, *noksan-ı arz* was collected by the provincial council on behalf of the imperial state as part of the district's annual dues. In 1857, this amounted to 138,589 guruş.[115] The monies were paid on confiscated land that the provincial councils and administrators rented out prior to selling and were collected along with the tithe.

From the perspective of the agrarian producers, *noksan-ı arz* referred to all additional extractions beyond the tithe set by the Tanzimat at 1/10. So when, for instance, producers were forced to pay dues from 1.5/10 to 2/10, up to as much as 1/2, all the shares beyond the 1/10 were described as *noksan-ı arz*. In some cases, *noksan-ı arz* was used interchangeably with *icare-i zemin*, which literally translates as soil rent paid in kind. There were complaints that, after the land sales started, the begs were seizing 1/3 of the harvest as the soil rent.[116]

A cursory glance at the petitions sent from Palu – or about Palu – show that Palu's agrarian producers, primarily the Armenians, saw *noksan-ı arz* as the biggest issue. But why did it become such a chronic issue in Palu's agrarian landscape at this time? Was there an observable and quantifiable increase in exploitation after the confiscation of the begs' lands? Or did the cultivators have greater opportunities to complain about the *noksan-ı arz* after the Tanzimat tithe regulations? The answer is both.

The Tanzimat discourse about instituting equal taxation and fixing the tithe at 1/10 resonated in Palu.[117] As soon as the region was brought under the Tanzimat programme in 1845, regardless of the actual intent or genuineness of the Tanzimat reformers to institute an equitable tax system, the agrarian population of Palu expected it to be put in effect. In their petitions, the *ahali* referred to 1848 (when the begs' lands were confiscated) as the date when *noksan-ı arz* was explicitly banned by the imperial state in Palu.[118] Thus, it was the combination of the two events (the confiscation and the 1/10 tithe) that was the legal/official basis for the *ahali*'s complaints about the *noksan-ı arz*. *Noksan-ı arz* was the way in which the producers articulated a moral economy of surplus extraction that referred to the Tanzimat, the way they could raise their voices about sharecropping terms and articulate their notion of fair taxation. And the imperial state sent several orders to the local administrators asking for the termination of this practice of *noksan-ı arz*.

The frequency of complaints about the *noksan-ı arz* was not just an effect of the legal-discursive space that Tanzimat opened up. It was also related to how the terms of surplus extraction got aggravated. In 1853, there were ongoing complaints that the begs were confiscating 1.5/10 in addition to the 1/10 tithe.[119] Despite the legal ratio, exploitation in the agrarian sector deepened. How did this happen? For one thing, there was the emergent problem of double-taxation – that is, paying rent and taxes at the same time. This was because, after the begs' lands were confiscated, the imperial state started to collect the tithe using multiple methods including trusteeship and farming out the lands, albeit inconsistently. At the same time, however, begs maintained their claims over land and its surplus – which meant that the producers found themselves expected to pay taxes to the state (i.e. the tithe) *and* other dues to the begs – and the latter was the *noksan-ı arz*.

Ultimately, the terms of the established sharecropping system did not change in the post-confiscation era. The agrarian population's complaints about the new Armenian landholders demonstrate this. Petitioners stated that, notwithstanding the efforts of the governors and other state officials, the misery caused by *noksan-ı arz* had continued for almost two decades.[120] In 1863, after the issue was discussed again at the Supreme Council, an inspector was dispatched to the district to investigate further. He produced a detailed inventory of the begs and aghas who collected *noksan-ı arz* and the names of the villages that paid these amounts for 1852–63 (Tables 6.3 and 6.4).

In Palu, up until this point the established system of extraction had been in kind. The amounts collected indicate a transition from in-kind to cash extraction. After the begs' lands were confiscated, two processes unfolded. On the one hand, sharecropping was still the dominant labour system. On the other, monetisation of surplus extraction in the area was

Table 6.3 Amount of money collected from all the non-Muslim villages of the Palu district (in *akçes*)[121]

Name of the Collector	Name of the Villages (v.) or Sub-districts (s.d).	Amount (*akçes*)
Şerif Beg	Haraba (s.d.)	60,000
Mehmed Sadık Beg		
Timur Beg		
Same as above	Nıbaşi [Nıbşi]	10,000
Hacı Tahir Beg	Yarımca, Yeni karye and other misc. villages	30,000
Cemşid Beg		
Mehmed Beg and his brothers	Kümbat (v.)	15,000
	Bağin (v.)	
	Srin (v.)	
Nuh Beg	Çayri Mezre	6,000
Said Beg	Neciran [Nacaran]	31,000
Haşim Beg	Tilik	
	Trkhe	
Azizoğlu	Karınca Mezresi	10,000
Osman Agha	Altıhan [Artıhan] (v.)	15,000
Hacı Tahir Beg	İsabeg	10,000
Aghas – the associates of begs	Karaçor (s.d.)	150,000
	Bulanık (s.d.)	
	Haraba	
Total		**687,000**

The Kurdish Nobility in the Ottoman Empire

Table 6.4 Amount of money collected from all the Muslim villages of the Palu district (in *akçe*s)[122]

Name of the Collector	Name of the Villages or Sub-districts	Amount (*akçe*s)
İbrahim Agha	Balka (بالقه) (v.) and Deste (دسته) (v.)	20,000
Said and Hacı Tahir Begs from İbrahim Beg's family	Hun (s.d.) and Weşin (s.d.)	72,000
Haşim Beg	ten villages (names not stated) and Kaziyani (s.d.) and Weşin (s.d.)	270,000
Hasan Efendi	Gökdere (s.d.)	20,000
Hamdullah Beg	Villages of Mezre (s.d.) and of Sivan	20,000
Mehmet Sadık Beg	Villages of Mezre (s.d.) and of Sivan	23,000
Necib Beg	Villages and sub-districts of Mezre (s.d.)	15,000
Mehmed, Abdullah, Baki, Mustafa, Gaffur and Malik Begs (Tayyib Beg's sons)	Mezre (sd). Seraçor (s.d.) Aşmuşad (s.d.)	40,000
Ahmed Beg's son Şerif Beg	Mezre (s.d.)	15,000
Ömer Beg	Sivan Mezre	5,000
Hurşid Begzade Said Beg	Mezre and sub-districts	3,000
Selim Beg and Timur Beg	Mezre Sivan	5,000
Total amount collected by the aghas – the associates of begs		80,000
Total		**340,000**

beginning. The loosening of the begs' hereditary control both intensified and transformed patterns of rural extraction.

The accounts also show that the extractions were made on the basis of village or sub-district – without specifying the cultivators. In many cases, more than one beg and/or agha's name appears as the extractor, which suggests the likelihood of double taxation – corroborating producers' complaints. Given that the imperial state also claimed dues from these areas, the burden on the agrarian producers seems to have deepened.

Significantly, the inspector prepared separate lists for Muslim and non-Muslim villages, suggesting that they both paid these levies. The majority of the Muslim villages and sub-districts paying were in the east and southeast of Palu, that is, Weşin, Karaçor, Gökdere, Hun, Saraçor and Sivan, the same areas previously defined by Ottoman administrators as Kurdish and tribal and unlikely to pay taxes. However, this homogenising description of the state fails to show the complexity of the socio-political organisation in different parts of Kurdistan. The table shows us a different reality:

noksan-ı arz was an agrarian levy and the Kurdish population of the area was paying substantial amounts of it – but not to the state. The agrarian population of these areas consisted primarily of Kurds who tilled the lands of various aghas and begs as sharecroppers – a fact that often gets lost in the Ottoman state's stereotypical description of the Kurds as a monolithic group as tribal and (semi-)nomadic.

The Armenian villages and sub-districts listed in Table 6.3 were located in the north and north-west, and the amount the non-Muslim villages paid (687,000 *akçe*s) was two times higher than that paid by the Muslim villages (340,000 *akçe*s). The reason for this stems mainly from the socio-economic organisation of agricultural production in Palu. The agrarian population of Palu was made up primarily, albeit not exclusively, of Armenians who tilled the fertile lands on the northern bank of the Murad/Arazdzani River. And after the begs' lands were sold, the purchasers were mainly Armenians. Thus, the higher number paid by the Armenians reflects the concentration of agrarian production in the areas where the Armenian population lived, and the sharecropping population being largely Armenian.

The problem was not just the begs, though. Another reason for intensified exploitation was that the purchasers of the confiscated land continued the existing terms of surplus extraction. Complaints about both 'Muslim and non-Muslim notables' reached the imperial state. The Muslim notables were the begs and aghas who continued to hold large amounts of land; non-Muslim notables were the wealthy Armenians who became new landowners.[123] Both were accused of extracting unfair fees – while it is clear that it was primarily the begs who imposed heavy dues in the rural sector. Nevertheless, while property relations were changing and more Armenian notables were acquiring land, the socio-economic rift within the Armenian population of Palu grew conspicuously, creating issues within the Armenian population. This is discussed in the last part of the chapter.

The Crisis of Representation

From the 1840s through the 1860s, Palu's name appeared in the Ottoman bureaucratic correspondence more often than it ever had, indicating a great number of conflicts. There were two reasons why the quantity of written records about Palu increased visibly in the mid-nineteenth century. First, the Ottoman imperial state developed an interest in the Kurdish east as it sought to consolidate its authority over land. An expanded provincial bureaucracy and the appointment of provincial administrators who were keen to convey local business to the imperial centre resulted in more Ottoman records related to Palu. Second, the Weşin incident and the subsequent land confiscation brought Palu before the Meclis-i Vâlâ several times.

Beyond these was a specific dynamic – Armenian notables' claims to represent the Armenian villagers. In other words, Palu featured frequently in government records, because of the deliberate efforts of Armenians from Palu based in Istanbul. Between the 1850s and 1860s, they flooded the imperial centre with petitions mostly related to property relations in the Palu countryside. While claiming to represent the interests of the villagers, they also had a vested interest in the Palu land – they hoped to acquire land from the confiscated lands.

After the death of Abdullah Beg, these financiers became ever more visible. They appealed to the Ottoman authorities about the begs' unpaid debts dating from before the land confiscation. During Abdullah Beg's time, the credit nexus that connected the begs to these financiers had tightened through the tax-farming and *mübaya* systems. Armenians served as creditors for the former and as purchasing agents for the latter. After the confiscation of the begs' lands, they assumed a new role as the representatives of the *ahali* in various Palu villages. Mardiros and others like him became the representatives of village communities, including the landless peasants and sharecroppers, before the Ottoman imperial state. They often claimed to represent the inhabitants of a specific village or 'non-Muslim inhabitants of Palu', and sometimes both Muslim and non-Muslim inhabitants. Often but not always, these representatives proved their right to speak on behalf of the community with a *vekâletnâme* given by the people – which the authorities accepted as genuine.[124] The issues they brought up revolved around land ownership, surplus extraction and the terms of sharecropping, and credit relations.

In the 1860s, Palu's agrarian population's indebtedness changed with the emergence of a new group of creditors, the *poliçecis*. These were Istanbul-based Armenian financiers who offered credit at extremely high interest rates. The opening of a land market after the confiscation of the Palu begs' lands, together with the resultant monetisation of surplus extraction with the *noksan-ı arz*, created the conditions for intensified peasant indebtedness. The *poliçeci*s loaned money at exorbitant interest rates, even charging interest on interest. In 1866, this rate was at 27 per cent, a dramatic increase over the 12 per cent rate that government regulations said was the maximum allowable rate.[125] When they could not collect their debts, the *poliçeci*s seized the homes, animals or lands of the indebted peasants.[126] These peasants found a voice in Mardiros, who appealed to the state on behalf of forty inhabitants in the hands of the *poliçecis*,[127] and managed to bring two *poliçecis* to the Commercial Court (*Ticaret Mahkemesi*) in the imperial capital.[128]

But the major preoccupation for Mardiros and others like him was land sales. They brought up issues such as the alliance between different elite groups in land registration and the collaboration between the begs and the surveyors, and between the begs and the Armenian notables, as well as the begs' reluctance to comply with the government orders on land sales.[129] These letters painted a dismal picture of the process, even though the situation on the ground was more complex than they indicated. The confiscation of the begs' lands happened abruptly, but the ensuing land sales were a bumpy process full of negotiations and setbacks. In the grand scheme of things, however, land sales were under way and land ownership in Palu had become more fragmented.

By appealing to the imperial centre about land sales, Mardiros and his associates forced the state to monitor land sales in Palu and act. The cases they raised were repeatedly heard by local and central councils. The Sublime Porte issued orders in 1848, 1852 and 1854 and in the 1860s to the provincial governors demanding that the local government intervene in the issues Mardiros had raised in his petitions.[130] The imperial state's plan to confiscate the begs' lands did not entail any considerations about what land organisation would look like afterwards; with their appeals to the state, these Istanbul-based Palu Armenians kept the land sales on the state's agenda. Pointing out the irregularities and chaos in the process, they repeatedly asked for cadaster (*mesaha*) in Palu. It was because of their appeals that the imperial centre dispatched investigators and surveyors who created detailed reports about the land sales. Their appeals pushed land sales into the realm of law and legality. But they were playing a double role: they had vested interests in undermining the economic power of the begs and breaking their long-lived control over land, even as they claimed to represent the *ahali*, particularly the Armenian sharecroppers in the fertile villages on the north and north-western banks of the Murad/ Aradzani River. This claim to representation, however, was not welcomed by all the parties involved and it did not go unchallenged.

Mardiros's claim to representation was disputed by some people in Palu, who were upset that he did not live in Palu. Besides, petitioners expressed their concern about Mardiros because he was presumably given a British passport.[131] In 1866, a petition was sent to the imperial state, signed by 'more than five hundred people from Palu who are now in Istanbul' and stating that Avedis and Mardiros did not represent them. The land issue, they said, had been resolved by selling the land and the appeals of these two were irrelevant and did not represent the Palu inhabitants.[132]

While it is not possible to know who penned this letter or whether it really reflects the view of 'five hundred' Palu inhabitants, it indicates a sense of anxiety over Avedis and Mardiros's claims to represent their interests. Clearly not everyone felt positive about their efforts to pull the government into local conflicts. To prevent them from continuing their appeals, the letter argued that the land surveys had been completed successfully, all land had been sold, and the land issue was resolved. The issue of the legitimacy of Mardiros's claim to represent the people also appeared in the begs' defence against him at the provincial council, which stated that his *vekaletname* was not legally valid.[133]

Mardiros stated that, on the basis of his role as the representative, he had brought land officials to the district five times and had managed to get the confiscated lands of begs put under *mîrî* status. He was disappointed not just because he felt his efforts were unappreciated, but because he had ended up spending 2,000 akçes. He wanted the *ahali* to repay him, which was probably why he became suspect in the eyes of many.[134] In 1871, Mardiros's frustration peaked, not just because he was broke and indebted, but because his *vekaletname* had been seized by a certain Ali Beg, the second clerk in the Meclis-i Vâlâ.[135] After this, he stopped reporting on the land question in Palu and disappeared from the scene. At this time, Palu was very different from in the 1830s when he had appeared as a creditor with solid financial links to the Palu nobility. Now, the Palu begs' hereditary land rights were gone, although agrarian exploitation remained, with multiple claimants vying for land and the new owners failing to improve the terms of surplus extraction. Land was fragmented, extraction was monetised and exploitation of the peasantry had intensified. The begs had lost their hereditary rights, but not their power; not only did they still have economic control over land, they had increasingly been incorporated into the local Ottoman administration. This process, however, was no less controversial than land re-organisation.

Conclusion

The abolition of the hereditary privileges of the Kurdish nobility within the context of the Tanzimat resulted in drastic changes in the socio-economic organisation of the region. The leadership position of the Kurdish elites received a big blow with the Ottoman state's frontal attack starting from the 1820s. The existing historical accounts of this critical period of Kurdistan's history have focused solely on the conflicts between the imperial state and the Kurdish elites. In addition to being a transformative moment in terms of the Kurdish elite's relations with the imperial state, abolishing the begs' hereditary privileges resulted in drastic changes within the locality, specifically in terms of the local property structures and power relations revolving around land ownership. This chapter examined the politics of land confiscation and demonstrated that both the Palu begs and agricultural producers worked to acquire or re-acquire land in the next few decades. The confiscation of the begs' lands brought to the fore discussions about the legitimacy of their fiscal privileges over land and its revenues. A highly detailed analysis of the process demonstrated that what shaped the path of the land programme and the prospects of the Palu nobility were largely the provincial negotiations and struggles rather than a blueprint imposed by the central Ottoman state.

For agricultural producers, the Palu nobility's hereditary position meant an exploitative labour system in land based on sharecropping. The begs' claim to unhindered control over agrarian surplus was at the heart of the conflict, and the rural population's resistance to sharecropping for the begs became more vocal after the land confiscation. Exploitation in the rural sector became deeper and more monetised. As their grip over land loosened with the confiscation, the begs and the aghas imposed monetary extractions (or a form of rent called *noksan-ı arz*) on the rural population.

But the impact of the abolition of the begs' hereditary privileges on the local population varied. Armenian financial bourgeois based in Istanbul came to the historical stage as potential buyers paving the way for protracted disputes between them and the begs for the next decades. Using their connections with itinerant Armenian merchants and the Armenian Patriarchate in Istanbul, these Palu Armenians became active parties in the government's land confiscation scheme.

This chapter has also shown the tensions of the process through which the buyers' private ownership claims confronted the begs' insistence that they still controlled the land in a hereditary fashion. Interestingly, even as the begs continued to justify their claims on the basis of their privileged status as a noble family, that is, as a group, their individual claims over land were based on their individual ownership. This was part of the process of establishing the grammar of private property which was overtaking ideas of communal property at all levels of the local society by the mid-nineteenth century. Even though the land continued to be under the Palu begs' control at large, there was a widespread notion of the illegitimacy of their hereditary claims over land among the local population.

The abolishment of the begs' hereditary privileges, while influencing land ownership patterns in this manner, also had repercussions in terms of the administration of the district. The next chapter focuses on the bureaucratic realm to demonstrate the making of a new administrative order in Palu as the position of *hâkim* (ruler) lost its erstwhile uncontested authority.

Notes

1. BOA.İ.MVL 139/3859, 24 Cemâziyelevvel 1265 [17 April 1849].
2. Deringil, '"They Live in a State of Nomadism and Savagery": The Late Ottoman Empire and the Post-Colonial Debate'.
3. BOA.A.MKT 220/9, 5 Ramazan 1265 [25 July 1849].
4. BOA.A.MKT.MVL 18/6 29 Ramazan 1265 [18 August 1849].
5. BOA.İ.MVL 150/4258 11 Şevval 1265 [30 August 1849].
6. BOA.A.MKT.MVL 19/82 10 Zilkade 1265 [27 September 1849]. This is one of the rare instances of the local şer'iyye court being mentioned as a mechanism of conflict resolution.
7. BOA.MVL 84/38, Document # 1 4 Rebîülevvel 1266 [18 January 1850].
8. BOA.MVL 84/38, Document # 1 4 Rebîülevvel 1266 [18 January 1850].
9. BOA.İ.MVL 162/4721, Document # 1 22 Rebîülâhir 1266 [5 February 1850].
10. BOA.İ.MVL 237/8388, Document # 5 15 Rebîülevvel 1268 [8 January 1852].
11. BOA.İ.MVL 237/8388, Document # 5 15 Rebîülevvel 1268 [8 January 1852].
12. BOA.İ.MVL 237/8388, Document #8, 7 Receb 1268 [27 April 1852].
13. Özok-Gündoğan, 'Counting the Population and the Wealth in an "Unruly" Land' (28 March 2020).
14. BOA.İ.MVL 237/8388, Document # 2, Evail-i Şevval 1257 (c. 16 November 1841).
15. KFD-Temlikname (1535). The imperial diploma (*temlîk*) given to Cemşid Beg in 1535 by Sultan Suleyman I. The relevant section reads: '*Hâkim-i Palu Cemşid Beg dâmet ma'aliyehü nün hakkında dahi mezîd-i inâyetim zuhûra getirip vech-i mesfûr üzere cümle kal'aların ve şehirlerin ve mezra'alaların ile kaffe-i mahsûrat-ı âbidesi ile kendüye oğul oğlu neslen ba'de neslin temlîk ve ihsân eyleyüp oğul oğlu neslen ba'de neslin mülkiyet üzere mutasarrıf ola bi râdetillahi allahü te'âlâ kendisi intikâl ederse eyâleti nakz olunmayup cümle hudûdun ile mülknameleri mûcebince bitamâmiha oğlu bir olursa oğluna ve eğer müte'addid olursa kendileri ihtiyar ettikleri üzere eger vâki' olan kal'alar ve yerleri aralarında tevzî' olunmağladır ve eğer âhar tarîkledir bi'l-cümle rızaları tevcîhle olur ise ve Kürdistan beglerin ne tarîkle vech ve münâsib görürler ise ana göre virile. Onlar dahi mülkiyyet tarîkıyla ila ebedi'd-devrân mutasarrıf ola ve eğer şöyleki aslâ ve kat'â kimsesi kalmayup kudret-i rabbânî ile ocakları hali kalacak olur ise*

dahi ol vakit eyâleti haricinden olanlara ve ecnebîlere verilmeyüp cümle Kürdistan begleri ile müşâveret ve ittifâk olunup anlar ma'rifeti ile gerü ol diyârın beglerinden ve begzâdelerinden her kime verilmek münâsib ve layık görürler ise ol kimse tevcih olunup verile bu mu'ahede-i hümâyûnun te'kîdi ve emr-i celîlü'l-kadrimin takrîr ve temhîri içün eline bu mülk-nâme-i behcet-âyât ve meserret-nümâyânı verdim ve buyurdum ki min ba'd eyâlet-i mezbûre hudûd-i mu'ayyene ve sınûr-i mübegyinesi ile kendünün mülkü olup mâlikâne mutasarrıf ola.'

16. BOA.İ.MVL 237/8388, Document #2, Evâil-i Şevval 1257 [c. 16 November 1841].
17. BOA.İ.MVL 237/8388, Document #2, Evâil-i Şevval 1257 [c. 16 November 1841].
18. BOA.İ.MVL 237/8388, Document #2, Evâil-i Şevval 1257 [c. 16 November 1841].
19. Haim Gerber, *The Social Origins of the Modern Middle East* (Boulder, CO: Lynne Rienner, 1987), 11.
20. Mundy and Smith, *Governing Property, Making the Modern State*, 14.
21. Gerber, *The Social Origins of the Modern Middle East*, 11.
22. Roger Owen and Martin P. Bunton eds, *New Perspectives on Property and Land in the Middle East* (Harvard CMES, 2000), xi.
23. Kenneth M. Cuno, *The Pasha's Peasants: Land, Society and Economy in Lower Egypt, 1740–1858* (Cambridge: Cambridge University Press, 1992), 13.
24. Peter Sluglett and Marion Farouk-Sluglett, 'The Application of the 1858 Land Code in Greater Syria: Some Preliminary Observations', in *Land Tenure and Social Transformation in the Middle East* ed. Tarif Khalidi (Beirut: American University of Beirut, 1984).
25. Owen and Bunton, *New Perspectives on Property and Land in the Middle East.*
26. Owen refers to Aricanli and Thomas for this point. Tosun Aricanli and Mara Thomas, 'Sidestepping Capitalism: On the Ottoman Road to Elsewhere', *Journal of Historical Sociology* 7, no. 1 (1994): 25–48.
27. The nature of land ownership in the Ottoman Empire and the related question of the relations of production in the agrarian sector were widely-debated issues among the Turkish scholars from the 1960s onwards. State control over land vs private land ownership was a central issue in these debates. For an overview of different positions on this debate, see Alp Yücel Kaya, 'Türkiye'de Mülkiyet Tartışmaları ve Çalışmaları', *Ayrıntı Dergi* Güz, no. 32 (2019): 59–69.
28. Mehmet Ali Ünal, 'XVI. Yüzyılda Palu Hükümeti', *Ondokuz Mayıs Üniversitesi Eğitim Fakültesi Dergisi* 7, no. 1 (1992): 253.
29. İnalcık, 'Temlîks, Soyurghals, Yurdluk-Ocaklıks, Mâlikâne-Mukâta'a and Awqaf', 112.
30. İnalcık, 115.

31. İnalcık, 128.
32. İnalcık, 128.
33. KFD-Temliknâme (1535). The imperial diploma (*temlîk*) given to Cemşid Beg in 1535 by Sultan Suleyman I.
34. Midhat Sertoğlu, *Sofyalı Ali Çavuş Kanunnamesi* ed. (İstanbul: Marmara Üniversitesi Yayınları, 1992), 19; M. Tayyip Gökbilgin ed., *Kavânin-i Âl-i Osman Der Hülâsa-i Mezâmin-i Defter-i Divan* (İstanbul: Enderun Kitabevi, 1979), 28–31.
35. Sertoğlu, *Sofyalı Ali Çavuş Kanunnamesi* ed., 19.
36. İnalcık, 'Temlîks, Soyurghals, Yurdluk-Ocaklıks, Mâlikâne-Mukâta'a and Awqaf', 113.
37. BOA.İ.MVL 237/8388, Document # 8, 7 Receb 1268 [27 April 1852].
38. BOA.A.MKT 31/97, 29 Zilhicce 1261 [29 December 1845].
39. BOA.ML.VRD 520, n.d.m 1257 [c. 1841].
40. BOA.İ.MVL 218/7299, 14 Şevval 1267 [12 August 1851].
41. BOA.İ.MVL 237/8388, Document # 1, no date.
42. BOA.İ.MVL 237/8388, Document # Evâil-i Şevval [November 1841].
43. BOA.İ.MVL 237/8388, Document # 2, Evâil-i Şevval [November 1841].
44. BOA.İ.MVL 237/8388, Document # 9, 27 Receb 1268 [17 May 1852].
45. BOA.MVL 134/29, no date.
46. Ibid.
47. BOA.İ.MVL 237/8388, Document # 6, 4 Receb 1268 [24 April 1852].
48. BOA.MVL 134/29, no date. There are two documents in this folder (not numbered by the archive). This is the one signed by all the begs and aghas promising to cover the expenses of the representatives in Istanbul.
49. BOA.İ.MVL 237/8388, Document #6, 4 Receb 1268 [24 April 1852].
50. Tribal structure in and around Palu is one of the least-known aspects of the area's socio-economic history. The Zaza tribes of Palu populated the Euphrates basin as settled agrarian groups and consisted of small kinship-based organisations. There were also Kurmanc tribes in different parts of the emirate. For more information of the tribes of Palu, see Yarman, *Palu-Harput, 1878*, 2: 144–8. As Khoury et al. argue, 'the term tribe has been used to describe many different kinds of groups or social formations'. Philip S. Khoury and Joseph Kostiner, 'Introduction: Tribes and the Complexities of State Formation in the Middle East', in *Tribes and State Formation in the Middle East* eds, Philip S. Khoury, and Joseph Kostiner (Berkeley, CA: University of California Press, 1990), 5. Similarly, it is not possible to come up with a singular definition of what 'tribe' means in Kurdistan. It has to be regionally, temporally and contextually specific. For a discussion on the conceptual issues surrounding the definition of tribe in the context of the Middle East, see Richard Tapper, 'Antropologists, Historians, and Tribespeople on Tribe and State Formation in the Middle East', in *Tribes and State Formation in the Middle East*: 48–73. For two classicial anthropological works on the Kurdish tribes, see: Martin van Bruinessen,

Agha, Shaikh and State: The Social and Political Structures of Kurdistan (London and New Jersey: Zed Books, 1992); Lale Yalçın-Heckmann, *Tribe and Kinship among the Kurds* (Frankfurt [etc.]: Peter Lang, 1991).

51. BOA.A.MKT.MVL 53/68 2 Ramazan 1268 [20 June 1852].
52. BOA.İ.MVL 237/8388, Document #7, not dated.
53. BOA.İ.MVL 237/8388, Document #6, 4 Receb 1268 [24 April 1852].
54. BOA.MVL 115/77, 21 Receb 1268 [11 May 1852].
55. BOA.İ.MVL 237/8388, Document # 7, no date.
56. BOA.MVL 115/77, 21 Receb 1268 [11 May 1852].
57. BOA.İ.MVL 237/8388 Document # 8 7 Receb 1268 [27 April 1852].
58. BOA.İ.MVL 237/8388, Document # 5 15 Rebîülevvel 1268 [8 January 1852].
59. BOA.A.MKT.MVL 53/68 2 Ramazan 1268 [20 June 1852].
60. BOA.İ.MVL 237/8388 Document # 8 7 Receb 1268 [27 April 1852].
61. BOA.İ.MVL 237/8388 Document # 8 7 Receb 1268 [27 April 1852].
62. BOA.İ.MVL 237/8388, 3 Şaban 1268 [23 May 1852].
63. BOA.MVL 143/26, 25 Zilkade 1269 [30 August 1853].
64. BOA.A.MKT.MVL 53/68 2 Ramazan 1268 [20 June 1852].
65. BOA.MVL.143/26, 25 Zilkade 1269 [30 August 1853].
66. BOA.İ.MVL 258/15097, 14 Zilkade 1268 [30 August 1852].
67. BOA İ.MVL 245/8911, 20 Zilkade 1268 [5 September 1852].
68. BOA İ.MVL 245/8911, 20 Zilkade 1268 [5 September 1852].
69. BOA İ.MVL 245/8911, 20 Zilkade 1268 [5 September 1852].
70. BOA.İ.MVL 237/8388, Document #8, 7 Receb 1268 [27 April 1852].
71. Huricihan Islamoglu, 'Modernities Compared: State Transformations and Constitutions of Property in the Qing and Ottoman Empires', *Journal of Early Modern History* 5, no. 4 (November 2001): 353–86.
72. BOA.İ.MVL 305/1253, 4 Şaban 1270 [2 May 1854]. When he died shortly after his arrival, the business of surveying was handed over to Şekib Efendi, who was to work with a local notable, Ali Agha. In a few years, it appeared that although Şekib Efendi was working hard, Ali Agha spent most of his time doing charitable work. His job was given to two separate clerks. BOA.MVL 353/74, 16 Rebîülâhir 1273 [14 December 1876].
73. BOA.A.MKT.UM, 107/43, 19 Şevval 1268 [6 August 1852].
74. BOA.A.MKT.UM 12 Rebîülâhir 1278 [17 September 1861].
75. For a study of the class conflicts within the Armenian community focusing on the *amira*s (i.e. a class of Istanbul-based bankers and bureaucrats), see Richard E. Antaramian, *Brokers of Faith, Brokers of Empire: Armenians and the Politics of Reform in the Ottoman Empire* (Stanford, CA: Stanford University Press, 2020), 28–33.
76. The definition of middle peasantry has long been a point of discussion for scholars in the field. Amid varying definitions of the concept in terms of land ownership, labour use and degree of market-orientation, it appears that the concept is historically and regionally defined. What is considered middle

peasantry in one context might not have analytical value in a different part of the world. As Charlesworth states, one needs to 'impos[e] qualifying limitations' while using the concept of middle peasantry. Besides, the concept is essentially used to explain peasant political activism – or lack thereof. I am using it to refer specifically to a group of rural cultivators who acquired land throughout the processes discussed here, as opposed to the *maraba* who were essentially landless labourers. Neil Charlesworth, 'The "Middle Peasant Thesis" and the Roots of Rural Agitation in India, 1914–1947', *The Journal of Peasant Studies* 7, no. 3 (1 April 1980): 266.

77. BOA.MVL 134/29, no date. There are two documents in this folder (not numbered by the archive). This is the one signed by all the begs and aghas promising to cover the expenses of the representatives in Istanbul. 18 Muharrem 1275 [28 August 1858].
78. BOA.MVL 183/47 18 Ramazan 1273 [12 May 1857].
79. He served as the governor of Harput from March 1849 until his death in August 1850. Ahmet Aksın, *Ondokuzuncu Yüzyılda Harput* (A. Aksın, 1999), 67.
80. The document says Eğin, but this is most probably a typo for Eğil. MVL 479/114, Document # 1, 4 Rebîülâhir 1282 [27 August 1865].
81. It is not clear on what legal grounds this negotiation took place, but it is clear that such efforts were revealed after the council reached a settlement about the confiscation of the begs' lands following Abdullah Beg's death. In the petitions they sent to the state, those who wanted to buy land in this new context frequently presented a brief history of their past efforts to render their claims legitimate. In response, the imperial state would mine the official records to verify the claims' truthfulness.
82. *Kalfa* literally means journeyman.
83. BOA.MVL 479/114, 12 Rebîülâhir 1281 [13 September 1865].
84. BOA.MVL 471/24 17 Zilhicce 1281 [13 May 1865].
85. The Çötelioğlus were a notable family based in Harput. Apparently, they also gained land from the Palu begs' confiscated property.
86. BOA.MVL 372/2, 3 Safer 1278 [10 August 1861].
87. BOA.A.MKT.MVL 119/57 14 Safer 1277 [1 September 1860].
88. BOA.A.MKT.MVL 119/57, 14 Safer 1277 [1 September 1860].
89. BOA.A.MKT.MVL 119/57 14 Safer 1277 [1 September 1860].
90. BOA.A.MKT.MVL 119/57, 14 Safer 1277 [1 September 1860].
91. Yarman, *Palu-Harput, 1878*, 2: 129.
92. BOA.MVL 366/16 Document # 3, 12 Receb 1277 [24 January 1861].
93. BOA.İ.MVL 237/8388, Document # 9, 27 Receb 1268 [17 May 1852].
94. BOA.MVL 366/16 Document # 4, Gurre Safer 1277 [19 August 1860].
95. BOA.MVL 715/31 Document # 2 22 Zilkade 1282 [8 April 1866].
96. BOA.İ.MVL 569/25574 Document # 6 3 Şaban 1283 [11 December 1866].
97. See Yapıcı, *Palu 1841 Nüfus ve Toplum Yapısı*.

After Abdullah Beg

98. Özok-Gündoğan, 'Counting the Population and the Wealth in an "Unruly" Land'.
99. BOA.MVL 739/3 5 Rebîülevvel 1284 [7 July 1867].
100. BOA.İ.MVL 569/25574 Document # 4 28 Receb 1283 [6 December 1866].
101. BOA.İ.MVL 569/25574 Document # 7 9 Zilkade 1283 [15 March 1867].
102. BOA.ŞD 1453/20 Document # 2 15 Şaban 1287 [10 November 1870].
103. BOA.A.MKT.MHM 56/49 12 Ramazan 1279 [3 March 1853]. See also BOA.İ.MVL 210/6804 Document # 1 27 Cemâziyelâhir 1267 [29 April 1851].
104. BOA.İ.MVL 210/6804 Document # 2 13 Receb 1267 [13 May 1851].
105. BOA.MVL 620/24 Document # 1 5 Cemaziyelevvel 1278 [8 November 1861].
106. BOA.MVL 2/50 5 Receb 1261 [10 July 1845].
107. BOA.MVL 2/50 5 Receb 1261 [10 July 1845].
108. BOA.İ.MVL 391/25856 Document # 7 12 Rebîülâhir 1274 [30 November 1857].
109. BOA.ML.EEM 36/55 c. 1876.
110. BOA.MVL 620/24 Document # 1 5 Cemâziyelevvel 1278 [8 November 1861].
111. For a discussion on symbolic capital as one of the constituents of the state, see Pierre Bourdieu, 'Rethinking the State: Genesis and Structure of the Bureaucratic Field', trans. Loic Wacquant and Samar Farage, *Sociological Theory* 12, no. 1 (1994): 18. Bourdieu argues that '[t]he state is the culmination of a process of concentration of different species of capital: capital of physical force or instruments of coercion (army, police), economic capital, cultural or (better) informational capital, and symbolic capital'.
112. BOA.İ.DH 391/25856 Document # 2 15 Muharrem 1274 [5 September 1857].
113. W. Padel and L. Steeg, *Corps de droit ottoman: recueil des codes, lois, règlements, ordonnances et actes les plus importants du droit intérieur, et d'études sur le droit coutumier de l'Empire ottoman* (Clarendon Press, 1906), 71.
114. Sinan Culluk and Yılmaz Karaca eds, *Osmanlı Arşivi'nde Şeyhülislam Fetvaları* (İstanbul: Başbakanlık Devlet Arşivleri Genel Müdürlüğü, 2015), 155.
115. BOA.İ.DH 391/25856 Document # 1, 1857.
116. BOA.A.MKT.MVL 119/57 14 Safer 1277 [1 September 1860].
117. BOA.İ.MVL 237/8388 Document #3 9 Rebîülevvel 1264 [14 February 1848].
118. BOA.MVL 484/56 7 Cemâziyelâhir 1282 [28 Ekim 1865].
119. BOA.MVL 142/61 19 Zilkadar 1269 [24 August 1853].
120. BOA.MVL 429/10, 26 Cemâziyelâhir 1280 [8 December 1863].
121. BOA.MVL 429/10, n.m.d. 1280 [1864].
122. BOA.MVL 429/10, n.m.d. 1280 [1864].

123. BOA.MVL 479/114 4 Rebîülâhir 1282 [27 August 1865].
124. BOA.A.MK.UM 414/43 26 Zilhicce 1276 [15 July 1860].
125. Mehmet Akif Berber, 'From Interest to Usury: The Transformation of Murabaha in the Late Ottoman Empire' (MA thesis, Istanbul, Istanbul Şehir University, 2014), 63.
126. BOA.MVL 493/85 26 Şevval 1282 [14 March 1866].
127. BOA.MVL 493/85 26 Şevval 1282 [14 March 1866].
128. BOA.MVL 514/71 24 Cemâziyelâhir 1283 [3 November 1886].
129. BOA.MVL 771/24 17 Zilhicce 1281 [13 May 1865]. He must be referring to the regulations issued in 1864 which aimed to prohibit usury. Berber, 'From Interest to Usury: The Transformation of Murabaha in the Late Ottoman Empire', 66–8.
130. BOA.MVL 376/3, 12 Rebîülevvel 1278 [17 September 1861].
131. BOA.İ.MVL 569/25574 Document # 5 2 Şaban 1283 [10 December 1866].
132. BOA.MVL 520/87 20 Recep 1283 [29 November 1866].
133. BOA.MVL 531/140 24 Muharrem 1282 [19 Haziran 1865].
134. BOA.ŞD 2862/17 Document # 2, 23 Receb 1288 [8 October 1871] and Document # 4, 24 Receb 1288 [9 October 1871].
135. BOA.ŞD 2862/17 24 Receb 1288 [9 October 1871].

Chapter 7

Provincial Administration after the Palu Nobility

In July 1852, the Porte received a petition sent by the Palu inhabitants about the *müdür* (district governor) İsmail Beg – a Palu noble. İsmail Beg was unpopular among Palu's rural population, mainly because of the excessive taxes he imposed on them. They were also unhappy because his handling of the lottery-based military recruitment (*kur'a-i şer'iyye*) was corrupt: lottery exclusions could be bought for cash. Such petitions always used graphic language; this one claimed that those who could not pay would be dragged out of the warm beds of their wives for military service. What choice do we have, the petitioners asked, other than fleeing to Iran, Russia or Istanbul?[1]

This petition, while particularly vivid, was by no means the only one raising issues related to the *müdür* of the district. From the 1850s through the early 1860s, the questions of who would be the *müdür*, what the traits of a good *müdür* were and who would determine his appointment (the provincial administration vs the imperial centre) preoccupied the local population and the local Ottoman administration. The question was especially thorny in Palu. Just as the hereditary rights of the Kurdish begs came under attack, the *müdürs*' role became more critical in local administrative processes. Different sectors of the local population became actively involved in the process of appointing the *müdür* and there was a lot of turnover in the position. *Müdürs* served for short periods, then left, either because of complaints like this one or because of pressure from local administrators, particularly those based in neighbouring Harput. The first part of the chapter looks at the fierce struggles between the begs, the Armenian notables and the ordinary people as well as the provincial Ottoman administrators. The chapter argues that after the hereditary rights of the begs were abolished, the *müdür* appointment became the battleground for how this early stage of the bureaucratisation of provincial administration was handled.

From the 1860s on, the position of *müdür* was replaced by the *kaymakam*, a very different office. More importantly, it was usually filled by the centre, as opposed to being chosen locally. The transition from *müdürlük* to *kaymakamlık* is a notable move in terms of the bureaucratisation of provincial administration in Palu, the imperial centre's efforts towards bringing provincial bureaucracy under its control, and a budding notion of meritocracy. The second part of the chapter examines the politics surrounding the appointments of the Palu *kaymakam*s from the 1880s to early 1900 and the central Ottoman administration's efforts to remove local actors from the decision-making process.

In the struggle over appointments, alliances were volatile, and different groups tried to get the imperial state on their side to get their candidate appointed. While conflicts over land ownership continued in the background, there was also rivalry over who would administer the town, as both the economic and administrative authority of the Kurdish nobility had dwindled. However, the Palu begs remained, and were contenders for and holders of both *müdür* and *kaymakam* positions.

Tax Collector/Local Administrator: The Political Economy of Müdürlük

The Ottoman state's efforts to establish an efficient system of tax collection was an underlying theme of the Tanzimat restructuring from its earliest years through the rest of the nineteenth century. The question of maximising the imperial treasury's access to the agrarian surplus, however, was not just a matter of choosing between direct or indirect forms of tax collection. It also entailed a re-organisation of the provincial bureaucracy that paved the way to new institutions, administrative positions, and new power configurations and conflicts in the provincial periphery. One key aspect was reforming the district (*kaza*) administration. Once a mainly administrative and judicial unit, in the Tanzimat era the *kaza* gained a new character.[2] It was now the smallest administrative unit after the village and was run by a *müdür* (lit. director). New regulations on *müdür* appointments issued in 1842 clearly show that at the heart of this re-organisation was the regulation of tax collection; the *kaza/müdür* system came about because of dissatisfaction with the centrally-appointed tax-collector (*muhassıl*) system. To collect the tithe, the *muhassıl*s had to appoint several people from a given region, and their compensations siphoned off more than half of the tithe revenues. Cultivators also objected, as the system frequently resulted in delays in the harvest.[3] The Meclis-i Vâlâ's solution was to re-assign the task of tithe collection to local actors. Starting in March 1842, *kaza*s would be administered by *müdürs* who were responsible for the collection of the tithe. Essentially, the *müdür* was a tax collector whose subsistence depended on tax revenues, not a salaried provincial administrator.[4] Therefore, complaining about poverty, the *müdürs* constantly demanded a regular salary.[5]

The regulations stated that the *müdürs* would be chosen from among the notables of the districts (*eşraf-ı hanedan*) by the notables themselves. They would be compensated with salaries paid by the taxes of inhabitants of the district.[6] In practice, however, there were various ways in which *müdürs* were appointed. Some sanjak governors (*kaymakam*) or provincial governors (*vali*) appointed their clients; sometimes the imperial state appointed the *müdür* directly from the centre. For the next two decades, the *müdürs* would be key administrative actors in the districts, and local actors would be heavily invested in their selection and appointment processes.

The question of the *müdür* appointment was not just the administrative one of who governed the district; it was about who had the upper hand in the collection of the tithe. From the time they accepted Ottoman suzerainty until the Tanzimat, the begs had been collecting the agrarian dues with no obligation to transfer them to the imperial centre. As the begs' hereditary prerogatives came under attack, the position of the *müdür* was critical in deciding who would control the farming out of agrarian dues – the question at the heart of the conflict between the governor and the begs.

MÜDÜR APPOINTMENTS

When the Ottoman administrators were discussing the abolition of the hereditary rights of the Kurdish nobles in Kurdistan, there was a widespread belief that the begs had to be compensated for their losses in order to control their resentment. One suggestion was to appoint the begs as salaried *müdürs* of the areas that had been under their hereditary control.[7] While this idea had support in principle, there were complications, including the difficulty of appointing a separate *müdür* for each area taken from the begs. To solve this problem, the Ottoman administration considered merging several areas and appointing one *müdür* from among the begs to administer the resulting sizeable unit consisting of confiscated lands of multiple begs. But this solution was deemed risky, as the begs who were not given a position might turn against the state.[8]

Palu was a sizeable and agriculturally fertile emirate – a fact repeatedly mentioned in the reports the provincial administrators sent to the imperial centre. This made it worthy of being a separate entity with its own *müdür*.⁹ From 1845 until 1849, the *müdür* of Palu was appointed from among the begs, creating a long-standing perception that *müdür* was merely a new name for *hâkim*.¹⁰ In 1845, the appointed *müdür* was none other than Abdullah Beg of the infamous Weşin incident.¹¹ In 1846 and 1847, another Palu beg, Tayyib Beg's son Mehmed Beg, served in the post. For reasons that are unclear, he was dismissed the same year and in his stead another beg, Tahir, was appointed. Muslim notables of Palu increasingly got involved in the appointment processes of the *müdür*s. This appointment was quickly disputed by sixty-eight people describing themselves as 'the *ulemâ suleha, e'imme, huteba*, and others', who sent a group petition (*mahzar*) to the centre. The signatories were the imams of various mosques, Muslim notables (*vücuh*), holders of the *timar*, and several Armenians who signed as *ahali* (commoners). They were upset that Mehmed Beg had been dismissed, claiming that he had been meticulous in overseeing the consistency of the Tanzimat practices and had brought stability to the district's governmental business.¹² Tahir Beg, the new *müdür*, was, they said, only a child (*sabi*) of thirteen or fourteen and unqualified to hold the position. Their concern was shared by the *qadi* and *na'ib* (judge and deputy judge), who wrote to the imperial capital to say that, due to his age, Tahir Beg could not conduct legal cases (*deavi-i şer'iyye*) properly.¹³ Dismayed that former *müdür* Mehmed Beg had left, they asked that he return and take over the duty again.

The petition is an example of the local notables' rise as influential actors in the administration of the district and their active involvement in the process of appointing *müdür*s. At this point, there was no complaint about the practice of appointing begs; rather, the petitioners were stating their preference for one beg over the other. No provincial officials outside Palu were involved in the process – the *müdür* appointment was decided by local actors within Palu. Shortly, however, things would change, and the begs' positions in the provincial bureaucracy would be contested by the provincial Ottoman administrators. The Ottoman administrators' discontent over the begs' appointments came at the same time as the begs' hereditary rights came under greater scrutiny. By now it should be clear that with the Tanzimat, provincial governors were the major figures seeking to undermine the economic and administrative power of the Kurdish nobility. The governors were also behind the initial push to remove the Kurdish begs from eligibility to be *müdür*. At the time of Weşin, Tahir Beg – another beg from the same family – was the *müdür*.¹⁴ Referring to Abdullah Beg's case, but broadening the issue, the governor of Harput, Mustafa Sabri, presented the appointments of Palu emirs as *müdür* as a problem requiring state intervention. Emboldened by Abdullah Beg's exile and the ongoing investigation of Weşin, Mustafa Sabri sought to convince the imperial state to appoint a non-beg from the area to be *müdür*. For the first time, the imperial state adopted a more hands-on approach to *müdür* appointment in Palu, appointing Abdullah Efendi, an Ottoman official (not to be confused with the Abdullah Beg), as the new *müdür*.[15] At the same moment, however, perhaps because communication takes time or because of the governor's speed in taking action against the begs, there was a parallel process of local *müdür* appointment. Before Abdullah Efendi arrived in the area, the governor had allied with other opponents of the begs to oust them from provincial administration. He sought the centre's say-so on this:

> The district of Palu had long been governed by the appointment of the *ûmera* as the *müdür*. The said *ûmera* and some *agavat* [pl. of *agha*, tribal chief] hid [some tax resources] during the survey of the district and saved them for their own benefit. The tax revenues of these households would have produced revenues for the Imperial Treasury.[16]

The problems surrounding the census of wealth and income in the early Tanzimat era were not unique to Palu, but by referring to these problems the governor was trying to spotlight issues caused by the begs' holding the *müdür* position. Apparently, he had already been cooking up an alliance with notables in the neighbouring Harput district. His strategy was to support members of elite families from outside Palu to be *müdür*, appointing a member of the Keşşafzade dynasty, a notable family from Harput, as *müdür*.

Palu's inhabitants were not just passive observers of this fierce dispute about the *müdür* position; some challenged the governor's agenda. As an outsider, the *müdür* was not welcomed by the people, despite the support he received from the governor. A crowd gathered in front of the *müdür*'s residence and threw rocks at it.[17] Seeing that his attempt to control Palu's administration had backfired, the governor once again resorted to the imperial state. Writing to report the incident, he asked for military deployment to ease the processes of *müdür* appointment, military conscription and property surveys.

The imperial state, however, wanted more information. The Meclis-i Vâlâ wrote to the Ottoman military officials in the region inquiring about the seriousness of the case. Mehmed Reşid, the commander of the Anatolian Army, responded. He stated his discontent with the begs' hereditary authority in Palu and echoed the governor's concern about their appointment as *müdür*.[18] But then he parted ways with the governor: he did not support either the begs or someone from the notable families of

Harput for the position. Instead, he wanted the Ottoman centre to send an appointee from Istanbul. Only in this way, he said, would it be possible to institute security in the area and save the poor *ahali* from the menace of the begs and the aghas.[19]

As the begs' authority and wealth came under attack in the context of the Tanzimat, the *müdür* took over the administrative and fiscal roles once held by the *hâkim*. Because Palu was a sizeable and wealthy district, multiple claimants from inside and outside Palu tried to seize the *müdür*-hood. With the insistent efforts of the Harput governor, the begs were increasingly pushed aside as candidates for the position – even though the imperial state had initially envisioned granting them the *müdür* position as compensation. A group of local notables from Palu – both Muslim and Armenian – emerged and frequently got involved in the *müdür* selection process via the petitions they sent to the imperial centre.

The governor of Harput sought to farm out Palu's lands to claimants from outside Palu through auctions (i.e. it went to the highest bidder) conducted in Harput, while the begs were seeking to keep the process and the claimants within Palu.[20] In addition to its significant administrative authority, the position of *müdür* was critical for both the local actors and provincial Ottoman administrators because it stood at the centre of collection of the tithe. The *müdür* position was not only the embodiment of the proxy war that the governor of Harput and his allies from the Harput dynasties waged against the Palu begs and their local allies, but also a lucrative position that granted its holder great authority to tap into the area's agrarian dues.

Rush to Müdür-hood

The politics revolving around the appointment of the *müdür* continued after Abdullah Efendi, the government appointee, arrived at the district, although things were quiet from February to October of 1849. In October, the notables of the district raised their voice again and complained about Abdullah Efendi. In a group petition, they provided a detailed account of Abdullah Efendi's oppression and misdeeds, saying 'he was not capable of distinguishing between right and wrong'.[21] Their account was corroborated by the local judge. The petition convinced the imperial state that Abdullah Efendi was unwanted, but, in a blow to the Harput governor, the Meclis-i Vâlâ approved the appointment of Mustafa Şükrü Beg from the Palu nobility.[22] It was a win for the begs and the Muslim notables of Palu.

As these appointments, resignations and re-appointments indicate, in the post-Weşin era starting in 1849, the *müdür* appointment was highly contested, with local actors clashing with each other and the imperial state. One curious aspect was parallel appointments (as we saw above) from the centre and the locality. In one case, İsmail Beg (whose name will appear again in this chapter) was the *müdür*, as seen from the petition dated November 1850 that inhabitants wrote complaining about him.[23] A document from December 1851, however, reported the resignation of Hasan Beg from the position of *müdür* and mentioned 'his lack of rapport with the district'.[24]

As the position of the *müdür* turned into a tug-of-war between the actors based in Palu and those based in Harput (mainly the provincial governor and his network of patronage for tax farms), other claimants, mainly members of the other noble families in the Palu vicinity, emerged. After the resignation of Hasan Beg, the governor of Harput continued his efforts to control the *müdür* appointment. This time, he suggested Mehmed Beg, a member of the neighbouring Kiği nobility.[25] It is striking how the governors of Harput sought to strip the begs of Palu of their noble titles, even as they allied with other begs in the vicinity and used their noble lineage to argue that they should be appointed to administrative positions. Mehmed Beg's appointment was also approved by the Harput council and the Commander of the Anatolian Army (*müşir*), who petitioned the Meclis-i Vâlâ to confirm him. However, the council would not. Palu deserved special attention, the council said, which meant that Palu's *müdür* would be appointed by Istanbul. It appointed Fahri Beg, a former scribe in the Dîvân-ı Hümâyun (*hâcegân-ı Dîvân-ı Hümâyun*) and the current *müdür* of Malatya. But a few months later, it gave in and authorised Mehmed Beg's appointment.[26] Little did the council know that he had already been ruling the district for the past few years through a proxy. Mehmed Beg was the *müdür* of Kiği in the north-east of Palu. But since he was also the deputy *kaymakam* of Siverek district, he delegated his son İsmail Beg to Palu as the *müdür*.[27] During his term as the *müdür* of the Kiği district in the north-west, Mehmed Beg's reputation for corruption reached Palu, and his son İsmail was also unpopular during his term as *müdür*. In two years, the Porte received several petitions – including the one that opened this chapter – from the inhabitants of Palu asking for İsmail Beg's dismissal.[28]

The issue was transferred to Meclis-i Vâlâ, which ordered the local administrators in Palu to find the petitioners and investigate the issue. In response, another letter was sent from Palu signed by the judge, the *müfti* and representatives of the Armenian community, stating that they could not find the petitioners. Nevertheless, they added, this fact should not be taken to mean that the content was insignificant. However, refuting the complaints of the petitioners, they stated that, from the day he started his job, the *müdür* had acted in complete accordance with the Tanzimat regulations and that the *ahali* was totally content with his rule.[29] They concluded by stating that from their conversation with the *ahali*, they could safely state that the said petition was '*bî-esâs ve asılsız* [baseless and unfounded]'.[30] This account was corroborated by the governor of Harput, who also sent a letter to the centre to refute the complaints about İsmail Beg. He also added that since İsmail Beg's father had returned to his primary position, the complaint about the former had become invalid.[31]

Let us look more closely at this episode. A petition sent by the *ahali* details the political economy of the *müdür* position and its effects on them. At the core of their complaint was the *müdür*'s unjust extractions. Moreover, the newly-instituted military conscription had become a source of revenue for the *müdür*, as those who bribed him did not have to serve. Thus, the position had become a source of exploitation and oppression for the agrarian population. Second, the position had apparently also become a lucrative enterprise for various actors outside of Palu. By the 1850s, the alliance between Palu notables, the Harput governor and the begs of the surrounding areas against the Palu begs had been consolidated. The nobles of Kiğı had secured the support of Palu district council and the Harput governor in exploiting the Palu *ahali*, who were at their wits' end because of the intensification of exploitation. Thirdly, Kurdish noble families' access to these positions was predicated upon the extent and nature of their alliance with the Ottoman administrators in the region, primarily the governors. Through his alliance with the Kurdish nobles of nearby Kiğı, the governor sought to undermine the Palu nobility's administrative and economic power in their hereditary lands.

The following year, Palu's inhabitants faced another moment of contention over the position of *müdür*. This time the *müdür* was Tecelli Efendi. The group of urban notables of Palu, who raised their voice about other *müdür*s, intervened again. The *ulemâ* sent a letter signed by ninety-nine people – thirty-four of whom were Armenians – complaining about Tecelli Efendi. Their main concerns about Tecelli Efendi were his lack of engagement with district security and problems with the collection of the tithe. The petition specifically stated that the problems had distressed many other people whose names did not appear in the petition.[32] Around the same time, another petition reached the Meclis-i Vâlâ, this one defending Tecelli Efendi and stressing how content and grateful the signatories were for his service.[33] The ensuing interrogation revealed that the *ahali*'s discontent with Tecelli Efendi stemmed from problems related to the sales of the Palu begs' confiscated lands. And the *müdür* himself was unhappy with the lack of harmony in the district: Tecelli Efendi quit the job, left Palu and resettled in Harput.[34]

After Tecelli Efendi's departure, the Harput governor again tried to control Palu's *müdür* appointment, appointing a certain Mehmed Agha, former *müdür* of Çorum, a town more than 450 miles away from Palu, as the deputy *müdür* of Palu.[35] This, however, did not pass muster with the Meclis-i Vâlâ. Once again, the Council stated that 'Palu was a huge district worthy of special attention', adding that it did not have enough information about Mehmed Agha to appoint him. Instead, the Council appointed Abdülvahhab Agha, the former *müdür* of Malatya in Kurdistan.[36] The governor of Harput continued his efforts to influence the selection of Palu's *müdür*, in concert with the provincial council. The involvement of the Harput-based Ottoman administrators in Palu's *müdür* selection process was a corollary of a process that had been under way since the early Tanzimat in the 1840s, namely, the efforts of the Harput governors to undermine the Palu begs' economic and political power.

Why was there such rapid turnover in the Palu *müdür* position? First, as the Ottoman administrators repeatedly emphasised, Palu was a sizeable district with fertile agricultural lands that could potentially generate enormous tithe revenues for the imperial treasury. This made it a lucrative position for the *müdür*s. In addition to a salary, the *müdür* typically farmed out the district's revenues, meaning that he had the power to distribute lucrative revenue sources to potential tax farmers who would, of course, reward him. Throughout the 1850s, diverse candidates travelled from district to district across the empire, looking for *müdür* positions. If they failed in one district, they tried in another.[37] All these indicate that because of its wealth, Palu became a potentially lucrative source of income for various people, including the begs of the area, whose livelihood was now dependent on their income from the *müdür* position after the confiscation of their land.

But there was another reason for the rapid turnover in the *müdür* position: the active involvement of the local population. The notables of the district, Muslim and Armenian alike, regularly conveyed their opinions on who should be the next *müdür*. Often, they were competing with the governor of Harput who wanted someone in his circle to be appointed. He often supported people from outside of Palu, including nobility from the surrounding areas.

The notables of Palu were usually involved in the process, typically trying to get someone from Palu appointed. Sometimes, however, they supported the *müdür* merely because they were pleased with his service. In one letter, the notables of Palu spoke of the then current *müdür* Hasan Efendi in flattering terms that give significant insights into what a good *müdür* meant to the local population, particularly to the notables. Good morals, dedication, fairness, establishing order and security were the qualities they lauded in Hasan Efendi, in addition to his habit of resolving important issues in accordance with law and regulations.[38] These seem like the minimum that would be expected from every administrator, but there was another thing they mentioned: Hasan Efendi did not accept bribes; he lived on his salary, and did not seize funds from the taxes for himself.[39] With the Penal Code of 1840, the Ottoman state had defined the contours of corruption or bribery – a sign of an emerging discourse of equality in the bureaucracy.[40] Prior to this, in the absence of regular salaries, Ottoman administrators in the provinces were compensated with taxes and tributes in what could be defined as a gift economy. With the Tanzimat regulations, specifically the Penal Code of 1840, as Cengiz Kırlı states, what were once 'gifts' were redefined as 'bribery' overnight.[41] This emerging notion of a good provincial administrator who did not live on 'bribes' was echoed by Palu's inhabitants, who wanted an honest official.

After serving as *müdür* for about six months, Hasan Efendi resigned from his position and retreated to his residence in Tokat in the north. During his brief rule, however, he received the endorsement not only of the Muslim notables of Palu, but of the Armenian inhabitants as well. One year after Hasan Efendi left his position, a group petition signed by eighty-five people – the great majority of them Armenians – arrived at the Porte requesting his return. The reason for Hasan Efendi's sudden departure, according to this petition, was that the Palu begs and their allies, the Çötelizade family of Harput, had intimidated the *müdür* and forced him to resign. Hasan Efendi received the Armenians' endorsement because in addition to virtues like collecting the taxes fairly, 'he treated everyone, the old and young, rich and poor, and Muslim [non-Muslim]' in an equal manner.[42] In a year, a group of four Armenians residing in Çukurçeşme, Istanbul sent another petition, re-stating the wish that Hasan Efendi return.[43] Among this quartet was Mardiros, who apparently followed not only land sales, as detailed in the previous chapter, but also *müdür* appointments from afar. Furthermore, the Armenian patriarch in Istanbul, Kigork,[44] penned a letter to the Sublime Porte about these issues. He also requested Hasan Efendi's return to the position of *müdür*.[45] The involvement of the patriarch suggests how important the *müdür* position was to Palu's Armenians. But their efforts did not go unchallenged. In 1859 a group petition from Palu signed by twenty-three people – including eleven Armenians – requested that a certain Bahadır Mehmed Agha from one of the notable families of Divriği be appointed *müdür* of Palu.[46] In face of the Istanbul-based Armenians' unrelenting efforts to bring the aforementioned Hasan Beg back to this position, this group sought to grant this job to someone from the region.

Shortly after this, on the last day of August 1859, another group petition reached Istanbul. It was once again from Muslim *ulemâ* of the town and signed by 104 people, thirty-four of them Armenian. The petition expressed their dismay with the process of *müdür* appointment in the previous decade or so. The *müdürs* who had served in the previous ten years, they said, had fallen short of properly [*layıkıyla*] administering the district. Their suggestion was to go back to the days when the begs held the *müdür* post, specifically requesting that the late İsmail Beg's son Tahir Beg, who had served in this position a few times in the past, return to the job.[47] Their wish most likely was not honoured. What is certain, however, is that for the next few years turnover continued.[48] What would end the negotiations and struggle over *müdür*-hood was not a consensus on the ideal profile of the appointee, but rather the imperial state's changing policies towards provincial administration.

Transition to Kaymakamlık

The re-organisation of the provincial bureaucracy was a work-in-progress. From the 1840s through the 1860s, the Ottoman imperial state devised and tested various methods to control provincial governance – a process that went hand in hand with efforts to increase its share from the agrarian surplus. At different times in the 1840s and the 1850s, the Ottoman administration issued regulations defining the appointment and dismissal procedures and the duties and responsibilities of provincial administrators, including the *müdürs, kaymakams* and *mutasarrıfs*.[49] These efforts culminated in the Provincial Law of 1864 (*Vilâyet Nizamnamesi*), midwifed by Midhat Pasha who had previously served as the governor of Niš. The law merged three provinces – Silistre, Vidin and Niš – into a new province, Tuna (*Tuna Vilayeti*), which became the laboratory for the implementation of the new law under its governor Midhat Pasha. In 1867, the Provincial Law was extended to the empire at large, with a few exceptions.

The Law re-organised administrative units and redefined the administrative positions that would govern them. An *eyalet*, once the largest administrative unit governed by a *vali*, was renamed *vilayet*. Below that was *sancak* or *liva*, now governed by a *mutasarrıf* instead of *kaymakam*. At the level of *kaza*, the position of *müdür* was replaced by a *kaymakam*.[50] This entailed a reconfiguration of the *kaymakam* position: it was now appointed and paid for by the central state rather than by local notables or provincial governors (*vali*).

This change would have significant repercussions for the district administration of Palu. With the replacement of the *müdür* by the *kaymakam*, Palu's local administration entered a new phase. The Provincial Law of 1864 created a powerful *kaymakam* appointed by the centre and ideally not ensnared in local politics and power relations. But even before this official change, the administrative units and how they were governed were not rigid. It was common practice to transform a *kaymakamlık* into a unit administered by a *müdür* or disintegrate a unit governed as a *kaymakamlık* into its constituent *kaza*s under separate *müdür*s.[51] In all these changes, the calculations were essentially based on the potential revenues an administrative unit could bring versus the governmental expenses for its administration. When a place was deemed of special significance, its administrative status would be raised from a unit administered by a *müdür* to *kaymakamlık*. For Palu, this was the case. The central government always emphasised Palu's significance because of the revenues it would bring to the treasury. Additionally, the fact that its countryside was populated primarily by the 'Kurds and tribes' made it worthy of attention.[52] By the 1880s, Palu was administered by a government-appointed *kaymakam* as opposed to an elected *müdür*.

Palu and its Kaymakams

At the core of the provincial re-organisation in this new era was the state's explicit effort to establish a hierarchical provincial administration (i.e. *vilayet, liva* [*sancak*], *kaza, nahiye* and *village*), the components of which would be accountable to the highest local administrator, namely the *vali*, instead of each unit reporting to the imperial centre. In theory, this meant that lower-ranking administrators had less contact with the central state. But in actuality, the centre appointed the administrators, from the highest (*vali*) to the lowest (*kaymakam*).

For Palu's administrators, the transition from *müdürlük* to *kaymakamlık* was not just about scale or hierarchy; it also reflected a change in the underlying governmentality of provincial administration overall. The *müdürlük* of the early Tanzimat era was a direct outcome of the Ottoman state's attempt to establish a regular tax-collection system in its provincial periphery. It usually opted to appoint a local notable who would potentially succeed in collecting the tithe. The *müdür*'s position was primarily predicated upon his ability to tap into the agrarian revenues of the area and channel them to the centre.[53] *Müdür* selection took place in the locality, with the active involvement of the local population. The newly-configured position of the *kaymakam*, in contrast, was a product of the imperial state's emphasis on meritocracy, accountability, and lawfulness in provincial administration. Even though the *kaymakam*s continued to be responsible for the administration of tax collection in their jurisdiction, there was a growing awareness of, and a conspicuous effort to separate provincial administrators from, local power conflicts.

We might then ask how the Palu nobility was positioned in this new context. During the early Tanzimat era, from the 1840s through the 1860s, appointing local notables and members of the local dynasties as *kaymakam*s was fairly common. Their knowledge of the local population, including the local language, and their potential to collect taxes more easily were perceived as assets. This approach remained after the provincial law was put into effect, albeit with a more explicit emphasis on the background, education and experience of the potential appointee. The begs continued to seek positions in provincial administration after the Provincial Law, albeit with visibly limited success, especially near the end of the century.

In 1886, the *kaymakam* of Palu was Mehmed Necib Beg, the brother of the late Abdullah Beg. Most likely, he was the first *kaymakam* appointed in the early 1880s. Necib Beg appeared on the scene in the 1840s, when he claimed inheritance of his late brother's lands. He also represented the Palu nobility in Istanbul when the Ottoman administration was strategising over the confiscation of the begs' lands. He featured in several conflicts with the cultivators, particularly over issues related to taxation and agrarian relations of production. While his appointment as the *kaymakam* solidified his authority, it did not end conflicts with the local population, including the local elites. In one instance, he had a town crier announce that the meat slaughtered by Christians was not halal, causing the Armenian deputy (*murahhasa*) of Palu to reach out to the imperial state to protest. When the deputy judge of the Islamic court of Palu (*na'ib*) also pointed out the unlawfulness of this announcement, it was the straw that broke the camel's back. [54] Necib Beg was swapped with Hafız Hüseyin Efendi, the *kaymakam* of the Lice district a hundred miles south-east of Palu.[55] According to governmental correspondence, Necib Pasha's unprofessional (*laubali*) interaction with the people, which was due to his extended tenure in the post, was the reason for his transfer to Lice.[56] Necib Pasha was the last Palu beg to serve as *kaymakam*. After him, the position underwent a transformation in terms of who served, the appointment criteria, and the nature of the job itself.

What resulted in the decreased representation in provincial bureaucracy of the Palu begs was not just the complaints about Necib Pasha or the way he governed. It was also related to the Ottoman state's changing approach to provincial administration. There was an emerging notion of provincial administrators needing certain credentials, particularly prior experience in administrative service. Those who worked for the central bureaucracy in Istanbul or in various echelons of provincial bureaucracy were most likely to be appointed as *kaymakam*s. In fact, there was an internal recycling of staff within the government service, and the *kaymakam* position was usually filled by people who had served in equivalent posts.

This was true of the *kaymakam*s who succeeded Necib Pasha, with most of the Palu *kaymakam*s having experience as bureaucrats in nearby areas with a significant Kurdish population. Without exception, however, they had previously served in administrative posts in the Ottoman provincial bureaucracy. From 1850 on, there was an increased emphasis on providing government officials with official training. The outcome was *Mekteb-i Mülkiye-i Şâhâne*, a higher education institution established to train the essential administrative personnel in charge of implementing the Tanzimat reforms. The school was not big enough to meet the needs of the empire's gigantic provincial bureaucracy, and graduates of the *Mekteb-i Mülkiye* aspired much higher than a lower-tier *kaymakamlık* like Palu.[57] Yet even for Palu, there was a rising tendency to emphasise the credentials of candidates for these positions in relevant governmental correspondence. The *kaymakam*s' educational background, linguistic skills and previous experience in similar posts were detailed in résumé-like accounts.

Hafız Hüseyin Efendi, who replaced Necib Pasha, was the *kaymakam* of Lice, a predominantly Kurdish town in the south-east, before he came to Palu.[58] His background and credentials are fairly representative of the type of administrators appointed to be *kaymakam* after the Palu begs lost their grip on the post. Born in Diyarbekir, Hafız Hüseyin Efendi had studied some Arabic and Persian at high school. He could read and write in Turkish and he knew Kurdish.[59] His career in provincial administration started when he was appointed *müdür* of the Dirgöl district in Diyarbekir and continued for the next few decades. He served as an inspector for a couple of years before he was appointed as the *müdür* of the nearby Hani district. After a second term in Dirgöl, he became the *müdür* of Behramki, another district in Diyarbekir. In between *müdür* positions, he served as the deputy *kaymakam* of the Cîzre district for a while. His next destination was Eğil, again in Diyarbekir province, where he served as the *müdür* before taking a *kaymakam* position in Diyadin district further north-east in Erzurum province. In 1881 he was sent to Palu and exchanged with Necib Pasha. He stayed in this position for only a year before he was dismissed for reasons which were not clear. His long service in provincial bureaucracy ended in chagrin, with his desperate wife, Nefise Hanım, petitioning the state for a suitable position for him.[60]

Exchange (*becayiş*) of administrators between different districts was a common way the Ottoman administration resolved issues. Hüseyin Efendi's career is representative of this practice of shifting *kaymakam*s (and other provincial administrators) within the region. Sometimes *kaymakam*s would be removed from their posts because of incompatibility with the local population, or they would ask to be re-appointed elsewhere because they could not adapt to the weather. In such cases, they would more often than not be kept within the empire's eastern frontier. A set of appointments made in the 1890s exemplifies this practice. Osman Tal'at Efendi, the *kaymakam* of Nusaybin, in the south-east of Diyarbakir near Mardin, was removed from his post because he had left his post without authorisation. He was replaced by the *kaymakam* of Palu, Sırrı. In turn, the position in Palu was filled by the appointment of Mustafa Safvet, who had been Lice's *kaymakam*. Then Abdullah Efendi, the *kaymakam* of Midyat near Mardin, was appointed to Lice.[61]

With Palu's transition to *kaymakamlık* came the gradual formation of a new type of provincial administrator that was increasingly different from its predecessor, *müdürlük*. With *kaymakamlık*, the expectation that provincial governors differentiate their personal benefits and income from the public treasury was clearer. The biggest signs of this were protracted legal cases about the corruption of *kaymakam*s. A *kaymakam* could only be considered corrupt once he was a salaried official whose fortune did not depend on the amount of tax revenues collected from his district. He was now expected to be a public servant, not a shareholder in surplus extraction. If the process that the Ottoman state ambitiously initiated in the 1840s with the new penal code was the beginning of this changing governmentality, the restructured position of the *kaymakamlık* after the Provincial Law of 1864 was the peak of the state's efforts to establish this idea in its provincial bureaucracy.

One corruption case concerned Nazif Beg, who was briefly the *kaymakam* of Palu in the early 1890s. During his tenure, a court case related to his infractions during his previous position in Siverek began. Extensive correspondence about this case detailed the acts deemed unlawful, including seizing the extractions from the district, not giving receipts to taxpayers and accepting bribes from accused murderers. The investigation also put Nazif Beg's connections with members of the local elite on the table, suggesting that he condoned the postponement of certain tax farmers' treasury payments.[62] Each item mentioned needed investigation before warranting a court case. In the hundreds of pages about this case, which included rulings from the centre (the sultanic orders [*irade*], Şûrâ-yı Devlet decisions and the Interior Ministry) two points stand out. The first is legality, that is, whether the suspect's actions were lawful. The second is the numerous references to his 'personal benefit' (*menfa'at-i şahsiyye*).⁶³ The underlying theme in each aspect of the investigative process was whether he had used his position for his personal benefit and made unlawful material gains, including bribes or gifts, in return for doing favours. Nazif Beg was acquitted of these charges, but the investigation underscored the idea that a *kaymakam* was a public servant who could not conflate his personal benefit with his position and who needed to act according to all relevant laws and regulations.

The new expectations of the *kaymakam* were also evident in the duties and responsibilities expected of him. Unlike the *müdür*, and despite being responsible for tax collection as a centrally appointed and paid government official, the *kaymakam* was not a tax collector per se. His duties extended beyond tax collection and included developing the town by initiating projects of infrastructure and development. These services were often used as rationales for promotion and rewards. In the 1880s, the biggest project preoccupying the local population and the local administrators was the repair of a damaged bridge across the Murad River – Palu straddled the Murad River, a tributary of the Euphrates. Bridges were crucial to Palu, and whenever one of the bridges was damaged, inhabitants would appeal to the state asking it to meet the cost of repairs. Sometimes, repairs were paid by the revenues of a *vakıf*.⁶⁴ More often than not, local notables, Ottoman administrators and district inhabitants co-operated to cover the costs.⁶⁵ Later, overseeing this kind of infrastructural project became primarily the *kaymakams*' business. In 1891, during Mustafa Safvet's term as *kaymakam*, the repair of a bridge on Euphrates River became a fully-fledged enterprise under his and the *müftî*'s leadership.⁶⁶ When the project, which used both state funds and contributions from the local community, was completed successfully, both the *kaymakam* and the *müftî* were promoted.⁶⁷

The transition from *müdür* to *kaymakam* and the attempt to establish the latter as a salaried official with credentials apt for the work and independent from local interests attests to the move towards bureaucratisation and professionalisation of provincial administration after the Palu begs.

Deputy *Kaymakams* (*Kaymakam Muavini*) and the Representation of the Non-Muslims

The final decade of the nineteenth century represents a new era in terms of the re-organisation of provincial administration. From the 1890s on, provincial governance ceased to be a solely domestic business, gaining an international character. The internationalisation of the Armenian Question in the aftermath of the 1878 Berlin Treaty brought the issue of the non-Muslim representation in provincial administration under the scrutiny of the great powers. Article 61 of the Treaty committed the Ottoman Empire to undertake reforms in the six eastern provinces where the majority of its Armenian population resided. The impact this had on intercommunal relations in the six eastern provinces and its ramifications for the relations between Kurds and Armenians needs elaboration that go beyond the scope of this chapter. For the moment, suffice it to say that the reforms urged by Russia, Great Britain and France had aspects that concerned Armenian representation in provincial administration.

In 1895, a new reform memorandum was offered by the consulates of these three powers in Istanbul.[68] At the centre of the suggested reforms for administrative re-organisation was an attempt to ensure representation of non-Muslims in provincial bureaucracy, including the local administrative councils, commensurate with their population in a given administrative unit.[69] This approach would also be used in selecting administrators for all units of the provincial hierarchy, from village to province. As far as *kaymakam*s were concerned, there was a requirement that 'if a kaymakam is a Muslim his deputy should be non-Muslim and vice-versa'.[70] In November 1896, communications from the Diyarbekir, Mamuretulâziz, Sivas and Erzurum provinces informed the centre of the appointment of non-Muslims to deputy *kaymakam* (*kaymakam muavini*) in accordance with the reform memorandum (*ıslahat layihası*).[71] In Palu, the new deputy *kaymakam* was Melkon Said Efendi, a Catholic Syriac. In a few months, the Porte received complaints from the Armenian Patriarchate saying that he had incited tension among Muslims and Christians by spreading unfair rumours about the Armenians. The governor refuted this in a detailed letter to the centre that stated that the matter could be solved with some advice.[72] Melkon Efendi stayed in the job until his death two years later. In his place, someone from outside Palu, an Armenian from Kayseri, Armenak Efendi, was appointed. At the time of his appointment, he was in his late twenties. After attending Mekteb-i Sultânî for two years, he enrolled in the high school section of the Mekteb-i Mülkiye-i Şâhâne, eventually graduating. He knew Arabic and Persian, and spoke and wrote Turkish, French and Armenian. His résumé also stated that he was familiar with Greek and Bulgarian.[73] After serving as the deputy *kaymakam* of Palu for a year, he was appointed to Pazarköy district. His position was filled by Abdülmesih Efendi, most likely a Syriac, who had previously been a clerk in Mardin.[74] When he died soon after his appointment, he was succeeded by Katole Efendi, who was born in Monastir and was of Vlach (Ulah) origin. After studying at the Vlach School of Monastir (Manastır Ulah Mektebi), he attended Law School (*Mekteb-i Hukuk-ı Şâhâne*) for three years. He spoke and wrote Turkish, French, Vlach and Greek and spoke Bulgarian. Like most other provincial bureaucrats, Katole Efendi served in various echelons of Ottoman bureaucracy in different parts of the empire before coming to Palu.[75] But he did not want to go to Palu and asked to be exempted from this position. His request was denied by the Commission of Public Officials (*Me'mûrîn-i Mülkiye Komisyonu*), even though there was a strong impression that some of the information in his résumé might not have been genuine.[76] Only six months after he took up the post, he resigned. His successor, Kirişyân Dikran Efendi, was an Armenian from Sivas who had attended Armenian schools in Sivas and Galata (Istanbul). He had graduated from the Ermeşe (Armaş) Armenian Monastery in İzmit and spoke and wrote Turkish, Armenian and French.[77] He had previously served as a clerk in the Armenian patriarchate (*murahhasa*) in Sivas.[78] Like the *kaymakam*s, the tenure of the deputy *kaymakam*s was fairly short, in most cases around a year or two. Dikran Efendi, however, stayed in the post for almost six years, longer than any of his predecessors. The last name that appeared in the governmental record was that of a certain Haralambo Efendi who had previously served as a clerk in the nearby Maden district. Haralambo Efendi's term ended only a few months after he had started because the position of deputy *kaymakam* was abolished altogether in 1909.[79]

It is not clear why the deputy *kaymakam* position was abolished; the reason might have been budgetary concerns.[80] But its abolition meant the disappearance of a post reserved for non-Muslims. Once the position was abolished, a significant venue for non-Muslim representation disappeared in Palu.

Conclusion

In Kurdish historical writings, as mentioned previously, the period after the abolition of the Kurdish emirates is usually narrated as a period of loss, fragmentation, and at times anarchy. It is undeniable that the dissolution of a socio-political organisation that prevailed for several centuries with a conscious government policy would have had severe ramifications for the history of Kurds and Kurdistan. Yet, this historical narrative of loss and disintegration does not show the complexity of the institutions, processes and relations that emerged after the disappearance of the Kurdish emirates from the historical scene. This chapter has examined the making of a new administrative order in Palu with the position of the *hâkim* (ruler) losing its erstwhile authority after the Tanzimat reforms took effect in the region in this new period.

After abolishing the begs' hereditary position, the Ottoman imperial state set out to restructure provincial administration in Palu. As mentioned previously, from the sixteenth century until the Tanzimat, Palu maintained its *maktû'ü'l-kadem* position in the Ottoman politico-administrative system, which meant that there were no governors, tax collectors or military troops in the emirate. The *hâkim* was the highest military and administrative authority, and abolishing this position led to the building of a provincial administrative organisation in the locality. In this context, Palu was being changed from an emirate ruled by a *hâkim* into a district with a budding provincial bureaucracy governed by a *müdür* – a position that embodied the Ottoman state's goal of restructuring provincial administration to maximise revenue extraction. The first part of this chapter focused on the establishment of the *müdür* position in Palu and provided a granular account of the conflicted process of *müdür* appointments. The Palu begs did have claims over this position, and they served as *müdür*s several times. This analysis in this chapter showed that far from being a top-down process, *müdür* appointments took place within the contested scene of local power configurations and involved various provincial actors who had a stake in changing the fiscal, military and administrative structures in the district.

From the 1860s onwards, the Ottoman imperial state embarked upon another episode of bureaucratic re-organisation in its provinces. This new set of reforms resulted in the transformation of the Palu's administration from a *müdürlük* to a *kaymakamlık*. The chapter examined the making of this new position as one primarily appointed by the imperial centre. Unlike the *müdür*, the *kaymakam*'s role was not envisioned as that of a tax collector but as that of a provincial administrator representing the state's authority in the locality. With this came a budding notion of meritocracy in the sense that the *kaymakam*s were expected to have a set of skills and training. By examining the politics surrounding the appointments of the Palu *kaymakam*s from the 1880s to early 1900s, the chapter illustrated the central Ottoman state's efforts to remove local actors from the decision-making process in the provincial administration.

The Palu nobility, however, was not out of this power game within the provincial bureaucracy. The chapter introduced the career of Necib Beg as an example of the Palu begs' manoeuvres in this new context. Like his brother Abdullah Beg thirty years earlier, he received his authority not just from his large landholdings but from his ability to acquire positions in the Ottoman provincial organisation. Abdullah Beg served as tax collector (*voyvoda* or *mütesellim*), while Necib Beg served as the *kaymakam*. After him, the begs no longer served in this position, but their desire for power did not end. Necib Beg and his two sons sought to revitalise their family's power by acquiring more lands and building warm relations with the local Ottoman military and bureaucratic elite. They also sought to turn around the processes that had caused fragmentation of their family's lands – a goal that would bring them into conflict with their relatives, on the one hand, and with the Armenians who had acquired land in the past few decades, on the other. From the 1890s on, Palu would once again be ensnared in land disputes. These conflicts, however, took place in a context defined by two new dynamics. First, Armenians in certain villages of Palu became increasingly suspect to the Ottoman state because of their increasing politicisation. Second, the Ottoman state's reform policy towards the eastern provinces where Armenians lived came under international scrutiny under the Berlin Treaty (1878). In the fall of 1895, along with several other areas in the empire, Palu became the site of violent massacres of the Armenian population. The final chapter examines this bloody episode.

Notes

1. BOA. İ.MVL 247/8989 19 Ramazan 1268 [7 July 1852].
2. Çadırcı, *Tanzimat Döneminde Anadolu Kentlerinin Sosyal ve Ekonomik Yapıları*, 240–1.
3. Çadırcı, 241.
4. Çadırcı, 248.
5. Köksal, *The Ottoman Empire in the Tanzimat Era*, 115.
6. Çadırcı, *Tanzimat Döneminde Anadolu Kentlerinin Sosyal ve Ekonomik Yapıları*, 241.
7. BOA İ.MVL 66/1254, Document # 5 11 Rebîülevvel 1261 [20 March 1845].
8. BOA İ.MVL 66/1254, Document # 5 11 Rebîülevvel 1261 [20 March 1845].
9. BOA.A.MKT 31/97 29 Zilhicce 1261 [29 December 1845].
10. BOA.A.MKT.UM 368/9 7 Safer 1276 [9 August 1859].
11. BOA.MVL 2/60 7 Receb 1261 [12 July 1845].
12. BOA.MVL 29/31 Document # 1 [c. October 1847].
13. BOA.MVL 29/31 Document # 2, 25 Şevval 1263 [6 October 1847].
14. BOA.İ.MVL 131/3491, Document # 11, 1 Zilkade 1264 [29 September 1848].
15. BOA.A.MKT.MVL 12/33 6 Safer 1265 [1 January 1849].
16. BOA.MVL 30/34 11 Safer 1265 [6 January 1849].
17. BOA.MVL 30/34 11 Safer 1265 [6 January 1849].

18. BOA.MVL 32/26 11 Rebîülevvel 1265 [4 February 1849].
19. BOA.MVL 32/26 11 Rebîülevvel 1265 [4 February 1849].
20. BOA.MVL 106/50 3 Zilkade 1267 [29 September 1851].
21. BOA.A.MKT.MVL 20/61, Document # 3 [c. October 1849].
22. BOA.A.MKT.MVL 20/61, Document # 2 1 Zilhicce 1265 [18 October 1849].
23. BOA.A.MKT.MVL 57/54 26 Zilhicce 1266 [2 November 1850].
24. BOA.İ.MVL 230/7973 3 Rebîülevvel 1268 Document # 1 [27 December 1851].
25. BOA.İ.MVL 230/7973 3 Rebîülevvel 1268 Document # 1 [27 December 1851].
26. BOA.A.MKT.MVL 50/87 12 Cemâziyelâhir 1268 [3 April 1852].
27. BOA.MVL 254/56 Document # 2 21 Rebîülevvel 1269 2 January 1853.
28. BOA. İ.MVL 247/8989 19 Ramazan 1268 [7 July 1852].
29. BOA.MVL 254/56 Document # 1 21 Safer 1269 [4 December 1852].
30. BOA.MVL 254/56 Document # 1 21 Safer 1269 [4 December 1852].
31. BOA.MVL 254/56 Document # 2 21 Rebîülevvel 1269 [2 January 1853].
32. BOA.İ.MVL 329/14095 Document #3, no date.
33. BOA.A.MKT.UM 164/70 28 Zilhicce 1270 [21 September 1854].
34. BOA.İ.MVL 329/14095 Document #4 Gurre Safer 1271 [24 October 1854].
35. BOA.İ.MVL 329/14095 Document #13 16 Receb 1271 [4 April 1855].
36. BOA.İ.MVL 329/14095 Document #13 16 Receb 1271 [4 April 1855].
37. Former *müdür* of the Çemişgezek district Abdurrahman is a good example. A beg of the Çemişgezek dynasty, he made a living as the *müdür* of various districts of the Harput province for over fifteen years. In 1858, he asked to be appointed *müdür* of Palu. BOA.A.MKT.UM 338/23 Document #2 5 Cemâziyelevvel 1275 [11 December 1858]. Mir Adil Agha from the Kemah dynasty (a district 160 miles north-west of Palu) also requested to be appointed to the position. BOA.MVL 589/85 7 Safer 1276 [5 September 1859]. The former *müdür* of Palu, Mustafa Efendi, petitioned the imperial state asking for a suitable job, saying that he was in dire economic circumstances now that his term as *müdür* was over. BOA.A.MKT.UM 261/92 Gurre Rebîülevvel 1274 [19 November 1857].
38. BOA.MVL 590/31 c. November 1857.
39. BOA.MVL 590/31 19 Rebîülevvel 1274 [7 November 1857].
40. Cengiz Kırlı, 'Yolsuzluğun İcadı: 1840 Ceza Kanunu, İktidar ve Bürokrasi', *Tarih ve Toplum* 4 (2006): 50.
41. Kırlı, 52.
42. BOA.MVL 575/8 23 Muharrem 1275 [2 September 1858].
43. BOA.MVL 586/54 11 Zilkade 1275 [12 June 1859].
44. Kevork II. Keresteciyan (1858–1860) http://www.turkiyeermenileripatrikligi.org/site/patriklerimiz-patriklik-makami/(last accessed 1 August 2020).
45. BOA.MVL 585/28 10 Şevval 1275 [13 May 1859].
46. BOA.MVL 587/55 26 Muharrem 1276 [25 August 1859].
47. BOA.MVL 589/72 3 Safer 1276 [1 September 1859].

48. In 1862, the Porte appointed a certain Osman Beg, an ethnic Georgian who had previously served in the Istabl-i Âmire [Imperial Stables] in the capital. BOA.A.MKT.MVL 140/39 29 Receb 1278 [30 January 1862].
49. Mehmet Güneş, 'Osmanlı Taşra İdaresinin Değişim Sürecinde Kaymakamlık Kurumu (1842–1871)' (Ph.D. dissertation, Marmara University, 2013), 26.
50. Çadırcı, *Tanzimat Döneminde Anadolu Kentlerinin Sosyal ve Ekonomik Yapıları*, 251–2. In reality, even before the changes of the Provincial Law, it was not unusual to see *kaymakam*s being appointed to the *kaza*s, especially sizeable ones. Güneş, 'Osmanlı Taşra İdaresinin Değişim Sürecinde Kaymakamlık Kurumu (1842–1871)', 24. But with this arrangement, the common practice of *kaza*s being administered by elected *müdür*s was replaced by having centrally-appointed *kaymakam*s as the governors of the *kaza*s.
51. Güneş, 'Osmanlı Taşra İdaresinin Değişim Sürecinde Kaymakamlık Kurumu (1842–1871)', 24–7.
52. BOA. Y.PRK.UM 3/3 Document # 2 11 Şevval 1297 [16 September 1880].
53. Çadırcı, *Tanzimat Döneminde Anadolu Kentlerinin Sosyal ve Ekonomik Yapıları*, 248.
54. BOA.DH.MKT 1378/99 19 Safer 1304 [16 November 1886].
55. BOA.DH.MKT 1410/79 12 Recep 1304 [6 April 1887].
56. BOA.DH.MKT 1386/30 23 Rebîülevvel 1304 [20 December 1886].
57. BOA.DH.MKT 519/7 Document # 2 28 Safer 1320 [5 June 1902].
58. BOA.DH.MKT 1410/79 12 Receb 1304 [6 April 1887].
59. BOA.İ.DH 1024/80779 Document # 13 Cemâziyelevvel 1304 [7 February 1887].
60. BOA.DH.MKT 1512/60 4 Şevval 1505 [14 June 1888].
61. BOA.DH.MKT 1701/66 2 Receb 1307 [22 February 1890].
62. BOA.DH.MKT 151/1 Document # 5 19 Mart 1309 [31 March 1893].
63. BOA.DH.MKT 151/1 Document # 5 19 Mart 1309 [31 March 1893].
64. BOA.A.MKT.NZD 78/58 4 Şaban 1271 [22 April 1855].
65. BOA.A.MKT.MHM 61/88, 27 Safer 1271 [19 November 1854].
66. BOA.DH.MKT 1820/3 8 Şaban 1308 [19 March 1891]. For the plan of the bridge, see BOA.Y.PRK.TNF 3/5 5 Cemâziyelâhir 1308 [16 January 1891].
67. BOA.DH.MKT 1820/3 8 Şaban 1308 [19 March 1891]; BOA.DH.MKT 1695/93 15 Cemâziyelâhir 1307 [6 February 1890].
68. Fuat Dündar, *Crime of Numbers: The Role of Statistics in the Armenian Question (1878–1918)* (Routledge, 2018), 36.
69. Dündar, 36.
70. Quoted in Dündar, 38.
71. BOA.DH.TMIK.S. 2/120 12 Cemâziyelâhir 1324 [18 November 1896]; BOA.DH.TMIK.S. 2/92 10 Cemâziyelâhir 1314 [16 November 1896].
72. BOA.DH.TMIK.M. 49/49 Document # 3, 16 Zilhicce 1315 [8 May 1898].
73. BOA. I.TAL. 211/41 Document # 1 No date; Document # 2 16 Zilkade 1317 [17 March 1900].
74. BOA. İ.DH. 1384/59 5 Safer 1319 [23 May 1901].

75. BOA. İ.DH. 1403/4 Document # 1, no date.
76. BOA. İ.DH. 1403/4 Document # 3 17 Cemâziyelâhir 1320 [20 September 1902].
77. BOA. İ.DH. 1406/42 5 Zilkade 1320 [3 February 1903].
78. BOA. İ.DH. 1406/42, no date.
79. BOA.DH.MUI 20/63 21 Eylül 1325 [4 October 1909].
80. Güneş, 'Osmanlı Taşra İdaresinin Değişim Sürecinde Kaymakamlık Kurumu (1842–1871)', 232.

Chapter 8

The Beginning of the Endgame? The Road to the 1895 Massacres in Palu

The five years between 1890 and 1895 are critical for Palu, a laboratory for understanding the ramifications of the key historical dynamics this book has investigated: the transformation of the Palu begs' noble position within the locality; the privatisation of land ownership and the resulting land disputes; and the state formation that was the politico-administrative context in which these changes took place. In this period, fragmentation within the Palu nobility reached its apex, with grave conflicts among the begs over land ownership. For the Palu begs, this was also a time to settle their accounts with the Armenians, who were putting up ever-stronger resistance to the begs' efforts to regain their land and political power. But this was occurring in the new context defined by the internationalisation of the Armenian Question. As mentioned, the Berlin Treaty of 1878 made the Ottoman policy towards the eastern provinces where Armenians resided the subject of international treaties. The Sublime Porte pledged to initiate these reforms under Great Power supervision. As Palu was ensnared in protracted conflicts over land ownership, this new context set the ground for a harsher political climate that rendered Armenians more vulnerable to Muslim rage. In 1895, Armenians in Palu became the target of deadly attacks, forced conversions, and seizure and destruction of their property.

In the fall of 1895, Palu experienced one of a number of massacres against Armenians in towns throughout the empire. The attacks started shortly after the Sultan bowed to the pressure of Armenian revolutionary organisations and the European powers and proclaimed a reform programme. While this was what triggered the attacks, it was the local power configurations that set the ground for the unfolding of violence. In Palu, the immediate background of the massacres was the deepening of land disputes between the begs and Armenian villages, the Ottoman state's centralisation policies, and the growing politicisation of local Armenians from the 1880s on. This chapter examines Palu's socio-economic and political panorama on the eve of the massacres, showing that the massacres resulted from the coalescence of short-term political dynamics (i.e. the internationalisation of the Armenian Question and the increased politicisation of Palu Armenians) with the ongoing socio-economic and political tensions that together created what Edip Gölbaşı described as a 'climate of violence' in Palu from the 1890s onwards.[1]

The Begs

The period from the confiscation of the Palu begs' lands in the 1850s through the 1880s was one of drastic transformation in terms of both the begs' position locally and their relations with the imperial state. As discussed, when they came under ideological and political attack in the Tanzimat context, it was the economic implications of their privileges that was the main problem for the government. But while the begs lost some land, the government plan left a third of their land intact. This, along with the land they bought from the portions opened up for sale, meant they were by no means impoverished by the land confiscation process. In an 1880 Ottoman document that listed the notable people of the Mamûretülâziz province, the first six names were Palu begs.[2]

Initially, the administrative transformations that came with the Tanzimat provided opportunities for the Palu begs. The *müdürlük* period made it easy for them to gain positions in the local bureaucracy, but this changed after the transition to *kaymakamlık*, when the begs' representation in provincial bureaucracy diminished drastically. Having lost their grip over surplus extraction and some of their lands, the Palu begs now found the doors of the provincial bureaucracy only half open to them.

By the 1890s, we observe roll-back in the two realms that constituted the Palu begs' economic and political power: land ownership and provincial bureaucracy. Behind this process was Necib Beg and his two sons. He had experienced the times when the Palu begs still held power and prestige but he had also witnessed the processes that undermined their hereditary privileges. Almost forty years later, his actions increasingly mimicked the old days during which one beg accumulated political authority and wealth and led the emirate as the *hâkim*. In a way, he sought to resurrect what looked like a micro-*hanedanlık* from the ashes of the Palu emirate, mainly by ensuring his and his sons' access to governmental positions. He also worked to retrieve the lands the begs had lost. His actions led to increased conflict between the begs and the Armenians.[3]

Necib Beg first came to the scene back in the 1850s after his brother's death in exile – his brother was Abdullah Beg of the Weşin incident. Necib Beg inherited half of his brother's land, thanks to his unrelenting appeals to the state insisting that since the brother had been childless, he, Necib, was the heir. In this new context, he secured his position by staying in close proximity to the Ottoman power elites and seeking recognition for his service and loyalty, rather than by insisting on his hereditary rights. He even provided military service, which had long been obsolete as a bond between the Palu begs and the imperial Ottoman state. Along with a relative, Tahir Beg, Necib Beg received a medal for service during the Crimean War.[4] Significantly, when the Armenians complained about the begs' increasing encroachment on land, this moment would be recounted as a turning point in the begs' return to their former exploitative practices.[5]

In the 1880s, as discussed previously, Necib Beg served an extended term as the *kaymakam* of the district, but was not particularly popular among the population. He was dismissed from the post, but continued his efforts to gain recognition within the Ottoman administrative system. Dervish Pasha, the *yaver-i ekrem* (aide-de-camp) to the Sultan, recommended that the imperial state raise Necib Beg's rank to *mirülûmera* to recognise his service. Derviş Pasha pointed out that not only had Necib Beg brought and led 500 men during the Crimean War, but that he had donated his mansion (valued at 45,000 guruş) to be used for the military station (*kışla*) to be built in Palu.[6] The promotion came with the title of *pasha*.[7] Necib Pasha's sons received positions in the provincial bureaucracy. But as they accumulated power, Necib Pasha and his family also attracted the fury of various local actors. In 1890, a telegraph with noticeably strong language was sent from Palu to the Porte, protesting Necib Pasha and his sons' appointments to the governmental positions and referring to serious offences they had committed.[8] A few months later, when Necib's oldest son İbrahim Beg was re-appointed to the membership of the court of first instance (*bidayet mahkemesi*), similar complaints were made about his actions during his previous tenure in the position.[9] In the same year, the appointment of Necib's younger son Rüşdü Beg to the local administrative council (*idare meclisi*) of the district brought complaints from local notables that he was ineligible because he was only eighteen years old.[10] This was later refuted by his birth records, but it indicates an ongoing pattern of resentment towards Necib Pasha and his family.

Along with acquiring governmental positions, Necib Pasha and his sons predicated their ambitious efforts towards creating a micro-*hanedanlık* on force or the threat of force. Reportedly, İbrahim Beg protected and used the armed men of the famous bandit Mahmud from the Beritan tribe.[11]

These men wreaked havoc in the villages under orders from İbrahim Beg, and when the helpless villagers appealed to him for protection, he demanded a quarter of the harvest as a protection fee.[12] İbrahim Beg's demand for protection money was reminiscent of the days when the begs held standing troops that they used against the recalcitrant tribes to protect the settled agrarian populations. At this time, however, he was offering protection from insecure conditions that he had created.

Necib Pasha's family also intensified their attempts to retrieve the lands that they had lost, even as disputes among the begs over land were increasing.[13] It was within this context that the lands of the Yarımca (Armujan) village became the subject of a fierce dispute between Necib Pasha and the descendants of Haşim Beg – another branch of the Palu family. The conflict started with Haşim Beg's death. His sister Azize Hanım inherited his lands in the village, but Necib Pasha claimed that the lands were part of the *vakıf* dedicated to the *Ravza-i Mutahhara-i Hazret-i Risâlet* (the tomb of the Prophet Muhammad).[14] Azize Hanım's husband Şerif Beg – another member of the Palu beg family – served as her legal representative. The long legal dispute over Yarımca was the peak of fragmentation within the Palu nobility: both begs were allied with provincial administrators, and they used legal means against each other for over ten years. In their fierce struggle over the fertile lands of Yarımca, the parties delved into past accounts to question the legitimacy of each other's land ownership. Şerif Beg and his allies from the local administration filed a complaint asserting that Necib Pasha's seizure of his late brother Abdullah Beg's lands forty years earlier was fraudulent, which led to a thorough investigation by the imperial centre. The Ministry of the Interior dug through old records and found one from 1852 that stated that Necib Beg's acquisition of his brother's lands accorded with rules and regulations. The investigation concluded that the said lands had been given to Necib Pasha at the time because of the *me'zûniyet-i kadîm* (ancient diplomas) held by the Kurdish begs – that is, the privileges granted to them by the Sultan back in the sixteenth century.[15] Although this approach failed, the case over Yarımca concluded in favour of Şerif Beg's family – only to be reopened a few years later. In face of a later investigation and a potential court case pushed by a coalition of local administrators, the judge and his rival family members, Necib Pasha fled to Istanbul – reportedly taking a considerable amount of cash with him (100,000–150,000 guruş).[16] His long career as a landed noble in Palu ended, but his two sons remained in Palu.[17]

These family conflicts revealed that the Palu begs no longer functioned as a collectivity with shared interests and goals. With the disappearance of the *hâkim* position as the highest authority within the family and the emirate, the begs had completely lost their ability to solve their disputes using internal mechanisms. Instead, protracted disputes between the begs over family lands kept ending up in court. Allying with local administrators, appealing to Ottoman administrators in Istanbul and pursuing legal action against each another, the begs deployed all available elements of the Ottoman bureaucracy in their disputes, all this while continuing to justify their rights over land by referring to their historical rights based on their noble descent. Yet the meaning of this claim had transformed dramatically: while they still claimed property rights on the basis of their noble lineage, they now demanded these rights on an individualised, not a collective, basis. They were making individual property claims based on the institutions, relations and contracts of the collective idea of an *ancien régime* – a tension they never resolved.

While the begs clashed over land ownership with each other, the conflicts between them and Armenian villages also intensified.[18] As various scholars have discussed, the late nineteenth century was a period of increased land disputes that mainly involved the Armenian population and the Kurdish landowners throughout the eastern provinces and intensified the dispossession of the Armenian population. Mehmet Polatel argues that the nature of the land conflicts involving Armenians changed markedly after the 1880s. Before the Hamidian era, he argues, these conflicts 'were confined to disputes between local powerholders and Armenian peasants and villages'.[19] After the 1880s, the conflicts stemmed mostly from the seizure of large chunks of land, and the disputes were not just between the local elites and the Armenians any more: the role of the ordinary Muslim population in land grabs increased. This gave the dispute an ethno-religious character as Armenians versus Muslims.

In Palu, of course, the disputes between the begs and the Armenian villages had been going on since the 1850s. When two-thirds of their land was opened up for sale, the begs either repurchased the land or simply continued to treat land purchased by others as their own. They rented or sold these lands and gave the buyers *sened*s (sales receipts) in lieu of title deeds. According to a report prepared by a commission appointed by the Armenian National Assembly, in 1876 several Armenian villages including Havav, Çınaz, Yeniköy and İsabeg, in addition to others seized by Muslim notables of the district, came under the begs' control.[20] These were the villages where the Armenians were able to claim lands after the begs' lands were confiscated. The report's findings indicate that the begs reversed this process and seized those lands that the Armenians had bought a few decades back. Typically, the begs sold land to buyers and granted them sale receipts that were not officially valid. The conflict would come to fore mostly after the death of the original seller. His descendants disputed the transaction's genuineness and claimed ownership referring to his historical rights.[21] Without a valid title deed, the buyer became vulnerable to dispossession. Such conflicts need to be seen as part of a continuum with the processes that had resulted in the fragmentation of the Palu begs' lands with the Tanzimat policies four decades earlier and the begs' attempts to get these lands back.

The begs' increased efforts to regain the land also led to a deepening of land disputes with Armenians. The begs were motivated by a sense of revanchism, an effort to reverse the processes that had resulted in the Armenians' acquisition of lands starting in the 1840s. The villages that actively resisted the begs' efforts to seize these properties included Havav, Kapıaçmaz (Tset) and Yeniköy (Nor Kiugh). The lands of the Kapıaçmaz and Sakrat villages became the subject of increasing tension between the inhabitants and the begs. Kapıaçmaz village was one place where the government's plan back in the 1850s had been implemented, resulting in a real change in land ownership. In accordance with the government plan, while the begs kept one-third of their previous land, the remaining two-thirds was opened up for sale.[22] In the summer of 1895, fifty Armenian inhabitants of Kapıaçmaz and Sakrat petitioned the Diyarbekir governorate, complaining about İbrahim and Rüşdü begs' encroachment upon the lands of the village.[23] The begs in turn filed a petition claiming that these villages had refused to pay the annual soil rent (*icare-i zemin*).[24]

Other villages' land disputes were more complicated. When the government opened up the begs' lands for sale, some properties were exempt because of their *vakıf* status (as opposed to private property or *mülk* status).[25] The village of Yeniköy was in this position. In the 1880s, villagers complained about the begs extracting taxes from the lands of villages that had been given *vakıf* status decades previously. The petitioners emphasised the unlawfulness of this, since the Tanzimat changes made the documents the begs held null and void. The question here was when these lands had acquired *vakıf* status, given that they were Palu begs' property before the Tanzimat. In 1866, when a land surveyor came to Palu, the Palu district council demanded that the lands of Yeniköy (along with tens of others) be exempt because of the village's *vakıf* status.[26] But further investigation by the Ministry of Pious Foundations revealed that the lands were not recorded as *vakıf*. In 1876, however, the lands of Yeniköy were usurped by Hacı Tahir Beg (who was Şükrü Beg's father).[27] The most likely explanation is that back in the 1860s, when the land sales were continuing, Hacı Tahir Beg tried to prevent these lands from confiscation by getting them *vakıf* status. This failed, but sometime between 1866 and 1872, however, as the Patriarchate's report indicates, Tahir Beg must have re-acquired the land and succeeded in getting it *vakıf* status. This might explain his family's continuing possession of Yeniköy's lands from the 1860s through the 1890s. This explanation is also lent credence by the petitioners' accounts stating that around 1848, they started to pay the tithe to the government. At some point, however, the begs reverted to their old practices of outrageous extractions.[28] The dispute continued for about a decade after the 1880s appeal. In 1895, the villagers took matters into their own hands, and Şükrü Beg complained to the state about the Armenians' attack on his home, which, he said, wounded his maid and let the villagers encroach on his land.[29]

Havav was the most persistent of all the Armenian villages in its resistance to the begs' efforts to control the village and its lands. The villagers refused to accept the traditional symbols of Şerif Beg's authority over their land, refusing to allow him to reside in his *konak* in the village. The villagers appealed to the governor, who supported their kicking the beg and his family out of the village and their refusal to comply with his orders to, for instance, bring him firewood. While it is not clear how he did it, Şerif Beg sold the lands to someone, but the villagers did not let the purchaser base himself in the village.[30]

The deepening of the clashes with the Armenian villages was a corollary of the begs' weakened collective identity. The conflicts of individual begs with specific Armenian villages indicates the disappearance of two aspects of the begs' local position, particularly with respect to the Armenians. First, the conflicts show that by the 1890s, the Armenian villagers no longer saw the begs' hereditary claims to land as authoritative. They not only refused to pay the begs dues, but also kept them from residing in their villages. Secondly, the disappearance of the collective identity and the symbolic authority of the begs meant the loss of their authority over power nodes in the area, including the tribes. As discussed, the Kurdish begs in general, and Palu begs in particular, were initially granted hereditary rulership and property rights for providing military service. This role entailed not only participating in military campaigns when summoned, but also keeping order and security in the locality. In the 1850s, even as they pushed for the abolition of the begs' hereditary control over land, Armenians were concerned that this could lead to the end of the protection the begs provided. And indeed, as their military leadership became obsolete, the begs' role of providing security to settled Armenian populations, particularly against armed tribal groups, also disappeared, along with their ability to do so.

The State

The question is where that left the Ottoman state when the local status quo was being renegotiated by local actors.

The State

From the 1840s through the 1870s, the Ottoman state's administration of its eastern provinces combined military means to curtail the power of the Kurdish elites and institutional restructuring to consolidate its infrastructural power. From the 1870s onward, however, the character of the Ottoman administration of the region changed. The Treaty of Berlin, signed in the aftermath of the Russo-Ottoman War of 1877–8, meant that the administration of the region was now linked to its policies towards the Armenian population, now the subject of international agreements. At issue were the reforms to be initiated by the Ottoman state to ameliorate conditions of Armenians in the six provinces (*vilayat-i sitte*), Bitlis, Diyarbekir, Mamüretülâziz, Sivas, Erzurum and Van, in the east where most Armenians lived.

The reforms originated within the Armenian community. After the proclamation of the Armenian National Constitution in 1863, the Armenian National Assembly – the governing body of the Armenian community in the Ottoman Empire – discussed Armenian grievances and possible solutions and appointed a special commission to examine the complaints coming from across the empire.[31] The commission presented its findings to the Sublime Porte in two reports in 1872 and 1876.[32] In these reports, issues related to taxation (unequal imposition of taxes, extra-legal and cash extractions, forced labour used to transport agricultural produce, etc.) were among the biggest problems Ottoman Armenians faced.[33] The reform agenda specifically mentioned the Kurdish begs' hereditary privileges as needing to be addressed. For example, a reform scheme seeking Russian support stated that '[t]he Kurdish *derebeg*s will be removed and the privileges granted to Kurds and *derebeg*s will be rescinded'.[34] In 1878, the British presented a memorandum to the Sublime Porte urging the implementation of the reform programme in the six provinces.[35] From the 1880s through the 1890s, reform in the eastern provinces became a tug of war between European powers claiming to protect rights of minority Ottoman Christians, the Ottoman state wary of Western states' involvement, and a growing Armenian nationalist movement.

The internationalisation of the Armenian Question changed Sultan Abdülhamid II's rule (1876–1909) of the Kurds and Kurdistan. Janet Klein has argued that Sultan Abdülhamid II established the Hamidiye Light Cavalry in 1890, an irregular militia composed of select Kurdish tribes, with the mission of '[s]ettling and controlling the tribes, creating bonds of loyalty, centralizing remaining Ottoman dominions, [and] protecting them from the "Armenian threat"'.[36] However, Zaza tribes, who made up the majority of tribes in Palu and its surroundings, were not recruited to the Hamidiye Light Cavalry because they were subject to recruitment by the regular army (*ahz-ı asker*).[37] This meant that the Hamidiye Light Cavalry, the centre of the Hamidian regime's policies towards the Kurds and Kurdistan from the 1890s on, had no role in Palu. In fact, instead of arming the tribes there, the Ottoman state had, since the 1840s, sought to disarm them and bring the region under its centralising control. The state had issued regulations aimed at the confiscation of the tribes' weapons, but, as of the 1890s, the state had not established a monopoly on violence there.

Along with the reform discourse associated primarily with the Armenian Question in international politics, the reform efforts of the 1880s need to be considered in a continuum with Ottoman efforts to bring the areas hitherto ruled by the Kurdish nobles under state control. The Ottoman administrators, especially those based in the eastern provinces, wanted reform, as they felt that the state's lack of authority was an urgent problem. In the words of the Mamüretülâziz governor, establishment of order in this region was contingent upon 'fortifying the authority of the government and disseminating justice [*takviye-i nüfûz-i hükûmet ve neşr-i adâlet*]'.[38] Local authorities perceived the unruliness of the 'Kurds and tribes [*ekrad ve aşâyir*]' as the major indicator of the state's lack of symbolic authority in the region. In 1891, the government planned to build three police stations (*karakolhane*) there.[39] The efforts to build military barracks for the Ottoman Fourth Army began in 1889, with Mirliva Mustafa Na'im Pasha arriving in Palu to supervise their construction.[40] The barracks were completed by the end of the year and soldiers sent there.[41] But these were only baby steps, as, given the power of armed tribal groups, the state lacked the monopoly on force in the region.

From the 1880s on, and especially after the Berlin Treaty, population figures were an essential component of the state's reform discourse. The state needed to know which provinces and districts contained enough Armenians for the Ottoman state to have to initiate reforms. According to Fuat Dündar, these discussions were nothing less than 'wars of statistics' between the Ottoman state, the Armenians and the Great Powers.[42] In 1881–2, the Ottoman administration set out to conduct an empire-wide population census; it dragged on for almost a decade. According to Kemal Karpat, it is impossible to state precisely when (or if) the census of 1881–2 ended, but the records were not submitted to the Sultan until 1893.[43] In the province of Diyarbekir, the census was conducted in March 1892.[44]

Ottoman documents say that the population of Palu was counted then, but the registers never arrived at the imperial centre.[45] By 1893, when, after several requests from the centre, the registers of Palu still had not been sent to Istanbul, the government dismissed the district's census official.[46] Mustafa Efendi, the census registrar, claimed that he had sent the registers, but offered no proof.[47] Interestingly, there are no archival records on the implementation of the census in Palu. Normally, a population census would cause an increase in correspondence between the imperial centre and the provinces because of the intensified contact between government officials and local actors. The lack of such a correspondence renders the question of whether the census was implemented in Palu an open one.

In March 1893, the Ottoman administration dispatched military forces to conduct the census in neighbouring Dersim (including Hozat, Ovacık, Pax and Kızılkilise).[48] Even then, there was no mention of nearby Palu's census. Interestingly, Karpat uses Ottoman census registers to cite Palu's population as of the 1881/2–1893 census.[49] The registers he is citing must have contained only estimates for Palu, given the lack of evidence that the census was ever done. Karpat also says that the Sultan himself demanded the accurate completion of the census.[50] With the population figures of interest internationally, it is even more surprising that Palu, which had a substantial Armenian population, might have been excluded from the census. At the same time, the Ottoman administration was growing wary of the Russian efforts to determine the population of the eastern provinces. In 1887, a cipher telegram sent by the Diyarbekir governor to the Ministry of the Interior reported that the Russian Consul in Erzurum had conducted a population census in Palu. Armenian priests were also recording the male population in the district and collecting money from the Armenians per person written down.[51] This telegram was a manifestation of the state's increasing suspicion of Palu Armenians who were engaged in political activities, which I discuss later in the chapter.

The security concerns of the state associated with unruly tribes and Armenians notwithstanding, Palu's fertile agrarian potential was still the focus of state interest in the district. Collection of the tithe was the most significant agenda item for the Ottoman administrators, and the local elite's grip over the agrarian surplus required constant attention.[52] This problem was accompanied by widespread peasant indebtedness to creditors (some Muslim, the majority Armenian) which exacerbated the risk of peasant dispossession. The establishment of an itinerant commission to determine the credit needs of the agricultural population and the opening of Agricultural Bank branches in the region were suggested as ways to address peasant indebtedness.[53]

While land disputes continued, the Ottoman administration worked to get an accurate picture of the agrarian taxes that the Palu lands could potentially generate. In 1890, the Ministry of Finance asked the Diyarbekir Governor to present updated information on how much of *mîrî* (state) lands were vacant (i.e. not being tilled) in Palu.[54] The government had been trying to increase tithe revenues since the 1840s, but the plan for how to achieve this changed according to local power configurations. By the 1890s, the Palu begs had lost their monopoly over the expropriation of agrarian surplus, but the Ottoman administration had still not established centralised tax-collection infrastructure. Generally, tithe collection was either delegated to a trustee (*emâneten*) or assigned to the villages at a fixed price (*maktû'an*).[55] This latter system did not function smoothly since 'villagers generally lacked the means to pay the fixed price for the tithe-collection opportunity. In practice, an influential villager – an elder or religious leader – generally took the initiative and acted as tax farmer.'[56] This was the case in Palu in the late nineteenth century, which meant that along with the two systems, tax farming was also used, with the farmers mostly local Muslims.

As the Ottoman state's attempts to confiscate agrarian surplus continued, Palu underwent a severe drought. From 1890 through 1893, cultivators produced less than one-fifth of what they had in previous years and grain prices increased dramatically, causing a widespread famine in the Palu countryside. The misery of the rural population was so extreme that, according to one account, more than five hundred families left the region in search of livelihood.[57] In her study of the nineteenth-century famines in the Ottoman Empire, Özge Ertem states that in the eastern provinces, the great majority of famine-related deaths affected the nomadic Kurdish tribes who lived on animal husbandry.[58] After three years of drought, because of the logistical difficulties of exporting grains from Diyarbekir to Palu, the local administration opted to provide credit at the Agricultural Bank (*Ziraat Bankası*) to those affected.[59] The drought and the resultant famine increased the tension in the rural sector and rendered the settled agricultural populations more vulnerable to the potential attacks of the nomadic pastoralist groups.

The Armenians

In his study of the relationship between land ownership and intercommunal violence, Stephan Astourian points out the difference between Eastern Anatolia and Cilicia – referring to an area in south-central Anatolia that extends north-east of the Mediterranean – in terms of Armenian ownership of land. He argues that while, in the former, the Armenian peasantry faced massive dispossession, in the latter, their ability to buy large chunks of land attracted the fury of the Muslim population. In both cases 'niche overlap', meaning 'competition for the same resource environment', created polarisation between the communities and eventually violence and massacres.[60] As Astourian argued, understanding changing land ownership patterns is paramount for determining what strained intercommunal relations in the areas where large-scale massacres took place in the fall of 1895. But while regional differences are important in understanding the correlation between land ownership and intercommunal violence, the Armenian population was not a monolithic entity. Along with differences between town and city or different provinces in terms of property and wealth configurations, there were large variations *within* the Armenian populations of small towns. As we saw in Chapter 6, in Palu, the sale of the begs' former lands deepened class differences within the Armenian community. Both Armenian middle peasants and the Armenian merchant and/or financial bourgeoisie were able to buy land, but the continuing complaints of cultivators and the reports of Ottoman officials indicate that exploitative relations of production in the agrarian sector did not change along with the owners. And even with land acquisition by the Armenian population, the majority of both Armenians and Muslims in Palu's villages were sharecroppers. Peasant indebtedness was chronic. By the 1860s, the rural credit network was extremely complex. As mentioned, *sarraf*s were a central component of the rural fiscal regime, serving as financiers to tax farmers and government officials, but also lending cash to cultivators at outrageous interest rates. In time, the credit network got more sophisticated – and more exploitative – with the emergence of the widespread practice of promissory notes (*poliçe*). The *sarraf*s started to transfer debt to other financiers, who imposed even higher interest rates on the borrowers. Debt collection could involve violence and dispossession, with borrowers frequently losing houses, animals and land to the *poliçeci*s.[61] As the *sarraf*s of olden times became the *poliçeci*s of the late nineteenth century, rural conflicts intensified. The increasing complexity of the credit network attests to the growth of monetisation, commodification of land and intensified stratification within the Armenian community at the turn of the century.

This noticeable differentiation within the rural community was also related to the extraordinary mobility of the Palu Armenians. From the eighteenth century on, they had solid links with local provincial towns and Istanbul. Some worked as labourers in construction or ports; others were *sarraf*s in the capital. In his study of Armenian migration to the United States from Harput, sixty miles away from Palu, David Gutman demonstrates that the socio-economic changes taking place in the rural sector created a vibrant regional economy and increasing rates of Armenian land ownership in and around Harput. Coupled with the evolution of steamship technology and the flooding of the region with American Protestant missionaries, these changes made Harput the epicentre of Armenian migration to North America at the end of the nineteenth century. Palu Armenians were equally mobile, but with a different pattern. Before the twentieth century, there was no noticeable immigration from Palu to the United States. There were cases, but the numbers of Palu Armenians' migrating to America was not comparable to the numbers for Harput. Instead, Palu Armenians mostly migrated to provincial towns such as Diyarbekir or Cilicia, or to Istanbul. They began emigrating to the United States in the early twentieth century, after the social, economic, demographic and psychological damage of the pogroms. The reasons for the difference between the Palu and Harput migratory patterns need further analysis that is beyond the scope of this study, but for Palu Armenians, labour migration heavily influenced the economic, socio-cultural, and eventually the political life in the district in the late nineteenth century. Whether in the cotton fields of Cilicia or the ports of Istanbul, Palu Armenians pursued their livelihoods outside of Palu.[62] This mobility, however, did not erode their ties with their home town; they closely followed the changes in Palu, specifically in relation to land and taxation. As discussed, it was Istanbul-based Palu Armenians who continuously brought the land disputes with the begs to the attention of the Ottoman imperial state. It was mainly through monies accumulated by labouring far from their homeland that they purchased land from the begs' confiscated acreage. Those who went back and forth from Istanbul to their homeland contributed to the making of an enlightened community of Armenians in the villages such as Havav or Kapıaçmaz. Descendants of those who remained in Istanbul constituted notable personalities on the capital's vibrant cultural and intellectual scene.[63]

By the 1880s, this cultural transformation had created an informed political culture in the Palu villages, providing fertile ground for the revolutionary ideologies of the budding Armenian political organisations. The village of Havav stood out in this respect. In 1885 Hampartsum Garian established an organisation called the 'National Association'.[64] While in Istanbul, he received letters from his townsmen about the bandit attacks and plundering they were suffering. He returned to Havav to empower village inhabitants, emphasising self-defence. Five founding members of the organisation (Garian, Priest Toros, teacher Ohan Vosgeyan, Yiğit Vartan Boyajıyan and Sarkis Maligyan) constituted the central committee, which organised weekly secret meetings that included village notables and youth, who also received arms drill training for self-defence.[65]

Towards the end of the nineteenth century, Ottoman Armenians' political scene saw the establishment of revolutionary organisations.[66] The first was the Social Democratic Hnchak Party, established in 1887 in Geneva with a socialist-revolutionary agenda. Next came the Armenian Revolutionary Federation (*Dashnaktsutiun*) established in Tblisi in 1890. These two organisations stood at the centre of Armenian political activism.[67] Palu Armenians were aware of the new parties; many members of the Hnchak Party were originally from Palu. Besides being active in the organisation's activities in the capital, these Armenians also established branches in their native villages.[68] Hnchak members from Palu included Azarig Koloyian from the village of Kapıaçmaz and Bedros Varjabedian (Bedre) from the Sakrat village. As mentioned, the epicentre of Armenian political consciousness in Palu was the village of Havav. After the 1908 Revolution, which deposed Sultan Abdülhamid II and reinstated the Ottoman constitution, *Dashnaksutyun* opened a branch in Havav. Looking at the villages from where these politicised Armenian men emerged reveals a clear pattern. The villages – Tset (Kapıaçmaz), Sakrat, Havav, Khoşmat and Sıgam – were the same villages that appeared in Ottoman governmental records of land conflicts in the second half of the nineteenth century. Residents of these villages petitioned the Ottoman state, followed up the cases in the Ottoman administrative machinery, and even took the begs to court.

The political activities of the Palu Armenians, both in Istanbul and in the villages of Palu, were not lost on Abdülhamid II's huge machinery of intelligence; from the 1890s onwards, their activities were closely monitored. Ottoman administrators found Armenian mobility suspicious. The state not only policed but also tried to halt migration of Armenians from Harput and nearby to the United States because of its enormous concern about Armenian revolutionary activism.[69] In 1891, the deputy governor of Erzurum province sent a dispatch informing the Ottoman centre of the movements of Armenians. He stated that thirty-seven Armenians from Palu, Kiği and Çarsancak had passed through Erzincan and arrived in the capital in a period of sixteen days.[70] Palu Armenians are almost always mentioned in such correspondence as one of the groups whose movements needed monitoring. They were subjected to property searches during their movements. For instance, an Armenian woman named Kogida living in Adana set out to go to Palu, her native town, with her son. When they passed through Osmaniye, their belongings were searched and a suspicious document was retrieved. According to the Adana governor, the document mentioned books (with Armenian dates on them) talking about 'oppression and tyranny (*zulm ve taaddi*)' which the suspects had hidden in a friend's home back in Palu before moving to Adana. The governor wanted the latter's house searched for this material.[71]

The Ottoman state also policed communications – letters and telegrams – among Armenians. As the Armenian revolutionary groups' activities became more and more suspicious in the eyes of the Ottoman state, correspondence to and from Palu was policed by the state.[72] For example, a certain Karabet from Palu sent a telegram to a Palu Armenian, Adam Mesrobyan, who was based in Çukurçeşme Hanı in Istanbul. A copy of the telegram was immediately sent to the Ministry of Police (*Zaptiye Nezareti*) so its content could be scrutinised.[73] The telegram sent by Ohannes Esmeryan based in the Kebir Han of Çukurçeşme in Istanbul to Karabet in Palu was similarly investigated.[74] There is no way of knowing if the Ottoman administrators found any suspicious political content in these letters, but none of the cases has a follow-up to the initial investigation, suggesting nothing was found that warranted further inquiry.

By the 1890s, Havav village stood out in governmental records as Ottoman administrators focused on it as a potential node of Armenian political activities. Havav was known in Palu for its educated population. According to Baron Majlan, an inhabitant of Havav, many of its (male) inhabitants 'knew how to read and almost all of them spent more or less time in Constantinople [and] had obtained some knowledge of the world'.[75] Furthermore, many teachers in the region's Armenian schools came from the village, which one British observer called 'the most enterprising village of the district'.[76] Not only did influential Armenians based in Havav flood the capital with letters asking the Ottoman administration to intervene in the land disputes with the begs,[77] they also responded fiercely whenever a beg tried to build a mansion (*konak*) in the village. This resistance made the village an attractive place of refuge for Armenians from surrounding areas.[78] It was a natural place for Armenian revolutionaries to start organising in.

As movement in and out of Havav became more visible, local Ottoman administrators became more and more wary. Ciphered messages raised particular concern about the Havav Armenians' connections with those in the neighbouring Mazgird district of Dersim. In one case, an Armenian from Palu, Bedros, was suspected of having facilitated Mazgird Armenians' entry to Havav in the guise of *poliçecilik*. The Diyarbekir deputy governor demanded an investigation to unearth the real reasons for their visits to Havav.[79]

The Beginning of the Endgame?

Another thing that concerned Ottoman administrators was the appeals made by Armenians to foreign representatives, particularly the British, French and Russians, about their treatment. Ottoman spies closely followed the actions and movements of Havav Armenians, and their intelligence reports indicated that Armenian notables gathered weekly in Havav to plot against the Ottoman state (*devlet-i aliyye aleyhinde akd-i cemiyet eden Ermeniler*).[80] The Ottoman administration believed that behind this were the Russian and British consuls and the Armenian patriarch. The spies also reported that seven people from these countries had come to the district to cause sedition (*fesad*) and that the patriarch was instilling similar ideas in Palu Armenians.[81] The report continued, saying that two Armenians at the church had said: 'We are tired of this state. British consul is here. Whatever it takes, let's do it and be done with it [*Bu devletten usandık. İngiliz konsolosu buradadır. Ne yapmak lazım ise hemen yapıp kurtulalım*].'[82] The next day, they gathered at the house of a certain Avadis Efendi to discuss the issue further. The interrogation report of the Ministry of Police said that the British consul translator had been at the gathering place and that the gathering had been provoked by the British consul's translator and the clergy.[83] One of the Armenians interrogated, Hampartsum, stated that they were told '*Fesad çıkarınız, kan dökünüz. İngiliz devleti hududunuzu tayin edecektir* [Stir turmoil, spill blood; the British government will determine your limits]'.[84] The procedures required that everyone who had participated in the gathering, the consul's translator and those affiliated with the Protestant school in the district all be interrogated, a gruelling process. And bringing the consul to the court risked creating tension with foreign states. Nevertheless, the investigation established that three Armenians, Setrak, Kakosyan and Hampartsum, had tried to cause a disturbance[85] and indicated that the Armenian patriarch should be reprimanded for his involvement.[86] The case eventually came in front of the Sultan. In a letter that he wrote to the British Queen in response to her memorandum asking for the amelioration of the Christians' situation, the Sultan brought up the case of the Palu Armenians:

> His Majesty to-day received another telegram from the Mutesarrif of Dersin [*sic*], stating that in the district of Pallo [*sic*], at a village called Havav, the Armenians, who on a former occasion addressed Her Majesty's Embassy, assembled secretly last Monday and prepared a paper (probably a programme of revolution), and opened a subscription with the object of collecting money for soldiers in the cause, who were to be paid 10 piasters a-head.[87]

The Sultan's use of the Havav case to exemplify the Armenians' 'open acts of rebellion' shows how the Palu Armenians were suspected due to their political activities. From the 1890s on, Ottoman administrators focused their attention on the Palu Armenians' possession of arms, with local administrators often reporting to the imperial centre about Armenians firing guns. This anxiety culminated in a protracted court case that became essentially a showcase to punish politically active Palu Armenians. According to government correspondence, one night, after having heard the gunfire of Muslims, a crowd of Armenians fired rifles two hundred times. When the police rushed to the area, the Armenians tore one of their shirts. Thirteen Armenians were arrested and sent to court. An interrogation at the police station established that the reason for their gathering and the rifle fire was related to a burglary, but the Diyarbekir governor said this had not been confirmed and insisted on finding out the real reason for the gathering and sending the suspects to court.[88] Zeki Pasha, commander-in-chief of the Fourth Army Corps, got involved in the case, writing a harsh (and ciphered) letter to the centre.[89] The two letters were similar. The governor wrote that the Armenians had fired guns 'at night' (*leylen*), clearly talking about a specific and recent incident.[90] Zeki Pasha's letter replaced 'at night' with 'every night' (*beher gece*) and said that Armenians carried arms every night under the pretext of their houses being robbed. Zeki Pasha added a detail that was not in the governor's telegraph: that the majority of Armenians flooding the streets were armed (*Ermenilerin ekserîsi müsallah sokaklara dökülüp*). The governor had said 'a lot of people' were shooting, and thirteen of them were roaming the streets (*tüfenk endâht edenler bir çok kesân olup bunlardan müsellehan sokaklarda dolaşanlardan on üç neferi...*), not the majority of Armenians.[91] With these two small changes, Zeki Pasha pushed the scale of the event to one implying the existence of a continuous problem involving a large number of armed Armenians. Not surprisingly, Zeki Pasha informed the Ottoman imperial administration that those who were involved were sent to court.

Six months later, this incident came to the attention of the British consulate, when the Criminal Court in Ergani Maden sentenced several people to seven years imprisonment. In a dispatch sent to Acting Consul Hampson, British Vice-Consul Thomas Boyadjian provided a rather detailed account of this incident:

> It appears that six months ago cases of burglary occurred in certain quarters of Palu inhabited by the Armenians of the place, and in order to give alarm and frighten away the thieves, guns, as was their custom under such circumstances, were fired for several nights by the tenants of the houses in the quarters abovementioned; one night, however, they fired without intermission several hundred times. The report of firing and tumult caused by it alarmed the *Kaimakam*,

and he thought something was going wrong in the town, so, accompanied by several gendarmes, he hastened to the spot, where he found a large number of Armenians, armed and in an excited state, assembled in the streets, whereupon he caused the arrest of seventeen of them as ringleaders and lodged them in prison, notwithstanding their protests of innocency [sic] and statement of the cause of their excitement.[92]

This was in line with the governor's account of the events that night – which he learned through a letter from the *kaymakam* of Palu. According to the British Vice-Consul, the general sentiment was that the convicted Armenians did not commit anything that could be considered 'treason' – a prevalent belief among the Ottoman administrators – and that the evidence presented by the Public Prosecutor did not prove anything like that. At the trial, which took place in open court, according to Boyadjian, a large number of people were present, suggesting that the case had become important to Palu inhabitants. The defendants' last hope was to petition the Sultan for forgiveness – which did not work. After being imprisoned in Maden for two years, they were transferred to Diyarbekir where they were bailed conditionally and then re-imprisoned.[93]

Concerns about Armenians' getting arms were widespread. In 1891, just a couple of months before this court case, Boyajian's local informants provided him with a worrying description of affairs in the Palu and Harput districts. According to his informant, 'Armenians are procuring arms to a considerable extent, and talk of the need of spilling blood that they may obtain freedom ... They [Armenians] affirm that over 100,000 Armenians under foreign officers are fully armed and drilled, and ready for an advance upon the Turks this spring.'[94] Armenians, the informant also added, were confident that England, France or Russia were 'coming to their aid this spring'.[95] As the Palu Armenians fell increasingly under suspicion, the level of surveillance increased, along with arrests of Palu Armenians on political charges.[96] It is not possible to determine the actual scale of weapons held by Armenians or whether these revolutionary thoughts appealed widely to Palu Armenians. One thing was clear, though, according to Boyajian: 'the Armenians in general are in constant apprehension, either with or without cause, of suddenly having their houses, books, and papers searched and of being on some trifling pretext imprisoned and, perhaps, condemned as political exiles'.[97]

In the early 1890s, another contributor to tensions in Palu's countryside was the increased prevalence of banditry and tribal attacks on the area's settled agrarian villages. News of Kurdish groups plundering settled villages and stealing their animals and the notorious bandits from the Dersim area wreaking havoc in the Armenian villages reached both the

Ottoman administrators and the British authorities. The 'economy of plunder' was a common source of livelihood for tribal forces throughout Kurdistan.[98] Famine and drought intensified the discontent of groups with no access to land or other productive resources between 1890 and 1893. In 1890, Acting Consul Hampson wrote in his dispatch that in Palu, the Kurds were at 'open war among themselves'.[99] Otherwise, he added, things were remarkably quiet in the country. Coming to 1891, however, the reports about Palu became more negative. Writing in September, Vice-Consul Boyajian presented a gloomy picture of affairs there, mentioning that 'gangs of marauders' had attacked the settled villages and seized their livestock.[100] These brigands terrorised both Muslim and Christian inhabitants of the area, creating, according to Boyajian, a general 'lawlessness'.[101] Problems worsened in the next months, resulting in the dismissal of the *kaymakam* and two other officials.[102] These tensions contributed to the deterioration of relations between Muslims and Armenians. It was at this moment of mutual distrust that news of the reform programme arrived in the locality and became the spark for violence against the Armenians.

On 30 September 1895, the Hnchak party held a demonstration in Istanbul to press the government to implement the reforms in the eastern provinces. The event turned violent after the Ottoman officials intervened, which was reciprocated by some of the protestors. This was followed by violent attacks on Armenians in the capital, which triggered a series of massacres of Armenians in different provinces, starting with Trabzon in early October, then followed by other eastern provinces including Diyarbekir, Sivas, Bitlis and Mamûretulaziz. In late October, Sultan Abdülhamid II (r. 1876–1909) approved the proclamation of the reform programme with a decree. The reform programme included policies related to provincial administrative organisation, the representation of non-Muslims in provincial governmental bodies, administration of justice, and the police and gendarmerie in the six eastern provinces.

It also included policies to control the movements of nomadic Kurds, to curtail the power and authority of the Hamidiye regiments and to collect taxes.[103]

As we have seen, even before the promulgation of the reforms, local administrators viewed Armenians with suspicion. By March 1895, British Consul Graves' reports about intercommunal relations in Palu became even more negative, as he conveyed his dismay at the 'ill treatment of the Christians by the police and the other authorities'.[104] In August 1895, the governor told the Christian notables that 'the Sultan had decided to introduce reforms, but that the reforms would be with the sword',[105] a comment that

The Beginning of the Endgame?

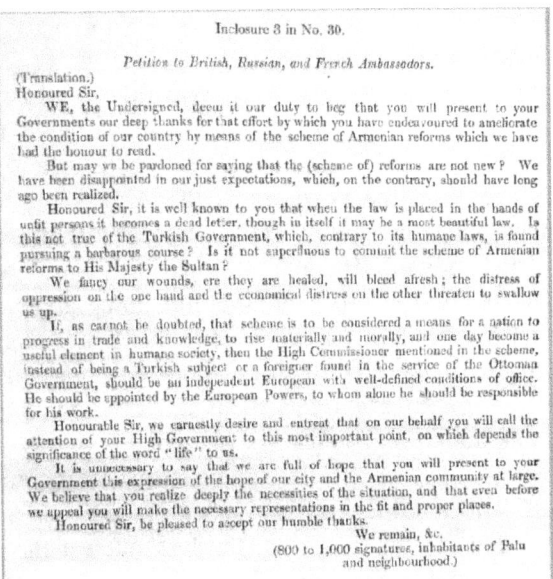

Figure 8.1 The Palu Memorial

cost him his job. In this tense environment, Havav village again came to the state's attention. This time the *kaymakam* of Palu received intelligence that arms and ammunition were concealed in the village. Searches by the police resulted in several arrests.[106] In September 1895, only a few months before the massacres, the government's suspicion of Palu Armenians grew when a certain Nışan was caught with suspicious documents. He had four letters written by Havav Armenians Vartan, Karabet, Bedros and Nışan to Armenians in Harput and Kiği.[107] The letters were intended to be signed by the inhabitants of twenty Armenian villages and the bishop of Palu, as well as the village headmen and the members of the council of the elderly (*ihtiyar heyeti*) and were intended to be sent to the British, French and Russian consuls. The governor said that the plan had been made by the Havav Armenians and arrested all four involved.[108] Though the Armenians involved were imprisoned, Dr Barnum, an American missionary, was able to transmit a copy of the letter to the British consul, Graves, who described it as the 'Palu Memorial[109] and shared copies with his French and Russian colleagues.

The letter claimed to convey the voices of a sizeable group of Armenians (twenty villages – 800 to 1000 inhabitants) including community leaders. The fact that it was addressed to foreign representatives was alarming to the Ottoman state, which feared the involvement of European powers, given the conditions of the Berlin Treaty. The signatories soon complained to Dr Barnum about ill treatment by the authorities.[110]

Relations between the begs and the Armenians were also difficult in this period. The begs were trying to re-gain the lands they had lost to the Armenians, and an increasingly vocal Armenian population was resisting. The begs told the government that Havav was collaborating with Kapıaçmaz village in their resistance, which further exacerbated the government's suspicions of Havav.[111] Around this time, the Armenians of Havav sent a telegram to the Sultan complaining about the two begs of Palu.[112] In September 1895, in response to the Armenians' appeals, the state conducted yet another investigation about the situation. It turned out, however, that the investigation was focused on the complainants rather than on the complaints; it summarily concluded that Havav Armenians had harboured malicious ideas for a while and that their complaints about the begs were slander, which warranted legal action.[113] The more Palu Armenians fell under state suspicion, the less interest the state took in their complaints about land issues. Locally, villagers overseeing land disputes with the begs were pressed by the government to settle the cases, sometimes even being imprisoned.[114]

In March 1895, American missionary Dr Barnum provided a dismal picture of the intercommunal relations in Palu and its vicinity, saying that '[d]uring a residence of thirty-six years I have never known such a desperate condition as the present'.[115] With hindsight, Barnum's gloomy description sounds accurate, as six months from this, the district would be embroiled in a massacre.

Violence and Massacres

Compared to the case for provincial centres or nearby Harput, the paucity of testimonies and historical records about events in Palu in the fall of 1895 is striking.[116] The death of British vice-consul Boyajian shortly before the 1895 massacres dramatically decreased British coverage of Palu. There is limited information from the Protestant missionaries, because Palu was an out-station for missionaries based in Harput. Missionaries went to Palu rarely, and certainly not during the massacres. The most detailed source about Palu during the 1895 Massacres is a collection of letters sent by Armenians from around the empire and published in 1896 in France as *Les Massacres d'Arménie, témoignages des victimes*. This book provides fairly detailed information about how the events unfolded in Palu, together with the responsibility of the begs, tribes and local administrators regarding the massacres.[117] Ottoman archival records fail to provide detailed information on the events in the locality. In his study of the language used in the official correspondence of the 1895 Massacres, Edip Gölbaşı demonstrated that Ottoman administrators consistently described the events as either *şûriş* (turmoil) or, mostly, *iğtişaşat* (pl. of *iğtişaş*, meaning disturbance, turbulence or disorder). By using this vocabulary together with the systematic passive voice, the Ottoman authorities concealed the collectively violent character of the events, portraying them as 'unorganized mass conflict, spontaneous outbursts of popular anger, or happenstances that were triggered by the "seditious" actions of the Armenians'.[118] Official correspondence employed in relation to the massacres in Palu also fitted with this pattern, describing the events in a way that gives no hint as to who the actors were or what their motivations might have been. Therefore, while demonstrating the Ottoman administrators' approach to the issues, the Ottoman official correspondence is not too useful in providing information on the events in the locality, the actors, and the scope of the massacres.

Shortly after the reform programme was announced in October, news of its promulgation and of the massacres in Istanbul, Trabzon and Erzincan reached Palu. Even before these episodes of violence, the Sasun massacres of 1894 had already had a negative impact on intercommunal relations.[119] Vice-Consul Boyajian observed that around Diyarbekir, the feeling of hostility was noticeable, particularly among the lower classes, after Sasun.[120] In early October 1895, Palu Armenians heard the news of violent attacks on Armenians in nearby Kiğı, only an hour away, and realised that the violence was getting closer.[121] According to contemporary accounts, the impact of the violence on local actors in Palu was virtually immediate. Turkish and Kurdish armed bands began to roam the area. As of 21 October, the atmosphere in Palu was already tense, with crowds gathering around the Armenian villages.

By 23 October,[122] the sense of terror and insecurity in the town reached such a level that people did not even leave their houses. Around this time, the Turkish inhabitants and soldiers of the regular army attacked shops in the centre of Palu, while Armenians hid in their houses.[123] The attacks then spread to the countryside. Assailants led by the Kurdish begs and the Muslim notables and armed with Martini rifles, daggers and axes laid siege to the Armenian villages.[124] When night came, Palu Armenians experienced fires, killings and raids, all accentuated by the sounds of bugling – a detail that is consistent across accounts of the different massacres of 1895. The carnage continued for at least another ten days. On 26 October, the chief commander authorised one division of the four battalions on the way to Harput to be directed to Palu because, he said,

Palu was becoming increasingly important.[125] There was no indication as to why Palu was deemed to be important.

By 4 November, Enis, the governor of Diyarbekir, was asking for military support, stating that the Kurds were attacking the Armenian villages of Palu.[126] Meanwhile, Armenian shops were closed and plundering was continuing. A sheikh was preaching a crusade against the Christians in the town.[127] At this point, the governor sent a cipher telegram to the centre stating that they had received news of '*iğtişaşat*' from Palu, but since the telegraph lines to Palu were broken he had sent special cavalrymen to investigate.[128]

The governor's account of what happened in Palu is reminiscent of the standard plot that authorities provided about the beginning of massacres elsewhere.[129] According to this official narrative, Armenians had gathered at the church and fired on the Muslim neighbourhood, forcing Muslims to reciprocate (*mukabeleye mecbur eylediklerinden*), which resulted in the deaths of three Armenians and three Muslims.[130] The commander of the Fourth Army, Zeki Pasha, sent a dispatch the same day informing the centre of this *iğtişaşat* in the town and stated that military units had been sent to suppress it.[131] The governor also declared that the town was surrounded by the Kurds planning an attack on the town and that he was in communication with Muslim notables of the town advising them to maintain order. In a few days, Diyarbekir governor Enis informed the centre that tribes in Palu and Dersim were attacking villages in the countryside.[132] The governor said that in addition to sending military force, he was working with the local notables to appease the tribes. Two days later, the governor stated that the *ekrad* had raided the town, causing *şûriş* and *iğtişaşat*.[133] Lacking information on the outcome of the *iğtişâşât*, the governor added, he was providing subsistence to those placed in a dire situation because of the *şûriş* (*şûriş sebebiyle zarûrete düşmüş olanların i'âşesine hükûmetçe bakılmakda idiği*).[134] He did not provide any information on how the government was providing help without knowing what had happened in the district. The next day, the Diyarbekir governor wrote that a certain Agop from Palu had been arrested for causing *iğtişaş* by firing a rifle twice.[135] Around 14 November, the Ministry of Foreign Affairs stated dismay about the news featured in the German press that one thousand souls had been killed in Ankara and Palu.[136]

The Diyarbekir governor's coverage of events in Palu ended with this last letter on 12 November. In fact, except for a dispatch sent by the military commander in the area on 27 November, there is no further governmental correspondence about events in Palu. The military dispatch stated that order had been established, but also mentioned that the tribes of the Dersim area had passed the Murad River and were planning an assault – suggesting that the region was far from tranquil.[137] None of the contemporaneous accounts of the Palu massacre provided any substantial information about what was actually happening in the district. The governor's accounts were brief, written in a bureaucratic language with no real information on local actors and events – other than the attacks of the Kurdish tribes.

Writing in December 1895, a missionary from Harput stated that '[i]n the villages which I have around Peri and Palu we have no particulars. The sum total must be dreadful in the extreme.'[138] The available records indicate that in Palu in the fall of 1895 there were two happenings after 20 October. On the one hand, there was tension in the city centre after the reform programme was proclaimed. The town's Muslim population, joined by the regular army soldiers, attacked and looted the Armenian shops. As mentioned, the government accounts claimed that the Armenians had fired first, provoking the Muslim reaction.[139] Other records, however, do not mention any such shooting, and instead say that the Armenians, terrified by the tense climate, had closed their shops and hidden in their houses.

Secondly, the town was surrounded by Kurdish groups who at some point entered the city and participated in the looting and the massacres.[140] Their attacks continued throughout the countryside, resulting in deaths, villages being destroyed, and houses and churches being burnt. One testimony claimed that sixteen villages on the banks of the Aradzani (Murad) River had been severely affected by the attacks.[141]

The role of local administrators in the 1895 massacres was critical, as it significantly influenced the extent of violence and casualties. In many places, particularly in the provincial centres, provincial administrators did not just condone the attacks, but encouraged the assailants. In the few areas where local administrators intervened, Armenians were spared violence.[142] A few months before the events, the district governor (*kaymakam*) of Palu was dismissed due to corruption. During the massacres, an interim governor was in charge. Available accounts mention his encouragement of the assailants.[143] Lower-level administrators also acted to foster an atmosphere of impunity for atrocities committed against the Armenians.[144] There are accounts of local administrators promising protection to Armenians while allying with the assailants. And, as mentioned, members of the army participated in the assaults and violence inflicted upon the Armenians.[145]

It is no coincidence that Havav village was attacked early in the massacres, given that it had long been seen as a hotbed of Armenian political activism. One European observer reported that the 'Turks said they would make this village a "field"'.[146] Early in October the conflict between the begs and the Havav village was re-ignited, with the begs asking to extract the entire yearly harvest – the year before, the begs could not collect the tithe because of the government's decision that took it away from the begs.[147] The village refused. The begs' exploitative demands for agrarian surplus were not new, but the massacres likely emboldened them and made them expect less resistance from formerly resistant villages. The villages which had had protracted conflicts with the begs, namely Havav and Tset (Kapıaçmaz), became the sites of score-settling. The begs threatened the Armenian population with a 'general massacre'.[148]

Around 29 October, Kurdish tribes began attacking Havav village. The villagers' initial resistance quickly faded, and they fled to nearby churches and monasteries.[149] Reportedly, Tayfur Beg arrived in the village after the killings and set fire to the houses of his enemies. A certain Ali Çavuş, who was infamous for brutality, took it upon himself to set fire to the church of Surp Asdvadzadzin and the parish school in the village.[150] Some begs had a vindictive attitude towards the Armenians during the massacres because of prior conflicts. One example is the Armenian Fermanian family, whose members were attacked by Hacı Timur Beg's servants. Tayfur Beg wanted to settle accounts with his foes in the Havav village and burnt down their houses, once the killings had ended.

There were also reports of begs providing refuge to Armenians fleeing persecution. The role played by İbrahim Beg (the late Necib Pasha's son) was critical during the tumultuous weeks of Fall 1895 in Palu. As the attacks on Armenians began, İbrahim Beg and his brother Rüşdü escorted the Armenian caravan that was fleeing to Sakrat village.[151] This earned him the reputation of being the protector of the Armenians and turned Sakrat into a refuge for thousands of Armenians fleeing from atrocities across Palu.[152] But the begs' role as protectors would later prove controversial: İbrahim Beg transformed protection into a profitable enterprise by asking the Armenians seeking entrance to the village to pay five piasters per person.[153] İbrahim Beg chased inhabitants of Kapıaçmaz village who had taken refuge in Kurdish villages and forced them into Sakrat in return for fees.[154] As Armenians from all around Palu flooded Sakrat seeking protection, hundreds of tribal chiefs and a brigade of soldiers also gathered there. Some accounts suggest that while commercialising protection in this manner, İbrahim Beg, together with the police officer and army commander, were nothing other than spectators when crowds looted the Armenians who took refuge in the village.[155]

The cases of two other villages offer a clearer account of the begs' roles. According to a British account, the Armenians of the Yeniköy village took refuge with Şükrü Beg. Of the 185 Armenian inhabitants of the village, ten were killed, and the beg and his servants raped all the women.[156] The relatively small number of Armenian deaths must have been because the begs extended some protection to the Armenians fleeing the tribal groups. In Havav, in contrast, 180 of the 220 Armenian houses were burnt and seventy people killed. British sources mentioned that, after the massacres, Tayfur Beg (Şerif Beg's son) 'extorted £T. 160 in money from the villagers as the price of his protection and demanded that the land of the village be transferred to him. The people are afraid to ask for his removal [from the village] as he would then set the Kurds on them.'[157]

The begs' extension of protection to the Armenians was a money-making enterprise. Shortly after the massacres, the British vice-consul wrote: '[İbrahim Beg] was charged to obtain the restitution of the stolen property to the Christians. He went round the villages extorting money from those who had stolen property and taking receipts from the Christians who have thus recovered nothing while he has enriched himself to the extent of several hundred pounds.'[158] It is obvious that most begs saw this as an opportunity to profit by extorting protection fees from the Armenians. The question that is equally important is whether, if the begs had genuinely tried to protect the Armenians, they could have done so. Notwithstanding İbrahim Beg's efforts to revitalise role of the *hâkim* and act as the highest authority in the area, those days were long gone. As the Palu nobility's military and economic power dwindled in visible ways as a result of the centralisation policies of the imperial state, they lost their authority over other power groups, tribal or otherwise, in the area. In the past, they had acted as the commander of the military forces that consisted of armed tribal men, standing atop the local power hierarchy and representing the tribal groups to the Ottoman state. But by the mid-nineteenth century, they had already lost their military roles vis-à-vis the tribes. As the modern Ottoman state made inroads into Kurdistan, the economic and symbolic aspects of the begs' rulership faded. By the 1890s, despite the begs being recognised by the state with medals or positions in the bureaucracy, their ability to exercise authority over the local actors had vanished. It is very unlikely that İbrahim Beg or other begs actually wanted to give the Armenians a safe refuge in the middle of this tragedy, but even if they did, they had neither the military power nor the symbolic capital to do so.

Conclusion

In British accounts of the massacres, Palu was mentioned as one of the two districts of Diyarbekir where the Armenians suffered the most. Six villages with a total of 181 houses were entirely burnt; seven villages were more than half burnt. Every Armenian house was plundered.[159] Along with deaths, destruction of property and psychological trauma, many Armenians were also forced to convert to Islam. According to one account, in Palu 3,000 Armenians were forcefully converted.[160]

Along with the human toll and socio-cultural effects, the 1895 massacres had an impact on land ownership and relations of production in the agrarian sector. The unprecedented mass violence they went through rendered the Armenians economically vulnerable. The massacres provided the begs with an unparalleled opportunity to seize lands in the villages with which they had had prolonged disputes. As we have seen, the village of Kapıaçmaz had been in conflict with İbrahim Beg over land since the 1850s. After the massacres, he re-instituted his control over the village's lands and the villagers went back to the practice of tilling the lands for him as sharecroppers.[161] He tried to put a legal imprint on this de facto situation by forcing the Armenians to testify in court that they had sold their lands to the begs.[162] Adding insult to injury, the Armenians also lost their cattle, which was stolen during the massacres.[163]

Palu Armenians were practically reduced to serfdom in the aftermath of 1895. 'Even when there is any harvest to reap', British consul Hallward wrote, 'many of them have neither implements, nor cattle, nor place to settle the harvest, and it seems impossible that they should be able to subsist another winter under present conditions.'[164] After the massacres, the begs began levying outrageous exactions on the Armenians,[165] and tax farmers' complaints about not being able to collect the tithe became ever louder.[166]

All in all, this moment of mass violence reset the agrarian relations of production back to the era when the begs had the undisputed upper hand in land ownership and surplus extraction. Even though the begs' de jure hereditary rights over land had become obsolete, this moment of revanchism helped them reinstate their control, albeit without the military power and symbolic authority that had once come with it. A more than half-century-long policy of Ottoman state-building resulted in the destruction of the *hâkim* position. This had far-reaching consequences for local power structures and relations. For better or worse, the *hâkim*s had long been the leaders of the local community – a role which involved not just surplus extraction and coercion but also arbitration of disputes, especially between the tribal groups. The Ottoman state brought the hereditary position of the *hâkim* to end with all of its components. But the military, fiscal and administrative restructuring in the locality was far from being consistent, comprehensive and authoritative. The Palu inhabitants met the tense imperial political atmosphere that came after the Berlin Conference as they were dealing with the ramifications of this strife-ridden process of the liquidation of the *ancien régime*'s institutions in the locality. The violence and massacres that plagued the region in 1895 were an outcome of these profound changes.

Notes

1. Edip Gölbaşı, '1896 Katliamları: Doğu Vilayetlerinde Cemaatler Arası 'Şiddet İklimi' ve Ermeni Karşıtı Ayaklanmalar', in *1915: Siyaset, Tehcir ve Soykırım*, eds Oktay Özel and Fikret Adanır 140–63.
2. BOA.Y.PRK.UM 4/5 24 Şevval 1297 [29 September 1880].
3. In her study on the Hamidiye Light Cavalry, Janet Klein has shown that a similar process was at play in other parts of Kurdistan. Tribal chiefs who accumulated wealth and power mostly through the tribal regiments increased their efforts to dispossess the Armenians of land in this tense political environment of increased suspicisons towards Armenians. Klein, *The Margins of Empire*, 2011, 143.
4. BOA.A.DVN.MHM 25/32 Evâsıt-ı Şaban 1274 [26 March 1858].
5. BOA. ŞD. 2480/6 Doc # 3 4 Zilkade 1300 [5 Eylül 1883].
6. BOA.Y.MTV 56/13 6 Rebîulâhir 1309 [9 November 1891].
7. The construction of this military station gave many other notables an opportunity to show their support for the Ottoman military. Along with Necib Beg, his son İbrahim Beg, a certain Mıgırdiç Efendi from the local notables, other Palu begs including Şükrü Beg (Necib Pasha's son-in-law) and Said Beg were also recognised for their help in constructing the station. BOA.DH.MKT 1929/24 4 Şaban 1309 [4 March 1892].
8. BOA.DH.MKT 2066/85 19 Şevval 1311 [25 April 1894].
9. BOA.DH.MKT 323/63 27 Cemâziyelâhir 1313 [26 December 1894].
10. BOA.DH.MKT 146/50 Document # 5 24 Nisan 1310 [6 May 1894].
11. BOA.DH.MKT 146/50 Document # 3 11 Ağustos 1309 [23 August 1893].
12. BOA.DH.MKT 146/50 Document # 3 11 Ağustos 1309 [23 August 1893]. The sums paid by the Armenians to the Kurdish tribes for protection (*hafir*) represented an existing practice in Kurdistan. Polatel observes that in and around Sasun, Armenians paid protection money to Kurdish tribes who would take up arms to defend them from the nomadic Kurdish tribes. Mehmet Polatel, 'The Complete Ruin of a District: The Sasun Massacre of 1894', in *The Ottoman East in the Nineteenth Century: Societies, Identities, and Politics* (London; New York: I. B. Tauris, 2016), 187.
13. See, among others, BOA.Y.PRK.MYD 13/71 5 Rebîulâhir 1311 [16 September 1893]; BOA.DH.MKT 217/38 12 Ramazan 1311 [19 March 1894]; BOA.DH.MKT 402/78 [28 July 1895].
14. BOA.DH.MKT 232/45 15 Muharrem 1312 [19 July 1894].

15. BOA.DH.MKT 146/50 Document # 4 16 Receb 1311 [23 January 1894].
16. BOA.DH.MKT 146/50 Document # 3 11 Ağustos 1309 [23 August 1893].
17. Necib Pasha's land holdings remained controversial even after his death in 1898 in Istanbul. He was survived by his second wife Emîne Habîbe and two children he had with her – Fazıl Beg and Seniha Hanım – in Istanbul, as well as by two sons based in Palu, İbrahim and Rüşdü Begs. After her husband's death, Emîne Habîbe appealed to the state complaining that the two elder sons had not given anything to her and her children from her husband's revenues and property in Palu.
18. See, among others, BOA.DH.MKT 401/67 2 Safer 1313 [2 Temmuz 1895]; BOA.DH.MKT 402/34 3 Safer 1313 [25 July 1895]; BOA.DH.MKT 416/50 Selh-i Safer 1313 [21 August 1895]; BOA.DH.MKT 426/19 21 Rebîülevvel 1313 [11 September 1895]; BOA.BEO 1591/119316 11 Şaban 1318 [4 December 1900].
19. Mehmet Polatel, 'Armenians and the Land Question in the Ottoman Empire, 1870–1914' (Ph.D. dissertation, Boğaziçi University, 2017), 110.
20. Armenian National Assembly, 'Second Report on the Oppression of the Armenians in Armenia and Other Provinces of Asiatic Turkey Presented to the Armenian National Assembly by the Commission Appointed for That Purpose' (London: Official Publication of the Armenian National Patriarchate in Constantinople, September 17, 1876), 56.
21. BOA.ŞD. 2480/6 Document # 2 14 Cemâziyelevvel 1298 [12 April 1881].
22. BOA. A.MKT.MVL 119/57 14 Safer 1277 [1 September 1860].
23. BOA.DH.MKT42/34 3 Safer 1313 [25 July 1895].
24. BOA.DH.MKT 401/67 2 Safer 1313 [2 July 1895]; BOA.DH.MKT 416/50 Selh-i Safer 1313 [21 August 1895].
25. BOA.MVL 522/94 18 Cemâziyelâhir 1283 [28 October 1866].
26. BOA.MVL 522/94 18 Cemâziyelâhir 1283 [28 October 1866].
27. Armenian National Assembly, 'Second Report on the Oppression of the Armenians in Armenia and Other Provinces of Asiatic Turkey Presented to the Armenian National Assembly by the Commission Appointed for That Purpose', 56.
28. Many accounts describe the period after the Crimean War as the time when the begs went back to their previous exploitative practices. See, for example, BOA.ŞD 2864/8 10 Zilkade 1288 [21 January 1872].
29. BOA.DH.MKT 430/32 29 Rebîülevvel 1313 [19 September 1895]; Also, Y.PRK.BŞK 43/22 28 Rebîülevvel 1313 [19 September 1895].
30. Dikran S. Papazian, *History of Palu's Havav Village* [*Badmutyun Palu Havav kyughi*], published by Mshag, Beirut, 1960.
31. Polatel, 'Armenians and the Land Question in the Ottoman Empire, 1870–1914', 75.
32. Armenian National Assembly, 'Second Report on the Oppression of the Armenians in Armenia and Other Provinces of Asiatic Turkey Presented to the Armenian National Assembly by the Commission Appointed for That

Purpose'. For a recent discussion on the Ottoman state's reform programme from the perspective of the Armenian community, see Antaramian, *Brokers of Faith, Brokers of Empire*.

33. Esat Uras and Cengiz Kürşat, *The Armenians in History and the Armenian Question* (Documentary Publications, 1988), 432–3.
34. Blue Book, Turkey, No. 1, 1897, 41, cited in Uras and Kürşat, 449.
35. Ali Karaca, *Anadolu Islahâtı ve Ahmet Şakir Paşa, 1838–1899* (İstanbul: Eren, 1993), 39.
36. Janet Klein, *The Margins of Empire: Kurdish Militias in the Ottoman Tribal Zone* (Stanford: Stanford University Press, 2016), 51.
37. Abdüsselam Ertekin, 'Hamidiye Alayları ve Sosyo-Politik Etkileri (1890–1908)' (Ph.D. dissertation, Mardin Artuklu University, 2019), 99.
38. BOA. Y.PRK. UM 3/3 Doc # 2 Şevval 1297 [16 September 1880].
39. BOA.DH.MKT 1809/111 7 Receb 1308 [16 February 1891].
40. BOA.Y.PRK.ASK 54/31 23 Mart 1305 [4 April 1889].
41. BOA.DH.MKT 1683/21 24 Rebîülâhir 1307 [18 December 1889].
42. Dündar, *Crime of Numbers: The Role of Statistics in the Armenian Question (1878–1918)* (New York: Routledge), 11.
43. Karpat, 'Ottoman Population Records and the Census of 1881/82–1893', 33.
44. BOA.DH.MKT 1976/105 29 Zilhicce 1309 [25 July 1892].
45. BOA.DH.MKT 1976/29 Zilhicce 1309 [25 July 1892].
46. BOA.DH.MKT 2044/79 2 Receb 1310 [20 January 1893].
47. BOA.DH.MKT 2044/79 2 Receb 1310 [20 January 1893].
48. BOA.DH.MKT 1303/20 20 Şaban 1310 [9 March 1893].
49. Karpat, 'Ottoman Population Records and the Census of 1881/82–1893', 134.
50. Karpat, 33.
51. BOA.DH.ŞFR 4/12 4 Şubat 1302 [16 February 1887].
52. BOA.Y.PRK.UM 3/3 11 Şevval 1297 [16 September 1880].
53. BOA.Y.PRK.UM 3/3 11 Şevval 1297 [16 September 1880].
54. BOA.ML.EEM 27 Kanun-i Sani 1305 [8 February 1890].
55. BOA.BEO.1003/75203 3 Rebîülâhir 1315 [1 September 1897].
56. Özbek, 'Tax Farming in the Nineteenth-Century Ottoman Empire', 234.
57. BOA.BEO 227/16968 Document # 3 11 Haziran 1309 [23 June 1893].
58. Özge Ertem, 'Fiyatı Alidir!: Diyarbakır'da Kıtlık, Yokluk ve Şiddet, 1879–1880', in *Diyarbakır ve Çevresi Toplumsal ve Ekonomik Tarihi Toplantısı* (Istanbul: Hrant Dink Vakfı Yayınları, 2013), 73.
59. BOA.BEO 227/16968 Document # 7 28 Ağustos 1309 [9 September 1893].
60. Stephan H. Astourian, 'The Silence of the Land: Agrarian Relations, Ethnicity, and Power', in *A Question of Genocide: Armenians and Turks at the End of the Ottoman Empire* (Oxford: Oxford University Press, 2011), 55. In his study of Ayntab, Ümit Kurt argues that the economic ascendancy of the Armenians over their Muslim population was the underlying reason

behind the pogroms in this town in 1895. Ümit Kurt, 'The Breakdown of a Previously Peaceful Coexistence', in *Armenians and Kurds in the Late Ottoman Empire*, ed. Ümit Kurt and Ara Sarafian (Fresno, CA: California State University Press, 2020), 45–70.

61. BOA.MVL 493/85 26 Şevval 1282 [14 March 1866]; BOA.MVL 0514/71 24 Cemâziyelâhir 1283 [3 November 1866]; BOA.MVL 518/16 21 Receb 1283 [29 November 1866]; BOA.MVL 531/105 1 Muharrem 1284 [5 May 1267]; BOA.MVL 739/3 11 Rebîülevvel 1284 [13 July 1867].
62. 'Palu: Population Movements', https://www.houshamadyan.org/mapotto manempire/vilayetdiyarbekir/palu/locale/population-movements.html (last accessed 14 June 2019).
63. 'Palu: Population Movements'.
64. 'Palu: Political Parties', https://www.houshamadyan.org/en/mapottomanem pire/vilayetdiyarbekir/palu/political-life/political-parties.html (last accessed 18 October 2020). Around the same time, there was another organisation named *Haigazian*, which probably referred to the same organisation as the National Association since the founding members and major agenda of both organisations were identical.
65. Papazian, *History of Palu's Havav Village*.
66. For a study which examines the Armenian Revolutionary groups' local organisations and their engagement with local actors, see Toygun Altıntaş, 'Crisis and (Dis)order: Armenian Revolutionaries and the Hamidian Regime in the Ottoman Empire, 1887–1896' (Ph.D. dissertation, University of Chicago, 2018). Altıntaş demonstrates that in the Muş plain and Sasun region, the Armenian revolutionaries sought to help the peasantry in their fight against the Kurdish landowners. In his study on the 1895 Massacres in Aintab Ümit Kurt emphasises the role of the Armenian revolutionary political organisations, particularly the Hunchakian, in the political awakening of Armenians. Ümit Kurt, 'Reform and Violence in the Hamidian Era: The Political Context of the 1895 Armenian Massacres in Aintab', *Holocaust and Genocide Studies* 32, no. 3 (2018): 404–23.
67. For more information on the Armenian revolutionary parties in the Ottoman Empire, see Louise Nalbandian, *The Armenian Revolutionary Movement: The Development of Armenian Political Parties through the Nineteenth Century* (Berkeley, CA: University of California Press, 2018); Gerard J. Libaridian, 'What Was Revolutionary about Armenian Revolutionary Parties in the Ottoman Empire?', in *A Question of the Genocide: Armenians and Turks at the End of the Ottoman Empire*, ed. Ronald Grigor Suny, Norman M. Naimark and Fatma Müge Göçek. (Oxford; New York: Oxford University Press, 2011), 82–112. For a recent critique of the historiography of the Armenian revolutionary movement in the Ottoman Empire, see Varak Ketsemanian, 'Ideologies, Paradoxes, and Fedayis in the Late Ottoman Empire: Historiographical Challenges and Methodological Problems in

the Study of the Armenian Revolutionary Movement (1890–1896)', in *Armenians and Kurds in the Late Ottoman Empire*, 119–60.
68. Palu: Political Parties, https://www.houshamadyan.org/en/mapottomanempire/vilayetdiyarbekir/palu/political-life/political-parties.html (last accessed 18 October 2020).
69. For an analysis of the Ottoman state's attempts to prohibit Armenian migration to the United States, see David Gutman, 'Travel Documents, Mobility Control, and the Ottoman State in an Age of Global Migration, 1880–1915', *Journal of the Ottoman and Turkish Studies Association* 3, no. 2 (2016): 347–68.
70. BOA.DH.MKT 151/121 29 Teşrinievvel 1307 [10 November 1891].
71. BOA.DH.MKT 297/58 9 Rebîülâhir 1312 [10 October 1894].
72. BOA.DH.MKT 1778/140 23 Rebîülevvel 1308 [6 November 1890].
73. BOA.DH.MKT 1754/105 9 Muharrem 1308 [25 August 1890].
74. BOA.DH.MKT 1778/141 23 Rebiülevvel 1308 [6 November 1890].
75. Woman's Board of Missions, *Life and Light for Heathen Women.*, vol. IV (Boston: Woman's Board of Missions, 1874), 322.
76. Inclosure 2 in No. 349. 'Letter addressed to Consul Graves', Kharput, 9 March 1895. United Kingdom House of Commons. Parliamentary Papers. Turkey. 1896 [C.8108] Turkey. No. 6 (1896). *Correspondence relating to the Asiatic provinces of Turkey: 1894–95. [In continuation of 'Turkey no. 3 (1896)': c. 8015.]*, 265.
77. See, among others, BOA.MVL 496/155 4 Muharrem 1283 [19 May 1865]; BOA. MVL 483/5 1 Muharrem 1282 [27 May 1865]; BOA.MVL 522/94 18 Cemâziyelâhir 1283 [28 October 1866] BOA.DH.MKT 1497/41 15 Receb 1305 [27 March 1888].
78. https://www.houshamadyan.org/mapottomanempire/vilayetdiyarbekir/palu/locale/history.html (last accessed 23 October 2020).
79. BOA.Y.PRK.A 9/66 29 Teşrin-i Sâni 1310 [11 December 1894].
80. BOA.A.MKT.MHM 750/13 Document # 10 18 Cemâziyelevvel 1312 [17 November 1894].
81. BOA.Y.MTV 108/45 23 Teşrinievvel 1310 [4 November 1894].
82. BOA.A.MKT.MHM 750/13 Document # 10 18 Cemâziyelevvel 1312 [17 November 1894].
83. BOA.A.MKT.MHM 750/13 Document # 10 18 Cemâziyelevvel 1312 [17 November 1894].
84. BOA.A.MKT.MHM 750/13 Document # 10 18 Cemâziyelevvel 1312 [17 November 1894].
85. BOA.A.MKT.MHM 750/13 Document # 10 18 Cemâziyelevvel 1312 [17 November 1894].
86. BOA.İ.HUS 31/6 4 Cemâziyelevvel 1312 [3 November 1894].
87. United Kingdom Foreign Office (FO) 881/6583, 'Reply of His Majesty the Sultan to Preceding Memorandum' (1894).
88. BOA.Y.PRK.UM 20/11 5 Kanunuevvel 1306 [17 December 1890].

89. BOA.Y.PRK.ASK 68/19 6 Cemâziyelevvel 1308 [18 December 1890].
90. BOA.Y.PRK.UM 20/11 5 Kanunuevvel 1306 [17 December 1890].
91. BOA.Y.A.HUS 242/13 6 Cemâziyelevvel 1308 [18 December 1890].
92. 'Vice Consul Boyadjian to Acting Consul Hampson', 21 June 1891. Great Britain House of Commons. Parliamentary Papers. 1892 [C.6632] *Turkey. No.1 (1892). Further correspondence respecting the condition of the population in Asiatic Turkey in continuation of 'Turkey No. 1 (1891)': C.6214*, 61.
93. Acting Vice-Consul Boyajian provided the names of all seven Armenians: Asdour Kaisarlian, Kapriel Kaisarlian, Arakel Kaisarlian, Nerses, Kikor Boudoukian, Nigoghos Fariskian and priest Kevork (Kigork). UK FO 881/6595 Inclosure 2 in No. 153. 'Memorandum by Action Vice-Consul Boyajian' (1895).
94. 'Vice-Consul Boyadjian to Acting Consul Hampson', 13 April 1891. Great Britain House of Commons. Parliamentary Papers. 1892 [C.6632] *Turkey. No.1 (1892). Further correspondence respecting the condition of the population in Asiatic Turkey [In continuation of 'Turkey No. 1 (1891)': C.6214]*. 47.
95. 'Vice-Consul Boyadjian to Acting Consul Hampson', 13 April 1891.Great Britain House of Commons. Parliamentary Papers. 1892 [C.6632] *Turkey. No.1 (1892). Further correspondence respecting the condition of the population in Asiatic Turkey [In continuation of 'Turkey No. 1 (1891)': C.6214]*. 47.
96. UK FO 881/6647 'Consul Graves to Sir A. Nicolson' (received at the Foreign Office, 21 July), Erzeroum, 28 June 1893.
97. 'Vice-Consul Boyajian to Sir Clare Ford' (received at the Foreign Office 12 May) Diarbekir, 18 April 1893. Great Britain House of Commons. Parliamentary Papers. 1896 [C.8015] Turkey. No. 3. (1896). *Correspondence relating to the Asiatic provinces of Turkey*, 98.
98. Özbek, 'The Politics of Taxation and the "Armenian Question" during the Late Ottoman Empire, 1876–1908', 795.
99. Great Britain House of Commons. Parliamentary Papers Turkey. No. 66. 'Acting Consul Hampson to Mr. Fane', Erzeroum, 1 August 1891 (received at the Foreign Office 21 August) *Turkey. No. 1 (1892). Further correspondence respecting the condition of the population in Asiatic Turkey [In continuation of 'Turkey No. 1 (1891)': C.6214]*, 69.
100. 'Acting Vice-Consul Boyajian to Acting Consul Hampson' (received at the Foreign Office 16 October), Harput, 19 September 1891. Great Britain House of Commons. Parliamentary Papers. 1892 [C.6632] *Turkey. No. 1 (1892). Further correspondence respecting the condition of the population in Asiatic Turkey [In continuation of 'Turkey No. 1 (1891)': C.6214]*, 77–8.
101. UK FO 881/6583 Inclosure in No. 13. 'Vice-Consul Boyajian to Consul Graves', Diarbekir, 28 November 1893.
102. UK FO 881/6172 No. 1111 'Vice-Consul Boyajian to Consul Hampson' (received at the Foreign Office, 25 December).

103. Uras and Kürşat, *The Armenians in History and the Armenian Question*, 596–606.
104. Inclosure in No. 387. 'Consul Graves to Sir P. Currie', Erzeroum, 5 April 1895. Great Britain House of Commons. Parliamentary Papers. 1896 [C.8108] Turkey No. 6 (1896). *Correspondence relating to the Asiatic provinces of Turkey: 1894–95. [In continuation of 'Turkey no. 3 (1896)': c. 8015.]*, 249.
105. Edwin Munsell Bliss, *Turkey and the Armenian Atrocities; a Reign of Terror, from Tartar Huts to Constantinople Palaces* ... ([n.p.], 1896), 484.
106. Inclosure in No. 317. 'Consul Graves to Sir P. Curie', Great Britain House of Commons. *Parliamentary Papers. 1896 [C.8108] Turkey No. 6 (1896). Correspondence relating to the Asiatic provinces of Turkey: 1894–95. [In continuation of 'Turkey no. 3 (1896)': c. 8015.]*, 247.
107. BOA.DH.ŞFR 180/10 2 Eylül 1311 [14 September 1895].
108. BOA.DH.ŞFR 180/15 3 Eylül 1311 [15 September 1895].
109. UK FO 881/6820 Inclosure 1 in No. 30. 'Consul Graves to Sir P. Currie', Erzeroum, 20 September 1895.
110. UK FO 881/6820 Inclosure 1 in No. 30. 'Consul Graves to Sir P. Currie', Erzeroum, 20 September 1895.
111. Inclosure 2 in No. 349. 'Letter addressed to Consul Graves', Kharput, 9 July 1895 Great Britain House of Commons. Parliamentary Papers *1896 [C.8108] Turkey No. 6 (1896). Correspondence relating to the Asiatic provinces of Turkey: 1894–95. [In continuation of 'Turkey no. 3 (1896)': c. 8015.]*, 382.
112. Inclosure 3 in No. 493. 'Acting Vice-Consul Boyajian to Consul Graves', Kharput, 9 March 1895. Great Britain House of Commons. Parliamentary Papers *1896 [C.8108] Turkey No. 6 (1896). Correspondence relating to the Asiatic provinces of Turkey: 1894–95. [In continuation of 'Turkey no. 3 (1896)': c. 8015.]*, 265.
113. BOA.DH.MKT 432/25 2 Eylül 1311 [14 September 1895].
114. UK FO 891/6695 Inclosure 2 in No. 71. 'Extract of Letter from Dr. Barnum', Kharput, 9 March 1895.
115. UK FO 891/6695 Inclosure 2 in No. 71. 'Extract of Letter from Dr. Barnum', Kharput, 9 March 1895. In the second half of the nineteenth century, one of the new actors that appeared in the local scene of Palu and its surrounding was the Protestant missionaries from the American Board of Commissioners for Foreign Missions (ABCFM). With its sizeable Armenian population, Palu got onto the Protestant missionaries' radar after the establishment of the Harput mission in 1855. Later Palu became one of the out-stations of the Harput mission. Missionaries touring the area passed by Palu, mostly on their way to Harput, and occasionally visited it. From the 1850s through the late 1860s, the missionaries' effort to gain the hearts and minds of the Palu inhabitants proved largely futile. Two decades of work finally bore a modest fruit with the establishment of a church of thirteen members in 1869.

According to the Armenian accounts, the begs wanted to capitalise on the presence of the Protestant missionaries to create fissures within the Armenian community. One of the begs brought a certain Mardiros Çulcuyan from Harput, a pastor who had just converted to Protestantism. The beg organised a meeting at his house where the pastor would talk about Christianity, which failed to create the expected outcome. His audience showed no interest and even rebuffed his claims to teach them what true Christianity was. Overall, in Palu, mission work largely failed, and the Armenians overwhelmingly stayed within the Armenian Apostolic Church. See *Historical Sketch of the Missions of the American Board of Commissioners for Foreign Missions in European Turkey, Asia Minor and Armenia* (New York, 1866), 39; 'Letter from Eastern Turkey', *Missionary Papers*. Chicago: American Board of Commissioners for Foreign Missions, pub. by the district secretary, 13 October 1867, 26; 'Letter from Barnum (November 7, 1865)', American Board of Commissioners for Foreign Missions. *Missionary Herald*, Vol. 62 (Boston, 1866); *The Missionary Herald, Containing the Proceedings of the American Board of Commissioners for Foreign Missions with a View of Other Benevolent Operations*, for the year 1869. Vol. LXV (Cambridge: Riverside Press, 1869), 129; Dikran S. Papazian, *History of Palu's Havav Village* [Badmutyun Palu Havav kyughi], published by Mshag, Beirut, 1960.

116. Recently, the literature on the unfolding of violence in specific provinces and towns has expanded. One of the first historians who emphasised the significance of the local context in understanding the 1895 Massacres is Jelle Verheij. See 'Les frères de terre et d'eau': sur le rôle des Kurdes dans les massacres arméniens de 1894–1896', *Islam des Kurdes* (special issue of *Les Annales de l'Autre islam)*, eds Martin van Bruinessen and Joyce Blau (Paris: Institut national des langues et civilisations orientales, 1998); 'Diyarbekir and the Armenian Crisis of 1895' in *Social Relations in Ottoman Diyarbekir, 1870–1915*, eds Jelle Verheij and Joost Jongerden (Leiden; Boston: Brill, 2012).

117. This book is frequently attributed to Archag Tchobanian (Armenian scholar and poet, 1872–1954) as the person who compiled the letters that the Ottoman Armenians sent. However, there is no concrete evidence that proves this. Some of the letters published in this book are copies of letters located in the Armenian Patriarchate archives in the Nubar Library in Paris. Private conversation with historian Jelle Verheij of the University of Amsterdam. 16 April 2021.

118. Edip Gölbaşı, 'The Official Conceptualization of the Anti-Armenian Riots of 1895–1897. Bureaucratic Terminology, Official Ottoman Narrative, and Discourses of Revolutionary Provocation', *Études Arméniennes Contemporaines*, no. 10 (30 March 2018): 37.

119. The Sasun Massacre which took place in the summer of 1894 was the first instance of mass atrocities against the Armenians. Polatel, 'The Complete

Ruin of a District'; Owen Miller, 'Rethinking the Violence in the Sasun Mountains (1893–1894)', *Études Arméniennes Contemporaines*, no. 10 (30 March 2018): 97–123.
120. UK FO 891/6695 Inclosure in No. 87. 'Vice-consul Boyajian to Sir P. Currie', Diarbekir, 26 March 1895.
121. *Les massacres d'Arménie: témoignages des victimes* (Édition du Mercure de France, 1896), 181.
122. Other accounts describe 25 October as the day that attacks on the Armenians peaked, especially in the countryside. D. S. Gregory, *The Crime of Christendom; or The Eastern Question, from Its Origin to the Present Time* (New York, [c1900]), 203, http://hdl.handle.net/2027/njp.32101073313304 (last accessed 15 September 2019).
123. *Les massacres d'Arménie*, 181.
124. *Les massacres d'Arménie*, 186.
125. BOA.A.MKT.MHM 636/5 6 Cemâziyelevvel 1313 [25 October 1895].
126. BOA.DH.ŞFR 183/41 23 Teşrînievvel 1311 [4 November 1895].
127. Bliss, *Turkey and the Armenian Atrocities; a Reign of Terror, from Tartar Huts to Constantinople Palaces …* , 441.
128. BOA.DH.ŞFR 183/83 25 Teşrînievvel 1311 [6 November 1895].
129. See the contributions to the special issue of the *Études Arméniennes Contemporaines* 'The Massacres of the Hamidian Period (I): Global Narratives and Local Approaches', eds Boris Adjemian and Mikaël Nichanian, no. 10. December 2017.
130. BOA.Y.PRK.UM 33/58 26 Teşrînievvel 1311 [7 November 1895].
131. BOA.Y.MTV 131/72 26 Teşrînievvel 1311 [7 November 1895].
132. BOA.Y.PRK.UM 33/69 29 Teşrînievvel 1311 [10 November 1895].
133. BOA.DH.ŞFR 31/9 Teşrînievvel 1311 [12 November 1895].
134. BOA.DH.ŞFR 31/9 Teşrînievvel 1311 [12 November 1895].
135. BOA.DH.ŞFR 184/5 1 Teşrînisani 1311 [13 November 1895]. This information is confirmed in Tchobanian, who states that two young men, Agop Gurdjian and Agop Terzian, were imprisoned. [Archag Tchobanian], *Les Massacres d'Arménie, témoignages des victimes*. (Paris: Édition du Mercure de France, 1896), 186.
136. BOA.HR.SYS 2734/14 25 Cemâziyelevvel 1313 [14 November 1895].
137. BOA.DH.TMIK 1/30 10 Cemâziyelâhir 1313 [27 November 1895].
138. Enclosure in No. 741. Harpoot, 12 December 1895. *Papers Relating to the Foreign Relations of the United States* (Washington: Government Printing Office, 1896), 1426.
139. BOA.Y.PRK.UM 33/58 26 Teşrînievvel 1311 [12 November 1895].
140. BOA.DH.ŞFR 183/134 [12 November 1895].
141. *Les massacres d'Arménie*, 196.
142. Gölbaşı, '1896 Katliamları', 156.
143. *Les massacres d'Arménie*, 186.
144. On the question of impunity, see Gölbaşı, '1896 Katliamları', 162.

145. James Wilson Pierce, *Story of Turkey and Armenia* (Baltimore, 1896), 486.
146. Bliss, *Turkey and the Armenian Atrocities; a Reign of Terror, from Tartar Huts to Constantinople Palaces* ..., 439–40.
147. *Les massacres d'Arménie*, 182.
148. *Les massacres d'Arménie*, 180.
149. Bliss, *Turkey and the Armenian Atrocities; a Reign of Terror, from Tartar Huts to Constantinople Palaces* ..., 439–40. See also Archag Tchobanian, *Les Massacres d'Arménie: Témoignages Des Victimes* (Édition du Mercure de France, 1896), 188.
150. *Les massacres d'Arménie*, 212–13.
151. https://www.houshamadyan.org/mapottomanempire/vilayetdiyarbekir/palu/locale/history.html (last accessed 20 July 2020). See also *Les massacres d'Arménie*, 189.
152. UK FO 881/6824 Inclosure 2 No. 135. 'Report on the state of Affairs in the Vilayet of Maamuret-ul-Aziz'.
153. *Les massacres d'Arménie*, 192.
154. *Les massacres d'Arménie*, 189–91.
155. *Les massacres d'Arménie*, 191.
156. Inclosure in No. 140. 'Vice-Consul Hallward to Consul Cumberbatch', Diarbekir, 17 March 1896. Great Britain House of Commons. Parliamentary Papers *1896 [C.8273]. Further correspondence relating to the Asiatic provinces of Turkey. [In continuation of 'Turkey no. 2 (1896)': c.–7927.]*, 127.
157. Inclosure in No. 140. 'Vice-Consul Hallward to Consul Cumberbatch', Diarbekir, 17 March 1896, Inclosure in No. 182. 'Vice-Consul Hallward to Sir P. Currie', Diarbekir, 21 April 1896, *House of Commons Parliamentary Papers*, Turkey. No. 8 (186). 127.
158. Inclosure in No. 140. 'Vice-Consul Hallward to Consul Cumberbatch', Diarbekir, 17 March 1896, Inclosure in No. 182. 'Vice-Consul Hallward to Sir P. Currie', Diarbekir, 21 April 1896, *House of Commons Parliamentary Papers*, Turkey. No. 8 (186). *Further correspondence relating to the Asiatic provinces of Turkey. [In continuation of 'Turkey no. 2 (1896)': c.–7927.]*, 128.
159. Inclosure in No. 140. 'Vice-Consul Hallward to Consul Cumberbatch', Diarbekir, 17 March 1896, Inclosure in No. 182. 'Vice-Consul Hallward to Sir P. Currie', Diarbekir, 21 April 1896, *House of Commons Parliamentary Papers*, Turkey. No. 8 (186). *Further correspondence relating to the Asiatic provinces of Turkey. [In continuation of 'Turkey no. 2 (1896)': c.–7927.]*, 127.
160. UK FO 881/6823 No. 270. 'Sir P. Currie to the Morquess of Salisbury' (received 9 March), Constantinople, 9 March 1896. For the mass conversions within the context of the 1895–6 massacres, see Selim Deringil, *Conversion and Apostasy in the Late Ottoman Empire*, reprint edn (New York: Cambridge University Press, 2015).

161. Inclosure in No. 182. 'Vice-Consul Hallward to Sir P. Currie', Diarbekir, 21 April 1896, *House of Commons Parliamentary Papers*, Turkey. No. 8 (186). *Further correspondence relating to the Asiatic provinces of Turkey. [In continuation of 'Turkey no. 2 (1896)': c.–7927.]*, 162.
162. Ibid.
163. 'Sir P. Currie to the Marquess of Salisbury' (received 18 May), Pera, 14 May 1896. *House of Commons Parliamentary Papers*, Turkey. No. 8 (1896). *Further correspondence relating to the Asiatic provinces of Turkey. [In continuation of 'Turkey no. 2 (1896)': c.–7927.]*, 170.
164. Inclosure in No. 242. 'Vice-Consul Hallward to Mr. Herbert', Diarbekir, 26 May 1896. *House of Commons Parliamentary Papers*, Turkey. No. 8 (1896). *Further correspondence relating to the Asiatic provinces of Turkey. [In continuation of 'Turkey no. 2 (1896)': c.–7927.]*, 201.
165. Inclosure in No. 368. 'Vice-Consul Hallward to Mr. Herbert', Diarbekir, 21 July 1896. *House of Commons Parliamentary Papers*, Turkey. No. 8 (1896). Further correspondence relating to the Asiatic provinces of Turkey. [In continuation of 'Turkey no. 2 (1896)': c.–7927.]*, 298.
166. BOA.DH.MKT 2154/34 15 Şaban 1316 [29 December 1898].

Conclusion: The End of the Nobility in Kurdistan

In 1920, Rüşdü Beg, a member of a Palu noble family, ran to be the representative of the Ergani district in the National Assembly (1920–3) convened in Ankara, the embryonic parliament of the Turkish state founded on the ashes of the Ottoman Empire. His namesake Rüşdü, the chief scribe (*tahrirat müdürü*) of the district, was also a candidate. When the ballots were counted, the latter protested the result, demanding an investigation because, he claimed, his votes had been attributed to his namesake's total. The Palu administrators' response was that although the voters did not formally specify which Rüşdü they meant, when they said Rüşdü Beg, they meant the late Necib Beg's son, since the other one was known as Rüşdü *Efendi*. Rüşdü Efendi lost, and Rüşdü Beg won, serving as the Ergani representative in the National Assembly until 1923.[1]

This book has shown the making and unmaking of the Palu begs as a noble family with de jure hereditary privileges within the Ottoman realm. Rüşdü Beg's career exemplifies the drastic changes members of this family underwent in the late Ottoman Empire. Rüşdü was born in 1876; Abdullah Beg, who attacked the Weşin village in 1848, was his paternal uncle. His father was Necib Pasha, the former *kaymakam* of Palu and a Crimean War veteran discussed in this book. Rüşdü Beg appeared on the historical stage when he was appointed to the local administrative council (*idare meclisi*) of the district at the age of eighteen. Throughout the 1890s, even though his brother İbrahim Beg was more prominent, Rüşdü Beg's name also came up repeatedly in land disputes with local Armenians, especially of the Tset (Kapıaçmaz) and Sakrat villages. During the 1895 Massacres, he and his brother demanded fees from Armenians who were desperately searching for safe refuge in Sakrat village. After being mainly his brother's sidekick, Rüşdü Beg entered politics, serving first as an MP in the last, short-lived (January–March 1920) Ottoman parliament (Meclis-i Mebûsan), then in

Conclusion

the National Assembly mentioned above. Four centuries after his ancestor Cemşîd Beg entered the Ottoman realm as a Kurdistan beg with hereditary privileges, Rüşdü Beg was a member of the Turkish parliament as the Ottoman Empire was on its deathbed.

From the day they acknowledged Ottoman suzerainty until after the empire's disintegration, the Palu begs maintained their identity as a noble family – the belief that they, as nobles, 'stood above other men'.[2] This sense of a noble past pre-dated the Ottoman suzerainty, but the begs justified their noble privileges by referring to imperial decrees granted by the Ottoman sultans. The content and the extent of their privileges changed over time, but until the frontal attack of the Tanzimat state, the hereditary character of the Palu begs' privileges remained unchanged. By examining the noble position of the Palu begs, this book challenged one of the foundational assumptions of Ottoman historical writing: that the Ottoman state categorically rejected the hereditary nobility. According to this view, unlike Europe, the Ottoman politico-administrative system was inherently inimical to hereditary nobilities. The system was meritocratic; the ruling elites were the slaves of the sultans; and there was no way of transferring property across generations since the Ottoman state confiscated property. Underlying these views is a set of assumptions about the absoluteness of the Ottoman state's authority. More recently, revisionist approaches to the Ottoman state have demonstrated the flexibility of Ottoman ruling strategies and demystified the notion of the all-powerful Ottoman state. Nevertheless, the argument that hereditary nobility was absent stems from the continuing impact of ahistorical and essentialised views of Ottoman state power that has origins in European political thought. From the Renaissance thinkers to Weber, European observers and thinkers emphasised the meritocratic system and the patrimonial character of Ottoman rule.[3] Euro-centric accounts of the Ottoman state reproduced these notions and treated the Ottoman Empire and Europe as dichotomous, highlighting what the former lacked compared to the latter.[4] Relatedly, both Ottoman and European historians based their examinations of the Ottoman elites on concepts, ideas and assumptions derived from an ideal-type portrayal of the nobility and, in the absence of this European-type ideal, jumped to the conclusion that there was no nobility at all. Even though recent studies have taken issue with this Euro-centric perspective on state formation in the Ottoman Empire, they have not challenged the accepted view that there were no hereditary nobilities in the Ottoman state.

Drawing on the revisionist literature that has demonstrated the protean character of the concept of nobility, this book examined the Palu begs as a noble group with hereditary privileges within the Ottoman realm.

Deploying a historical, as opposed to an ideal-type, approach to the notion of nobility, this book has shown what nobility entailed and how it was transformed and then disappeared in the Ottoman context. This contributes to recent literature that has revealed the flexible character of Ottoman ruling strategies and challenged previously accepted notions of absolute state power. Diachronic and synchronic research on other elite groups' noble identity, positions and privileges can provide a more complete picture of what nobility entailed in the Ottoman politico-administrative system.

The prevalent views on Kurdish elites in the Ottoman Empire are shaped by ahistorical state-versus-society or centre-versus-periphery dichotomies and nationalist teleologies. These accounts simplify the relationship between the Kurdish elites and the Ottoman state into a reductionist narrative of the centralising state versus the unruly Kurdish emirs that ends with the inevitable demise of the Kurdish emirates. This book challenged these accounts in two ways. First, it demonstrated that while the Palu begs saw themselves as having a noble pedigree that pre-dated the Ottomans, their position as a noble group with de jure privileges came from their position within the Ottoman administrative system. Rather than being antagonistic, the relationship between the Kurdish elites and the Ottoman state was actually symbiotic and contextual. Their privileges were shaped by the context of their interactions and negotiations with the Ottoman state – not in constant reaction to it. Second, the book has exposed the multi-faceted nature of the socio-economic and political conflicts that made and unmade the Kurdish begs' positions within the Ottoman realm. Local actors – Muslim notables, provincial Ottoman administrators, agricultural producers and financiers – engaged in the processes through which the Kurdish begs' noble privileges were redefined and eventually abolished. By examining the complex local power structures and relations over a period of two centuries, this book has provided a granular account of the Kurdish nobility in the Ottoman Empire.

This book also contests the established narrative about the impact abolishing the emirates had on Kurdish society. The prevalent narrative – not supported by solid empirical research – is that the dwindling economic and political authority of the Kurdish begs in the mid-nineteenth century caused a power vacuum in Kurdistan that was marked by lawlessness and tribal strife. According to this perspective, this lawlessness empowered religious sheiks to become the new political leadership within Kurdish society. While the impact of these transformations on the Kurdish tribes and political leadership in Kurdistan still awaits serious historical scrutiny, the existing argument overlooks the diversity of political actors, their strategies, and the plurality of institutional milieux within which these

Conclusion

actors competed and negotiated. As the analysis of the Weşin incident demonstrates, Tanzimat councils became arenas in which villagers settled accounts with the begs and challenged their fiscal, military and symbolic authority. To this picture we can add the contested process of *müdür* appointments, which demonstrate a nascent deliberative process among the local actors over who would administer the district and how. Looking at these local disputes and negotiations over land, taxes and bureaucratic positions, this book shows that the lawlessness argument fails to capture the complexity of political life in Kurdistan in the aftermath of the land reform. Further historical research can build on this to shed more light on the contours of day-to-day politics in Kurdistan within the context of modern state-making.

Land ownership stands at the heart of the Palu begs' noble identity. As this book has shown, from the time Cemşîd Beg captured the Palu castle from the Safavid forces in the sixteenth century, the Palu begs exercised political and economic control over the Palu land. Politically, the ruler (*hâkim*) descended from the Palu begs. Economically, the begs were defined as the owners of the land (*mülkiyet üzere*) and controlled its revenues. As this book has shown, neither the political nor the economic aspects of their control were static. While the Palu begs held onto their noble identity for several centuries, their control over land underwent drastic changes that began in the late eighteenth century and accelerated in the Tanzimat era. At the core of this transformation were the intertwined processes of state-making and the privatisation of land ownership in Kurdistan. This book has examined two stages of the Palu begs' changing land ownership. The first took place in the late eighteenth century and was caused mainly by economics: as their cash needs increased, the Palu begs farmed out or leased out their lands. While the land was becoming more commodified, the begs still retained their hereditary ownership. The second episode of land fragmentation – from the 1850s on – resulted from political processes. After more than three centuries, the Ottoman state unleashed a frontal attack on the Kurdish begs and their autonomous realms. Palu's fertile agricultural land made it desirable, and the government saw its revenue potential. The Palu begs' privileges, which included inalienable control over land and its surplus, came under attack so that the state could further its goals of confiscating agricultural surplus through a centralised system and a bureaucratising provincial administration. The logical move was to confiscate the begs' lands.

Studies of land tenure in the Ottoman Empire have focused largely on the Land Code of 1858 as the significant turning point in the codification of private land ownership. However, in Palu, land privatisation preceded the

Land Code by almost a decade. The move towards private land ownership began in 1850 when the begs' lands were confiscated and opened up for sale. The new owners involved claimed individual ownership over land, which caused, as this book shows, tensions when these claims were met with the begs' insistence that they still controlled the land. However, even that is less simple than it seems, as the begs themselves, even while justifying their claims on the basis of their status as a noble family (i.e. as a group), made land claims based on individual ownership. All this was part of the process of establishing the grammar of private property, which by the mid-nineteenth century was overtaking ideas of familial and communal property ownership at all levels of the local society.

By situating this process of changing land tenure at the centre of its inquiry, this book provides a unique political economy perspective that analyses of the Ottoman state's policies towards Kurdistan have lacked. Economic calculations were made with an eye to the potential symbolic ramifications of annulling the imperial decrees that had granted the begs their hereditary estates. The state established itself as a party in surplus extraction, abolishing the long-standing tax-exempt status of the begs' lands. Further research on other parts of Kurdistan can provide a more holistic perspective on the political economy of Ottoman state-making in Kurdistan.

Finally, the book examined the 1895 Massacres within the context of these changes taking place in the locality in terms of land ownership, power configurations, and ongoing tensions between the begs and local Armenians, primarily over land. Despite changes in the fiscal, administrative and political realms, the begs continued to claim ownership over Palu land. Their disputes with the Armenian villages lasted several decades, as the begs refused to recognise the ownership rights of those who purchased their confiscated lands. They continued to impose sharecropping on the cultivators. The begs were adamant about reversing the process and subduing villagers all the way up to the last decade of the nineteenth century. Meanwhile, the internationalisation of the Armenian Question and the politicisation of the Palu Armenians put the inhabitants of these villages under the spotlight. This book has shown that the violence and massacres that plagued Palu in 1895 took place against the backdrop of these ongoing conflicts. The begs saw the empire-wide anti-Armenian climate as an opportune moment to settle their scores with the Armenian villages. In the aftermath of the massacres, most of the Armenian population were once again forced to work as sharecroppers, tilling the begs' lands. Future research can shed more light on the period between the 1895 Massacres and the Armenian Genocide in 1915 regarding the relations between the begs and the Armenians.

Notes

1. BOA.DH.I.EK 120/2 26 Kanun-i Sâni 1336 [26 January 1920].
2. Lukowski, *The European Nobility in the Eighteenth Century*, 1.
3. Haldén, 'The Ubiquitous and Opaque Elites of the Ottoman Empire c.1300–c.1830'.
4. For a critique of this view, see Islamoglu and Perdue, 'Introduction'.

Postscript

On a hot summer day in 2013, one of the descendants of the Palu begs took me to a mansion built by one of his ancestors, presumably in the 1950s. The house stood in the middle of hundreds of acres of fertile agricultural land and orchards. In the front yard was an unkempt fountain with a weak flow of water. A line of pine trees encircled the backyard. The meticulously constructed irrigation canals below the pine trees were clogged with debris. As I looked at the beautiful details of the house, the descendant told me about the uncle who had built it – a learned man with a passion for bringing modern agricultural techniques and machinery to his estate. All the details inside and outside of the mansion showed that the ancestors of this man had once been wealthy. No more. The unkempt courtyard and desolate fields as far as the eye could see did not reflect the glorious past of this noble family.

Palu, once the stronghold of the begs, a place of ethnic and religious diversity, witnessed a series of dramatic events from 1896 (the year at which this book ends) on, events that changed it into an ethno-religiously homogenised, culturally conservative and economically deprived place. These transformations reflected the tumultuous processes leading up to the dissolution of the Ottoman Empire. After the 1895 Massacres, the Armenian population of Palu in the countryside was reduced to servile agricultural labourer status. However, the 1908 Revolution opened up a new chapter in the ongoing story of Armenian dispossession. Throughout the empire, Armenians demanded that the new regime address the issue of the lands they had lost during the Hamidian era.[1] Like Armenians elsewhere, the Palu Armenians appealed to local and central administrators for the return of their land. Their inquiries were mostly ensnared in local bureaucracy and bore little or no fruit. This brief moment of hope disappeared with the tense political climate unleashed with the Balkan Wars and the First

Postscript

World War, and then the 1915 genocide of the Armenian population removed Armenians from Palu altogether. The begs remained, but without the glory that once accompanied their title.

Note

1. Mehmet Polatel, 'Land Disputes and Reform Debates in the Eastern Provinces', *World War I and the End of the Ottomans: From the Balkan Wars to the Armenian Genocide*, eds Hans-Lukas Kieser, Kerem Öktem and Maurus Reinkowski (London: I. B. Tauris, 2015), 169–87; Nilay Özok-Gündoğan, 'A "Peripheral" Approach to the 1908 Revolution in the Ottoman Empire: Land Disputes in Peasant Petitions in Post-Revolutionary Diyarbekir', in *Social Relations in Ottoman Diyarbekir, 1870–1915*, eds Joost Jongerden and Jelle Verheij (Leiden; Boston: Brill, 2012): 179–215.

Glossary

Abdullah Beg: One of the Palu begs. He inherited his lands from his father Hacı Ali Beg in 1841 and became the *hâkim* of the emirate in 1843. In 1848, he had a violent encounter with the Weşin village and was exiled to Tekfurdağı. He died in exile.

Beg/Bey: An honorific title used to address the male descendants of the Kurdish noble families.

Cemşîd Beg: The first ruler of the Palu emirate in the Ottoman realm. He fought alongside the Ottoman forces against the Safavids during the Çaldıran Battle (1514) and saved the Palu fortress from the Safavid forces. He participated in Sultan Süleyman I's Iraqi campaign in 1533–5. He was granted a *temlîknâme* by the sultan, which put Palu under his hereditary rule.

Defterdar: Treasurer appointed by the imperial state to each province to oversee fiscal affairs during the Tanzimat era.

Hâkim: The ruler of a *hükümet*.

Hükümet: Special administrative designation granted to the Kurdish emirates in the Ottoman Empire. *Hükümet* status recognised the hereditary rule of the Kurdish nobles over the emirate.

İdris-i Bidlîsî (1457–1520): A bureaucrat and scholar. He came from a respectable Sufi family from Bidlis. He served first in the Akkoyunlu and then in the Ottoman court. He accompanied Selim I during his campaign against the Safavids and worked towards unifying the Sunni Kurds on behalf of the Ottoman sultan. He secured the majority of the Kurdish nobles' support.

Glossary

İltizam: Tax farming. In this tax-collection system, a private person undertakes the collection of taxes from a revenue source in return for a certain annual lump sum paid to the state determined with an auction.

Kaymakam: The administrator of a district (*kaza*) or a sanjak.

Ma'âdin-i Hümâyun Emâneti: A special fiscal and administrative body established in 1775 to oversee the administration of the Keban and Ergani mines.

Mâlikane: A new form of tax farming that emerged in 1695. It was different from regular tax farming in two ways. First, the annual tax amount of a revenue source was determined by the treasury, not with an auction. Second, these were lifelong tax farms rather than farms with a limited (one-to-three-year) term.

Meclis-i Vâlâ-i Ahkâm-i Adliyye (The Supreme Council of Judicial Ordinances): A council established in 1838 to make the legal changes within the scope of the Tanzimat and oversee the implementation of the reforms.

Mefrûzü'l-kalem and ***Maktû'ü'l-kadem***: Designations that granted fiscal, administrative and military autonomy to Kurdish *hükümet*s. The former meant that the Ottoman state could not implement land and population surveys or grant fiefs to cavalrymen. The latter meant that the state could not have military and civilian Ottoman administrators (i.e. tax collectors, governors and the Janissary troops) installed in the *hükümet*s.

Mîr (emîr): The ruler of a Kurdish emirate.

Müdür: The administrator of a district. This position was restructured during the Tanzimat period to increase the imperial state's authority over local administration.

Müşir: Upper-level military commander charged with performing both military and administrative functions. With the establishment of the *müşirlik* of Diyarbekir (1838), the *müşir* became the highest provincial administrator of the province.

Necib Pasha: Abdullah Beg's brother. He inherited half of his brother's lands after he died in 1840. Over the next four decades, he increased his power. Appointed as the *kaymakam* of Palu in 1880. He was granted the *pasha* title by the state after donating his mansion for the construction of an Ottoman army barracks in Palu.

***Noksan-ı arz*:** Originally referred to a fee paid to the landowner to cover the difference between land's pre-harvest and post-harvest value. In the second half of the nineteenth century, it came to refer to extra dues that the begs and the aghas imposed on the peasantry in and around Palu.

Sublime Porte (Bâb-ı Âli): Referred to the central government of the Ottoman Empire. The term came from the splendid gate of the complex where the major departments of the budding Ottoman bureaucracy were based during the Tanzimat era.

***Tahrir*:** Periodic surveys of land and population carried out in the early centuries of the empire in order to determine the tax-bringing revenue sources of the newly-conquered areas.

Tanzimat: A period of intense fiscal, military and administrative reforms in the Ottoman Empire that began in 1839 with the issuance of the Gülhane Imperial Rescript (*Gülhane Hattı Hümayunu*).

***Temlîknâme/Temlîk/Mülknâme*:** A title deed given by the ruler, granting ownership of specific lands in return for a service.

***Timar*:** The main military, fiscal and administrative institution of the Ottoman Empire, based on granting the revenues of state-owned lands to cavalrymen in return for military and administrative service.

***Vali*:** The administrator of a province (*eyalet*; later *vilayet*).

***Yurtluk-ocaklık*:** Hereditary estates granted to the Kurdish begs in return for their military service. Contrary to the *hükümet*s, the Ottoman state conducted *tahrir*s in the *yurtluk-ocaklık* areas.

Yusuf Ziya Pasha: Served two terms (1786–99 and 1807–11) as the superintendent of the Mine Administration (Ma'âdin-i Hümâyun Emâneti). He also served as the governor of several provinces in Kurdistan, including Erzurum, Diyarbekir and Malatya. He was steadily raised in the Ottoman bureaucracy and became the grand vizier. He commanded the Ottoman army against the French forces in Egypt in 1798.

Select Bibliography

Archival Sources

BAŞBAKANLIK OSMANLI ARŞIVI (BAŞKANLIK OSMANLI ARŞIVI)

Ali Emiri Abdülhamid I (AE.SABH I)

Cevdet
   Adliye (C.ADL)
   Askeriye (C.AS)
   Dahiliye (C.DH)
   Darbhane (C.DRB)
   İktisat (C.İKT)
   Maliye (C.ML)

Bâb-ı Âli Evrak Odası (BEO)

Dahiliye
   Islahat (DH.TMIK.S)
   İdare-i Umumiye Ekleri (DH.I.UM.EK)
   Mektubi Kalemi (DH.MKT)
   Muamelat (DH.TMIK.M)
   Muhaberat-ı Umumiye İdaresi (DH.MUI)
   Şifre Kalemi (DH.ŞFR)

Hariciye Siyasi (HR.SYS)

Hatt-ı Hümayûnlar (HAT)

İbnülemin
  Dahiliye (IE.DH)
  Tevcihat (IE.TCT)

İrade
  Dahiliye (İ.DH)
  Hususi (İ.HUS)
  Meclis-i Vâlâ (İ.MVL)
  Mesail-i Mühimme (İ.MSM)
  Taltifat (I.TAL)

Maliye Nezareti
  Emlak-ı Emiriyye Müdürüyeti (ML.EEM)
  Vâridat Muhasebesi Defterleri (ML.VRD.d)

Meclis-i Vâlâ (MVL)

Nüfus Defterleri (NFS.d)

Sadaret
  Amedi Kalemi Evrakı (A.AMD)
  Deavi Evrakı (A.MKT.DV)
  Divan Kalemi Evrakı (A.DVN)
  Meclis-i Vâlâ Evrakı (A.MKT.MVL)
  Mektubi Kalemi Evrakı (A.MKT)
  Mühimme Evrakı (A.DVN.MHM)
  Mühimme Kalemi Evrakı (A.MKT.MHM)
  Nezaret ve Devair Evrakı (A.MKT.NZD)
  Umum Vilayat Evrakı (A.MKT.UM)

Şura-yı Devlet (ŞD)

Topkapı Sarayı Müzesi Evrakı (TS.MA.e)

Yıldız
  Askeri Maruzat (Y.PRK.ASK)
  Mütenevvi Maruzat (Y.MTV)
  Ticaret ve Nafia Nezareti Maruzatı (Y.PRK.TNF)
  Umumi (Y.PRK.UM)
  Yaveran ve Maiyyet-i Seniyye Erkan-ı Harbiyye Dairesi (Y.PRK.MYD)

NATIONAL ARCHIVES (FORMERLY BRITISH NATIONAL ARCHIVES) (BNA), LONDON

Records of the Foreign Office (FO)

Select Bibliography

Periodicals

Missonary Herald
The Contemporary Review

Collections of Documents and Published Primary Sources

American Board of Commissioners for Foreign Missions (1866). *Historical Sketch of the Missions of the American Board of Commissioners for Foreign Missions in European Turkey, Asia Minor and Armenia.* New York.

American Board of Commissioners for Foreign Missions, Woman's Board of Missions (1874). *Life and Light for Heathen Women.* Boston, MA: Press of Geo. R. Rand & Avery, no. 3, Cornhill.

American National Red Cross (1896). *Report: America's Relief Expedition to Asia Minor under the Red Cross.* [S.l.].

Armenian National Assembly (1876). 'Second Report on the Oppression of the Armenians in Armenia and Other Provinces of Asiatic Turkey Presented to the Armenian National Assembly by the Commission Appointed for That Purpose'. London: Official Publication of the Armenian National Patriarchate in Constantinople, 17 September.

Badger, George Percy (1852). *The Nestorians and Their Rituals with the Narrative of a Mission to Mesopotamia and Coordistan in 1842–1844, and of a Late Visit to Those Countries in 1850: Also, Researches into the Present Condition of the Syrian Jacobites, Papal Syrians, and Chaldeans, and an Inquiry into the Religious Tenets of the Yezeedees.* London: Gregg.

Banse, Ewald (1915). *Die Türkei; Ein Moderne Geographie.* 3. aufl. Braunschweig [etc.].

Behesnilian, Krikor (1903). *Armenian Bondage and Carnage; Being the Story of Christian Martyrdom in Modern Times.* London: Gowans Bros.

Blis, Edwin Munsell (1896). *Turkey and the Armenian Atrocities; a Reign of Terror, from Tartar Huts to Constantinople Palaces.* Philadelphia, PA: Edgewood.

Boyes W. J., F. J. N. Mackenzie, R. H. Fawcett, Sir Charles Metcalfe MacGregor and M. H. Saward (1877). *Routes in Asia: Routes in Asia Minor, Armenia, Kurdistan, Georgia, Mesopotamia, and Part of Western Persia.* Office of the Superintendent of Government Printing.

Boyajian, Nazareth A. (c. 1923). *Heart of Euphrates.*

Brownrigg, H. S., M. H. Saward, C. MacGregor, C. Metcalfe, R. H. Fawcett, F. J. N. Mackenzie and W. J. Boyes (1877). *Routes in Asia.* Calcutta: Office of the Superintendent of Government Printing.

Bury, John Bagnell, Stanley Arthur Cook and Frank Ezra Adcock (1925). *The Cambridge Ancient History: The Assyrian Empire.* Vol. 3. Cambridge: Cambridge University Press.

Celalzade Mustafa (1990). *Selimname*, ed. Ahmet Uğur and Mustafa Çuhadar. Ankara: Kültür Bakanlığı Yayınları.

Chesney, Francis Rawdon (1850). *The expedition for the survey of the rivers Euphrates and Tigris: carried on by order of the British Government in the years 1835, 1836, and 1837; preceded by geographical and historical notices of the regions situated between the rivers Nile and Indus.* London: Longman, Brown, Green, & Longmans.

Dwight, H. G. O. (2016). *Christianity Revived in the East, Or, a Narrative of the Work of God among the Armenians of Turkey.* New York: Baker & Scribner.

Filian, George H. (1896). *Armenia and Her People; or, The Story of Armenia by an Armenian.* Hartford, CT: American Pub. Co.

Gabrielian, M[ugurdich] C[hojhauji (1892). *Gabrielyan, M. C. The Armenians or, The people of Ararat: a brief historical sketch of the past and the present condition of Armenia, the Armenians, their religion, and missions among them.* Philadelphia: Allen, Lane & Scott.

Gaidzakian, Ohan (1898). *Illustrated Armenia and the Armenians.* Boston: B. H. Aznive.

Great Britain Parliament (1905). House of Commons, *Parliamentary Papers.* H.M. Stationery Office.

Great Britain. Foreign Office (1884). 'Reports from Her Majesty's Consuls on the Manufactures, Commerce, &c. of Their Consular Districts'. London: Harrison & Sons.

Greene, Frederick Davis (c. 1896) Armenian Massacres: Or the Sword of Mohammed. Philadelphia; Chicago: National Publishing Co.

Gregory, Daniel S. (1900). *The Crime of Christendom, Or, the Eastern Question from its Origin to the Present Time.* New York: Abbey Press.

Hammer-Purgstall, Josef von (1840). *Geschichte des Osmanischen Reiches: grossentheils aus bisher unbenützten Handschriften und Archiven.* Pesth: C.A. Hartleben's Verl.

Harland, Marion (1896). *Home of the Bible: What I Saw and Heard in Palestine.* New York: Christian Herald.

Harris, J. Rendel (1897). *Letters from the Scenes of the Recent Massacres in Armenia.* New York [etc.].

Henson P. (1896). *The Armenian Amphitheater and Its Bloody Arena.* Chicago: Fleming H. Revell Company.

Hewitt, John Haskell (c. 1914). *Williams College and Foreign Missions: Biographical Sketches of Williams College Men Who Have Rendered Special Service to the Cause of Foreign Missions.* Boston: Pilgrim Press.

Hilprecht, Hermann Vollrat (1896). *Recent Research in Bible Lands: Its Progress and Results.* J. D. Wattles & Co.

Hogarth, D. G. (1896). *A Wandering Scholar in the Levant.* London: John Murray.

Hogarth, D. G. (1896). *The Nearer East.* London: H. Frowde.

İzgöer, Ahmet Zeki (2016). *Divan-ı Hümâyûn sicilleri Diyarbekir ahkâm defterleri. Cilt. 1 numaralı defter (H. 1155–1167/M. 1742–1754).* Diyarbakır: Dicle Üniversitesi İlahiyat Fakültesi Yayınları.

Select Bibliography

İzgöer, Ahmet Zeki (2016). *Divan-ı Hümâyûn sicilleri Diyarbekir ahkâm defterleri. 1 numaralı defter (H. 1155–1167/M. 1742–1754)*. Diyarbakır: Dicle Üniversitesi İlahiyat Fakültesi Yayınları.

İzgöer, Ahmet Zeki (2018) *Divan-ı Hümâyûn Sicilleri Diyarbekir Ahkâm Defterleri -2 numaralı defter* (H. 1167–1176 / M. 1754–1763). Diyarbakır: Dicle Üniversitesi İlahiyat Fakültesi.

İzgöer, Ahmet Zeki (2013). *Divan-ı Hümâyûn Sicilleri Diyarbekir Ahkâm Defterleri -3- numaralı defter* (H.1176–1198/ M. 1763–1784). Diyarbakır: Dicle Üniversitesi İlahiyat Fakültesi.

İzgöer, Ahmet Zeki (2013). *Diyarbekir Şer'iyye Sicilleri: Âmid Mahkemesi. Cilt 2. 3709 Numaralı Sicil (H. 1145/M. 1732), 3712 Numaralı Sicil (H. 1145–1212/ 1732–1798)*. Diyarbakır: Dicle Üniversitesi İlahiyat Fakültesi Yayınları.

İzgöer, Ahmet Zeki (2014). *Diyarbekir Şer'iyye Sicilleri: Âmid Mahkemesi. Cilt 3 3754 Numaralı Sicil (H. 1151–1154/1738–1741)*. Diyarbakır: Dicle Üniversitesi İlahiyat Fakültesi Yayınları.

İzgöer, Ahmet Zeki (2015). *Diyarbekir Şer'iyye Sicilleri: Âmid Mahkemesi. Cilt 4 756 Numaralı Sicil (H. 1151–1152/1739), 3744 Numaralı Sicil (H. 1169–1170/1756), 3773 Numaralı Sicil (H. 1170–1296/1757–1879), 3796 Numaralı Sicil (H. 1172–1173/1758–1760)*. Diyarbakır: Dicle Üniversitesi İlahiyat Fakültesi Yayınları.

İzgöer, Ahmet Zeki (2015). *Diyarbekir Şer'iyye Sicilleri: Âmid Mahkemesi. Cilt 5 3743 Numaralı Sicil (H. 1181–1182/M. 1767–1768), 3757 Numaralı Sicil (H. 1202–1203/M. 1788), 3675 Numaralı Sicil (H. 1203/M. 1788–1789), 3753 Numaralı Sicil (H. 1204–1205/M. 1790)*. Diyarbakır: Dicle Üniversitesi İlahiyat Fakültesi Yayınları.

İzgöer, Ahmet Zeki (2015). *Diyarbekir Şer'iyye Sicilleri: Âmid Mahkemesi. Cilt 6 3725 Numaralı Sicil (H. 1205–1206 / M. 1790–1791)*. Diyarbakır: Dicle Üniversitesi İlahiyat Fakültesi Yayınları.

İzgöer, Ahmet Zeki (2015). *Diyarbekir Şer'iyye Sicilleri: Âmid Mahkemesi. Cilt 7 3823 Numaralı Sicil (H. 1197–1206 / M. 1782–1792), 3749 Numaralı Sicil (H. 1208–1209/M. 1793–1794), 3797 Numaralı Sicil (H. 1214–1215/M. 1800), 3798 Numaralı Sicil (H. 1215–1216/M. 1800–1802), 3698 Numaralı Sicil (H. 1210–1217/M 1795–1802)*. Diyarbakır: Dicle Üniversitesi İlahiyat Fakültesi Yayınları.

İzgöer, Ahmet Zeki (2016). *Diyarbekir Şer'iyye Sicilleri: Âmid Mahkemesi. Cilt 8. 3750 numaralı sicil (H. 1218/M. 1803), 3716 numaralı sicil (H. 1219–1222 / M. 1805–1807), 3787 numaralı sicil (H. 1232–1233/ M. 1817–1818)*. Diyarbakır: Dicle Üniversitesi İlahiyat Fakültesi Yayınları.

İzgöer, Ahmet Zeki (2017). *Diyarbekir Şer'iyye Sicilleri: Âmid Mahkemesi. Cilt 9. 3746 numaralı sicil (H. 1136–1264/M. 1724–1848), 3745 numaralı sicil (H. 1237–1239/M. 1822–1824), 3685 numaralı sicil (H. 1239–1241/ M. 1823–1825)*. Diyarbakır: Dicle Üniversitesi İlahiyat Fakültesi Yayınları.

İzgöer, Ahmet Zeki (2018). *Diyarbekir Şer'iyye Sicilleri: Âmid Mahkemesi. Cilt 10. 3742 numaralı sicil (H.1236–1240 / M. 1821–1824), 3718 numaralı* sicil (H.1242–1243/M. 1827–1828), 3714 numaralı sicil (H.1154–1155/M. 1741–1742). Diyarbakır: Dicle Üniversitesi İlahiyat Fakültesi Yayınları.

İzgöer, Ahmet Zeki, Sıbğatullah Kaya and Ali Kaya (1999). *Salname-i Diyarbekir*. Diyarbakır: Diyarbakır Büyükşehir Belediyesi Yayınları.

Karajian, Hagop (1915). *Regional Geology and Mining of Armenia*. New York City: The Nerso Press.

Karajian, Hagop (1920). *Mineral Resources of Armenia and Anatolia*. New York: Armen Technical Book Co. 1st edn.

Koch, Karl Heinrich Emil (1846). *Wanderungen Im Oriente, Während Der Jahre 1843 Und 1844*. Weimar: Druck und Verlag des Landes-Industrie-Comptoirs.

Layard, Austen Henry (1849). *Nineveh and Its Remains: With an Account of a Visit to the Chaldean Christians of Kurdistan, and the Yezidis, or Devil-Worshippers; and an Inquiry into the Manners and Arts of the Ancient Assyrians*. New York, G. P. Putnam.

Lepsius, Johannes ([1897]). *Armenië En Europa. Een Schriftelijke Aanklacht*. Rotterdam: Daamen.

Les massacres d'Arménie: témoignages des victimes (1896) Édition du Mercure de France.

Lynch, H. F. B. (1901). *Armenia, Travels and Studies*. Vol. 2. London: Longmans, Green and Co.

[MacDonald, Alexander] (1893). *The Land of Ararat; Or, Up the Roof of the World by a Special Correspondent [I.E.]*. (Paperback) London: Eden, Remington & Co.

Machiavelli, Niccolò. *The Prince*. Trans. W. K. Marriott. EBook #1232. Project Gutenberg Ebook, 1998. https://www.gutenberg.org/files/1232/1232-h/1232-h.htm#chap04.

Meyrier, Gustave (2000). *Les massacres de Diarbékir: correspondance diplomatique du vice-consul de France, 1894–1896*. [Caen]: Inventaire.

Moltke, Helmuth (1893). *Essays, Speeches, and Memoirs of Field-Marshal Count Helmuth von Moltke*. New York: Harper & Bros.

Murray (Firm), John (1895). *Handbook for Travellers in Asia Minor, Transcaucasia, Persia, Etc*. London: J. Murray.

Peçevî, İbrahim and Bekir Sıtkı Baykal (1982). *Peçevi Tarihi*. Ankara: Başbakanlık Matbaası.

Percy, [Henry Algernon George Percy] (1901). *Highlands of Asiatic Turkey*. London: E. Arnold.

Pierce, James Wilson (1896). *Story of Turkey and Armenia*. Baltimore: R. H. Woodward Co.

Ravndal, G. Bie (1926). *Turkey: A Commercial and Industrial Handbook*. Washington: G.P.O.

Rogers, Robert William ([1915]). *A History of Babylonia and Assyria*. 6th edn. New York, Abingdon Press.

Şerefhan (1990). *Şerefname: Kürt Tarihi*. 3. Baskı. Istanbul: Hasat Yayınları.

Şeref Han Bitlisi (2018). *Şerefname* (trans. Abdullah Yegin). Istanbul: Nûbihar Yayınları.

Select Bibliography

Smith, Benjamin E. (Benjamin Eli) and William Dwight Whitney (1896–1910). *The Century Dictionary and Cyclopedia; a Work of Universal Reference in All Departments of Knowledge, with a New Atlas of the World.* Rev. edn. New York: The Century Co.

Smith, Warrington (1843). 'Geological Features of the Country Around the Mines of the Taurus in the Pashalic of Diarbekir Described from Observations Made in the Year 1843'. *Quarterly Journal of the Geographical Society of London* I, no. 1,845: 330–40.

Southgate, Horatio (1840). *Narrative of a Tour through Armenia, Kurdistan, Persia, and Mesopotamia: With Observations on the Condition of Mohammedanism and Christianity in Those Countries.* London: Tilt and Bogue.

Strong, Elnathan Ellsworth (1885). *Mission Stories of Many Lands: A Book for Young People. With Three Hundred and Forty Illustrations.* Boston: American Board of Commissioners for Foreign Missions.

Sykes, Mark (1915). *The Caliphs' Last Heritage*; London: Macmillan.

Tozer, Henry Fanshawe (1990). 1829–1916. *Turkish Armenia and Eastern Asia Minor.* Astoria, NY: J. C. & A. L. Fawcett.

Tupper, H. Allen (1896). *Armenia, Its Present Crisis and Past History.* Baltimore: Murphy & Co.

West, Maria A. ([188?]). *The Romance of Missions in the Land of Ararat.* Boston: J. J. Arakelyan.

Wheeler, C. H. (1868). *Letters from Eden; or, Reminiscences of Missionary Life in the East.* Boston: Boston: American Tract Society.

Wheeler, Charles Henry ([c. 1888]). *Odds and Ends; or, Gleanings from Missionary Life.* Boston: Congregational Sunday-school and Publishing Society.

Wheeler, S. A. (1899). *Missions in Eden; Glimpses of Life in the Valley of the Euphrates.* New York: Fleming H. Revell Co.

Wheeler, Wilmot Henry (1899). *Self-Support Churches and How to Plant Them. Illustrated by the Life and Teachings of Rev. C.H. Wheeler.* Grinnel, IA: Better Way Pub. Co.

Williams, Augustus Warner (1896). *Bleeding Armenia: Its History and Horrors under the Curse of Islam.* Chicago: Publishers Union.

Williams, Charles (1878). *The Armenian Campaign: A Diary of the Campaign of 1877, in Armenia and Koordistan.* London: C. K. Paul & Co.

Wilson, Charles William (1895 [1905]). *Handbook for Travellers in Asia Minor, Transcaucasia, Persia,* London: J. Murray.

Secondary Sources

Abbasi, Mustafa (2005). 'The "Aristocracy" of the Upper Galilee: Safad Notables and the Tanzimat Reforms', in *Ottoman Reform and Muslim Regeneration*, edited by Itzchak Weismann and Fruma Zachs. London: New York: New York: I. B. Tauris.

Abou-El-Haj, Rifa'at Ali (2005). *Formation of the Modern State: The Ottoman Empire, Sixteenth to Eighteenth Centuries*, 2nd edn. (Syracuse, NY: Syracuse University Press).

Abou-El-Haj, Rifa'at Ali (1988). *The Ottoman Nasihatname as a Discourse over 'Morality'* In *Mélanges Professeur Robert Mantran*, edited by A. Temini, 17–30. Zaghouan, Tunis: Centre d'Études et de Recherches Ottomanes, Morisques, de Documentation et d'Information.

Abu-Manneh, Butrus (2015). 'Two Concepts of State in the Tanzimat Period: The Hatt-ı Şerif of Gülhane and the Hatt-ı Hümayun'. *Turkish Historical Review* 6, no. 2 (26 November): 117–37.

Adams, Julia (2007). *The Familial State: Ruling Families and Merchant Capitalism in Early Modern Europe*. 1st edn. Ithaca, NY: Cornell University Press.

Adanır, Fikret (2006). 'Semi-Autonomous Provincial Forces in the Balkans and Anatolia'. In *The Cambridge History of Turkey: The Later Ottoman Empire*, edited by Suraiya Faroqhi, 157–85. Cambridge: Cambridge University Press.

Adjemian, Boris and Mikaël Nichanian (2018). 'Rethinking the "Hamidian Massacres": The Issue of the Precedent'. *Études Arméniennes Contemporaines*, no. 10 (30 March): 19–29.

Ágoston, Gábor (2014). 'Firearms and Military Adaptation: The Ottomans and the European Military Revolution, 1450–1800'. *Journal of World History* 25, no. 1 (1 August): 85–124.

Ágoston, Gábor (2010). 'Ulema'. In *Encyclopedia of the Ottoman Empire*, edited by Gabor Agoston and Bruce Masters, 577–8. New York: Facts on File, Inc.

Agoston, Gabor and Bruce Alan Masters eds (2010). *Encyclopedia of the Ottoman Empire*. Infobase Publishing.

Akiba, Jun (2009). 'The Local Councils as the Origin of the Parliamentary System in the Ottoman Empire'. In *Development of Parliamentarism in the Modern Islamic World*, edited by Tsugitaka Sato, 176–204. Tokyo: Toyo Bunko.

Aksan, Virginia H. (2014). *Ottoman Wars, 1700–1870: An Empire Besieged*. London: Routledge.

Aksan, Virginia H. and Daniel Goffman eds (2007). *The Early Modern Ottomans: Remapping the Empire*. Cambridge: Cambridge University Press.

Aksın, Ahmet (1999). *19. Yüzyılda Harput*. Elazığ: Ceren Ofset.

Aksoy, Gürdal (1996). *Tarihi Yazılmayan Halk: Kürtler*. Istanbul: Avesta.

Akyel, Salih and Savaş Sertel (2015). 'Osmanlı Nüfus Defterlerinin Tarih Yazımındaki Yeri: 1840 Tarihli Çarsancak Kazası Gayrimüslim Nüfus Defteri Örneği'. *Journal of History and Future* 1, no. 1 (December): 78–98.

Alagöz, Mehmet (2003). 'Old Habits Die Hard: A Reaction to the Application of Tanzimat and Bedirhan Bey's Revolt'. MA thesis, Boğaziçi Üniversitesi.

Alan, Ahmed (2017). *Hetawî Kurd (1913–1914)*. Istanbul: Avesta.

Alanoğlu, Murat (2017). 'Osmanli İdârî Sistemi İçerisinde Palu Hükûmeti'. Ph.D. dissertation, Istanbul University.

Alanoğlu, Murat (2019). 'Zaza Beylikleri, Şeyhler ve İslam'. *Tarih ve Gelecek Dergisi* 5, no. 3 (27 December): 792–804.

Select Bibliography

Alanoğlu, Murat (2019). 'Zazalar'. In *TDV İslam Ansiklopedisi*, Ek-2: 688–90. Ankara: Türkiye Diyanet Vakfı. Last accessed 10 May 2021 https://islamansiklopedisi.org.tr/zazalar.

Alsancakli, Sacha (2018). 'Historiography and Language in 17th-Century Ottoman Kurdistan: A Study of Two Turkish Translations of the Sharafnāma'. *Kurdish Studies* 6, no. 2: 171–96.

Alsancakli, Sacha (2017). 'Matrimonial Alliances and the Transmission of Dynastic Power in Kurdistan: The Case of the Diyādīnids of Bidlīs in the Fifteenth to Seventeenth Centuries'. *Eurasian Studies* 15, no. 2 (26 April): 222–49.

Alsancakli, Sacha (2017). 'What's Old Is New Again: A Study of Sources in the Šarafnāma of Šaraf Xān Bidlīsī (1005–7/1596–99)'. *Kurdish Studies* 5, no. 1 (11 May): 11–31.

Altıntaş, Toygun (2018). 'Crisis and (Dis)order: Armenian Revolutionaries and the Hamidian Regime in the Ottoman Empire, 1887–1896'. Ph.D dissertation, University of Chicago.

Anastasopoulos, Antonis (2003). 'Introduction'. In *Halcyon Days in Crete V: A Symposium Held in Rethymno: Provincial Elites in the Ottoman Empire*, edited by Antonis Anastasopoulos, xi–xxviii. Rethymnon: Crete University Press.

Anastasopoulos, Antonis ed. (2003). *Provincial Elites in the Ottoman Empire: Halcyon Days in Crete V: A Symposium Held in Rethymnon 10–12 January 2003*. Rethymnon: Crete University Press.

Anscombe, Frederick F. (1997). *The Ottoman Gulf: The Creation of Kuwait, Saudi Arabia, and Qatar*. New York: Columbia University Press.

Anscombe, Frederick F. (2014). *State, Faith, and Nation in Ottoman and Post-Ottoman Lands*. New York: Cambridge University Press.

Antaramian, Richard E. (2020). *Brokers of Faith, Brokers of Empire: Armenians and the Politics of Reform in the Ottoman Empire*. Stanford, CA: Stanford University Press.

Aricanli, Tosun and Mara Thomas (1994). 'Sidestepping Capitalism: On the Ottoman Road to Elsewhere''. *Journal of Historical Sociology* 7, no. 1: 25–48.

Arslantaş, Yasin (2017). 'Confiscation by the Ruler: A Study of the Ottoman Practice of Müsadere, 1700s–1839' Ph.D. dissertation, London School of Economics and Political Science.

Asch, Ronald G. (2003). *Nobilities in Transition 1550–1700: Courtiers and Rebels in Britain and Europe*. London: New York: Bloomsbury USA.

Aslanian, Sebouh D. (2014). 'The Marble of Armenian History: Or Armenian History as World History'. *Études Arméniennes Contemporaines*, no. 4 (15 December): 129–42.

Astourian, Stephan H. (2011). 'The Silence of the Land: Agrarian Relations, Ethnicity, and Power'. In *A Question of Genocide: Armenians and Turks at the End of the Ottoman Empire*, edited by Ronald Grigor Suny, Norman M. Naimark, and Fatma Müge Göçek. 55–81. Oxford: Oxford University Press.

Ates, Sabri (2014). 'In the Name of the Caliph and the Nation: The Sheikh Ubeidullah Rebellion of 1880–81'. *Iranian Studies* 47, no. 5: 735–98.

Ates, Sabri (2015). *Ottoman–Iranian Borderlands: Making a Boundary, 1843–1914*. Cambridge: Cambridge University Press.

Atmaca, Metin (2013). 'Politics of Alliance and Rivalry on the Ottoman–Iranian Frontier: The Babans (1500–1851)'. Ph.D. dissertation, Albert Ludwigs University of Freiburg.

Atmaca, Metin (2017). 'Three Stages of Political Transformation in the 19th Century Ottoman Kurdistan'. *Anatoli. De l'Adriatique à La Caspienne. Territoires, Politique, Sociétés*, no. 8 (1 October): 43–57.

Ay, Tuncay (2015). 'Tanzimat'ın Hakkâri'de Uygulanması'. MA thesis. Bitlis Eren University.

Aydın, Mahir (1990). 'Sultan II. Mahmud Döneminde Yapılan Nüfus Tahrirleri'. In *Sultan II. Mahmud ve Reformları Semineri*. Istanbul: Edebiyat Fakültesi Basımevi.

Aykan, Yavuz (2016). *Rendre la justice à Amid: Procédures, acteurs et doctrines dans le contexte ottoman du XVIIIème siècle*. Leiden: Brill.

Aykan, Yavuz and Boğaç Ergene (2019). 'Shari'a Courts in the Ottoman Empire before the Tanzimat'. *The Medieval History Journal* 22, no. 2 (1 November): 203–28.

Aymes, Marc (2013). *A Provincial History of the Ottoman Empire: Cyprus and the Eastern Mediterranean in the Nineteenth Century*. London: Routledge.

Aymes, Marc (2007). 'The Voice-over of Administration: Reading Ottoman Archives at the Risk of Ill-Literacy'. *European Journal of Turkish Studies. Social Sciences on Contemporary Turkey*, no. 6 (12 December).

Aytekin, E. Attila (2009). 'Agrarian Relations, Property and Law: An Analysis of the Land Code of 1858 in the Ottoman Empire'. *Middle Eastern Studies* 45, no. 6 (1 November): 935–51.

Aytekin, E. Attila (2009). 'Historiography of Land Tenure and Agriculture in the Nineteenth Century Ottoman Empire'. *Asian Research Trends New Series* 4: 1–24.

Aytekin, E. Attila (2013). 'Tax Revolts during the Tanzimat Period (1839–1876) and before the Young Turk Revolution (1904–1908): Popular Protest and State Formation in the Late Ottoman Empire'. *Journal of Policy History* 25, no. 3 (July): 308–33.

Aytekin, E. Attila (2016). 'The Production of Space during the Period of Autonomy: Notes on Belgrade Urban Space, 1817–67'. *Journal of Balkan and Near Eastern Studies* 18, no. 6 (1 November): 588–607.

Aytekin, E. Attila (2012). 'Peasant Protest in the Late Ottoman Empire: Moral Economy, Revolt, and the Tanzimat Reforms'. *International Review of Social History* 57, no. 2: 191–227.

Aytekin, E. Attila (2021). 'Cultivators, Creditors and the State: Rural Indebtedness in the Nineteenth Century Ottoman Empire: *The Journal of Peasant Studies* 35, no 2.

Bacqué-Grammont, Jean-Louis and Chahryar Adle (1986). *Quatre lettres de Seref Beg de Bitlis (1516–1520): Études Turco-safavides, XI*. W.

Select Bibliography

Bahadıroğlu, Yavuz (2005). *Mısır'a Doğru*. Istanbul: Nesil Yayinlari.

Bajalan, Djene and Sara Zandi Karimi (2014). 'The Kurds and Their History: New Perspectives'. *Iranian Studies* 47, no. 5 (3 September): 679–81.

Bajalan, Djene Rhys (2012). 'Şeref Xan's Sharafnama: Kurdish Ethno-Politics in the Early Modern World, Its Meaning and Its Legacy'. *Iranian Studies* 45, no. 6: 795–818.

Bajalan, Djene Rhys (2013). 'Between Conformism and Separatism: A Kurdish Students' Association in Istanbul, 1912 to 1914'. *Middle Eastern Studies* 49, no. 5 (1 September): 805–23.

Bajalan, Djene Rhys (2013). 'Early Kurdish "Nationalists" and the Emergence of Modern Kurdish Identity Politics: 1851–1908'. In *Turkey's Kurdish Question*, edited by Fevzi Bilgin and Ali Sarihan, 3–28. New York: Rowman & Littlefield.

Bajalan, Djene Rhys (2016). 'Princes, Pashas and Patriots: The Kurdish Intelligentsia, the Ottoman Empire and the National Question (1908–1914)'. *British Journal of Middle Eastern Studies* 43, no. 2 (2 April): 140–57.

Bajalan, Djene Rhys (2012). 'Şeref Xan's Sharafnama: Kurdish Ethno-Politics in the Early Modern World, Its Meaning and Its Legacy'. *Iranian Studies* 45, no. 6 (1 November): 795–818.

Bajalan, Djene Rhys and Sara Zandi Karimi eds (2015). *Studies in Kurdish History: Empire, Ethnicity and Identity*. London; New York: Routledge.

Balla, Eliana and Noel D. Johnson (2009). 'Fiscal Crisis and Institutional Change in the Ottoman Empire and France'. *The Journal of Economic History* 69, no. 3: 809–45.

Bang, Peter Fibiger and C. A. Bayly eds (2011). *Tributary Empires in Global History*. 2011 edn. New York: Palgrave Macmillan.

Barkan, Ömer Lütfi (2015). 'H. 933–934 (M. 1527–1528) Mali Yılına Ait Bir Bütçe Örneği'. *İstanbul Üniversitesi İktisat Fakültesi Mecmuası* 15, nos 1–4 (13 August).

Barkan, Ömer Lütfi (1943). 'Kanunnâme-i Boz Ulus'. In *XV ve XVI Incı Asırlarda Osmanlı İmparatorluğunda Ziraı Ekonominin Esasları. Birinci Cilt: Kanunlar*, 1: 140–44. Istanbul: Bürhaneddin Matbaası.

Barkan, Ömer Lütfi (1941). 'Mülk Topraklar ve Sultanların Temlik Hakkı'. In *İstanbul Hukuk Fakültesi Mecmuası*, VII: 157–76.

Barkan, Ömer Lütfi. (1980) 'Timar'. In *Türkiye'de Toprak Meselesi: Toplu Eserler*, 805–72. Istanbul: Gözlem Yayınları.

Barkan, Ömer Lütfi (1980). 'Türk Toprak Hukuku Tarihinde Tanzimat ve 1274 (1858) Tarihli Arazi Kanunnamesi'. In *Türkiye'de Toprak Meselesi*, 291–375. İstanbul: Gözlem Yayınları.

Barkan, Ömer Lütfi (1939). 'Türk-İslam Toprak Hukuku Tatbikatının Osmanlı İmparatorluğu'nda Aldığı Şekiller: Malikane-Divanı Sistemi'. In *Türk Hukuk ve İktisat Tarihi Mecmuası*, 2: 119–84.

Barkan, Ömer Lütfi (1943). *XV ve XVI Incı Asırlarda Osmanlı İmparatorluğunda Ziraı Ekonominin Esasları. Birinci Cilt: Kanunlar*. Vol. 1. Istanbul: Bürhaneddin Matbaası.

Barkan, Ömer Lütfi (1980). 'Feodal Düzen ve Osmanlı Tımarı'. In *Türkiye'de Toprak Meselesi: Toplu Eserler*, Vol. 1. Istanbul: Gözlem Yayınları.
Barkey, Karen (1994). *Bandits and Bureaucrats: The Ottoman Route to State Centralization*. Ithaca, NY: Cornell University Press.
Barkey, Karen (2008). *Empire of Difference: The Ottomans in Comparative Perspective*. Cambridge: New York: Cambridge University Press.
Barsoumian, Hagop (1982). 'The Dual Role of the Armenian Amira Class within the Ottoman Government and the Armenian Millet (1750–1850)'. In *Christians and Jews in the Ottoman Empire: The Functioning of a Plural Society*, edited by Benjamin Braude and Bernard Lewis, 171–84. Teaneck: Holmes & Meier.
Başar, Fahameddin (1997). *Osmanlı Eyalet Tevcihatı (1717–1730)*. Ankara: TTK Yayınları.
Basarir, Özlem (2013). 'Diyarbekir Voyvodası Mustafa Ağa'nın Terekesi Üzerine Bazı Düşünceler. *Bilig* 65: 23.
Basarir, Özlem (2011). 'Diyarbekir Voyvodalığı Aklâmı Malikânecileri Örneğinde XVIII. Yüzyılda Yatırımcıların Kimlikleri Üzerine Bir Değerlendirme'. *Hacettepe Üniversitesi Türkiyat Araştırmaları Dergisi*, Güz, no. 15: 39–61.
Basarir, Özlem (2009). 'XVIII. Yüzyılda Diyarbekir Voyvodalığı'nın Mekânsal Örgütlenmesi'. *The Journal of International Social Research* 4, no. 18: 196–229.
Bayerle, Gustav (1997). *Pashas, Begs, and Effendis: A Historical Dictionary of Titles and Terms in the Ottoman Empire*. Istanbul: Isis Press.
Bayraktar, Uğur (2020). 'Reconsidering Local versus Central: Empire, Notables, and Employment in Ottoman Albania and Kurdistan, 1835–1878'. *International Journal of Middle East Studies* 52, no. 4 (November): 685–701.
Bayraktar, Uğur (2017). 'Erken 19. Yüzyılda Kürt-Osmanlı İlişkileri: Zirki Beyleri ve Hazro'da Yerel Siyaset'. In *Osmanlı Devleti ve Kürtler*, edited by İbrahim Özcoşar and Shahab Vali 135–54. Istanbul: Kitap Yayınevi.
Bayraktar, Uğur (2015). 'Periphery's Centre: Reform, Taxation, and Local Notables in Diyarbakir, 1845–1855'. Ph.D. dissertation, Boğaziçi University.
Becker, Seymour (1986). *Nobility and Privilege in Late Imperial Russia*. DeKalb, IL: Northern Illinois University Press.
Behrens, Betty (1963). 'Nobles, Privileges and Taxes in France at the End of the Ancien Régime'. *Economic History Review*: 15, no. 3: 451–75.
Khalidi, Tarif (1984). *Land Tenure and Social Transformation in the Middle East*. Beirut: American University of Beirut.
Berber, Mehmet Akif (2014). 'From Interest to Usury: The Transformation of Murabaha in the Late Ottoman Empire'. MA thesis, Istanbul Şehir University.
Berktay, Halil (1987). 'The Feudalism Debate: The Turkish End – Is "Tax-vs.-Rent" Necessarily the Product and Sign of a Modal Difference?' *The Journal of Peasant Studies* 14, no. 3 (1 April): 291–333.
Berktay, Halil (1991). 'The Search for the Peasant in Western and Turkish History/Historiography'. *The Journal of Peasant Studies* 18, no. 3–4 (1 April): 109–84.

Select Bibliography

Berktay, Halil and Suraiya Faroqhi eds (2016). *New Approaches to State and Peasant in Ottoman History*. New York: Routledge.

Beşirli, Mehmet (1999). '385 Numaralı Harput Şer'iye Sicili'nin Tanıtımı ve Osmanlı Şehir Tarihi Açısından Önemi'. *OTAM* 10: 3–25.

Bidlīsī, Sharaf Khān (1971). *Şerefname: Yazan Şeref Han, Arapçadan çeviren, Mehmet Emin Bozarslan*. Ant Yayinlari.

Bidlīsī, Sharaf Khān and Mehrdad R. Izady (2005). *The Sharafnamâ, or, The History of the Kurdish Nation, 1597*. Costa Mesa, CA: Mazda.

Bitton, Davis (1969). *The French Nobility in Crisis, 1560–1640*. Stanford, CA: Stanford University Press.

Bloch, Marc (1961). *Feudal Society*. Trans. L. A. Manyon. 1st edn. London: Routledge & Kegan Paul.

Blomley, Nicholas (2003). 'Law, Property, and the Geography of Violence: The Frontier, the Survey, and the Grid'. *Annals of the Association of American Geographers* 93, no. 1: 121–41.

Blumi, Isa (2011). *Reinstating the Ottomans: Alternative Balkan Modernities, 1800–1912*. New York: Palgrave Macmillan.

Blumi, Isa (2017). *Foundations of Modernity: Human Agency and the Imperial State*. London: Routledge.

Bohanan, Donna (2001). *Crown and Nobility in Early Modern France*. 2001 edn. New York: Palgrave.

Bois, Thomas, V. Minorsky and D. N. MacKenzie (2012). 'Kurds, Kurdistān'. In *Encyclopaedia of Islam*, 2nd edn. Leiden: Brill.

Boris, James (2014). 'Arab Ethnonyms ('Ajam, 'Arab, Badū and Turk): The Kurdish Case as a Paradigm for Thinking about Differences in the Middle Ages'. *Iranian Studies* 47, no. 5: 683–712.

Bossenga, Gail (ed.) (2012). 'A Divided Nobility: Status, Markets, and the Patrimonial State in the Old Regime'. In *The French Nobility in the Eighteenth Century: Reassessments and New Approaches*, 1st edn, 43–75. University Park, PA: Penn State University Press.

Bourdieu, Pierre, Loic J. D. Wacquant and Samar Farage (1994). 'Rethinking the State: Genesis and Structure of the Bureaucratic Field'. *Sociological Theory* 12, no. 1: 1–18.

Bozarslan, Hamit (2003). 'Some Remarks on the Kurdish Historiographical Discourse in Turkey (1919–1980)'. In *Essays on the Origins of Kurdish Nationalism*, 14–39. Costa Mesa, CA: Mazda.

Braddick, Michael (1996). 'The Early Modern English State and the Question of Differentiation from 1550 to 1700'. *Comparative Studies in Society and History* 38, no. 1: 92–111.

Bragg, John (2014). *Ottoman Notables and Participatory Politics: Tanzimat Reform in Tokat, 1839–1876*. New York: Routledge.

Brenner, Neil (2001). 'The Limits to Scale? Methodological Reflections on Scalar Structuration'. *Progress in Human Geography* 25, no. 4 (1 December): 591–614.

Brooke, John L., Julia C. Strauss and Greg Anderson (2018). *State Formations: Global Histories and Cultures of Statehood*. New York: Cambridge University Press.

Bruinessen, Martin van (1992). *Agha, Shaikh and State: The Social and Political Structures of Kurdistan*. Zed Books.

Bruinessen, Martin van (2016). 'The Kurds as Objects and Subjects of Historiography – Turkish and Kurdish Nationalists Struggling over Identity'. In *Identität Ethnizität und Nationalismus in Kurdistan – Festschrift zum 65. Geburtstag von Prof. Dr. Ferhad Ibrahim Seyder*, edited by Fabian Richter, 13–61. Munster: Lit Verlag.

Bruinessen, Martin van (2003). 'Ehmedi Xani's Mem u Zin and Its Role in the Emergence of Kurdish National Awareness'. In *Essays on the Origins of Kurdish Nationalism*, edited by Abbas Vali, 40–57. Costa Mesa, CA: Mazda.

Bruinessen, Martin van and Hendrik Boeschoten eds (1988). *Evliya Çelebi's Book of Travels: Evliya Çelebi in Diyarbekir*. Leiden; New York: Brill Archive.

Burbank, Jane and Frederick Cooper eds. (2010). *Empires in World History: Power and the Politics of Difference*. Princeton, NJ: Princeton University Press.

Burke, Peter ed. (2001). *New Perspectives on Historical Writing*. 2nd edn. University Park, PA: Penn State University Press.

Burke, Peter (2014). 'The Language of Orders in Early Modern Europe'. In *Social Orders and Social Classes in Europe since 1500: Studies in Social Stratification*, edited by M. L. Bush 1–12. London and New York: Routledge.

Burney, C. A. (1957). 'Urartian Fortresses and Towns in the Van Region'. *Anatolian Studies* 7 (December): 37–53.

Bush, M. L. (1983). *Noble Privilege*. Manchester: Manchester University Press.

Bush, M. L. (1988). *Rich Noble, Poor Noble*. Manchester: Manchester University Press.

Bush, M. L. ed. (2014) *Social Orders and Social Classes in Europe since 1500: Studies in Social Stratification*. Routledge.

Çadırcı, Musa (1991). *Tanzimat Döneminde Anadolu Kentlerinin Sosyal ve Ekonomik Yapıları*. Ankara: TTK.

Çadırcı, Musa (2018). 'Hurufat Defterlerine Göre 18. Yüzyılda Palu'. *Vakıflar Dergisi*, no. 49: 21–41.

Çakar, Enver, Kürşat Çelik and Yavuz Kısa eds (2018). *Uluslararası Palu Sempozyumu (Elazığ 11–13 Ekim 2018) Bildiriler Kitabı*. Vol. 1. Elazığ: Fırat Üniversitesi Harput Uygulama ve Araştırma Merkezi.

Can, Selman (2010). 'Osmanlı Diplomatikasında Kozalaklar'. *Güzel Sanatlar Enstitüsü Dergisi*, no. 7.

Canbakal, Hülya (2005). 'On the Nobility of Urban Notables'. In *Provincial Elites in the Ottoman Empire: Halcyon Days in Crete V: A Symposium Held in Rethymnon 10–12 January 2003*, edited by Antonis Anastasopoulos, 39–50. Rethymnon: Crete University Press.

Canbakal, Hülya (2009). 'The Ottoman State and Descendants of the Prophet in Anatolia and the Balkans (c. 1500–1700)'. *Journal of the Economic and Social History of the Orient* 52, no. 3: 542–78.

Select Bibliography

Cannadine, David (1999). *The Decline and Fall of the British Aristocracy*. Trade paperback edn. New York: Vintage.

Cannon, John (1995). 'The British Nobility, 1660–1800'. In *The European Nobilities in the Seventeenth and Eighteenth Centuries: Western Europe 1*, edited by H. M. Scott, 61–91. London; New York: Longman.

Canpolat, Sibel and Ahmet Aksın (2007). '1832–1840 Tarihli Eğin Şer'iyye Sicilinin Belge Özetleri'. *Fırat Üniversitesi Sosyal Bilimler Dergisi* 17, no. 1: 275–300.

Cardoso, José Luís (2013). *Paying for the Liberal State: The Rise of Public Finance in Nineteenth-Century Europe*. Reprint edn. Cambridge: Cambridge University Press.

Centeno, Miguel Angel (2002). *Blood and Debt: War and the Nation-State in Latin America*. University Park: Penn State Press.

Çetinsaya, Gökhan (2001). 'Türkiye'de Osmanlı Tarihçiliğinin Son Çeyrek Yüzyılı: Bir Bilanço Denemesi'. *Toplum ve Bilim* 91, no. Kış (2001): 8–37.

Ceylan, Ebubekir (2008). 'Bağdat Eyalet Meclisleri (1840–1872)'. In *Selçuklu'dan Cumhuriyete Şehir Yönetimi*, edited by Erol Özvar and Arif Bilgin 337–54. İstanbul: Türk Dünyası Belediyeler Birliği.

Cezar, Yavuz (2011). 'Tanzimat'da Malî Durum'. *İstanbul Üniversitesi İktisat Fakültesi Mecmuası* 38, no. 3–4 (7 October).

Cezar, Yavuz (2005). 'The Role of the Sarrafs in Ottoman Finance and Economy in the Eighteenth and Nineteenth Centuries'. In *Frontiers of Ottoman Studies*, edited by Colin Imber, Keiko Kiyotaki, and Rhoads Murphey 1: 61–6. London: I. B. Tauris.

Chakrabarty, Dipesh (1998). 'Minority Histories, Subaltern Pasts'. *Economic and Political Weekly* 33, no. 9: 473–9.

Charlesworth, Neil (1980). 'The "Middle Peasant Thesis" and the Roots of Rural Agitation in India, 1914–1947'. *The Journal of Peasant Studies* 7, no. 3 (1 April): 259–80.

Chaussinand-Nogaret, Guy (1985). *Noblesse Au XVIIIe Siècle. Anglais*. Cambridge; New York: Cambridge University Press.

Cheyette, Fredric L. (1968). *Lordship and Community in Medieval Europe, Selected Readings*. 1st edn. New York: Holt, Rinehart & Winston.

Christoph, Herzog and Raoul Motika (2000). '"Alla Turca": Late 19th/Early 20th-Century Ottoman Voyages into the Muslim "Outback"', *Die Welt Des Islams* 40, no. 2: 139–95.

Çiçek, M. Talha (2016). 'Negotiating Power and Authority in the Desert: The Arab Bedouin and the Limits of the Ottoman State in Hijaz, 1840–1908'. *Middle Eastern Studies* 52, no. 2 (3 March): 260–79.

Çiftçi, Erdal (2018). 'Migration, Memory and Mythification: Relocation of Suleymani Tribes on the Northern Ottoman–Iranian Frontier'. *Middle Eastern Studies* 54, no. 2 (4 March): 270–88.

Çizakça, Murat (1996). *A Comparative Evolution of Business Partnerships: The Islamic World and Europe, with Specific Reference to the Ottoman Archives*. Leiden: Brill.

Clark, Samuel (1995). *State and Status: The Rise of the State and Aristocratic Power in Western Europe*. 1st edn. Montreal: Buffalo: Queen's School of Policy Studies.

Conermann, Stephan and Gül Sen eds (2020). *The Mamluk–Ottoman Transition: Continuity and Change in Egypt and Bilad Al-Sham in the Sixteenth Century*, Vol. 2. Göttingen: V & R Unipress GmbH.

Cooper, Adrienne (1983). 'Sharecroppers and Landlords in Bengal, 1930–50: The Dependency Web and Its Implications'. *The Journal of Peasant Studies* 10, no. 2–3 (1 January): 227–55.

Cooper, Frederick (2004). 'Empire Multiplied. A Review Essay'. *Comparative Studies in Society and History* 46, no. 2: 247–72.

Cooper, Frederick and Jane Burbank (2010). 'Imperial Trajectories'. In *Empires in World History: Power and the Politics of Difference*, edited by Frederick Cooper and Jane Burbank Princeton, NJ: Princeton University Press.

Creighton, Oliver (2015). *Early European Castles: Aristocracy and Authority, AD 800–1200*. London: Bloomsbury.

Cuno, Kenneth M. (1992). *The Pasha's Peasants: Land, Society and Economy in Lower Egypt, 1740–1858*. Cambridge: Cambridge University Press.

Dağlı, Yücel, Seyit Ali Kahraman and İbrahim Sezgin eds (2001). *Evliya Çelebi Seyahatnâmesi*. Vol. III. Yapı Kredi Yayınları.

Dalyan, Murat Gökhan (2009). '19. Yüzyılda Nasturiler (İdari Sosyal Yapı ve Siyasi İlişkileri)'. MA, Süleyman Demirel University.

Davis, Natalie Zemon (2011). 'Decentering History: Local Stories and Cultural Crossings in a Global World'. *History and Theory* 50, no. 2: 188–202.

Dehqan, Mustafa (2007). 'Nehrî Documents from the Institute of Persian National Records: A Catalogue'. *Middle East Studies Association Bulletin* 41, no. 2: 157–63.

Dehqan, Mustafa and Vural Genc (2018). 'Kurds as Spies: Information-Gathering on the 16th-Century Ottoman–Safavid Frontier'. *Acta Orientalia Academiae Scientiarum Hungaricae* 71, no. 2 (1 June): 197–231.

Dehqan, Mustafa and Vural Genç (2017). 'A Document on the Kurdish Hakkārī Claim to 'Abbāsid Descent'. *Fritillaria Kurdca. Bulletin of Kurdish Studies*, no. 19–20: 4–13.

Demirtaş, Feyzullah (2005). *Mirdasi Hükümdarları: 'Palu ve Eğil hükümetleri' ve Çermik beyliği*. İstanbul: F. Demirtaş.

Der Matossian, Bedross (2007). 'The Armenian Commercial Houses and Merchant Networks in the 19th Century Ottoman Empire'. *Faculty Publications, Department of History*, 1 January. http://digitalcommons.unl.edu/historyfacpub/130.

Deringil, Selim (2009). '"The Armenian Question Is Finally Closed": Mass Conversions of Armenians in Anatolia during the Hamidian Massacres of 1895–1897'. *Comparative Studies in Society and History* 51, no. 2 (April): 344–71.

Deringil, Selim (2003). '"They Live in a State of Nomadism and Savagery": The Late Ottoman Empire and the Post-Colonial Debate'. *Comparative Studies in Society and History* 45, no. 02: 311–42.

Select Bibliography

Dıvrak, Uysal (2015). 'XIX Yüzyılın İlk Yarısında Çemişgezek Köylerinin Müslüman Nüfusu'. *Journal of International Social Research* 8, vol. 8, issue 41 (December).

Dölek-Sever, Deniz (2017). 'Policing the "Suspects": Ottoman Greeks and Armenians in Istanbul, 1914–18'. *Middle Eastern Studies* 53, no. 4 (4 July): 533–50.

Douki, Caroline and Philippe Minard (2007). 'Global History, Connected Histories: A Shift of Historiographical Scale?' *Revue d'histoire Moderne et Contemporaine* No 54-4bis, no. 5: 7–21.

Doumani, Beshara (1995). *Rediscovering Palestine: Merchants and Peasants in Jabal Nablus, 1700–1900*. Berkeley, CA: University of California Press.

Doumanis, Nicholas (2012). *Before the Nation: Muslim–Christian Coexistence and Its Destruction in Late-Ottoman Anatolia*. 1st edn. Oxford: Oxford University Press.

Duggan, Anne (1998). 'Introduction: Concepts, Origins, Transformations'. In *Nobles and Nobility in Medieval Europe: Concepts, Origins, Transformations*, edited by Anne J. Duggan, 1–16. King's College London: Boydell & Brewer.

Duguid, Stephen (1973). 'The Politics of Unity: Hamidian Policy in Eastern Anatolia'. *Middle Eastern Studies* 9, no. 2: 139–55.

Duman, M. Şahin (2018). *Belgelerle tarihte İzoli: İzollular ve İzoli aşireti*. Bilgeoğuz Yayınları.

Dündar, Fuat (2018). *Crime of Numbers: The Role of Statistics in the Armenian Question (1878–1918)*. New York: Routledge.

Dündar, Fuat (2015). 'Empire of Taxonomy: Ethnic and Religious Identities in the Ottoman Surveys and Censuses'. *Middle Eastern Studies* 51, no. 1 (2 January): 136–58.

Dursun, Selçuk (2007). '*Forest and the State: History of Forestry and Forest Administration in the Ottoman Empire*'. Ph.D. dissertation, Sabancı University.

Eley, Geoff (2005). *A Crooked Line: From Cultural History to the History of Society*. Ann Arbor, MI: University of Michigan Press.

Eley, Geoff (1989). 'Labor History, Social History, "Alltagsgeschichte": Experience, Culture, and the Politics of the Everyday – a New Direction for German Social History?' *The Journal of Modern History* 61, no. 2: 297–343.

Eley, Geoff (1980). 'Some Recent Tendencies in Social History'. In *International Handbook of Historical Studies: Contemporary Research and Theory*, edited by Georg G. Iggers and Harold T. Parker, 55–70. London: Methuen.

Emecen, Feridun Mustafa (2010). *Osmanlı Klâsik Çağında Savaş*. Istanbul: Timaş.

Epözdemir, Şakir. *1514 Amasya Antlaşması Kürt-Osmanlı İttifakı ve Mevlana İdris-i*. Bitlisi Istanbul: Pêrî Yayınları, 2005.

Eppel, Michael (2008). 'The Demise of the Kurdish Emirates: The Impact of Ottoman Reforms and International Relations on Kurdistan during the First Half of the Nineteenth Century'. *Middle Eastern Studies* 44, no. 2 (1 March): 237–58.

Eppel, Michael (2018). 'The Kurdish Emirates', in *Routledge Handbook on the Kurds*, edited by Michael M. Gunter, 1–10. London and New York: Routledge: 37–47.

Erkutun, Mehmet İlkin (2004). 'Darendeli İzzet Hasan: Ziyânâme (Sadrazam Yusuf Ziya Paşa ve Fransızların İşgali Üzerine Yapılan Osmanlı Devleti'nin Mısır Seferi 1798–1802)'. Ph.D dissertation, Istanbul University.

Erler, Mehmet Yavuz (2008). 'Osmanlı'da "Asil Kan" Aristokrasisinin XIX. Yüzyıldaki Yansımalarına Dair Birkaç Örnek: Cengiz Han ve Ramazanoğlu Soyu'. *Journal of International Social Research* 1, no. 2.

Ertekin, Abdüsselam (2019). 'Hamidiye Alayları ve Sosyo-Politik Etkileri (1890–1908)'. Ph.D. Dissertation, Mardin Artuklu University.

Ertem, Özge (2013). 'Fiyatı Alidir!: Diyarbakır'da Kıtlık, Yokluk ve Şiddet, 1879–1880'. In *Diyarbakır ve Çevresi Toplumsal ve Ekonomik Tarihi Toplantısı*, 73–9. Istanbul: Hrant Dink Vakfı Yayınları.

Evans, Peter B., Dietrich Rueschemeyer and Theda Skocpol eds (1985). *Bringing the State Back In*. Cambridge: Cambridge University Press.

Faroqhi, Suraiya ed. (2008). *Merchants in the Ottoman Empire*. Paris; Dudley, MA: Peeters.

Faroqhi, Suraiya, Bruce McGowan and Sevket Pamuk (1994). *An Economic and Social History of the Ottoman Empire, 1300–1914*. Cambridge: Cambridge University Press.

Fass, Paula S. (2003). 'Cultural History/Social History: Some Reflections on a Continuing Dialogue'. *Journal of Social History* 37, no. 1: 39–46.

Fedyukin, Igor (2016). 'Nobility and Schooling in Russia, 1700s–1760s: Choices in a Social Context'. *Journal of Social History* 49, no. 3: 558–84.

Filipović, Nedim (1986). 'Ocaklik Timars in Bosnia and Herzegovina'. *Prilozi Za Orijentalnu Filologiju*, no. 36: 149–80.

Finkel, Caroline (2007). *Osman's Dream: The History of the Ottoman Empire*. 3/25/07 edn. New York: Basic Books.

Fitzgerald, Timothy (2016). 'Rituals of Possession, Methods of Control and the Monopoly of Violence: The Ottoman Conquest of Aleppo in Comparative Perspective'. *The Mamluk–Ottoman Transition*: edited by Stephan Conermann and Gul Sen, 250–73. Göttingen: V&R unipress.

Fleischer, Cornell H. (2014). *Bureaucrat and Intellectual in the Ottoman Empire: The Historian Mustafa Ali (1541–1600)*. Princeton, NJ: Princeton University Press.

Forster, Robert (1963). 'The Provincial Noble: A Reappraisal'. *The American Historical Review* 68, no. 3: 681–91.

Fouracre, Paul (1998). 'The Origins of the Nobility in Francia'. In *Nobles and Nobility in Medieval Europe: Concepts, Origins, Transformations*, edited by Anne Duggan. 17–24. King's College London: Boydell & Brewer.

Fuccaro, Nelida (2011). 'The Ottoman Frontier in Kurdistan in the Sixteenth and Seventeenth Centuries'. In *The Ottoman World*, edited by Christine Woodhead, 237–50. London: Routledge.

Gaborieau, Marc, Aleksandar Popović and Thierry Zarcone eds (1990). *Naqshbandis: Cheminements et Situation Actuelle d'un Ordre Mystique Musulman*. Istanbul: Isis.

Select Bibliography

Gelvin, James (2011). *The Modern Middle East*. 3rd edn. New York; Oxford: Oxford University Press.

Gelvin, James L. (2006). 'The "Politics of Notables" Forty Years After'. *Middle East Studies Association Bulletin* 40, no. 1: 19–29.

Genç, Mehmet (2000). 'Iltizam (إلتزام)'. In *TDV İslâm Ansiklopedisi*, 22: 154–8. İstanbul: Türkiye Diyanet Vak. Accessed 25 September 2020. https://islamansiklopedisi.org.tr/iltizam--vergi.

Genc, Vural (2019). *Acem'den Rum'a Bir Bürokrat ve Tarihci Idris-i Bidlîsî*. Ankara: Türk Tarih Kurumu.

Genc, Vural (2019). 'Rethinking Idris-i Bidlisi: An Iranian Bureaucrat and Historian between the Shah and the Sultan'. *Iranian Studies* 52, no. 3–4 (4 July): 425–47.

Genc, Vural (2011). *Iranli Tarihcilerin Kaleminden Çaldıran*. İstanbul: Bengi Yayınları.

Genell, Aimee M. (2016). 'Autonomous Provinces and the Problem of "Semi-Sovereignty" in European International Law'. *Journal of Balkan and Near Eastern Studies* 18, no. 6 (1 November): 533–49.

Gerber, Haim (1986). 'A New Look at the Tanzimat: The Case of the Province of Jerusalem'. *Palestine in the Late Ottoman Period*, Jerusalem: Yad Izhak Ben-Zvi, 30–45. Leiden: Brill.

Gerber, Haim (1987). *The Social Origins of the Modern Middle East*. Boulder, CO: Lynne Rienner.

Ghaderi, Farangis (2017). 'The Literary Legacy of the Ardalans'. *Kurdish Studies* 5, no. 1 (17 May): 32–55.

Ghereghlou, Kioumars (2015). 'Cashing in on Land and Privilege for the Welfare of the Shah: Monetisation of Tiyūl in Early Safavid Iran and Eastern Anatolia'. *Acta Orientalia Academiae Scientiarum Hungaricae* 68, no. 1 (1 March): 87–141.

Given-Wilson, Chris (1996). *The English Nobility in the Late Middle Ages: The Fourteenth-Century Political Community*. 1st edn. London: Routledge.

Gökbilgin, M. Tayyip (ed.) (1979). *Kavânin-i Âl-i Osman Der Hülâsa-i Mezâmin-i Defter-i Divan*. İstanbul: Enderun Kitabevi.

Gölbaşı, Edip (2011). '19. Yüzyıl Osmanlı Emperyal Siyaseti ve Osmanlı Tarih Yazımında Kolonyal Perspektifler'. *Tarih ve Toplum Yeni Yaklaşımlar* 13, no. Güz: 199–222.

Gölbaşı, Edip (1915). '1896 Katliamları: Doğu Vilayetlerinde Cemaatler Arası 'Şiddet İklimi've Ermeni Karşıtı Ayaklanmalar'. In *1915: Siyaset, Tehcir ve Soykırım*, edited by Oktay Özel and Fikret Adanır, 140–63. Istanbul: Tarih Vakfı Yurt Yayınları.

Gölbaşı, Edip (2018). 'The Official Conceptualization of the Anti-Armenian Riots of 1895–1897. Bureaucratic Terminology, Official Ottoman Narrative, and Discourses of Revolutionary Provocation'. *Études Arméniennes Contemporaines*, no. 10 (30 March): 33–62.

Gölbaşı, Edip (2008). 'The Yezidis and the Ottoman State: Modern Power, Military Conscription, and Conversion Policies, 1830–1909'. MA thesis, Boğaziçi University.

Gördük, Yunus Emre (2014). 'Eğil Emirliği'nin Kısa Tarihçesi ve Eğil Emirlerine Ait Şecere Metninin Tercümesi'. *OTAM* 35: 89–120.

Gorski, Philip S. (2003). *The Disciplinary Revolution: Calvinism and the Rise of the State in Early Modern Europe*. Chicago, IL: University of Chicago Press.

Göyünç, Nejat (1969). 'Diyarbekir Beylerbeyliği'nin ilk idari taksimatı'. *Tarih Dergisi* 22: 23–34.

Göyünç, Nejat (1991). 'Yurtluk-Ocaklık Deyimleri Hakkında'. In *Prof. Dr. Bekir Kütükoğlu'na Armağan*, 269–78. İstanbul: İ.Ü. Edebiyat Fak.

Gül, Abdülkadir (2016). *Dersim'deki Osmanlı*. Istanbul: İdil Yayınları.

Gümüş, Ercan (2018). '17. Yüzyılda Aşiret Geleneklerinin Şer'i Hukuktaki Yerine Dair Diyarbekir Mahkemesi'den Bir Örnek: Kan Davalarında Sulh Amacıyla Kız Verme Âdeti ve Aşiretli Toplumlar Hakkında Bazı Değerlendirmeler'. *Journal of Turkish Studies* vol. 13, issue 1 (1 January): 29–50.

Gündoğan, Azat Zana (2005). 'The Kurdish Political Mobilization in the 1960s: The Case of "the Eastern Meetings"'. MA thesis, Middle East Technical University.

Güneş, Mehmet (2013). 'Osmanlı Taşra İdaresinin Değişim Sürecinde Kaymakamlık Kurumu (1842–1871)'. Ph.D. dissertation, Marmara University.

Güran, Tevfik (2011). 'Tanzimat Dönemi Osmanlı Maliyesi'. *İstanbul Üniversitesi İktisat Fakültesi Mecmuası* 49 (1 October): 79–95.

Güran, Tevfik (2004). 'Temettüat Registers as a Resource about Ottoman Social and Economic Life'. In *The Ottoman State and Societies in Change: A Study of the Nineteenth Century Temettuat Registers*, edited by Hayashi, Kayoko, and Mahir Aydın, 3–14. London: Kegan Paul.

Gureghian, Aida (2010). 'Eternalizing a Nation: Armenian Hishatakarans in the Seventeenth Century'. *Church History* 79, no. 4: 783–99.

Gutman, David (2019). *The Politics of Armenian Migration to North America, 1885–1915: Migrants, Smugglers and Dubious Citizens*. Edinburgh: Edinburgh University Press.

Gutman, David (2016). 'Travel Documents, Mobility Control, and the Ottoman State in an Age of Global Migration, 1880–1915'. *Journal of the Ottoman and Turkish Studies Association* 3, no. 2: 347–68.

Haldén, Peter (2020). *Family Power: Kinship, War and Political Orders in Eurasia, 500–2018*. Cambridge: Cambridge University Press.

Haldén, Peter (ed.) (2020). 'The Ubiquitous and Opaque Elites of the Ottoman Empire c.1300–c.1830'. In *Family Power: Kinship, War and Political Orders in Eurasia, 500–2018*, 252–82. Cambridge: Cambridge University Press.

Haldon, John F. (1994). *The State and the Tributary Mode of Production*. London; New York: Verso.

Hanssen, Jens, Thomas Philipp and Stefan Weber eds (2002). *The Empire in the City: Arab Provincial Capitals in the Late Ottoman Empire*. Beirut and Würzburg: Ergon in Kommission.

Select Bibliography

Hassanpour, Amir (1992). *Nationalism and Language in Kurdistan, 1918–1985*. Illustrated edn. San Francisco, CA: Edwin Mellen.

Hassanpour, Amir (2003). 'The Making of Kurdish Identity: Pre-20th Century Historical and Literary Discourses. In *Essays on the Origins of Kurdish Nationalism*, edited by Abbas Vali 106–62. Costa Mesa, CA: Mazda.

Hathaway, Jane (2002). *The Politics of Households in Ottoman Egypt: The Rise of the Qazdaglis*. Cambridge: Cambridge University Press.

Hause, Steven C. (1996). 'The Evolution of Social History'. *French Historical Studies* 19, no. 4: 1,191–214.

Hayashi, Kayoko and Mahir Aydin eds (2004). *The Ottoman State and Societies in Change: A Study of the Nineteenth Century Temettuat Registers*. London; New York: Kegan Paul.

He, Wenkai (2013). *Paths toward the Modern Fiscal State*. Cambridge; London: Harvard University Press.

Yalçın-Heckmann, Lale (1991). *Tribe and Kinship among the Kurds*. Frankfurt [etc.]: Peter Lang.

Heftler, Victoria (1997). 'The Future of the Subaltern Past: Toward a Cosmopolitan History from Below'. *Left History* 5, no. 1.

Henning, Barbara (2018). *Narratives of the History of the Ottoman-Kurdish Bedirhani Family in Imperial and Post-Imperial Contexts: Continuities and Changes*. Bamberg: University of Bamberg Press.

Hickok, Michael (1997). *Ottoman Administration of 18th Century Bosnia*. Leiden; New York: Brill.

Hirschler, Konrad (2001). 'Defining the Nation: Kurdish Historiography in Turkey in the 1990s'. *Middle Eastern Studies* 37, no. 3: 145–66.

Hobsbawm, Eric (1971). 'From Social History to the History of Society'. *Daedalus* 100, no. 1: 20–45.

Hobsbawm, Eric (1997). *On History*. New York: The New Press.

Hobsbawm, Eric (1998). 'On History from Below'. In *On History*. New York: The New Press.

Hodgson, Marshall G. S. (1993). *Rethinking World History: Essays on Europe, Islam and World History*. Cambridge: Cambridge University Press.

Houston, Christopher (2009). 'An Anti-History of a Non-People: Kurds, Colonialism, and Nationalism in the History of Anthropology'. *The Journal of the Royal Anthropological Institute* 15, no. 1: 19–35.

Houston, Christopher (2007). '"Set Aside from the Pen and Cut off from the Foot": Imagining the Ottoman Empire and Kurdistan'. *Comparative Studies of South Asia, Africa and the Middle East* 27, no. 2 (18 September): 397–411.

Hovannisian, Richard G. (2006). *Armenian Tigranakert/Diarbekir and Edessa/Urfa*. Costa Mesa, CA: Mazda.

Hurewitz, J. C. (1975). *The Middle East and North Africa in World Politics: A Documentary Record: European Expansion, 1535–1914*. New Haven, CT: Yale University Press.

Idris-i Bidlisi (2016). *Selim Şah-Nâme*. Trans. Hicabi Kırlangıç. Ankara: Hece Yayinlari.

İlhan, M. Mehdi (1981). '1518 Tarihli Tapu Tahrir Defterine Göre Amid Sancağında Timar Dağılımı'. *İstanbul Üniversitesi Edebiyat Fakültesi Tarih Enstitüsü Dergisi* 12: 85–100.

İlhan, M. Mehdi (2000). *Amid (Diyarbakır): 1518 tarihli defter-i mufassal*. Ankara: Türk Tarih Kurumu Basımevi.

İlhan, M. Mehdi (1982). '1518 Tarihli Tapu Tahrir Defterine Göre Âmid Sancağında Timâr Dağılımı'. *Tarih Enstitüsü Dergisi* XII: 85–100.

Imber, Colin (2009). *The Ottoman Empire, 1300–1650: The Structure of Power*. 2nd edn. Basingstoke: Palgrave Macmillan.

Imber, Colin (1994). 'Canon and Apocrypha in Early Ottoman History'. In *Studies in Ottoman History in Honour of Professor of V.L. Menage*. edited by Colin Heywood and Colin Imber, 117–37. Istanbul: Isis Press.

İnalcik, Halil (1954). 'Ottoman Methods of Conquest'. *Studia Islamica*, no. 2: 103–29.

İnalcik, Halil (1976). *Application of the Tanzimat and Its Social Effects*. Lisse: Peter de Ridder Press.

İnalcik, Halil (2006). 'Temlîks, Soyurghals, Yurdluk-Ocaklıks, Mâlikâne-Mukâta'a and Awqaf'. In *History and Historiography of Post-Mongol Central Asia and the Middle East*. edited by John E. Woods and Ernest Tucker, 112–34. Wiesbaden: Harrassowitz.

İnalcik, Halil (1979). 'The Khan and the Tribal Aristocracy: The Crimean Khanate under Sahib Giray I'. *Harvard Ukrainian Studies* 3/4: 445–66.

İnalcik, Halil and Cemal Kafadar (1993). *Süleymân the Second and His Time*. Istanbul: Isis Press.

İnalcık, Halil and Mehmet Seyitdanlıoğlu (2006). *Tanzimat: Değişim Sürecinde Osmanlı İmparatorluğu*. Istanbul: Phoenix Yayınevi.

İpşirli, Mehmet (1992). 'Beylerbeyi'. In *TDV İslâm Ansiklopedisi*, 6: 69–74. Istanbul: Türkiye Diyanet Vakfı. Accessed 15 February 2020. https://islamansiklopedisi.org.tr/beylerbeyi.

İpşirli, Mehmet (2011). 'Temliknâme'. In *TDV İslâm Ansiklopedisi*, 40: 430–1. İstanbul: Türkiye Diyanet Vakfı. Accessed 25 September 2020. https://islamansiklopedisi.org.tr/temlikname.

İşbilir, Ömer (2013). 'Yük'. In *TDV İslâm Ansiklopedisi*, 44: 46–8. Istanbul: TDV. Accessed 1 February 2020. https://islamansiklopedisi.org.tr/yuk

İslamoğlu, Huri (ed.) (2004). *Constituting Modernity: Private Property in the East and West*. London ; New York: I. B. Tauris.

İslamoğlu, Huri (2001). 'Modernities Compared: State Transformations and Constitutions of Property in the Qing and Ottoman Empires'. *Journal of Early Modern History* 5, no. 4 (November): 353–86.

İslamoğlu, Huri (2004). 'Politics of Administering Property: Law and Statistics in the Nineteenth Century Ottoman Empire'. In *Constituting Modernity: Private Property in the East and West*, edited by Huri İslamoğlu, 276–319. London: I. B. Tauris.

Select Bibliography

İslamoğlu, Huri (2000). 'Property as a Contested Domain: A Reevaluation of the Ottoman Land Code of 1858'. In *New Perspectives on Property and Land in the Middle East*, edited by Roger Owen. London: Harvard University Press.

İslamoğlu, Huri (1994). *State and Peasant in the Ottoman Empire: Agrarian Power Relations and Regional Economic Development in Ottoman Anatolia During the Sixteenth Century*. Leiden: Brill.

İslamoğlu, Huri (2004). *The Ottoman Empire and the World-Economy*. Cambridge: Cambridge University Press.

İslamoğlu, Huri and Peter C. Perdue (2001). 'Introduction'. *Journal of Early Modern History* 5, no. 4 (1 January): 271–81.

İslamoğlu-İnan, Huri and Peter C. Perdue eds (2009). *Shared Histories of Modernity: China, India, and the Ottoman Empire*. Critical Asian Studies. New Delhi: Routledge.

Jennings, Ronald C. (1973). 'Loans and Credit in Early 17th Century Ottoman Judicial Records: The Sharia Court of Anatolian Kayseri'. *Journal of the Economic and Social History of the Orient* 16, no. 2/3: 168–216.

Jennings, Ronald C. (1978). 'Zimmis (Non-Muslims) in Early 17th Century Ottoman Judicial Records: The Sharia Court of Anatolian Kayseri'. *Journal of the Economic and Social History of the Orient* 21, no. 3: 225–93.

Jones, Michael ed. (1987). *Gentry and Lesser Nobility in Late Medieval Europe*. New York: Palgrave Macmillan.

Jongerden, Joost (2012). 'Elite Encounters of a Violent Kind: Milli İbrahim Paşa, Ziya Gokalp and Political Struggle in Diyarbekir at the Turn of the 20th Century'. In *Social Relations in Ottoman Diyarbekir, 1870–1915*, edited by Joost Jongerden and Jelle Verheij; 55–84. Leiden; Boston: Brill.

Jongerden, Joost and Jelle Verheij eds (2012). *Social Relations in Ottoman Diyarbekir, 1870–1915*. Leiden; Boston: Brill.

Joseph, Sabrina (2007). 'The Legal Status of Tenants and Sharecroppers in Seventeenth- and Eighteenth-Century France and Ottoman Syria'. *Rural History* 18, no. 1 (April): 23–46.

Jwaideh, Wadie (2006). *The Kurdish National Movement: Its Origins and Development*. Syracuse: Syracuse University Press.

Kaelble, Hartmut (2004). *The European Way: European Societies during the Nineteenth and Twentieth Centuries*. New York: Berghahn.

Kafadar, Cemal (1995). *Between Two Worlds: The Construction of the Ottoman State*. Berkeley, CA: University of California Press.

Kafadar, Cemal (1998). 'The Question of Ottoman Decline'. *Harvard Middle East and Islamic Review* 4: 30–75.

Kahveci, Gülay (1998). '29 Numaralı Mühimme Defteri'. MA thesis, Istanbul University.

Karabulut, Serdar (2017). 'Palu'nun Siyasi/Ekonomik Tarihi (XIV–XVIII. Yüzyıllar Arası) ve Palu Çarşısı'na Dâir Vakıfname Belgesi'nin Tercümesi'. *OTAM* 41, no. Bahar: 145–68.

Karabulut, Serdar (2017). 'Şeyh Alâeddin İbn-i Şeyh Pir Vakfiyeyi Tarihiyesi Üzerine Bir İnceleme'. *Bingöl Üniversitesi İlahiyat Fakültesi Dergisi* 5, no. 9: 263–78.

Karabulut, Serdar (2018). 'Şeyh Ali Sebtî ve Palu Çevresinde Hâlidîliğin Yayılmasındaki Yeri'. *AKADEMİAR Akademik İslam Araştırmaları Dergisi*, no. 4 (7 June): 145–75.

Karabulut, Serdar (2013). *Zazalar*. İzmit: Altın Kalem Yayınları.

Karaca, Ali (1993). *Anadolu Islahâtı ve Ahmet Şakir Paşa, 1838–1899*. İstanbul: Eren.

Karaman, Kıvanç and Şevket Pamuk (2013). 'Different Paths to the Modern State in Europe: The Interaction between Warfare, Economic Structure, and Political Regime, *American Political Science Review* 107(3), 603–26.

Karasu, Hamit (2018). 'Osmanlı Ayanları Üzerine Yapılan Çalışmalar (Tanzimata Kadar)', *Journal of Turkish Studies* 13 (1 January): 127–50.

Karataş, Mehmet (2012). 'Mahkeme Kayıtlarına Göre XVII. ve XVIII. Yüzyıllarda Diyarbekir'de Gayrımüslimler'. *Elektronik Sosyal Bilimler Dergisi* 11, no. 42: 393–422.

Karateke, Hakan T. (2019). 'The Peculiar Status of the Crimean Khans in Ottoman Protocol'. *Journal of the Ottoman and Turkish Studies Association* 6, no. 1: 103–20.

Karateke, Hakan T. and Maurus Reinkowski (eds) (2005). *Legitimizing the Order: The Ottoman Rhetoric of State Power*. 1st edn. Leiden: Boston: Brill.

Karimi, Sara Zandi (2017). 'History of Ardalānids (1590–1810) by Sharaf al-Dīn Bin Shams al-Dīn'. *Kurdish Studies* 5, no. 1 (11 May): 56–79.

Kármán, Gábor and Lovro Kunčević (2013). *The European Tributary States of the Ottoman Empire in the Sixteenth and Seventeenth Centuries*. Leiden; Boston: Brill.

Kawtharani, Wajih (2018). 'The Ottoman Tanzimat and the Constitution'. *Al Muntaqa* 1, no. 1: 51–65.

Kaya, Alp Yücel (2019). 'Türkiye'de Mülkiyet Tartışmaları ve Çalışmaları'. *Ayrıntı Dergi* Güz, no. 32: 59–69.

Kaya, Alp Yücel (2019). '19. Yüzyılda Batı Anadoluda Tarımsal Kapitalizmin Gelişiminde Güç Mücadelesi: Baltazzi Çiftlikleri ve Büyük Toprak Sahipliğinin Dönüşümü', *Türkiye Sosyal Bilimler Kongresi*, Ankara, Turkey.

Kaya, Alp Yücel (2012). 'Were Peasants Bound to the Soil in The Large Estates (Çiftliks) of the 19th Century Balkans? Reappraisal of the Question of New/Second Serfdom in the Ottoman Historiography', *Working in Greece and Turkey, A Comparative Labour History from Empires to Nation-States, 1840–1940*, edited by Leda Papastefanaki and M. Erdem Kabadayı, 61–112. New York: Berghahn.

Kaya, Alp Yücel and Mehmet Yücel Terzibaşoğlu (2009). 'Tahrirden Kadastroya 1874 İstanbul Emlak Tahriri ve Vergisi kadastro tabir olunur tahrir i emlak', *Tarih ve Toplum*, 9–58.

Select Bibliography

Kaya, Alp Yücel and Onur Peker (2019). 'Parga Çiftliği Kararnamesi (1875): Çiftlik Sahipleri ve Çiftçi 'Ahali' Arasında Mücadele', edited by Mustafa Öztürk ve Ayşe Değerli, 1–14. *İktisat Tarihi Kongresi Bildirileri* 1, İzmir 25–27 Nisan.

Kaya, Mehmed S. (2011). *The Zaza Kurds of Turkey: A Middle Eastern Minority in a Globalised Society*. London; New York: I. B. Tauris.

Kechriotis, Vangelis (2013). 'Postcolonial Criticism Encounters Late Ottoman Studies'. *Historein* 13: 39–46.

Ketsemanian, Varak (2020). 'Ideologies, Paradoxes, and Fedayis in the Late Ottoman Empire: Historiographical Challenges and Methodological Problems in the Study of the Armenian Revolutionary Movement (1890–1896)'. In *Armenians and Kurds in the Late Ottoman Empire*, edited by Ümit Kurt and Ara Sarafian 119–60. Fresno, CA: California State University Press.

Ketsemanian, Varak (2018). 'The Hunchakian Revolutionary Party and the Assasination Attempts against the Patriarch Khoren Ashekian and Maksudzade Simon Bey in 1894'. *International Journal of Middle East Studies* 50, no. 4 (November): 735–55.

Keyder, Çağlar and Faruk eds (1991). *Landholding and Commercial Agriculture in the Middle East*. Albany, NY: State University of New York Press.

Khodarkovsky, Michael (2004). *Russia's Steppe Frontier: The Making of a Colonial Empire, 1500–1800*. Bloomington, IN: Indiana University Press.

Khoury, Dina Rizk (2002). *State and Provincial Society in the Ottoman Empire: Mosul, 1540–1834*. Cambridge: Cambridge University Press.

Khoury, Dina Rizk eds (1991). 'The Introduction of Commercial Agriculture in the Province of Mosul and Its Effects on the Peasantry, 1750–1850'. In *Landholding and Commercial Agriculture in the Middle East*, edited by Çağlar Keyder and Faruk Tabak 155–72. Albany, NY: State University of New York Press.

Khoury, Dina Rizk (2006). 'The Ottoman Centre versus Provincial Power-Holders: An Analysis of the Historiography'. In *The Cambridge History of Turkey: The Later Ottoman Empire*, edited by Suraiya Faroqhi 135–56. Cambridge: Cambridge University Press.

Khoury, Dina and Dane Kennedy (2007). 'Comparing Empires: The Ottoman Domains and the British Raj in the Long Nineteenth Century'. *Comparative Studies of South Asia, Africa and the Middle East* 27 (1 January): 233–44.

Khoury, Philip S. (1990). 'The Urban Notables Paradigm Revisited', *Revue Des Mondes Musulmans et de La Méditerranée* 55, no. 1: 215–30.

Khoury, Philip S. and Joseph Kostiner (1990). 'Introduction: Tribes and the Complexities of State Formation in the Middle East'. In *Tribes and State Formation in the Middle East*, edited by Philip S. Khoury and Joseph Kostiner 1–22. Berkeley, CA: University of California Press.

Khoury, Philip S. and Joseph Kostiner eds (1990). *Tribes and State Formation in the Middle East*. Berkeley, CA: University of California Press.

Kieser, Hans-Lukas, Kerem Oktem and Maurus Reinkowski eds (2015). *World War I and the End of the Ottomans: From the Balkan Wars to the Armenian Genocide*. Sew edn. London New York: I. B. Tauris.

King, Diane E. (2014). *Kurdistan on the Global Stage: Kinship, Land, and Community in Iraq*. New Brunswick, NJ: Rutgers University Press.

Kiprovska, Mariya (2021). 'Power and Society in Pleven on the Verge of Two Epochs: The Fate of the Mihaloğlu Family and Its Pious Foundations (Vakf) during the Transitional Period from Imperial to National Governance'. *Bulgarian Historical Review:* 172–204.

Kisa, Yavuz (2020). 'M. 1679–1683 (H.1089–1092) Tarihli Harput Şer'iyye Sicilinin Tanıtımı ve Fihristi'. *Fırat Üniversitesi Sosyal Bilimler Dergisi* 30, no. 1 (31 January): 505–33.

Kiyotaki, Keiko (2019). *Ottoman Land Reform in the Province of Baghdad*. Leiden; Boston: Brill.

Kılıç, Orhan (1997). *18. yüzyılın ilk yarısında Osmanlı Devleti'nin idari taksimatı. Eyalet ve sancak tevcihatı*. Elazığ: Şark Pazarlama.

Kılıç, Orhan (2018). 'Klasik Dönem Osmanlı İdari Sisteminde Farklı Bir Unsur: Kürdistan Vilayeti/Eyaleti'. In *CIEPO 22 Uluslararası Osmanlı Öncesi ve Osmanlı Çalışmaları Komitesi Bildiriler Kitabı*, 547–64. Trabzon: Trabzon Büyükşehir Belediyesi.

Kırlı, Cengiz (2014). 'From Economic History to Cultural History in Ottoman Studies'. *International Journal of Middle East Studies* 46, no. 2 (May): 376–8.

Kırlı, Cengiz (2015). *Yolsuzluğun İcadı: 1840 Ceza Kanunu, İktidar ve Bürokrasi*. Istanbul: Verita.

Klein, Janet (1996). 'Claiming the Nation: The Origins and Nature of Kurdish Nationalist Discourse, a Study of the Kurdish Press in the Ottoman Empire'. MA thesis, Princeton University.

Klein, Janet (2007). 'Kurdish Nationalists and Non-Nationalist Kurdists: Rethinking Minority Nationalism and the Dissolution of the Ottoman Empire, 1908–1909'. *Nations and Nationalism* 13, no. 1: 135–53.

Klein, Janet (2010). 'Minorities, Statelessness, and Kurdish Studies Today: Prospects and Dilemmas for Scholars'. *Journal of Ottoman Studies/Osmanlı Araştırmaları Dergisi, Special Issue in Honor of Rifa'at Abou-El-Haj* 36: 225–37.

Klein, Janet (2000). 'Proverbial Nationalism: Proverbs in Kurdish Nationalist Discourse of the Late Ottoman Period'. *The International Journal of Kurdish Studies* 14, no. 1/2: 7.

Klein, Janet (2012). 'State, Tribe, Dynasty, and the Contest over Diyarbekir at the Turn of the 20th Century'. In *Social Relations in Ottoman Diyarbekir, 1870–1915*, edited by Joost Jongerden and Jelle Verheij 147–78. Leiden; Boston: Brill.

Klein, Janet (2011). *The Margins of Empire: Kurdish Militias in the Ottoman Tribal Zone*. Stanford, CA: Stanford University Press.

Koçunyan, Aylin (2014). '"Long Live Sultan Abdülaziz, Long Live the Nation, Long Live the Constitution ..."'. *Constitutionalism, Legitimacy, and Power:*

Select Bibliography

Nineteenth Century Experiences, edited by Kelly L. Grotke and Markus J. Prutsch 189–210. Oxford: Oxford University Press.

Köksal, Osman (2006). 'Osmanlı Hukukunda Bir Ceza Olarak Sürgün ve İki Osmanlı Sultanının Sürgünle İlgili Hattı-ı Hümayunları. 19(19)'. *Osmanlı Tarihi Araştırma ve Uygulama Merkezi Dergisi OTAM* 19, no. 19: 283–341.

Köksal, Yonca (2006). 'Coercion and Mediation: Centralization and Sedentarization of Tribes in the Ottoman Empire'. *Middle Eastern Studies* 42, no. 3: 469–91.

Köksal, Yonca (2002). 'Imperial Center and Local Groups: Tanzimat Reforms in the Provinces of Edirne and Ankara'. *New Perspectives on Turkey* 27: 107–38.

Köksal, Yonca (2002). 'Reform in the Province of Edirne: Ottoman Archives on Local Administration during the Tanzimat Period (1839–1878)'. *Peri Orakis, Epistimoniki Periodiki Ekdosi* 2.

Köksal, Yonca (1999). 'Tanzimat Döneminde Bulgaristan: Osmanlı'da Merkezî Devletin Oluşumu 1839–1878'. *Toplum ve Bilim* 83: 2000.

Köksal, Yonca (2010). 'Tanzimat ve Tarih Yazımı'. *Doğu Batı* 51: 193–216.

Köksal, Yonca (2019). *The Ottoman Empire in the Tanzimat Era: Provincial Perspectives from Ankara to Edirne*. London; New York: Routledge.

Köprülü, Mehmed Fuat (1941). 'Ortazaman Türk-İslam Feodalizmi'. *Belleten* V, no. 19: 319–34.

Köprülü, Orhan F. 'Bey'. In *TDV İslâm Ansiklopedisi*, 6: 11–12. Accessed 5 February 2020. https://islamansiklopedisi.org.tr/bey.

Köroğlu, Kemalettin and Ali M. Dinçol (1989).'Palu Yazıtı Üzerine Bir Not'. *Anadolu Araştırmaları*, issue 11: 123–9.

Köse, Muhammed (2016). '2688 Numaralı Palu Nüfus Defterine Göre 1841 Yılında Sivan Nahiyesinin Demografik ve Sosyal Yapısı', *Bingöl Araştırmaları Dergisi* 2, no. 2 (10 January): 87–128.

Kostopoulou, Elektra (2016). 'Autonomy and Federation within the Ottoman Empire: Introduction to the Special Issue'. *Journal of Balkan and Near Eastern Studies* 18, no. 6 (1 November): 525–32.

Kostopoulou, Elektra (2016). 'The Island That Wasn't: Autonomous Crete (1898–1912) and Experiments of Federalization'. *Journal of Balkan and Near Eastern Studies* 18, no. 6 (1 November): 550–66.

Kotsonis, Yanni (2014). *States of Obligation: Taxes and Citizenship in the Russian Empire and Early Soviet Republic*. University of Toronto Press.

Koyuncu, Mevlüt (2008). 'İlk İslâm Fetihleri Döneminde El-Cezire Bölgesi ve İslamlaşma Süreci'. *Sakarya Üniversitesi Fen Edebiyat Dergisi* 1: 131–40.

Koyuncu, Nuran (2014). 'Osmanlı Devleti'nde Sarrafların Mültezimlere Kefilliği'. *İnönü Üniversitesi Hukuk Fakültesi Dergisi* 5, no. 1: 295–326.

Królikowska-Jedlińska, Natalia (2018). *Law and Division of Power in the Crimean Khanate (1532–1774): With Special Reference to the Reign of Murad Giray (1678–1683)*. Leiden; Boston: Brill.

Kühn, Thomas (2007). 'Shaping and Reshaping Colonial Ottomanism: Contesting Boundaries of Difference and Integration in Ottoman Yemen' *Comparative Studies of South Asia, Africa and the Middle East* 27, no. 2: 315–31.

Kunt, İ. Metin (1983). *The Sultan's Servants: The Transformation of Ottoman Provincial Government, 1550–1650*. New York: Columbia University Press.

Kunt, İ. Metin (1978). *Sancaktan Eyalete: 1550–1650 Arasında Osmanlı Ümerası ve İl İdaresi*. İstanbul: Boğaziçi Üniversitesi Yayınları.

Kunt, Metin Ibrahim (1974). 'Ethnic-Regional (Cins) Solidarity in the Seventeenth-Century Ottoman Establishment'. *International Journal of Middle East Studies* 5, no. 3: 233–9.

Kunt, I. M. and Christine Woodhead eds (2014). *Suleyman the Magnificent and His Age: The Ottoman Empire in the Early Modern World*. London; New York: Routledge.

Kurt, Ümit and Ara Sarafian eds (2020). *Armenians and Kurds in the Late Ottoman Empire*. Fresno, CA: California State University Press.

Kurt, Ümit and Ara Sarafian (2018). 'Theatres of Violence on the Ottoman Periphery: Exploring the Local Roots of Genocidal Policies in Antep', *Journal of Genocide Research*, vol. 20, issue 3: 351–71.

Kurt, Ümit and Ara Sarafian (2018). 'Reform and Violence in the Hamidian Era: The Political Context of the 1895 Armenian Massacres in Aintab'. *Holocaust and Genocide Studies* 32, no. 3: 404–23.

Kurt, Ümit and Ara Sarafian (2020). 'The Breakdown of a Previously Peaceful Coexistence'. In *Armenians and Kurds in the Late Ottoman Empire*, edited by Ümit Kurt and Ara Sarafian 45–70. Fresno, CA: California State University Press.

Kushner, David ed. (1997). *Palestine in the Late Ottoman Period: Political, Social and Economic Transformation*. Jerusalem: Leiden: Brill.

Laçin, Bedirhan (2017). 'New Inclinations towards Land Usufruct in the 18th Century Anatolia'. MA thesis. Bilkent University.

Leibfried, Stephan, Evelyne Huber, Matthew Lange, Jonah D. Levy, Frank Nullmeier and John D. Stephens eds (2015). *The Oxford Handbook of Transformations of the State*. Oxford: Oxford University Press.

Leonhard, Jörn and Christian Wieland (2011). 'Noble Identities from the Sixteenth to the Twentieth Century: European Aristocratic Cultures in Law, Politics, and Aesthetics'. In *What Makes the Nobility Noble?: Comparative Perspectives from the Sixteenth to the Twentieth Century*, edited by Jörn Leonhard and Christian Wieland, 7–34. Vandenhoeck & Ruprecht.

Levy-Daphny, Tsameret (2015). 'To Be a Voyvoda in Diyarbakır: Socio-Political Change in an 18th-Century Ottoman Province'. In *Society, Law, and Culture in the Middle East*, 44–58, edited by Ehud Toledano and Dror Ze'evi De Gruyter Open.

Levy-Daphny, Tsameret (1965). 'The Ottoman Empire in the Mid-nineteenth Century: A Review'. *Middle Eastern Studies* 1, no. 3 (1 April): 283–95.

Select Bibliography

Libaridian, Gerard J. (2011). 'What Was Revolutionary about Armenian Revolutionary Parties in the Ottoman Empire?' In *A Question of the Genocide: Armenians and Turks at the End of the Ottoman Empire*, edited by Ronald Grigor Suny, Norman M. Naimark, and Fatma Müge Göçek, 82–112. Oxford: Oxford University Press.

Lindner, Rudi Paul (2007). *Explorations in Ottoman Prehistory*. Ann Arbor, MI: University of Michigan Press.

Lindner, Rudi Paul (1983). *Nomads and Ottomans in Medieval Anatolia*. Illustrated edn. Bloomington: Sinor Research Institute of Inner Asian Studies.

Lipp, Charles (2016). *Contested Spaces of Nobility in Early Modern Europe*. London; New York: Routledge.

Lowry, Heath W. (2012). *Nature of the Early Ottoman State*. Albany, NY: State University of New York Press.

Lowry, Heath W. (1986). 'Privilege and Property in Ottoman Maçuka in the Opening Decades of the Tourkokratia: 1461–1553'. In *Continuity and Change in Late Byzantine and Early Ottoman Society*, edited by Anthony Bryer and Heath W. Lowry 97–128. Birmingham: University of Birmingham, Centre for Byzantine Studies.

Ludtke, Alf (1995). *The History of Everyday Life: Reconstructing Historical Experiences and Ways of Life*. Princeton, NJ: Princeton University Press.

Lukowski, Jerzy (2003). *The European Nobility in the Eighteenth Century*. Houndsmills, Basingstoke, Hampshire; New York: Palgrave Macmillan.

Makdisi, Ussama (2002). 'Ottoman Orientalism'. *The American Historical Review* 107, no. 3: 768–96.

Makdisi, Ussama (1997). 'Reclaiming the Land of the Bible: Missionaries, Secularism, and Evangelical Modernity'. *The American Historical Review* 102, no. 3: 680–713.

Makdisi, Ussama (2002). 'Rethinking Ottoman Imperialism: Modernity, Violence and the Cultural Logic of Ottoman Reform'. In *The Empire in the City: Arab Provincial Capitals in the Late Ottoman Empire*, edited by Jens Hanssen, Thomas Philipp, and Stefan Weber. 29–48. Beirut and Würzburg: Ergon in Kommission.

Malmîsanij (2004). *Diyarbekirli Cemilpaşazadeler ve Kürt Milliyetçiliği*. İstanbul: Avesta.

Malmîsanij (2009). *Cizira Botanlı Bedirhaniler ve Bedirhani Ailesi Derneği'nin Tutanakları*. 1. baskı. Istanbul: Avesta.

Mardin, Şerif (1969). 'Power, Civil Society and Culture in the Ottoman Empire'. *Comparative Studies in Society and History* 11, no. 3: 258–81.

Masters, Bruce (2006). 'Semi-Autonomous Forces in the Arab Provinces'. In *The Cambridge History of Turkey: The Later Ottoman Empire*, edited by Suraiya Faroqhi, 186–206. Cambridge: Cambridge University Press.

Masters, Bruce (2013). *The Arabs of the Ottoman Empire, 1516–1918: A Social and Cultural History*. Cambridge: Cambridge University Press.

Matuz, Josef (1982). 'The Nature and Stages of Ottoman Feudalism'. *Asian and African Studies* 16: 281–92.

Maxwell, Alexander and Tim Smith (2015). 'Positing "Not-yet-Nationalism": Limits to the Impact of Nationalism Theory on Kurdish Historiography'. *Nationalities Papers* 43, no. 5: 771–87.

McGowan, Bruce (1994). 'The Age of the Ayans, 1699–1812'. In *An Economic and Social History of the Ottoman Empire, 2: 1600–1914*, edited by Halil Inalcik and Donald Quataert Cambridge: Cambridge University Press.

Menchinger, Ethan L., Frank Castiglione and Veysel Şimşek eds (2020). *Ottoman War and Peace Studies in Honor of Virginia H. Aksan*. Leiden; Boston: Brill.

Ménage, V. L. (1966). 'Some Notes on the "Devshirme"'. *Bulletin of the School of Oriental and African Studies, University of London* 29, no. 1: 64–78.

Menek, Abdulkadir (2011). *Kürt Meselesi ve Said Nursi*. Yenibosna, İstanbul: Nesil.

Mikhail, Alan and Christine M. Philliou (2012). 'The Ottoman Empire and the Imperial Turn'. *Comparative Studies in Society and History* 54, no. 04: 721–45.

Miller, Owen (2018). 'Rethinking the Violence in the Sasun Mountains (1893–1894)'. *Études Arméniennes Contemporaines*, no. 10 (30 March): 97–123.

Miller, Owen (2017). '"Back to the Homeland" (Tebi Yergir): Or, How Peasants Became Revolutionaries in Muş'. *Journal of the Ottoman and Turkish Studies Association* 4, no. 2: 287–308.

Minawi, Mostafa (2016). 'Telegraphs and Territoriality in Ottoman Africa and Arabia during the Age of High Imperialism'. *Journal of Balkan and Near Eastern Studies* 18, no. 6 (1 November): 567–87.

Minawi, Mostafa (2016). *The Ottoman Scramble for Africa: Empire and Diplomacy in the Sahara and the Hijaz*. Stanford, CA: Stanford University Press.

Mitchell, Timothy (1990). 'Everyday Metaphors of Power'. *Theory and Society* 19, no. 5: 545–77.

Mongia, Radhika V. (2007). 'Historicizing State Sovereignty: Inequality and the Form of Equivalence'. *Comparative Studies in Society and History* 49, no. 02 (April): 384–411.

Mukhopadhyay, Dipali (2014). *Warlords, Strongman Governors, and the State in Afghanistan*. Cambridge: Cambridge University Press.

Mundy, Martha and Richard Saumarez Smith eds (2007). *Governing Property, Making the Modern State: Law, Administration and Production in Ottoman Syria*. London: I. B. Tauris.

Murphey, Rhoads (2011). *Exploring Ottoman Sovereignty: Tradition, Image and Practice in the Ottoman Imperial Household, 1400–1800*. London: Continuum.

Murphey, Rhoads (1985). *Kanun-Name-i Sultani Li'Aziz Efendi: Aziz Efendi's Book of Sultanic Laws and Regulations: An Agenda for Reform by a Seventeenth-Century Ottoman Statesman*. Cambridge, MA: Harvard University Press.

Select Bibliography

Murphey, Rhoads (2006). *Ottoman Warfare, 1500–1700*. London: Routledge.

Murphey, Rhoads (1993). 'Süleyman's Eastern Policy'. In *Süleymân the Second and His Time*, edited by Cemal Kafadar and Halil Inalcik Istanbul: Isis Press.

Nalbandian, Louise (2018). *The Armenian Revolutionary Movement: The Development of Armenian Political Parties through the Nineteenth Century*. Berkeley, CA: University of California Press.

Nirenberg, David (2015). *Communities of Violence: Persecution of Minorities in the Middle Ages*. Updated edn with a new preface by the author. Princeton, NJ: Princeton University Press.

Nutini, Hugo G. (2004). *The Mexican Aristocracy: An Expressive Ethnography, 1910–2000*. Austin, TX: University of Texas Press.

Nutini, Hugo G. (1995). *The Wages of Conquest: The Mexican Aristocracy in the Context of Western Aristocracies*. Ann Arbor, MI: University of Michigan Press.

Ohanian, Daniel (2017). 'Collaboration in Ottoman Governance: The c. 1907 Imperial Census and the Armenian Apostolic Patriarchate of Istanbul'. *Journal of the Ottoman and Turkish Studies Association* 4, no. 2: 365–80.

Okkar, Emine (2010). 'Çarsancak Tarihi'. *Türk Dünyası Araştırmaları*, no. 186: 53–74.

Oktay, Adnan (2016). *Terceme-i Tevarih-i Şeref Han*. İstanbul: Nûbihar Yayınları.

Olson, Robert (1989). *The Emergence of Kurdish Nationalism and the Sheikh Said Rebellion, 1880–1925*. Austin, TX: University of Texas Press.

Olson, Robert (2000). 'The Kurdish Rebellions of Sheikh Said (1925), Mt. Ararat (1930), and Dersim (1937–8): Their Impact on the Development of the Turkish Air Force and on Kurdish and Turkish Nationalism'. *Die Welt Des Islams* 40, no. 1: 67–94.

Öncel, Fatma (2017). 'Land, Tax and Power in the Ottoman Provinces: The Malikane-Mukataa of Esma Sultan in Alasonya (c. 1780–1825)'. *Turkish Historical Review* 8, no. 1: 54–74.

Ortaylı, İlber (1974). *Tanzimattan sonra mahalli idareler (1840–1878)*. Ankara: TODAİE.

Ortner, Sherry B. (1995). 'Resistance and the Problem of Ethnographic Refusal'. *Comparative Studies in Society and History* 37, no. 1 (January): 173–93.

Osterhammel, Jürgen (2015). *The Transformation of the World: A Global History of the Nineteenth Century*. Princeton University Press.

Owen, Roger and Martin P. Bunton eds (2000). *New Perspectives on Property and Land in the Middle East*. Harvard Middle Eastern Monographs, 34. Cambridge, MA: Distributed for the Center for Middle Eastern Studies of Harvard University by Harvard University Press.

Öz, Mehmet (2003). 'Ottoman Provincial Administration in Eastern and Southeastern Anatolia: The Case of Bidlis in the Sixteenth Century'. In *Ottoman Borderlands: Issues, Personalities, and Political Changes*, edited by Kemal H. Karpat and Robert W. Zens, 145–156. Madison, WI: University of Wisconsin Press.

Özbek, Nadir (2015). *İmparatorluğun bedeli: Osmanlı'da vergi, siyaset ve toplumsal adalet (1839–1908)*. Istanbul: Boğaziçi Üniversitesi Yayınevi.

Özbek, Nadir (2018). 'Tax Farming in the Nineteenth-Century Ottoman Empire: Institutional Backwardness or the Emergence of Modern Public Finance?'. *The Journal of Interdisciplinary History* 49, no. 2 (1 August): 219–45.

Özbek, Nadir (2012). 'The Politics of Taxation and the "Armenian Question" during the Late Ottoman Empire, 1876–1908'. *Comparative Studies in Society and History* 54, no. 4: 770–97.

Özcan, Abdülkadir. (2001). 'Kapıcı'. In *TDV İslâm Ansiklopedisi*, 24: 345–7. İstanbul: Türkiye Diyanet Vakfı. Accessed 1 March 2021 https://islamansiklopedisi.org.tr/kapici

Özcan, Abdülkadir (2007). 'Redif'. In *TDV İslâm Ansiklopedisi*, 34: 524–6. İstanbul: Türkiye Diyanet Vakfı. Accessed 1 March 2021 https://islamansiklopedisi.org.tr/redif--ordu.

Özgül, İbrahim and Nazım Kartal (2019). *Osmanlı'da yerel yönetimlerin gelişimi ve yerel yönetim metinleri*. Istanbul: Hiperlink Eğitim.

Özil, Ayşe (2019). 'Whose Property Is It? The State, Non-Muslim Communities, and the Question of Property Ownership from the Late Ottoman Empire through the Turkish Nation State'. *Journal of the Ottoman and Turkish Studies Association* 6, no. 1: 211–35.

Özkaya, Yücel (1977). *Osmanli İmparatorluğu'nda Ayanlık*. Ankara: Ankara Üniversitesi Basimevi.

Özkaya, Yücel (1992). 'Anadolu'daki Büyük Hanedanlıklar'. *Belleten* 56: 809–46.

Özoğlu, Hakan (2004). *Kurdish Notables and the Ottoman State: Evolving Identities, Competing Loyalties, and Shifting Boundaries*. Albany, NY: State University of New York Press.

Özoğlu, Hakan (1996). 'State–Tribe Relations: Kurdish Tribalism in the 16th- and 17th-Century Ottoman Empire'. *British Journal of Middle Eastern Studies* 23, no. 1: 5–27.

Özok-Gündoğan, Nilay (2012). 'A "Peripheral" Approach to the 1908 Revolution in the Ottoman Empire: Land Disputes in Peasant Petitions in Post-Revolutionary Diyarbekir'. In *Social Relations in Ottoman Diyarbekir*, edited by Joost Jongerden and Jelle Verheij, 179–215. *1870–1915*. Leiden; Boston: Brill.

Özok-Gündoğan, Nilay (2020). 'Can One Save the Voices of the Ordinary Kurds Fom the Enourmous Condescension of Posterity? An Agenda for Social History in Kurdish Historical Writings'. In *Armenians and Kurds in the Late Ottoman Empire*, edited by Ümit Kurt and Ara Sarafian 95–114. Fresno, CA: California State University Press.

Özok-Gündoğan, Nilay (2020). 'Counting the Population and the Wealth in an "Unruly" Land: Census Making as a Social Process in Ottoman Kurdistan, 1830–50'. *Journal of Social History* 53, no. 3 (1 March): 763–91.

Özok-Gündoğan, Nilay (2014). 'Ruling the Periphery, Governing the Land: The Making of the Modern Ottoman State in Kurdistan, 1840–70'. *Comparative*

Studies of South Asia, Africa and the Middle East 34, no. 1 (31 May): 160–75.
Özvar, Erol (2013). 'Voyvoda'. In TDV *İslam Ansiklopedisi*, 43: 129–31. Istanbul Türkiye Diyanet Vakfı.
Özvar, Erol and Arif Bilgin (2008). *Selçukludan Cumhuriyete Şehir Yönetimi*. Beykoz, İstanbul: TDBB: Türk Dünyasi Belediyeler Birliği.
Pakalın, Mehmet Zeki (1954). *Osmanli Tarih Deyimleri ve Terimleri sözlüğü*. Millî Eğitim Basımevi.
Pamuk, Şevket (2014). 'Fiscal Centralisation and the Rise of the Modern State in the Ottoman Empire'. *The Medieval History Journal* 17, no. 1 (1 April): 1–26.
Pamuk, Şevket (2012). 'The Evolution of Fiscal Institutions in the Ottoman Empire, 1500–1914'. In *The Rise of Fiscal States: A Global History, 1500–1914*, edited by Yun Casalilla, Bartolomé, Patrick O'Brien, and Francisco Comín Comín 304–31. Cambridge: Cambridge University Press.
Panaite, Viorel (2013). 'The Legal and Political Status of Wallachia and Moldavia in Relation to the Ottoman Porte'. In *The European Tributary States of the Ottoman Empire in the Sixteenth and Seventeenth Centuries*, edited by Gábor Kármán and Lovro Kunčević 7–42. Leiden: Brill.
Papazian, Dikran S. (1960). *History of Palu's Havav Village* [*Badmutyun Palu Havav kyughi*]. Mshag, Beirut.
Papp, Sándor (2013). 'The System of Autonomous Muslim and Christian Communities, Churches, and States in the Ottoman Empire'. In *The European Tributary States of the Ottoman Empire in the Sixteenth and Seventeenth Centuries*, edited by Gábor Kármán and Lovro Kunčević 375–419. Leiden: Brill.
Pearce, R. (1983). 'Sharecropping: Towards a Marxist View'. *The Journal of Peasant Studies* 10, nos 2–3 (1 January): 42–70.
Pekol, Fatih (2017). 'Zirki Beylikleri ve Beyleri Tarihi'. MA, Mardin Artuklu University.
Perdue, Peter C. 'China and Other Colonial Empires' (2009). *Journal of American–East Asian Relations* 16, no. 1–2 (1 January): 85–103.
Perdue, Peter C. (2010). *China Marches West the Qing Conquest of Central Eurasia*. Cambridge, MA: Harvard University Press.
Petrov, Milen V. (2004). 'Everyday Forms of Compliance: Subaltern Commentaries on Ottoman Reform, 1864–1868'. *Comparative Studies in Society and History* 46, no. 4: 730–59.
Pfeiffer, Judith and Sholeh A. Quinn eds (2006). *History and Historiography of Post-Mongol Central Asia and the Middle East: Studies in Honor of John E. Woods*. Wiesbaden: Harrassowitz Verlag.
Philliou, Christine (2008). 'The Paradox of Perceptions: Interpreting the Ottoman Past through the National Present'. *Middle Eastern Studies* 44, no. 5 (1 September): 661–75.
Pitcher, Donald Edgar (1973). *An Historical Geography of the Ottoman Empire: From Earliest Times to the End of the Sixteenth Century*. Leiden: Brill.

Poggi, Gianfranco (1978). *The Development of the Modern State: A Sociological Introduction.* 1st edn. Stanford, CA: Stanford University Press.
Polatel, Mehmet (2017). 'Armenians and the Land Question in the Ottoman Empire, 1870–1914'. Ph.D. dissertation, Boğaziçi University.
Polatel, Mehmet (2015). 'Land Disputes and Reform Debates in the Eastern Provinces'. *World War I and the End of the Ottomans: From the Balkan Wars to the Armenian Genocide,* edited by Hans-Lukas Kieser, Kerem Öktem, and Maurus Reinkowski 169–87. London: I. B. Tauris.
Polatel, Mehmet (2016). 'The Complete Ruin of a District: The Sasun Massacre of 1894'. In *The Ottoman East in the Nineteenth Century: Societies, Identities, and Politics,* edited by Yaşar Tolga Cora, Dzovinar Derderian, and Ali Sipahi, 179–98. London; New York: I. B. Tauris.
Prakash, Gyan (1990). 'Writing Post-Orientalist Histories of the Third World: Perspectives from Indian Historiography'. *Comparative Studies in Society and History* 32, no. 2 (April): 383–408.
Quataert, Donald (2006). *Miners and the State in the Ottoman Empire: The Zonguldak Coalfield, 1822–1920.* New York: Berghahn.
Quataert, Donald (2003). 'Ottoman History Writing and Changing Attitudes towards the Notion of "Decline"'. *History Compass* 1, no. 1: 1–9.
Quataert, Donald (1994). 'Overview of the Nineteenth Century'. In *An Economic and Social History of the Ottoman Empire, 1300–1914,* edited by Halil Inalcık with Donald Quataert 761–76. Cambridge: Cambridge University Press.
Quataert, Donald (2003). 'Recent Writings in Late Ottoman History'. *International Journal of Middle East Studies* 35, no. 1 (February): 133–9.
Quataert, Donald (2006). 'Tanzimat Dönemi'nde Ekonominin Temel Problemleri'. In *Tanzimat: Değişim Sürecinde Osmanlı İmparatorluğu.* edited by Halil İnalcık and Mehmet Seyitdanlıoğlu Trans. Fatma Acun, 447–55. Istanbul: Phoenix Yayınevi.
Rady, M. (2000). *Nobility, Land and Service in Medieval Hungary,* Basingstoke and New York: Palgrave Macmillan.
Redhouse, James W. (1890). *Turkish and English Lexicon.* Istanbul: Çağrı Yayınları.
Reid, James J. (2000). 'Rozhîkî Revolt, 1065/1655'. *Journal of Kurdish Studies* 3, no. 0 (1 January): 13–40.
Rogan, Eugene L. (2002). *Frontiers of the State in the Late Ottoman Empire: Transjordan, 1850–1921.* Cambridge; New York: Cambridge University Press.
Şahin, İlhan (1999). 'XV. ve XVI. Yüzyıllarda Osmanlı Taşra Teşkilâtının'. Özellikleri. *XV ve XVI. Asırları Türk Asrı Yapan Değerler,* Abdülkadir Özcan. İstanbul. İnsani İlimler Araştırma Vakfı: 233–58.
Sahiner, Araks (1995). 'The Sarrafs of Istanbul: Financiers of the Empire'. MA thesis, Istanbul: Boğaziçi University.
Saito, Kumiko (2018). '16. ve 17. Yüzyıllar Doğu ve Güneydoğu Anadolusu'nda Timarların Çeşitli Biçimleri: Farklı Uygulamalara Tek İsim Koymak'. *Osmanlı Araştırmaları* 51, no. 51 (20 April): 63–113.

Select Bibliography

Sakaoglu, Necdet (1988). *Köse Paşa Hanedanı*. Ankara: Tarih Vakfi.

Salzmann, Ariel (1993). 'An Ancien Régime Revisited: "Privatization" and Political Economy in the Eighteenth-Century Ottoman Empire'. *Politics & Society* 21, no. 4 (1 December): 393–423.

Salzmann, Ariel (1996). 'Measures of Empire: Tax Farmers and the Ottoman Ancien Regime, 1695–1807'. Ph.D. dissertation, New York University.

Salzmann, Ariel (2004). *Tocqueville in the Ottoman Empire Rival Paths to the Modern State*. Leiden: Brill.

Samuk, Hidayet (2017). 'Servi Bölgesi ve Köyleri', *Bingöl Araştırmaları Dergisi* 4, no. 1 (9 October): 9–40.

Saraçoğlu, M. Safa (2008). 'Some Aspects of Ottoman Governmentality at the Local Level: The Judicio-Administrative Sphere of the Vidin County in the 1860s and 1870s'. *Ab Imperio* 2008, no. 2: 223–54.

Saraçoğlu, M. Safa (2016). 'Resilient Notables: Looking at the Transformation of the Ottoman Empire from the Local Level 1'. In *Contested Spaces of Nobility in Early Modern Europe*, edited by Charles Lipp and Matthew P. Romaniello 257–77. Routledge.

Saraçoğlu, M. Safa (2018). *Nineteenth-century Local Governance in Ottoman Bulgaria: Politics in Provincial Councils*. Edinburgh: Edinburgh University Press.

Sariyannis, Marinos (2018). *A History of Ottoman Political Thought up to the Early Nineteenth Century*. Leiden; Boston: Brill.

Saul, Nigel (1987). *Scenes from Provincial Life: Knightly Families in Sussex, 1280–1400*. Oxford: New York: Oxford University Press.

Sayce, A. H. (1925). 'The Kingdom of Urartu (Van)'. In *The Cambridge Ancient History: The Assyrian Empire, 1925*, 3: edited by J. B. Bury, S. A. Cook, F. E. Adcock, M. P. Charlesworth and C. T. Seltman 169–86. Cambridge: Cambridge University Press.

Scalbert-Yücel, Clémence and Marie Le Ray (2006). 'Knowledge, Ideology and Power. Deconstructing Kurdish Studies'. *European Journal of Turkish Studies. Social Sciences on Contemporary Turkey*, no. 5 (31 December).

Schull, Kent and Christine Isom-Verhaaren eds (2016). *Living in the Ottoman Realm: Empire and Identity, 13th–20th Centuries*. Bloomington, IN: Indiana University Press, March.

Scott, H. M. ed. (2007). *The European Nobilities in the Seventeenth and Eighteenth Centuries*: Vol. 1: Western and Southern Europe 2nd edn. New York: Palgrave Macmillan.

Scott, H. M. and Christopher Storrs (2007). 'The Consolidation of Noble Power in Europe, c. 1600–1800'. In *The European Nobilities in the Seventeenth and Eighteenth Centuries, Vol. 1: Western and Southern Europe*, edited by H. M. Scott, 1–60. New York: Palgrave Macmillan.

Scott, James C. (1999). *Seeing Like a State: How Certain Schemes to Improve the Human Condition Have Failed*. New Haven, CT: Yale University Press.

Şener, Abdüllatif (1990). *Tanzimat Dönemi Osmanlı Vergi Sistemi*. Ankara: İşaret.

Şenyurt, Ali (2016). '18. ve 19. Yüzyıllarda Osmanlı Devleti'nde Poliçe Kullanımı ve Poliçeci Esnafı'. Ph.D. dissertation, Istanbul University.

Şenyurt, Ali (2016). 'Osmanlı Devleti'nde Poliçe Kullanımının Hukuki Esasları ve Uluslarası Lahey Konferansı'. *Tarih ve Uygarlık* 9: 143–61.

Sertoğlu, Midhat (1992). *Sofyalı Ali Çavuş Kanunnamesi.* İstanbul: Marmara Üniversitesi Yayınları.

Sevin, Veli (1994). 'Three Urartian Rock-Cut Tombs from Palu'. *Tel Aviv* 21, no. 1 (March): 58–67.

Seyitdanlıoğlu, Mehmet (1994). *Tanzimat devrinde Meclis-i Vâlâ, 1838–1868.* Ankara: Türk Tarih Kurumu Basımevi.

Şimşek, Veysel (2005). 'Ottoman Military Recruitment and the Recruit: 1826–1853'. MA thesis, Bilkent University.

Şimşek, Veysel (2015). 'The Grand Strategy of the Ottoman Empire, 1826–1841'. Ph.D dissertation, McMaster University.

Sinclair, T. A. (1989). *Eastern Turkey: An Architectural & Archaeological Survey, Volume III.* London: Pindar Press.

Sinclair, Thomas A. (2003). 'The Ottoman Arrangements for the Tribal Principalities of the Lake Van Region of the Sixteenth Century'. In *Ottoman Borderlands: Issues, Personalities, and Political Changes*, edited by Kemal H. Karpat and Robert W. Zens; 119–44. Madison: University of Wisconsin Press.

Sluglett, Peter and Marion Farouk-Sluglett (1984). 'The Application of the 1858 Land Code in Greater Syria: Some Preliminary Observations'. In *Land Tenure and Social Transformation in the Middle East*, edited by Tarif Khalidi, Beirut: American University of Beirut.

Smith, Jay M. (2006). 'Introduction: Nobility after Revisionism'. In *The French Nobility in the Eighteenth Century: Reassessments and New Approaches*, edited by Jay M. Smith 1–18. University Park, PA: Penn State University Press.

Smith, Jay M. ed. (2006). *The French Nobility in the Eighteenth Century: Reassessments and New Approaches.* University Park, PA: Penn State Press.

Sneath, David (2007). *The Headless State: Aristocratic Orders, Kinship Society, and Misrepresentations of Nomadic Inner Asia.* New York: Columbia University Press.

Solakzade, Mehmet Hemdemî Çelebi and Vâhid Çabuk (1989). *Solak-zâde tarihi.* Ankara: Kültür Bakanlığı.

Soleimani, Kamal (2016). 'Islamic Revivalism and Kurdish Nationalism in Sheikh Ubeydullah's Poetic Oeuvre'. *Kurdish Studies* 4, no. 1: 5–24.

Sönmez, Ebru (2006). 'An Acem Statesman in the Ottoman Court: İdris-i Bidlîsî and the Making of the Ottoman Polict on Iran'. MA thesis, Boğaziçi University.

Strayer, Joseph R. (2005). *On the Medieval Origins of the Modern State.* 2nd edn. Princeton, NJ: Princeton University Press.

Takamatsu, Yoichi (2004). 'Ottoman Income Survey (1840–1846)'. In *The Ottoman State and Societies in Change: A Study of the Nineteenth Century Temettuat Registers*, Hayashi Kayoko and Mahir Aydın, 15–45 London: Kegan Paul.

Select Bibliography

Taşkın, Ünal. 'Osmanlı Devletinde Kullanılan Ölçü ve Tartı Birimleri'. MA thesis, Fırat University.

Tezcan, Baki (2000). 'The Development of the Use of "Kurdistan" as a Geographical Description and the Incorporation of This Region into the Ottoman Empire in the 16th Century'. In *The Great Ottoman, Turkish Civilisation. Philosophy, Science and Institutions*, Vol. 3, edited by Kemal Çiçek, 540–53. Ankara: Yeni Türkiye.

Tilly, Charles (1993). *Coercion, Capital and European States: AD 990–1992*. Cambridge: Wiley-Blackwell.

Tilly, Louise A. (1980). 'Social History and Its Critics'. *Theory and Society* 9, no. 5: 668–70.

Tızlak, Fahrettin (1991). '*Keban-Ergani Yöresinde Madencilik (1775–1850)*'. Ph.D. dissertation, Fırat University.

Tızlak, Fahrettin (2013). 'XVIII. Yüzyıl Sonu İşe XIX. Yüzyılın İlk Yarısında Harput Çevresinde Madencilik Faaliyetleri', 349–65. Elazığ: Fırat Üniversitesi Harput Uygulama ve Araştırma Merkezi.

Toledano, Ehud R. (1997). 'The Emergence of Ottoman-Local Elites (1700–1900): A Framework for Research'. In *Middle Eastern Politics and Ideas: A History from Within*, edited by Ilan Pappe and Moshe Ma'oz 145–62. London: I. B. Tauris.

Tuncer, Orhan Cezmi (1999). 'Diyarbakır-Harput Kervan Yolu'. *Güzel Sanatlar Enstitüsü Dergisi* 5: 151–72.

Turan, Şerafettin (1961). 'XVII. Yüzyılda Osmanlı İmparatorluğu'nun İdari Taksimatı: H.1041/M.1631–32 Tarihli Bir İdari Taksimat Defteri'. In *Atatürk Üniversitesi 1961 Yıllığı*, 201–32. Erzurum: Atatürk Üniversitesi.

Türesay, Özgür (2013). 'The Ottoman Empire Seen through the Lens of Postcolonoal Studies'. *Revue d'histoire Moderne et Contemporaine* 60, no. 2 (February): 127–45.

Turhan, Fatma Sel (2014). *The Ottoman Empire and the Bosnian Uprising: Janissaries, Modernisation and Rebellion in the Nineteenth Century*. London: I. B. Tauris.

Ueno, Masayuki (2013). '"For the Fatherland and the State": Armenians Negotiate the Tanzimat Reforms'. *International Journal of Middle East Studies* 45, no. 1: 93–109.

Uğur, Ahmet (1988). 'Doğu ve Güneydoğu'da Bazı Yerlerin Osmanlı İmparatorluğuna Katılması'. *Erciyes Üniversitesi İlâhiyat Fakültesi Dergisi* 5.

Ünal, Mehmet Ali (1987). 'Osmanlı İmparatorluğu'nda Müsâdere'. *Türk Dünyası Araştırmaları Dergisi* 49: 95–111.

Ünal, Mehmet Ali (1994). 'XVI. ve XVII. Yüzyıllarda Diyarbekir Eyaletine Tabi Sancakların İdari Statüleri (1986), Ankara 1994, Ss. 2211–2220'. In *X. Türk Tarih Kongresi'ne Sunulan Bildiriler (1986)*, 5: 2,211–20. Ankara.

Ünal, Mehmet Ali (1992). 'XVI. Yüzyılda Palu Hükümeti'. *Ondokuz Mayıs Üniversitesi Eğitim Fakültesi Dergisi* 7, no. 1.

Ungor, Ugur Umit (2012). *The Making of Modern Turkey: Nation and State in Eastern Anatolia, 1913–1950*. 1st edn. Oxford: Oxford University Press.

Uras, Esat and Cengiz Kürşat (1988). *The Armenians in History and the Armenian Question*. Istanbul: Documentary Publications.

Vali, Abbas (ed.) (2003). *Essays on the Origins of Kurdish Nationalism*. Costa Mesa, CA: Mazda.

Vali, Abbas (2003). 'Genealogies of the Kurds: Constructions of Nation and National Identity in Kurdish Historical'. In *Essays on the Origins of Kurdish Nationalism*, edited by Abbas Vali 58–105. Costa Mesa, CA: Mazda.

Vali, Abbas (2003). 'Nationalism and the Question of Origins'. In *Essays on the Origins of Kurdish Nationalism*, edited by Abbas Vali 1–13. Costa Mesa, CA: Mazda.

Verheij, Jelle (1998). 'Les frères de terre et d'eau': sur le rôle des Kurdes dans les massacres arméniens de 1894–1896'. In *Islam des Kurdes* (special issue of *Les Annales de l'Autre islam*), edited by Martin van Bruinessen and Joyce Blau, 225–76. Paris: Institut national des langues et civilisations orientales.

Verheij, Jelle (2012). 'Diyarbekir and the Armenian crisis of 1895 – the Fate of the Countryside'. In, *Social Relations in Ottoman Diyarbekir, 1870–1915*, edited by Jelle Verheij and Joost Jongerden 333–44. Leiden [etc.]: Brill.

Verheij, Jelle (2018). '"The Year of the Firman": The 1895 Massacres in Hizan and Şirvan (Bitlis Vilayet)'. *Études Arméniennes Contemporaines*, no. 10 (30 March): 125–59.

Verheij, Jelle and Suavi Aydın (2012). 'Confusion in the Cauldron: Some Notes on Ethno-Religious Groups, Local Powers, and the Ottoman State in Diyarbekir Province, 1800–1870'. *Social relations in Ottoman Diyarbekir, 1870–1915*, edited by Jelle Verheij and Joost Jongerden (eds), 15–54. Leiden [etc.]: Brill.

Wasiucionek, Michal (2019). *The Ottomans and Eastern Europe: Borders and Political Patronage in the Early Modern World*. Bloomsbury.

Welskopp, Thomas (2010). 'Social History'. In *Writing History: Theory and Practice*, edited by Stefan Berger, Heiko Feldner and Kevin Passmore. 203–22. London: Bloomsbury Academic.

Winter, Stefan (2006). 'The Other "Nahdah": The Bedirxans, The Millîs and the Tribal Roots of Kurdish Nationalism in Syria'. *Oriente Moderno* 25 (86), no. 3: 461–74.

Woods, John E. (1999). *The Aqquyunlu: Clan, Confederation, Empire*. Revised, expanded edn. Salt Lake City: University of Utah Press.

Yadirgi, Veli (2017). *The Political Economy of the Kurds of Turkey: From the Ottoman Empire to the Turkish Republic*. Cambridge: Cambridge University Press.

Yapıcı, Süleyman (2018). '1841 Nüfus Defterlerinde Palu'. In *Fırat Üniversitesi Harput Uygulama ve Araştırma Merkezi Uluslararası Palu Sempozyumu Bildiriler Kitabı*, 1: 231–56. Elazığ: Fırat Üniversitesi Matbaası.

Yapıcı, Süleyman (2016). *Palu 1841 Nüfus ve Toplum Yapısı*. Elazığ: Süleyman Yapıcı.

Yapıcı, Süleyman (2004). *Palu: Tarih, Kültür, Idari ve Sosyal Yapı*. Elazığ: Süleyman Yapıcı.

Select Bibliography

Yarman, Arsen (2010). *Palu-Harput, 1878 Raporlar*. Vol. 2. Derlem.

Yaycıoğlu, Ali (2011). 'Provincial Power-holders and the Empire in the Late Ottoman World: Conflict or Partnership?' In *The Ottoman World*, edited by Christine Woodhead, 436–52. Abingdon: Routledge.

Yaycıoğlu, Ali (2019). 'Perdenin Arkasındakiler: Osmanlı İmparatorluğunda Sarraflar ve Finans Ağları Üzerine Bir Deneme'. *Journal of Turkish Studies* (Türklük Bilgisi Araştırmaları): Festschrift in Honor of Özer Ergenç, vol. 51 (December), 375–96.

Yaycıoğlu, Ali (2016). *Partners of the Empire: The Crisis of the Ottoman Order in the Age of Revolutions*. Stanford, CA: Stanford University Press.

Yıldız, Gültekin (2009). *Neferin adı yok: zorunlu askerliğe geçiş sürecinde Osmanlı devleti'nde siyaset, ordu ve toplum, 1826–1839*. Istanbul: Kitabevi.

Yılmazçelik, İbrahim (1995). *XIX. Yüzyılın İlk Yarısında Diyarbakır: (1790–1840): Fizikî, İdarî ve Sosyo-Ekonomik Yapı)*. Ankara: Türk Tarih Kurumu Basımevi.

Yılmazçelik, İbrahim (2019). *Osmanlı döneminde Diyarbakır üzerine bazı tespitler ve Diyarbakır Şer'iyye sicilleri: Katalog ve fihristleri*. Istanbul: Hiperlink Yayınlari.

Yun-Casalilla, Bartolomé, Patrick K. O'Brien, Patrick O'Brien and Francisco Comín Comín eds (2012). *The Rise of Fiscal States: A Global History, 1500–1914*. Cambridge; New York: Cambridge University Press.

Ze'evi, Dror and Ehud R. Toledano eds (2015). *Society, Law, and Culture in the Middle East: Modernities in the Making*. Warsaw/Berlin De Gruyter Open.

Zmora, Hillay (2002). *Monarchy, Aristocracy and State in Europe 1300–1800*. London; New York: Routledge.

Index

Note: f indicates figure, m indicates map, n indicates note, *t* indicates table

Abbas Agha, 86
Abbasids, 51, 64
Abbas Mirza, 66
ABCFM (American Board of Commissioners for Foreign Missions), 275n115
Abdülgafur Beg, 77, 85, 142
Abdülhamid II, 249–50, 255, 260
Abdullah Beg
  appointment as *müdür*, 222
  exile of, 3, 168–9, 177–8
  land distribution following death of, 178–84, 216n81, 245
  Meclis-i Vâlâ case, 166–9
  *sarraf*s and, 143
  tax farming and collection by, 84, 139–41, 146, 152, 202
  Weşin violence and, 1–2, 27, 157–71
Abdullah Efendi, 223, 224, 233
Abdüllatif (mine supervisor), 142
Abdülmecid I, 16, 120, 180
Abdülmesih Efendi, 235–6
Abdülvahhab Agha, 227
Abdürrahim Beg, 155n49
Abdurrahman Beg, 239n37
Abou-El-Haj, Rifa'at, 67
Abrank village, 24, 195–6, 196*t*
Adanır, Fikret, 7
*agha*s (tribal chiefs), 51, 66, 179, 183, 184–6, 188–9; *see also specific individuals*

Ágoston, Gábor, 47, 72
agrarian taxes
  Armenians and, 251–2
  competition over, 82–4
  Kurdish nobility's exemptions from, 80
  noksan-ı arz, 203–7, 205–6*t*
  sharecroppers and, 147–51
  Tanzimat programme and, 145–52, 201–3
Ahmed I, 96n16, 180
Ahmed Agha, 201
Ahmed Aziz, 101n128
Ahmed Beg, 91, 194
Ahmed Pasha, 134
Akiba, Jun, 150
Akkoyunlu confederation, 59n20, 60n39, 64
Alaaddin Beg, 66
Alanoğlu, Murat, 28n3, 30n11
Ali Agha, 86, 157, 215n72
Ali Beg, 210
Ali Çavuş, 266
Ali Efendi, 117
Ali Pasha Han, 155n53
Alsancakli, Sacha, 59n32
Altıntaş, Toygun, 272n66
American Board of Commissioners for Foreign Missions (ABCFM), 275n115
Anadolu Kumpanyası (professional association), 155n49

330

Index

Anatolian Army, 190
Aricanli, Tosun, 213n26
Armenak Efendi, 235
Armenian Revolutionary Federation (*Dashnaktsutiun*), 255
Armenians
  Berlin Treaty (1878) and, 235, 238, 242, 249
  crisis of representation for, 207–10
  Genocide of 1915, 22, 284
  *kaymakam*s and, 235–6, 238
  land purchases by, 191, 192–4, 199, 200
  Massacres of 1895, 27, 262–9, 284
  müdür appointments and, 228
  National Constitution (1863), 249
  noksan-ı arz and, 207
  Palu's historical geography and, 21–2
  as purchasers of confiscated lands, 20
  as *sarraf*s (creditors), 142–5, 154n43, 253
  Sasun Massacre (1894), 276n119
  sharecropping and, 187
arsenic sulphide (*zırnık*) mines, 112
Artuqid dynasty, 21
aşiret askeri (tribal forces), 66
Asiye Hanım, 179
Astourian, Stephan, 252–3
Ateş, Sabri, 6, 111, 124
Atmaca, Metin, 28–9n5, 32
avârız taxes, 81–2
Avedis (*sarraf*), 209–10
Azîz Efendi, 67, 68–9, 79, 84, 97n38
Azize Hanım, 245

Baban emirate, 2, 28–9n5
Bahadır Mehmed Agha, 228
Bahadıroğlu, Yavuz: *Mısır'a Doğru: Sefer-i Hümayûn*, 44
*baltacı*s, 74, 99n77
Barnum, Dr, 261–2, 275n115
Bayezid I, 7, 10
Becker, Seymour, 87
Bedirkhan Beg, 2, 111, 113, 124, 132, 177
Behlül Pasha, 124
Berktay, Halil, 11–12
Berlin Treaty (1878), 235, 238, 242, 249
beylerbeyi (governors), 55, 62, 75
beylik câizesi, 78, 84

Bidlîsî, İdris-i, 44, 46–7, 48, 52, 58n13, 58n18, 65
Bitlis emirate, 50, 119
Bloch, Marc, 51
Blumi, Isa, 93
Bohtan emirate, 2, 119
Bosnia and Herzegovina, 33n33, 33n35, 35n59
Bourdieu, Pierre, 217n111
Boyadjian, Thomas, 258–9, 260, 262, 263
Boyajıyan, Yiğit Vartan, 254–5
Boz Agha, 160
bribery, 199, 226, 228, 233–4
British model of nobility and aristocracy, 14
Bruinessen, Martin van, 173n48, 214
Burhan Beg, 77–8
Burke, Peter, 95n3
Bush, M. L., 52

Cafer Pasha, 66
câize, 78–9
Canbakal, Hülya, 91, 157
Cannon, John, 14
Çarsancak, 76, 79, 202, 255
Çelebi, Evliyâ, 20–1, 33n32
Cemşîd Beg
  Kurdish nobility descended from, 2, 43–5
  land ownership and sales by, 180, 182–3, 195–7
  military assistance to Ottomans by, 65, 66, 96n11
  *seyyid*s and, 91
  temlîknâme granted to, 53, 54, 56, 61n51, 65, 80, 96n15
census processes, 39n115, 117–19, 251
centralisation processes
  agrarian sector and, 145–51
  of mining operations, 133–6
  of tax collection, 136–41
  see also Tanzimat (Re-organisation) period
Charlesworth, Neil, 216n76
*çiftlik*s, 84, 87–90, 94
Commission of Public Officials (*Me'mûrîn-i Mülkiye Komisyonu*), 236

conscription, 108, 113, 115–16, 126, 130n48, 223
çorbacıs, 193–4
corruption, 68, 196, 219, 225, 228, 233–4, 265
Çötelioğlu Abdüllatif Efendi, 195, 216n85
Çötelioğlu Mutaf Agha, 78
Çötelizade Hacı İbrahim Pasha, 137
Çötelizade İshak Pasha, 137
Council of Financial Accounting (*Meclis-i Muhasabe*), 188
Crimean Khanate, 8, 35n59
Çukurçeşme Han, 193, 197
Cuno, Kenneth, 181

Darphane-i Âmire (Imperial Mint), 62, 72, 76
Defterhane (Imperial Registry), 119, 180, 190
Dehqan, Mustafa, 61n52
Demirtaş, Feyzullah, 29n7
Derviş Pasha, 244
devşirme (child-levy) system, 10, 34n45
*dirlik*s (fiefs), 81
Divan-ı Hümayûn registers, 70
Diyarbekir
  Müşirliği established in, 114, 137
  tax collection in, 137–8
  unregistered lands in, 119
Diyarbekir Beylerbeğliği (administrative unit), 48
draft lottery system (*kur'a-i şeriyye*), 116, 219
Dündar, Fuat, 250
Dursun, Selçuk, 153n12

Edebali, Sheikh, 57n9
El-Hac Abdurrahman Seyyid, 92
El-Hâc Ali Beg, 146
El-Hâc İbrahim Reşid, 101n128
El-Hac Mustafa Seyyid, 92
emanet (trusteeship) system, 72, 76, 165, 204
Emetullah Hanım, 102n140
Emîne Habîbe, 270n17
Emir Balak, 21
Enis (governor of Diyarbekir), 264

enregisterement (*tahrir*s), 7, 32nn29–30, 33n33, 47, 48
Erekli Han, 70
Ergani mine, 18–19, 25, 62, 71–80, 93, 133–4, 143, 153n11
Ertem, Özge, 252
Erzurum Treaty (1823), 112
Esat Pasha, 194
Esmeryan, Ohannes, 256
Es-Seyyid Ahmed Beg, 146
Es-Seyyid Hüseyin Efendi, 78
Europe
  models of nobility and aristocracy in, 13–14
  sharecropping in, 148
  state formation in, 110

Fahri Beg, 225
Farouk-Sluglett, Marion, 181
Fazıl Beg, 270n17
Ferhâd Beg, 66
Feyzullah Beg, 134, 135
fiefdoms *see timar*s
Fouracre, Paul, 13–14
French model of nobility and aristocracy, 13–14

Galip Pasha, 128n23
Garian, Hampartsum, 254–5
Genç, Vural, 58n18, 61n52
Gerber, Haim, 181
Gökdere, 201–2, 206
Gölbaşı, Edip, 243, 277n144
Gülhane Decree (1839), 29n8, 108, 159
Gurdjian, Agop, 277n135
Gutman, David, 254, 273n69

Hacı Ali Beg, 139, 143
Hacı Bekirzâde Ahmed Beg, 134
Hacı Devlet Şah Beg, 143
Hacı Hüseyin Seyyid, 91
Hacı Mehmed Agha, 157, 164
Hacı Tahir Beg, 247–8
Hacı Timur Beg, 266
Hafız Hüseyin Efendi, 231, 232–3
Hafız Mehmed Pasha, 137–9, 140, 141, 143, 146, 153n23
Hâfız Mustafa Pasha, 70, 76

Index

hâkim (ruler), 1, 16, 19, 27, 52, 54, 62, 77, 84, 122, 133, 138, 139, 146, 153n3, 222, 224, 237, 243, 246, 268, 283; see also specific begs
Haldén, Peter, 14–15
Halid Beg, 44
Halil Beg, 85, 91
Hallward, Vice-Consul, 268
Hamdullah Beg, 146, 194
Hamidiye Light Cavalry, 6, 249–50, 269n3
Hammer-Purgstall, Joseph von, 33n35
Hamza Beg, 66
Han Mahmud, 113, 128n23
haraçgüzâr (tributary), 8
Haralambo Efendi, 236
Harput
    dispute resolution in, 150–1, 156n81
    localisation of Ottoman policies in, 135
    sharecropping in, 149, 150
    tax collection in, 137–8
    unregistered lands in, 119
Hasan Beg, 66, 225, 229
Hasan Efendi, 227–8
Haşim Beg, 245
Hazine-i Âmire (Imperial Treasury), 72, 198, 200
Hekim Yanaki, 143, 155n50
Hnchak Party, 255, 260
Hoca Nişan, 185
Hoca Sadeddin, 48
Hodgson, Marshall, 45
Hourani, Albert, 4–5, 6
Houston, Christopher, 30n11
hükümet status
    justice administration and, 17
    land ownership and, 122
    military service linked to, 70
    mine operations and, 75
    Ottoman state's recognition of, 7–8, 48, 49*m*, 53
    tahrirs and, 7–8, 32n29
    taxes and, 80–1, 83
    timar system and, 7–8, 32n29, 50
Hûn, 201–2, 206
Hüseyin Beg, 77–8, 84
Hüseyin Efendi, 46

İbrahim Beg (Palu *hâkim* in the 18th century)
    beylerbeyi status granted to, 62, 75
    land ownership and, 85, 270n17
    military support to Ottomans by, 69, 269n7
    tax collection by, 85, 194
İbrahim Begs (Palu nobles, 19th century)
    Armenians and, 244–5, 247, 266–7, 268
    land ownership and, 270n17
    *sarraf*s and, 143
    tax collection by, 194
İbrahim Pasha, 53, 65, 113
İbrahim Seyyid, 91
Ilkhanids, 64
iltizam (tax farms), 82; see also tax farming
Imperial Mint (*Darphane-i Âmire*), 72, 76
Imperial Registry (*Defterhane*), 119, 180, 190
Imperial Treasury (*Hazine-i Âmire*), 72, 198, 200
İnalcık, Halil, 47, 53, 95n5, 159, 182
income surveys (*tahrir-i temettüât*), 118
institutional infrastructure, 114–20
İskender Beg, 77, 82, 134, 135
Ismail, Shah, 46
İsmail Agha, 184
İsmail Beg, 86, 88, 91, 102n140, 132, 219, 225–6
İzoli tribe, 134–5, 141, 154n38

Janissary Army, 139
Joseph, Sabrina, 147–8
Jwaideh, Wadie, 170–1, 173n48

Kadre Hanım, 179
Kafadar, Cemal, 57n4
Kapıcızade el-Hâc Mehmed, 85
kapıkulu (slave army), 66
Kapucuoğlu Osman, 78
Karabegân, 162, 167, 201–2
Karacimşit, Mehmet, 61n51
Karaçor, 201–2, 206
Karakoyunlu confederation, 59n20, 60n39
Karpat, Kemal, 250
Katole Efendi, 236

*kaymakam*s (provincial administrators), 220, 229–36, 237
Keban mine, 18–19, 25, 62, 71–80, 133–4, 143
*kelekçi*s, 25, 74, 77
Keşşafzade dynasty, 223
Keyder, Çağlar, 88
Khoşmat village, 24, 197, 255
Khoury, Dina, 6, 89, 214n50
Kiğı mines, 73
Kiğork (Armenian patriarch), 228
Kigork (*sarraf*), 144
Kirişyân Dikran Efendi, 236
Kırlı, Cengiz, 228
kızılbaş, 67
Klein, Janet, 5–6, 249, 269n3
Köksal, Yonca, 137
Koloyian, Azarig, 255
*kömürcübaşı*s, 74
Kunt, Metin, 34n49
Kurdish nobility
  genealogies of, 50–2, 60n38
  honorific titles of, 51
  land control and, 80–90, 120–5
  military role of, 63–71
  mine operations and, 71–80
  noble privilege of, 52–5
  in Ottoman politico-administrative system, 47–50
  see also Palu emirate; *specific individuals*
Kurmanc tribes, 214n50
Kurt, Ümit, 271n60, 272n66

Lâlâ Mustafa Pasha, 66
Land Code of 1858, 119, 181, 283–4
land ownership
  Abdullah Beg's lands following his death, 178–84
  competing claims on, 184–7
  hereditary, 120–5, 283–4
  purchases of land, 192–4
  sales of land, 194–201, 196*t*, 200*t*, 246–7
  Tanzimat programme and, 119–25
  taxes and, 183–4
  usufruct rights, 85–6, 88, 102, 181, 195

Latif Beg, 196–7
Latif Efendi, 196, 196*t*
Leonhard, Jörn, 15
localisation processes
  agrarian sector and, 145–51
  of mining operations, 133–6
  of tax collection, 136–41
Lowry, Heath, 33n33, 34n44

Ma'âdin-i Hümâyun Emâneti, 19, 22, 72–3, 75
Machiavelli, Niccolò, 11
Mahmud II, 116
Majlan, Baron, 256
maktû'ü'l-kadem, 7, 8, 48, 50, 80, 83
Maligyan, Sarkis, 254
malikâne (tax-farm) contracts, 76, 82–3, 84–7, 94, 101n128, 108, 129n42, 142
Mamûretülâziz province, 243
Mardiros (*sarraf*), 143, 194, 208–10, 228
Mardiros Çulcuyan, 276n115
Marx, Karl, 109
Masters, Bruce, 33n37
McDowall, David, 173n48
Meclis-i Muhasabe (Council of Financial Accounting), 188
Meclis-i Vâlâ-i Ahkâm-i Adliyye (Supreme Council of Judicial Ordinances)
  Abdullah Beg versus Weşin Village case, 160, 164, 166–9
  abolition of hereditary privileges of Kurdish nobility and, 19, 124, 185
  agrarian disputes and, 145
  census processes and, 117, 118
  establishment of, 37n92
  land ownership and, 119–21, 124, 177, 185
  land ownership disputes and, 187–9
  müdür appointments and, 223–4, 227
mefrûzü'l-kalem, 7, 8, 24, 48, 50, 80, 83, 180, 190
Mehmed II, 10, 11
Mehmed Agha, 227
Mehmed Beg, 85, 91, 142–4, 160, 185, 194, 222, 225
Mehmed Reşid Pasha, 137, 223–4
Mehmed Seyyid, 91
Mehmed Tahir Beg, 134, 143

Index

Mekteb-i Mülkiye-i Şâhâne, 232, 235
Melik II, 43
Melkon Said Efendi, 235
Me'mûrîn-i Mülkiye Komisyonu (Commission of Public Officials), 236
Mesrob Mashtots, 22
Mesrobyan, Adam, 256
Mevlânâ Hâlid-i Bağdâdî, 38n106
middle peasantry, 178, 193, 215–16n76, 253
Midhat Pasha, 229
Mihaloğulları family, 7
mines, 71–80, 112, 133–6, 142–3, 153n12
Mîr Abdullah, 118
Mir Adil Agha, 239n37
Mîr Ahmed, 118
Mîrdasi begs, 44
mîr-i mîrân, 62
mîrî (state) status of lands, 179–83
Mirliva Mustafa Na'im Pasha, 250
Mîr Mehmed, 118
Mîr Muhammad, 112–13
Mığırdiç Cezayirliyan, 154n41
Mığırdiç Efendi, 269n7
Mollâ Ahmed, 85
Molla Muhyiddin, 85–6
*müdür*s (district governors), 219–29, 237
Mughals, 45
Muhammed Beg, 50
muhassıllık system, 115, 220
Muhtar Efendi, 199–200, 200*t*
Muhyiddin Seyyid, 91
Mullah İsmail, 160, 163
Mundy, Martha, 130n65
Murad III, 180
Murad IV, 67
Murad/Aradzani River, 25, 89–90, 148
Murphey, Rhoads, 67
müsadere (confiscation of wealth), 10–11
*müşir*s (upper-level military commanders), 114, 123, 137
Mustafa IV, 133
Mustafa Beg, 82, 143, 144
Mustafa Efendi, 239n37, 251
Mustafa Sabri Pasha, 116, 165–7, 169, 177, 179, 222–3
Mustafa Safvet, 233, 234

Mustafa Şükrü Beg, 224–5
Müteferrika, İbrahim, 11

Nakşibendî-Hâlidiyye order, 22, 38n106
nasihatnâme literature, 67, 68
Nazif Beg, 233–4
Necib Beg (aka Mehmed Necib Beg)
  as *kaymakam*, 231–2, 238
  land ownership by, 184–5, 195, 197, 243–4, 270n17
  military support to Ottomans by, 269n7
  provincial administration and, 231, 244–5
  *sarraf*s and, 143, 144
  tax collection by, 179
Nefise Hanım, 232
nobility
  decline of, 17–20, 87
  as historical category of analysis, 9–17
  military purposes of, 63–7
  see also Kurdish nobility
*nöker*s (cavalrymen), 66
noksan-ı arz, 150, 203–7, 205–6*t*, 211
Numan Efendi, 77
Nurullah Beg, 112

Ömer Beg, 91, 146
Ömer Naîmi Efendi, 132
örfi (customary) taxes, 81, 115, 129n39
Osman Agha, 144
Osman Beg, 57n9, 240n48
Osman Gazi, 44
Osman Nuri Efendi, 198–9, 200
Osman Pasha, 66, 133
Osman Seyyid, 91
Osman Tal'at Efendi, 233
Osterhammel, Jürgen, 109
öşür see tithe
Ottoman imperial state
  census administration in, 39n115, 117–19, 251
  centralisation processes, 4, 133–41, 145–51
  emanet (trusteeship) system, 72
  Imperial Mint (*Darphane-i Âmire*), 72, 76
  Imperial Registry (*Defterhane*), 119, 180, 190

Ottoman imperial state (cont.)
　Imperial Treasury (Hazine-i Âmire), 72, 198, 200
　Keban-Ergani mines and, 71–80
　localisation processes, 5, 19–20, 133–41, 145–51
　post-colonial perspectives on, 31n22
Ottoman–Safavid Wars (1510s), 44–5, 55
Owen, Roger, 181, 213n26
Özbek, Nadir, 129n42
Özoğlu, Hakan, 32n25

Palu emirate
　genealogies of, 50–2, 60n38
　historical geography of, 20–6, 21f, 23m, 24t
　as hükümet, 7
　land control in, 80–90
　map of, 23
　Massacres of 1895, 27
　military role of, 63–71
　Muslim-Turkish identity and, 2
　noble privilege of, 52–5
　Ottoman recognition of hereditary rulership of, 1, 3
　see also Kurdish nobility; specific individuals
Pamuk, Şevket, 125–6
Panaite, Viorel, 8
Pazuki emirate, 44
Penal Code of 1840, 228
Polatel, Mehmet, 246, 269n12
poliçecis (creditors), 208, 253
poll tax (cizye), 129n39
Protestant missionaries, 275–6n115
provincial administration, 219–38
Provincial Law of 1864, 229–30, 240n50

qadi courts, 17, 37n86

Reşid Pasha, 113, 191
Rüşdü Beg, 244, 247, 266, 270n17, 280–1
Rüşdü Efendi, 280
Russo-Ottoman War (1768–74), 70
Russo-Ottoman War (1808), 133
Russo-Ottoman War (1828), 112
Russo-Ottoman War (1877–8), 249
Rüstem Beg, 66

Sadık Efendi, 192
Sadullah Pasha, 132
Safavids, 26, 45–6, 48, 64–5, 66
Said Beg, 143, 155n49, 269n7
Salih Pasha, 134, 135
Salzmann, Ariel, 82, 83, 88, 91–2, 94
sanjaks, 8
Saracoğlu, Safa, 150
Saraçor, 206
sarrafs (creditors), 78, 132, 142–5, 154n41, 155n49, 185, 193, 253
Scott, H. M., 35n64
Şekib Efendi, 215n72
Selim I, 43, 44, 46, 53, 65, 96n15
Selim Beg, 134, 135
Seljukids, 60n39, 64
Şem'i (scribe), 50
Seniha Hanım, 270n17
Şeref Han: Şerefnâme, 44, 50–1
Şerif Beg, 124, 185, 245, 248
şer'i (religious) taxes, 81, 129n39
Seyfullah Beg, 82, 91
Şeyhoğlu İbrahim Pashazade Mehmed Beg, 132
Seyyid el Hac Ibrahim, 84
seyyids, 90–2
Seyyit Diyab, 86
sharecroppers, 147–51, 152, 186–7, 193, 205, 211
Sheikh Mehmed, 102n140
Sheikh Said, 22, 170
Sheikh Ubeydullah, 170
Shi'ite Muslims, 46
Sivan, 201–2, 206
siyaseten katl (political execution), 11
Sırvantsdyants, Karekin, 22
Sluglett, Peter, 181
Smith, Richard Saumarez, 130n65
Social Democratic Hnchak Party, 255, 260
Soran emirate, 2
state formation, 109–11
Storrs, Christopher, 35n64
Sublime Porte
　Armenians and, 146, 235, 244, 249
　income surveys conducted by, 118
　land programme administration and, 119, 185, 192, 209

Index

military support from Kurdish nobility and, 126, 140
modern state formation and, 109, 116
petitions of complaint against Kurdish nobility, 91, 146, 150, 209, 219, 225, 228, 235, 244
provincial administration and, 219, 225, 240n48
*sarraf*s and, 144
Şükrü Beg, 247, 248, 267, 269n7
Suleyman I, 2, 53, 61n51, 65, 67, 80, 96n15, 180
Süleyman Beg, 132
Sunni Muslims, 46
Supreme Council of Judicial Ordinances
see Meclis-i Vâlâ-i Ahkâm-i Adliyye

Tahir Agha, 160
Tahir Beg, 144, 184–5, 195–7, 222, 244, 248
*tahrir*s (enregisterment), 7, 32nn29–30, 33n33, 47, 48
Tanzimat (Re-organisation) period
autonomy of Kurdish nobility and, 4, 26
conscription during, 115–16, 126
Gülhane Decree (1839), 29n8, 108, 159
institutional infrastructure in, 114–20
land ownership and, 22, 26, 119–25, 188
Meclis-i Vâlâ-i Ahkâm-i Adliyye and, 37n92
mines and, 133–6
modernity and, 128n16
sharecropping and, 149
state formation and, 110
tax collection centralisation, 114–15, 136–41, 204
tapu temessükatı (title deeds), 119, 120
taxes
avârız taxes, 81–2
census processes and, 117–18, 119
centralisation of, 136–41
collection of, 84, 94, 114, 115, 136, 138, 166, 184, 201–2, 220, 231, 234
exemptions from, 108, 114–15
hükümet status and, 80–1, 83
*kaymakam*s and, 231, 234
land ownership and, 183–4
mines and, 74

noksan-ı arz, 150, 203–7, 205–6t, 211
örfi (customary) taxes, 81, 115, 129n39
poll tax (*cizye*), 129n39
şer'i (religious) taxes, 81, 129n39
*seyyid*s and, 90–1
Tanzimat programme and, 114–15, 136–41, 204
see also agrarian taxes; tax farming; tithe (*öşür*)
tax farming
agrarian sector and, 146
land purchases and, 193–4
malikâne contracts, 76–7, 82–3, 84–7, 94, 101n128, 108, 129n42, 142
*sarraf*s and, 142–5
Tayfur Beg, 266, 267
Tazcan, Baki, 97n38
Tchobanian, Archag, 276n117, 277n135
Tecelli Efendi, 226–7
*temessüknâme*s, 46, 78, 86
temlîknâme, 9, 16, 33n40, 53–5, 56, 61n51, 65, 96n15
territorialisation, 111
Terzian, Agop, 277n135
Thomas, Mara, 213n26
Tilly, Charles, 109
tithe (*öşür*), 114, 129n39, 136, 145, 147–9, 185, 201, 204, 220–1
title deeds (*tapu temessükatı*), 119, 120
*timar*s (fiefdoms), 7, 11, 47, 48, 50, 81
Treaty of Berlin (1878), 235, 238, 242, 249
Treaty of Erzurum (1823), 112
tribal chiefs *see agha*s
trusteeship (*emanet*) system, 72
Turan Beg, 124

ulemâ, 91–2, 104n164
usufruct rights, 85–6, 88, 102, 181, 195
Uzun Hasan, 64

Van Beylerbegliği (administrative unit), 48
Varjabedian, Bedros, 255
Veli Pasha, 139
Verheij, Jelle, 276n116, 276n117
Vosgeyan, Ohan, 254–5
voyvodalık, 82–3

Wallachia, 8
Weber, Max, 5, 109
Weşin, 1, 3, 27, 28n1, 157–71, 201–2, 206
Wieland, Christian, 15

Yahya Agha, 201
Yansûr Beg, 50, 69, 71
Yaycıoğlu, Ali, 5, 13, 154n43
Yazıcıoğlu Hüdaverdi, 142
Yeni Han, 193

Yensûr Beg, 143
*yurtluk-ocaklık*s, 7, 32n29, 48, 53, 70, 122–3, 168–71, 177, 181
Yusuf Beg, 81
Yusuf, El-Hâc (aka Yusuf Agha/Yusuf Pasha), 75–80, 101n128, 194

Zazas, 28n3, 214n50, 250
Zeki Pasha, 258, 264
zırnık (arsenic sulphide) mines, 112

EU representative:
Easy Access System Europe
Mustamäe tee 50, 10621 Tallinn, Estonia
Gpsr.requests@easproject.com